*Women, Family, and Ritual in Renaissance Italy*

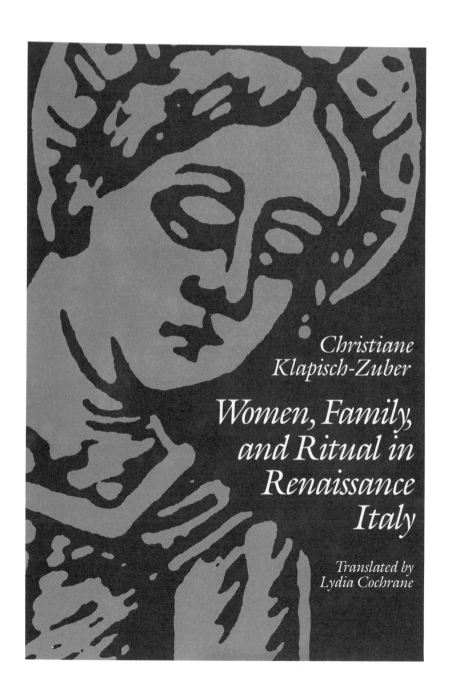

*Christiane
Klapisch-Zuber*

# *Women, Family,
and Ritual in
Renaissance
Italy*

*Translated by
Lydia Cochrane*

*The University of Chicago Press
Chicago and London*

The University of Chicago Press, Chicago 60637
The University of Chicago Press, Ltd., London

02 01 00 99 98 97 96 95 94 93      5 6 7 8 9

The publication has been supported by the National Endowment for the Humanities, a federal agency which supports the study of such fields as history, philosophy, literature, and languages.

*Library of Congress Cataloging in Publication Data*

Klapisch-Zuber, Christiane.
  Women, family, and ritual in Renaissance Italy.

  Includes index.
  1. Women—Italy—Florence—History—Addresses,
essays, lectures.   2. Family—Italy—Florence—History—
Addresses, essays, lectures.   3. Kinship—Italy—
Florence—History—Addresses, essays, lectures.
4. Florence (Italy)—History—1421–1737—Addresses,
essays, lectures.   5. Florence (Italy)—Social Life
and customs—Addresses, essays, lectures.   I. Title.
HQ1149.I8K57   1985      306'.0945'51      84-28061
ISBN 0-226-43926-7 (paper)

# Contents

# *Foreword*

Christiane Klapisch-Zuber ranks among the most imaginative and productive social historians of the Italian Renaissance. Her publications are well known and much admired in her native France and in Italy, and broadly across Europe. However, only a few of her short studies have up to now appeared in English. This has limited her audience in the English-speaking world to the comparatively few specialists in Italian, especially Florentine, history.

But this looks to be an *annus mirabilis,* in terms of her English-language publications. First, the English version of the big study, *Les Toscans et leurs familles* (1978), which we jointly authored, is scheduled for publication in 1985 by Yale University Press (under the title *The Tuscans and Their Families: A Study of the Florentine Catasto of 1427).* Second, we have before us English translations of her most important articles. In real measure, these short studies illustrate her style as a historian better even than our book. Large, joint enterprises inevitably impose a discipline on the participants, in dividing the research tasks, in developing conclusions acceptable to all. We both endorsed the conclusions of our book, but we both retain some reservations about particular interpretations it contains.

In this collection of short studies, Klapisch-Zuber speaks fully and freely in her own voice. And it's a voice that has much of importance to say about the society and social practices of Renaissance Italy, and about the methods historians should adopt in recapturing its life.

These studies admit analysis and intepretation at several levels. We can begin with a consideration of the sources Klapisch-Zuber principally utilizes. She frequently cites the famous Florentine *catasto* of 1427–30, as well as earlier tax surveys (notably from Prato) and later *catasti* from Florence and its countryside. These large surveys also served as the principal source of *Les Toscans*. They are inexhaustible mines of statistical information, here interpreted by one who knows them well.

More recently she has been systematically exploiting a very different type of source. This is the *ricordanze*, the family memoirs or domestic histories which most Florentine fathers maintained. In them they noted life cycle events—births, marriages, deaths—that affected their own families or those of close kin; they recorded sales and purchases; they set down almost everything that touched the fortunes of their households. Only a few of these *ricordanze* are published, and Klapisch-Zuber has read through hundreds of difficult manuscripts in order to gather the data contained in the following studies. This fact alone guarantees their freshness.

The *ricordanze*, like the surveys, are marvelously precise in the information they supply; they usually cite exact dates for the events recorded and exact prices for properties sold or acquired. They admit of some statistical manipulation, as Klapisch-Zuber's work in several places illustrates. But more interesting than the embedded numbers are the descriptions they offer of social practices, including social rituals. They show in detail how the Florentine family managed its domestic affairs, and they uniquely illuminate the ceremonial aspects of domestic life. They tell us, for example, how servants or wet nurses were selected, and who they were; they take us through the many rituals associated with marriages and christenings; and they show us the gifts exchanged between bride and groom, and their respective kin.

Finally, Klapisch-Zuber makes frequent use of a rare literary work, a contemporary effort to explain the rituals of marriage. The author is a Roman, Marcantonio Altieri, who in the early sixteenth century wrote a work called *Li nuptuali*. Contemporary interpretations of private rituals are extremely rare; Klapisch-Zuber found this nearly forgotten tract, recognized its value, and now uses it to complement the Florentine *ricordanze*.

A second level at which her studies can be analyzed is the methods she applies to these different kinds of sources. A graduate of the Ecole Normale Supérieure, she developed an early interest in the history of art. Her graduate training at the Ecole des Hautes Etudes brought her into contact with such scholars as Ruggiero Romano, Alberto Tenenti, and Fernand Braudel. Her first major historical work combined both her early interests in art history and the orientation toward economics and material life associated with the work of these prominent historians. Her *thèse de troisième cycle*, sustained at Paris in 1966, was a study of the marble quarries of Carrara in the Renaissance, and was published in 1969 as *Les maîtres du marbre: Carrare, 1300–1600*. Her most recent work indicates a return to art history, though in the service of ethnology much more than in that of aesthetics.

In the 1960s, the use of quantitative methods in historical research was attracting great interest among historians. In 1966, she and I began the collaboration which led, twelve years later, to the publication of *Les Toscans*. Several of the articles in this present collection manifest her quantitative skills and interests.

Another method which has exerted a profound influence upon her style as a scholar is historical ethnology. In this she follows a path laid out by several prominent French historians: Jacques Le Goff, who has long pleaded for "another Middle Ages" *(Pour un autre moyen âge* was the original title of his collection of essays published in translation by the University of Chicago Press in 1980); Georges Duby, whose recent work has drawn him deeply into the investigation of kinship groups, marriage, and sexuality in medieval northern France; and Emmanuel Le Roy Ladurie, best known in America for his celebrated study of the heretical community of Montaillou in the Pyrenees, in the early fourteenth century.[1] Through the publications of these scholars, the work of anthropologists—Claude Lévi-Strauss foremost among them —has penetrated into French historical studies. The program, to be sure, has proved difficult to implement within a medieval context, chiefly because materials of significant ethnographic content are so rare. Klapisch-Zuber alertly recognized the nearly unique value of the Florentine *ricordanze,* in the descriptions they offer of ritual behavior and of ritual objects. The studies printed here place the fruits of her insight and labor before us.

In introducing these studies to American readers, I hope that it is not inappropriate to express some reservations. As Duby does for twelfth-century northern France, Klapisch-Zuber stresses the paramount importance in Florentine society of the agnatic lineage or the patrilineage. Women, whether sisters, daughters, or wives, held only a marginal place in this form of kinship organization. The picture she presents of the position of Florentine women in a society dominated by these male fellowships tends to be bleak.

But have we not somewhat exaggerated the predominance of the lineage over and against other forms of kin organization, which persisted? As Jack Goody argues in his recent study of family and marriage in medieval

---

1. Jacques Le Goff, *Work, Time, and Culture in the Middle Ages* (Chicago, 1980); Georges Duby, *The Knight, the Lady and the Priest: The Making of Modern Marriage in Medieval France,* trans. Barbara Bray with an Introduction by Natalie Zemon Davis (New York, 1984); Emmanuel Le Roy Ladurie, *Montaillou: The Promised Land of Error,* trans. Barbara Bray (New York, 1978).

Europe, societies can and often do contain several types of kindred, both agnatic and cognatic.[2] Usually, they are organized to achieve certain specific functions. The agnate lineage seems primarily designed to protect the kindred's patrimony against ruinous divisions. Its involvement with property transactions lends it particular visibility in the surviving records. It did not replace but was rather superimposed upon the older, bilineal or cognatic descent group. This latter continued to exist as a community of support and even of affection. Klapisch-Zuber cites several instances in which matrilineal or affinal relatives participated in domestic ceremonies, as, for example, in welcoming the new bride into her husband's home. To read the letters of the Florentine matron Alessandra Macinghi Strozzi to her exiled sons urging them to marry is to gain this impression: Alessandra was not so much concerned to promote the lineage of her husband; she simply wanted descendants, grandchildren.[3] The bilineal descent group remained a community of affection.

We need, I believe, to pay more attention to these other, less visible forms of kin organization, in which women were far more important than in the agnatic lineage. Perhaps, as we come better to appreciate the importance of matrilineal ties, Florentine women may appear somewhat less marginal, and their experiences a little less harsh, than represented here.

On a still more basic level, these imaginative essays invite reflection on the nature and limits of historical ethnology. Its achievement to date has been the illumination of symbols, ritual life, and formal behavior, for which there has been little place in conventional historiography. Any method that saves neglected elements of past cultures must be applauded. On the other hand, can a method designed to study the societies of the living successfully explore the kingdoms of the dead? New methods in history require new controls, new ways of testing and evaluating proposed conclusions. Are they as yet entirely in place?

The problem principally derives from the often ambiguous, even impenetrable meanings conveyed by symbols or ritual acts. To be sure, even written records mask as well as display historical realities. The author may be misinformed or lying. But normally the basic message is clear, even if misleading or deceptive. Often, the basic message conveyed by a ritual gesture or symbol will not be clear. Even a contemporary, Marcantonio Altieri, as Klapisch-Zuber informs us, professed bafflement as to the meaning of some nuptial rituals at Rome. The ethnologist of living communities inquires from their members what the meaning of their rituals might be. The ethnologist of dead communities cannot.

Historians who work with these difficult materials must, in my opinion, gingerly find their way between two snares. If they are too cautious, they

2. Jack Goody, *The Development of the Family and Marriage in Europe,* Past and Present Publications (London and New York, 1983), 224–25.

3. *Lettere di una gentildonna fiorentina ai figliuoli esuli,* ed. C. Guasti (Florence, 1877).

may end up simply endorsing conclusions based on the more explicit literary and statistical evidence. And if they are too bold, they can indulge in speculations that are entirely beyond critical control. Professor Leonard E. Boyle, in his recent, mischievous, and ultimately deflating reassessment of the acclaimed *Montaillou,* includes among his recommendations:

> 10. *Keep your feet on the ground.* The greatest danger of all in the quest of *mentalité* . . . is that of playing fast-and-loose with the evidence . . . The . . . temptation is particularly attractive if one has read widely in anthropology, ethnology and kindred sciences, and is awed by the ease with which authors in these areas can turn a molehill into a mountain, or, to change the metaphor, can take off into the blue from a speck.
> There are several good examples of this in Montaillou.[4]

In my opinion, Christiane Klapisch-Zuber escapes these snares as well as any scholar and better than most. Let the reader decide, in perusing the following essays, whether this judgment is correct. And he or she should also observe that Klapisch-Zuber is not wedded to a single method. Rather, the quality which most distinguishes her work is versatility. When the documents permit it, she is a quantifier; when they contain much ethnographic substance, she adapts her method. In both arts—historical quantification and ethnology—she is unquestionably a pioneer and a master. Her essays may evoke reservations, but that is the predictable experience of pioneers. They will also evoke admiration and respect.

David Herlihy
*Harvard University*

---

4. "Montaillou Revisited: *Mentalité* and Methodology," in *Pathways to Medieval Peasants,* ed. J. A. Raftis (Toronto, 1981), 139.

# Preface

The articles brought together in this volume did not spring from a deliberate plan. They represent the gradual drift of my interests and, even more, the slow shifting of my approach to historical materials. Many of these studies were born of my surprise at a detail or an anomaly that had more to do with microhistory than with the quantitative history I was almost exclusively versed in up to that point. As David Herlihy recalls and as the first chapter of this volume confirms, I was then just emerging from a history heavy with figures and measurements. Here I leave such well-marked routes to explore more capricious trails. Although the questions to which I am seeking answers issued from a long acquaintance with demographic and familial phenomena and the study of massive amounts of data, and although they are elaborations of problems that have already been raised, they are in general questions that resist treatment by figures and graphs. I found that I had to call upon data of a more tenuous sort: fragments of statements that people had made about themselves or about those close to them; objects, names, or sentiments that families had passed on or modified; friendship or kinship networks that could be discerned radiating from an individual. I had to borrow analytical models from ethnologists, who take to the field to observe gestures and statements.

The clearest change to which this shift in procedures has led me, it seems to me, is to make it possible to approach the symbolic and its presence in the interplay of social and familial relations. To mention briefly one or two new perspectives that await further study, I hope to have suggested in some of the essays that follow the central place that ritual systems occupied in the shifting equilibrium between rival family groups and between the sexes in Florence. Competition, domination, and contractual relations deserve a new reading, perhaps in new terms, through these domestic or public rituals. What now awaits analysis, I would suggest, is the relationship between ideology and ritual—between the acknowledged systems for the interpretation of social phenomena and the accommodations people sought within the seemingly rigid but, in practice, extraordinarily flexible framework of ritualized behavior.

In quite another key, although I concur that there is an urgent need to bring women out of silent history into their rightful place in "audible" history, it seems to me of even greater urgency to analyze the interaction of sex-based differences and politics (in the broadest sense of the term) and to study the officially sanctioned representations of those gender differences. In short, to investigate how a set of gender-based symbols came to be written into a good part of history. From this point of view, any further investigation of Florentine society should seek meaningful comparison with neighboring societies, which, although close at hand, differed greatly in both their organization and their ambitions. The following articles represent stages, then, in an ongoing experiment.

I am deeply grateful to Julius Kirshner and to the University of Chicago Press for taking the risk of presenting the varied studies that make up this volume. They portray a route taken, sometimes with hesitant steps; more than reassuring answers, they represent a questioning. In the English-language dress tailored for them by Lydia Cochrane they may also offer the American public an insight into one stage of the dialogue that has taken place in France recently between historians and anthropologists. In this connection, I hasten to acknowledge my debt to Françoise Zonabend and André Burguière, among many others, since a good number of the themes treated here were first worked out and discussed in the seminars and workshops of the Ecole des Hautes Etudes en Sciences Sociales, where we could draw comparisons between our areas of research and share our fieldwork. It would be a more difficult task to name every person—American, Italian, and French—who has given me friendly encouragement by a suggestion or an objection, has directed me to a new source or a new argument, or has helped me to rein in my enthusiasm or to forge ahead. I hope they will all recognize my gratitude in my firm sense of community with them—a community founded on gift and exchange.

CHRISTIANE KLAPISCH-ZUBER

*Women, Family, and Ritual in Renaissance Italy*

# 1

## State and Family in a Renaissance Society: The Florentine Catasto of 1427–30

Certain periods, certain regions are lucky. The traces they left have served them so well that everything seems to have been said about them. So it is with Renaissance Florence. Artists and thinkers, patrician families and restive proletariat, commercial and financial networks, sharecropped farms hidden in olive groves and city guilds, political vicissitudes and clan showdowns: hasn't everything been probed, described, analyzed by a fertile—perhaps a proliferating—historiography? Historians have drawn magnificent portraits, but the background from which these images so clearly emerge remains blurred and out of focus— a regrettable state of affairs for a civilization that invented perspective. To know the entire population (not merely the rich or the city dwellers); to apply demographic measures to the masses of which the population is composed; to investigate the family (not just the patrician family and its lineage) as an institution; to determine the extent of wealth (not just the balance sheets of a few enterprises whose ledgers have been passed down to us)—these were some of the objectives that could be set up without fear of following too closely in the footsteps of other investigators. *Les Toscans et leurs familles,* which was published in 1978, gave concrete form to a dozen years of work on the part of an international team and undertook to set in perspective the two-dimensional figures that had held center

Originally published as "Etat et famille dans une société de la Renaissance," in *Le temps de la réflexion,* vol. 1 (Paris: Gallimard, 1980), 243–71.

stage.[1] What I intend to do here is to raise some questions concerning both the strides forward and the missteps involved in that undertaking.

The initial aim of that research was to grasp a society through its large-scale agglomerations rather than through individual, exceptional cases. The project was born of a document, largely unexploited by historians, drafted between 1427 and 1430 by the commune of Florence (which then dominated the major part of Tuscany, only Siena and Lucca escaping its sway). The *catasto* (cadastral survey), as the document is called, presents the tax declarations of all inhabitants of Tuscany who were subjects of Florence, from the richest to the very poorest—about 60,000 families comprising about 265,000 persons. Partial studies of this massive documentation had been made, as well as studies that drew on it only for information concerning a particular theme.[2] The whole, we could safely claim, remained intact: preliminary incursions and flyovers had exhausted neither its breadth nor its richness. The mission that the team set itself in 1966–67 was to explore this impressive lode in its entirety. In a form exceptional until our own time, the *catasto* offered abundant materials on families and on individuals and, at the same time, an ore no less precious concerning the wealth and the lifestyle of a whole population.

In 1966–67, when the project was launched, historians had recently become aware of the family as a domain of scholarship, thanks to studies in social anthropology and, particularly, to the works of Philippe Ariès.[3] Historical demography in turn had led many scholars to question the nature, the function, the autonomy, and the relations of this entity, the "family," which they constructed ideally as the progeny and fortunes of one couple.

Historians of economic or political life were concerned with more traditional questions, which they added to those of the demographic historians and attempted to resolve in monographs that focused on the greatness and the decline of merchant or aristocratic families. A model of the genre, for Florence, can be found in a 1968 work by Richard A. Goldthwaite.[4]

1. D. Herlihy and C. Klapisch-Zuber, *Les Toscans et leurs familles: Une étude du catasto florentin de 1427* (Paris: Presses de la Fondation Nationale des Sciences Politiques, 1978; to be published in 1985 in English translation by Yale University Press under the title *The Tuscans and Their Families: A Study of the Florentine Catasto of 1427*). The research was carried out by authors assisted by several collaborators, French and American, historians, statisticians, and students. It was financed by the Ecole des Hautes Etudes en Sciences Sociales and by the C.N.R.S. in France, and by the University of Wisconsin and by the National Science Foundation in the United States. The document is preserved in the State Archives in Florence and Pisa and several volumes were consulted.

2. I will cite only the study on agrarian structures by E. Conti, *La formazione della struttura agraria moderna nel contado fiorentino* (Rome, 1965), and the many studies by E. Fiumi on the demographic history of Florence, San Gimignano, and Prato.

3. P. Ariès, *L'enfant et la vie familiale sous l'Ancien Régime,* 1st ed. (Paris, 1960).

4. R. A. Goldthwaite, *Private Wealth in Renaissance Florence. A Study of Four Families* (Princeton, 1968).

Based on an examination of carefully preserved family archives, the book traces the fortunes of four families of the Florentine patriciate by means of a historical study of their patrimony and their investments in industry and commerce. Goldthwaite emphasizes the solidarities or the divergences of interest that maintained family unity or hastened division. He concludes that the nuclear family had emerged by the fifteenth century and that lineage ties had weakened, leaving couples and their immediate descendants isolated in their huge palaces, enclosed within their own privacy.

Could these conclusions be accepted as they stood when a number of studies in economic and political history were insisting on the solidarity among members of the family in its larger definition? On the other hand, was there not a risk of being deceived by the picture that the cultivated Florentines themselves supplied of their entourage when they analyzed —like Leon Battista Alberti in his famous *I libri della famiglia*—the network of alliances and blood ties necessary to their political and economic domination? Does not Alberti offer an image of the lineage and the family too specific to the urban haute bourgeoisie to be projected with total uniformity onto the whole of society? Such questions made it imperative to reach out beyond the studies of particular families and to avoid the fascination of the admirable literature that contemporaries themselves devoted to these matters, so that the hazier silhouettes, never highlighted in politics, business, or art, could be brought into clearer focus.

Access to large numbers, to the common masses, for example, is never an easy undertaking. It is even harder for the medievalist. Since his documentation is sparse, quantitative history rarely seems possible to him. Thus the availability of a survey as rich as the Florentine *catasto* encouraged questions that medievalists have often set aside, discouraged in advance by the unreliability of the responses they feel the material will elicit. The *catasto*, by contrast, offered a series of extraordinarily homogeneous and, within certain limits, dependable data. The basic unit for this survey is the household—that is, the domestic cell whose members share an estate. Each individual is thus situated in relation to those close to him in his daily life, but also in relation to his fellow citizens, since the tax officials wanted above all to place him on the scale of wealth and in the hierarchy of society. It is exceptional, for such an early period, to find every person identified not only by familial and social ties but also by personal characteristics, which medieval archival sources usually fail to give or reveal by other channels. Age and the precise kinship relation with the head of family are clearly given in the *catasto*. Even better, the more than a quarter-million persons described in this manner constituted an almost closed population and inhabited a province with an established political personality. Thus the historian can analyze the structure of this population and examine the bonds that linked one person to another without too much concern for the distortions that external exchanges bring to bear on a narrower community.

A description as complete as that of the *catasto* offers an approach to another sort of problem, one that has frequently been posed in Italian and Anglo-American historiography: the economic and political integration of a region that from the beginning of the fourteenth century was overshadowed by a single, dominant city. In this connection, an important question (which the studies of Marvin Becker in particular have refined and clarified) is that of the birth of the territorial state. It absorbed local privileges and the regional disparities that derived from a complex political heritage, and it came to define a community by means of the space it occupied.[5] When Florence imposed its domination over rival cities—repeating on a larger scale the model of its own relations with its *contado,* the immediately surrounding hills and plains of the Arno valley—the Florentine commune of the fourteenth century established the relations that it intended to maintain with those cities along fairly flexible lines, leaving a good deal to local autonomy. Marvin Becker has shown that the development of fiscal institutions and of civic ideology had kept pace with the growing financial burdens of the republic in a process that was, after all, classic in the formation of a state. To find a remedy for its permanent indebtedness to its citizens, who were taxed through "forced loans" and had thus become the state's creditors, the commune was obliged, even before the last decade of the fourteenth century, to put increased pressure on the *contado* and on the subject cities—a fiscal and political pressure that took some of the wind out of the sails of the regimes that enjoyed local autonomy. This pressure continued into the fifteenth century, aggravated by the armed conflict with Milan.

This sort of analysis rests primarily on a study of the revenues and expenditures of the machinery of state. Lacking data on the regional distribution of wealth, however, it cannot answer the problem of local variation in the global economic equilibrium on which a centralized tax policy was built, nor that of the imbalances this policy produced. Thus the description of wealth—movable goods, landholdings, credit extended, etc.—which was in theory universal and without exceptions in the *catasto* of 1427, invited global analysis of the regional or social distribution of the aggregates of wealth on which Florentine fiscal policy was founded and which were either diminished or accentuated by that policy. Naturally, the fiscal nature of the document introduces more than one bias in such a description. We had no alternative, however, if we wanted to leave open the possibility of measuring the real pressure that a state in the process of formation can exert on particular or collective interests.

These concerns led our research into the use of procedures that were more ambitious than we had realized at the outset. My description of research now completed may seem to suggest that the authors of the study

5. M. Becker, *Florence in Transition* (Baltimore, 1966–67).

never swerved from their initial intentions and followed a preestablished program point by point, holding fast to a clearly stated set of objectives and pursuing a questionnaire drawn up before they began. With humbler hindsight, I would have to confess to the second thoughts, mistakes, and abandoned directions that marked the progress of the investigation. What I intend to do here is to reflect on the strategies used in this research as they relate to the objectives that determined them, which were in turn constantly refashioned and realigned by those strategies. In this investigation, the movement from hypothesis to provisional results and back to hypothesis turned out to be accelerated, so to speak, by the methodological constraints inherent in an enormous document, a raw material as demanding as it was immense.

Should we, for example, have been satisfied with a cross section, with random samples taken from the whole of the data? To have taken notes on only one-tenth of the families would obviously have expedited our work. Perhaps our medievalists' reaction was too timid: the scarcity of the texts on which the medievalist usually works makes him unwilling to neglect any of them. When transported to the domain of large numbers he may still keep his reflex of exhaustiveness. In this case, in any event, I think the reflex was salutary. It permitted fine distinctions in the research by taking into account both the very small—the parish of ten souls, for example—and the exceptional—the family of forty-seven persons; such cases reveal, by their very exaggeration, traits that were less clearly expressed elsewhere. Above all, our procedure permitted internal comparisons and checks that a random selection would have made impossible. Let me add that, right at the start, the researchers decided against cutting into the mass of the document and taking out only what they judged to be statistically sufficient. We wanted to create easy access to this mine of information by providing an index to help others find what might interest them, and this argued in favor of an exhaustive survey of the data. In this sort of ocean, no one ever takes the same dive twice; now, anyone searching for some pearl will have a better idea of where to put down.

To find the answer, then, to the questions put to the *catasto* on economic, demographic, and familial structures in Tuscany, an enormous mass of data had to be manipulated. The main point of the undertaking, moreover, lay in counts, measurements, and relations to be established for a population of a size still to be determined when the investigation began. The nature of the research required a workable tool for analysis able to handle an enormous file of notes. In 1966 it was still unusual for a historian to sit down at a computer keyboard to attack his data. In the United States the use of computers had become common in certain disciplines in the social sciences, and the practice had spun off to a few historians accustomed to the methodology of sociology, electoral analysis, or demography. On the other side of the Atlantic the use of computers was limited to research centers that were capable of coherent policy and enjoyed sufficient means. Above all, machines offered an invitation to a new mind set, and medievalists were poorly prepared for that. Indeed, analyzing a body of homogeneous data or organizing serial data—even more, calculating and critiquing statistical indices and measuring the relations among phenomena—all constituted approaches newer to scholars trained in philological methods than to specialists in the modern period with some familiarity with economics or demography. Historians of the Middle Ages, on the other hand, can rarely make use of sources that are homogeneous (hence easily quantifiable), of extremely broad dimensions (which thus lend themselves naturally to automation), or very diversified in nature (which consequently demand an instrument that permits the interplay of a large number of variables). The die was cast: those elements of the document that could respond to the problems initially raised were thrown into the mold of computerized information.

Anyone using this method soon realizes that the operation is inherently reductive. In research that sets off with the goal of identifying hidden demographic and social structures and using them to clarify certain economic, political, or familial behaviors, one has to select the structures that can best serve as variables and will best lead to the necessary statistical measurements if the resulting information is to be coherent. The choice of these procedures inevitably involves the elimination of some information: if the reader is to judge the portion lost in this case, he will need to have the *catasto* presented in somewhat greater detail.

When the commune of Florence decided in 1427 to put into effect a thorough reform of its fiscal system, it based this reform on a precise evaluation of the possessions of those under its jurisdiction. The appraisal was done by means of a detailed description of all of the taxpayer's holdings, to be made out by the taxpayer himself or someone charged by him to do so. As far as real property was concerned, the smallest scrap of land was identified; meticulously described as to the crops it bore; measured in all its dimensions; situated in relation to surrounding landmarks; and evaluated for its market price, the amount of its annual harvest, and the value of its crops as estimated, based on a price scale fixed by the *catasto* officials. All this was then expressed in the aggregate for taxation purposes by a sum that represented the agricultural revenue capitalized at 7 percent. The resulting information makes up an inexhaustible reservoir on agrarian structures and land division in the Tuscan countryside. Anyone willing to take on the job could draw maps of every kind of specialized crop in the province. That was not our ambition. Not one of the specific items was retained. Only the total tax value of each entire estate appears in our working notes. An impoverishment as great as this undeniably cripples the historian's curiosity, but to fulfill his objectives he must resign himself to it.

Other information on individuals or households, their goods, and their tax rate was also eliminated. This sort of selection is based on choices governed, in the last analysis, by a principle of internal coherence whereby the data selected should line up with the sort of information most commonly found. Refusal to make such a selection leads to the juxtaposition of disparate and noncomparable blocks of information. In spite of Florence's attempt to make its own fiscal policy uniform, the 1427 reform still left profound regional disparities. The calculation of assessments was not based on the same elements in all places; the tax itself, which should have been in conformity with these assessments, was neither uniform nor always applied in the same manner. As the aim of our research belonged less to fiscal history than to social history, it seemed preferable to retain, as an indicator of wealth, the capital value of the estate rather than the ensuing tax assessments, calculated according to weightings that varied greatly from one region to another.

A total of twenty items was drawn up for each household of taxpayers, with five additional items concerning each household member—in all, no more than a minuscule part of what could conceivably be drawn from the *catasto*. The information from these twenty-five items was sufficient, however, to delineate the socio-professional status of each family; to situate it on the scale of wealth, providing some idea of the nature of its main sources of wealth; and, finally, to establish its structure and composition.

Another guiding principle in the collection of data was not to impose premature classifications on the family or the local community; all the categories and subdivisions of the document were thus respected throughout. This was a frustrating procedure, for it meant waiting for answers until all the data had been collected, and made it impossible to check information as we went along. It proved rewarding, however, since it prevented us from forcing an abundance of particular data into preestablished analytical categories.

At the cost of rigorous selection and deliberate restriction of its treasures, then, the *catasto* was explored for many arid years, as the information it contained was put onto file sheets and coded. The data-processing techniques that historians began to assimilate after 1965 still required punch cards and fixed formatting. The rigidity of these procedures did not encourage either the retention of information of varying content (hence of varying significance) or the introduction of new data that emerged unexpectedly after the procedures for scrutiny had been laid down.

The method chosen, however, aimed at more than a process of preliminary selection and successive reduction dictated by the need for uniformity. Let me close these methodological considerations by stressing that a vast body of data is acceptable only if the analyses make advantageous use of its very extensiveness in order to bring increased certainty to conclusions and a deeper comprehension of the complex relations among phenomena.

The statistical techniques that the medievalist employs are usually limited to calculating percentages or, at most, to very simple measurement. In the handling of masses of data, however, we cannot be satisfied with that sort of calculation, for results would soon proliferate and become as unintelligible as the basic data. Whether they like it or not, researchers are forced to refine their methods and to learn more elaborate statistical techniques. Although these methods enhance research, they have the drawback of repelling potential readers. It is certainly not a passion for statistics or an inherent faith in figures that prompts the poor historian, unprepared for such acrobatics, to turn to the calculation of correlation coefficients or factor analysis for reassurance that his first conclusions are valid. But he soon learns that these techniques have the advantage of letting him read relations clearly that he senses indistinctly. These techniques also permit translation of certain relations into graphs, which demonstrate clustering or highlight the most relevant factors. Although with simpler techniques —automatic cartography, for example—the computer can accurately translate the spatial diversity of statistical distributions, its major contribution is to enable us—thanks to calculations that would be impossible without its aid—to throw light on interrelations and to measure their strength. All this work, of course, is based on the researcher's intuition and, as a rule, merely corroborates first impressions derived from simple percentages. The more refined calculations encourage us to proceed with greater rigor, however, since they measure and compare such connections between phenomena as can be read according to the variables established. They help our investigation to go beyond description to interpretation founded on measurable quantity and its statistical representation.

The research that centered on the *catasto* did not originally follow paths this foreign to the medievalist. We first had to clear the underbrush in the best tradition of historical work. Data-processing techniques demand perhaps even more forcefully that the researcher know what the data represented in their original state, for contemporaries, so that he can understand what they represent in their coded state when he manipulates them today. The gap between these two states must always be taken into consideration, at the risk of working according to today's mental categories alone and neglecting past inflections of what we come to decree as historical reality.

In the case of the *catasto*, our critique of the source and of the elements selected from it led us, somewhat unexpectedly, to explore with great care certain problems of fiscal and administrative history that were not of top priority in our original objectives. The greater part of the archives of the administrative offices charged with the survey has fortunately been preserved in Florence. Through these archival materials we could know the decisions taken, day by day, by the directors of these new offices, who clarified or interpreted the law for the fiscal reform. The "*catasto* officials," who labored for three years to put together our document, headed a team that often numbered more than a hundred people. This bureaucracy, of varying composition but with a high degree of competence, did no more than repeat and refine the methods employed by other communal administrators who had managed state funds or set the tax base in earlier years. The study of the precise conditions of the drafting of the *catasto* between 1427 and 1430 later led us not only to a better understanding of how the document had been formulated but to an analysis of the activities of an administrative office, the recruitment of its personnel, and the powers that the organs of government in the commune granted to these annual magistracies. The various methods employed by those involved in this enormous compilation—house calls on private citizens, visits to their storerooms and examination of their account books, appeals for the denunciation of tax evaders, verification of collected information by comparison with other fiscal or financial government documents, repeated confrontation of the information given with the statements contained in other declarations—this whole arsenal of measures, this handbook of bureaucratic behavior, helped us to penetrate the daily reality of the machinery of a state in the process of formation.

This rather dry study, furthermore, gave us a glimpse of a political process involved with the establishment of a centralized state—a process that our preliminary research had shown to be a complex one. Fiscal reform was only one of the things at stake in a much larger political debate. The successive interpretations of the law that the magistrates responsible for directing the *catasto* translated into concrete decisions show that the adoption of the reform did not interrupt a debate astir among the politically active class and the common folk alike. The heightening conflict can plainly be seen in the revolution smouldering in some of the cities subjected to Florence, who pleaded their privileges and their autonomous status in refusing to hand in tax declarations. In one such city, Volterra, sullen resistance gave way to open revolt, which Florence was obliged to put down, not without bloodshed, with an armed expeditionary force.

These instances of resistance are an expression of the clash between different conceptions of public authority. The rebel cities denied Florence's right to liken their citizens to its own rural subjects, and they held fast to the "liberties" the capital city had guaranteed them by treaty when they came under its sway. When challenged by these communities, who were immovable on the question of their privileges, the Florentine commune sought to fuse the legal status of all its subjects, grounding its prerogative on a new idea of the common good developed by "civic humanism" after the end of the fourteenth century. But this affirmation of principle was nothing but a facade that covered acute tensions within the governing class. The two factions that struggled for power on the eve of the Medici principate (1434)—the Albizzi and the Medici—pursued the idea of equality before the tax laws more from political opportunism than from principle. In the Volterra affair the Albizzi faction pushed for repression, the Medici faction for compromise. These dissensions, when all was said and done, led to the failure of the *catasto* as an instrument of a new policy of centralization. Not only was Florence forced to accept that the tax declarations from the rebel cities were useless, but the various succeeding editions of the *catasto* after 1427 up to the end of the fifteenth century were limited to the city of Florence and its immediate surroundings, long subjected to its authority. Thus the chief ambition proclaimed in 1427 —to unify the disparate fiscal policies of Tuscany in order to hasten the political integration of the whole domain—was soon abandoned.

Our preliminary inquiry into the origins and the drawing up of the document ended up by clarifying, in its own way, the still limited nature of a conception of the public good, a conception shared by the greater part of the Florentine governing class yet in open contradiction, on many points, with the clan loyalties and the caste reflexes of that class. The vicissitudes of the fiscal reform as it was implemented are difficult to read through the grid of modern categories of class and party. Works subsequent to our study that have aimed at clarifying the structures of political behaviors[6] support our conclusions on this point: the centralizing conceptions that the oligarchical government of the 1420s reconfirmed as its own merely demonstrate their immaturity in practice.

The traces left by the day-to-day administration of the *catasto* are interesting for another reason. In reality, they clarify the reactions of the public to bureaucratic pressure. The Florentine "people" demanded a fiscal reform, seeing in it a less arbitrary instrument, since the tax would from then on be based, not on appraisal by citizen commissions more or less sympathetic toward the wealth of their neighbors, but on individual declarations—on standards of appraisal that were verifiable and universal. Similarly, the *catasto* abolished the collective responsibility that had forced neighbors to pay a share of the tax of someone who either could not pay or had devised a way not to pay. The assent of an overwhelming majority of the Florentines reduced fraud in 1427 to exceptionally modest proportions: this can be judged *a contrario* after 1430, when later versions of the *catasto* (which needed to be repeated every three years in Florence) relied on increasingly harsh measures to repress a resurgence of fraud. These positive reactions, however, did not wipe out all resistance to the investigations of the *catasto* officials. Not always conscious, this resistance was expressed in widespread underestimation of the sources of wealth on which the tax was calculated—agricultural revenues and capital investment in industry, banking, or commerce—or in a small-scale cheating with respect to the age, sex, or health of dependents to lessen the payable tax. We could see fathers increasing the amount of the dowry promised to a

6. Political behavior has been studied by D. Kent, in *The Rise of the Medici: Faction in Florence, 1426–1434* (Princeton, 1979).

daughter in order to deduct a larger amount from their taxable wealth, reporting another as younger in order to find a good match for her, adding a few years for a son to give him quicker access to certain well-paying municipal positions, and making another son younger to escape paying the head tax on him. There is no doubt that public morality did not impinge much upon these taxpayers, no matter how charmed they may have been by the egalitarianism of the new fiscal system; they maintained the reflexes of secrecy and petty thievery that the former regime of forced contributions had encouraged, even among associates or neighbors, while congratulating themselves that the *catasto* had come to "bring fortunes out into the light."

More subtly, administrative pressure contributed to a change in mentality through its repeated invitation to certain efforts of memory or thought. One example of this is the record that everyone keeps of the course of his own life and of his age. The series of surveys for which the Florentine commune asked those under its jurisdiction to give their age shows how this invitation was understood better and better, even deep in the countryside, between the end of the fourteenth and the end of the fifteenth centuries. Peasants and *popolo minuto* had no parish registers in which to verify their dates of birth, but merchants and even some artisans in the cities kept books in which they registered the birth dates of their children. This explains why the precision of the ages reported in the *catasto* varies greatly with social conditions. Nonetheless, an evolution, a real apprenticeship in precision, can be perceived, even in the imprecision that marks the declaration of ages in the less privileged classes throughout the century. Although ages still group massively around preferred numbers at the end of the fifteenth century, the obviously rounded numbers that clustered around the tens, in 1370, for nearly 40 percent of the declared ages, make up only one-sixth of the total a century later. No one, in 1427, ventured to claim before the tax officials that he "had nothing to declare but 130 years," as an old peasant had joked in 1370. A long familiarity with evaluation and, in urban circles, the spread of writing even to modest families permitted the head of family, accustomed to the pen and the document, to place himself on the age scale and to situate the members of his family in relation to himself.

After we had studied the reformers' ambitions and their political moves, looked at the kinds of reticence or resistance they encountered, and sifted through the afterthoughts and modifications that legislators or administrators wrote into the original proposal, we were in a position to draw some preliminary conclusions about the role of the reform in the political life of the "territorial state" and in the setting up of that state. The documentation itself offered other angles of attack. For example, it permitted a concrete grasp of the administrative organization of a vast territory —11,000 square kilometers (7,000 sq. mi.), roughly the equivalent of the state of New Jersey. This administrative geography, as well as the population distribution map that underlies it were unknown or barely charted. Thorough examination of the *catasto* made it possible, among other things, to map localities in Tuscany and to draw the approximate lines of the administrative districts into which they fitted. Here too, the research was based quite traditionally on a critical reconstruction of the most plausible boundaries between parishes or districts. This time-consuming task was performed all the more carefully because statistical cartography, which immediately simplifies contours, runs the risk of exaggerating errors of detail. The image that resulted from these topographical researches permitted us to measure the disparity between the administrative units grouped under the banner of Florence, a disparity that led back to differences in their legal status and to unequal demographic distribution—in other words, to the very different relations that human communities maintain with their environment.

At the center of the territory, the land within a forty-kilometer (twenty-five-mile) radius of Florence and long subject to it was characterized by very small, widely scattered communities, a pattern of dispersed habitations, high population density, and a tightly knit administrative network.[7] In the outlying areas, on the other hand, the territories of the subject cities that had felt the gravitational pull of Florence for a shorter time showed a more highly concentrated pattern of habitations, a population of varying density but generally of lower density than areas closer to Florence, and a less tightly knit administrative network. Although the Florentine *contado* still had a political framework based on the compact distribution of small parishes typical of the Early Middle Ages, settlement patterns and the administrative network on the periphery were organized on a more compartmentalized model into large communities that dominated a rural space without political personality. The heart of the Florentine territory, densely populated and tightly organized, was also the region that would suffer, along with Florentines themselves, all the consequences of the fiscal reform. Here documentation was not left to chance: this had long been the terrain that the bureaucracy of the commune found most to its taste, and here very few people indeed escaped the clutches of the fisc.

Within this landscape of administrative contrasts, one is struck by the internal disequilibrium, both of population and of wealth. In 1427, one inhabitant out of seven lived in Florence. The ratio of the population of the capital to that of the secondary cities gave Florence an exceptional advantage, if we can believe the geographers' theoretical studies. One might expect a much smaller gap between the chief city of a region and its subject cities, but Pisa numbered little more that 7,000 inhabitants at a time when Florence had approximately 40,000. This says a good deal about the hypertrophy of Florence, which concentrated in its hands—

7. The map of Tuscany has been published as *Una carta del popolamento toscano negli anni 1427–1430* by C. Klapisch-Zuber (Milan: Franco Angeli Ed., 1983).

along with nearly two-thirds of the taxable wealth of the entire area —roles and functions that went far beyond the relatively narrow limits of its own territory. Its international activities thus gave it a crushing supremacy within its own region. And this accumulation of wealth and power on the part of Florence seems to have increased even further, from the middle of the fourteenth century, in inverse relation to its demographic importance in the population of the region: in a territory enlarged by recent annexations, the place occupied by the population of Florence diminished slightly. We can understand better the difficulties faced by the subject cities in ensuring the respect of their relative autonomy before such a dazzling partner. The political domination of Florence was further hastened in the fifteenth century by the Florentines' growing hold on economic life, the penetration of their capital into the subject regions, and the accelerated concentration of properties lying beyond the old *contado* in the hands of citizens of Florence. All in all, this new picture of the distribution of wealth should lead to a reconsideration of the financial, political, and institutional history of Florence at the dawn of modern times.

In 1427, the wealth of Florence involved a small number of families and the contrast between the *popolo grasso* and the *popolo minuto* was no less striking than that between the capital and the provincial cities or between city and country. A handful of taxpayers—a hundred or so —enjoyed one-fifth of all of the wealth of Tuscany. The 3,000 richest Florentine families gathered into their hands alone more possessions than the remaining 57,000 households of the territory.

The debts of the urban proletariat and of men of the rural social strata who worked on share-cropped farms owned by Florentine proprietors give the lie to contemporary justifications of the system, which present the liberality of the rich as an ideal process that permitted wealth to circulate and to irrigate all of the branches of society. In reality, the new fiscal system was no more able than its predecessors to stop the continuing concentration of wealth in the hands of those who already held the greater part of it. Quite to the contrary: in totally exempting the dwelling place from taxation—be it a hovel or a palace—along with the furnishings that each family kept for its own personal use, the *catasto* encouraged the rich to multiply their unproductive investments and to construct ever more sumptuous residences, filling them with products of the goldsmith's skills, works of art, and valuable libraries. The glory of the Renaissance was built on heightened exploitation of indigent sharecroppers and provincials short of capital. Both of these groups continued to allow income and profits— an increasing share of which went to nourish artists and humanists—to flow toward the central city.

In Florence, the development of the state under the oligarchical regime of the beginning of the fifteenth century and then under the Medici principate was accompanied by a cultural and sumptuary investment that was both novel and covered by fiscal immunity. In the fourteenth century, the collectivity as a whole had financed the embellishment of the city through communal or corporative commissions: this tendency lessened in the fifteenth century. When the rich left only a part of their wealth visible and halted the admiring gaze of the common people at the imposing facades of their palaces, they kept for themselves, in the privacy of their homes, the enjoyment of works that formerly had been intended for the appreciation of all. The study of the reformed fiscal policy of the fifteenth century thus places these traits of Renaissance patronage, which have often been noted, in an economic perspective. The investment in cultural goods, in which Robert S. Lopez discerned a refuge for capital in periods of economic difficulties[8] was also the hidden revenge of a patriciate recoiling from the full force of the fiscal reform and showing that it could make its function of representing the community work to its own advantage. The patriciate offered its own image as that of the collectivity, an image of severe splendor cherishing hidden treasures.

Both the presence and the distribution of another fundamental aspect of the economic history of Tuscany, sharecrop farming *(mezzadria)* was clarified by the *catasto*. *Mezzadria*, which put such a durable mark on the Tuscan landscape, already had a long history by the fifteenth century. The juridical aspects of its origins and how and by what means it operated have been explored and described in an abundant scholarly literature. What is less known is its extent at that time and the stages of its establishment. Thus, even a summary study of the *catasto* data on the living conditions of most country dwellers provides an important benchmark in the plotting of the long itinerary of *mezzadria*. In the Florentine *contado*, one-quarter of the peasant houses were inhabited, in 1427, by families who gave half of their produce to their landlord. A more sensitive mapping of this sort of contract shows that it had not penetrated into the mountainous zones and that the hills to the south, southwest, and north of the city were much more touched by it than the suburbs of Florence and the Arno valley downstream from the city. While *mezzadria* regulated the life of three rural households out of four in certain zones close to Florence, it barely existed, in any event in its more clearly defined forms, in the lands near the subject cities and on the periphery of the territory. It could be said to be still an almost exclusively Florentine phenomenon. Samplings carried out in later censuses show an expansion of the *mezzadria* system to the northwest and southwest of the city: here in certain zones nearly all of the rural population came under this regime and worked lands owned by others, many of whom lived in Florence.

How can we explain the success of a contract that seems to have promised only poverty and indebtedness? Indeed, the *mezzadro* figures among

8. R. S. Lopez, "Hard Times and Investment in Culture," in *The Renaissance: A Symposium* (New York, 1953), 19–32.

the taxpayers who appear to be the most indigent. All that they possessed in their own right was simple furniture, some tools, and a few sheep, goats, or pigs or a "worthless old donkey." But the halo of poverty that they cast around the flourishing capital, if we can believe the *catasto,* must be taken with a grain of salt. They had, as compared to their companions in misery who lived in the regions where small landholdings or long-term peasant leases under emphyteusis prevailed, the enormous privilege of working a unified holding capable of nourishing, fairly generously, two families—that of the farmer and that of the landowner. Hard-hearted as the *mezzadri* might have thought the *oste*—who often did not hesitate to throw out a sharecropper couple too old to make the farm pay—they more often found in him a *padrone* who kept them from dying of hunger in times of scarcity, who married off their daughters, or who advanced them seed or the money to buy an ox. These close ties between the city dweller and the rustic—the townspeople's account books offer frequent evidence of their dealings—wove a network of obligations that the *catasto* translates crudely for us into terms of debts, advances, loans, and provisions. On the balance sheet, the rustic never seems to win. In reality, he knew how to make the best use of his work potential in a period of demographic penury that encouraged landlords to be more accommodating. In this way, the scarcity of rural manpower, to which the *catasto* gives ample evidence, furthered the establishment of modern agrarian structures in Tuscany in two ways: to the members of the bourgeoisie who wanted to invest in land, it opened up the possibility of reorganizing parcels of land into coherent and self-sufficient holdings, and it spared them the violent opposition of dispossessed peasants. Our fifteenth century sharecroppers were still capable of disputing the conditions of the contract, and if these were too rigorous or if their creditors—including the landlords—were too pressing, they simply would desert the farm, sure of finding another to work a little farther on.

The conditions that *mezzadria* offered—seemingly tough but conjuncturally advantageous for the peasant—played an important role in the demographic upswing of the fifteenth century. In this period of strong demographic pressure, rural families as well as scattered lands could be unified. These families were encouraged to reproduce and to remain together on the land. This was certainly not the case with the urban proletariat, or with the rural masses in the areas that *mezzadria* had not yet touched. The Florentine surveys, and the *catasto* in particular, clearly demonstrate the size of the population and its phases of decline and renewal. They also raise questions concerning the influence that living conditions exercised on the demographic response of the various social groups to the challenge of death.

Around 1338, Florence probably had a population closer to 120,000 inhabitants than to 90,000. By 1427, the fourteenth-century walls were too loose a fit for a population that had fallen to fewer than 40,000, and even by 1551 the city had not recovered more than half the population it had had at the beginning of the fourteenth century. The population of the Tuscan countryside had diminished at least as brutally, losing in three-quarters of a century up to two-thirds and even three-fourths of its size at the beginning of the fourteenth century. Moreover, this reduced population had suddenly aged, for the successive waves of plague had hit harder among the young. At the time of the *catasto,* the survivors of the more numerous generations of the third and fourth quarter of the fourteenth century still swell the upper part of an hourglass-shaped age pyramid. Adults and adolescents, on the other hand, are few enough to give this pyramid extremely steep sides at its midsection. Furthermore, although there were many children at its base, they were unable to give the pyramid the regularity typical of the young populations of the demographic Old Regime or of today's developing countries.

How are we to interpret observations of this sort, which apply, as we have seen, to more than a quarter million persons? In order to understand the simultaneous presence of two larger age groups—children and old people—which bracket more restricted groups of adults, we have to re-construct the movement of this population and see it as it evolves rather than keep to the static view offered by a census like that of 1427. We carried out test surveys, this time by random sample, in Florentine fiscal archives containing information on individuals similar to that of the *catasto.* In this way we were able to compare the age structure we had ascertained for 1427 to those illustrated in complementary studies for the period 1370–1480, a comparison that emphasized the extreme instability of the structures that the *catasto* had revealed. The slopes of the age pyramid of 1427 bear traces of the blows suffered by the population for six decades or more. After the Great Plague of 1348, this scourge returned roughly every ten years. In 1400 it carried off 30 people a day in Florence—at least 11,000 victims in all. Three years before our survey took place, the plague struck once more all around the city and killed a great many children, prompting a minor baby boom the following year. Each time the plague hit, the population seems to have reacted with an upsurge of marriages, and once the fear was past, conception picked up again. After each high in mortality, the birthrate leaped. But these more numerous children were the first victims of the next epidemic. As the younger part of the population dwindles, the age categories at the top of the pyramid become relatively larger; the population "ages."

Demographically, 1427 is about the bottom of the trough. During the fifteenth century, the epidemics of plague were less lethal and less frequent. The global population shows little further decline after the second decade. Its structure stabilizes slowly, and the ratio of one age class to another slowly comes back to normal. About 1470, the age pyramids for Florence and its immediate countryside return to a regular profile, without abnormal shrinkage in the adult generations. Here as elsewhere in Europe, the population was ready for a new start.

The rich in Florence and the poor *mezzadri* stand out quite clearly from the rest of the population, however, by several demographic traits, particularly by the youth of the groups they comprise. Not the last of the merits of the *catasto* is to have enabled us to recognize the social differences in the way the population was structured. In the privileged classes of the capital, the size of the younger age groups—children and adolescents —contrasts strongly to their meager place in the city's population as a whole. Rich families—and the vast majority of rich families in Tuscany lived in Florence, as we know—were overflowing with young people and children. One-half of the poor were twenty-five years old or younger when one-half of the rich were seventeen years old or younger. In the city this social group alone gives the impression of a vigorous population, capable of reproducing itself and of growing. It is easy to understand that the medieval image of happiness made such a strong connection between youth and wealth.

Analogous contrasts divide the rural regions of the Florentine territory. The heart of the Florentine *contado* also had a population younger and more dynamic than the peripheral regions around Arezzo, Pisa, and Volterra, which were more clearly stamped with the image of age. There appears to be a relation between the youth of the population of Florence's old *contado* and landholding structures: the network of prosperous farms under *mezzadria* allowed the families installed in them to raise more children, to marry their sons sooner and in greater number, and to house more grandchildren. It also facilitated the remarriage of family widowers, which ensured the presence of an adult couple on the farm. In this way, *mezzadria* held out a better hope of survival in a period of demographic collapse. It helped to stabilize the population and to keep it level. The demographic decline of the fourteenth century and the beginning of the fifteenth century was less violent in regions of *mezzadria* than at the periphery of the territory, where *mezzadria* was not practiced. But also the recuperation after 1470 was less vigorous there. *Mezzadria* therefore served as a brake to both population decline and population upturn: it undoubtedly played a stabilizing role before serving as a buffer to the upswing of population at the turn of the century.

From the synthetic picture we had for 1427, then, we were led to a diachronic investigation on much broader scale, based on other images taken throughout an entire century. This investigation alone could provide the key to the inherent features of the first *catasto*. It proved equally necessary when it came to interpreting domestic structure.

On the average, the domestic unit, the basis of the census, did not surpass 4.4 persons. But this rather low average does not faithfully reflect the diversity of the situations involved. In 1427, in fact, 11 percent of the population lived in households of more than ten persons, and over 50 percent in households of at least six. It is soon apparent that this average size varies a good deal according to social condition, profession, and residence, and the corresponding diversification of the internal structure of the domestic unit is just as great. In short, some Tuscan households consisted of very small families, especially in the city, and there was also a group—rather large for a European society—of households in which several couples and their children lived together. In the early 1970s, Peter Laslett and the Cambridge team of historical demographers proposed a typology that we could conveniently apply, in its broad lines, to the Tuscan example in order to bring some clarity into the confusion of domestic forms reflected in the *catasto*.⁹ As in England in the modern period, the dominant form in Tuscany in the fifteenth century remained the conjugal family: close to two-thirds of all of the households belong to this category. The presence of the smaller but substantial group—nearly one out of five—of composite households suggests, however, that the Tuscan domestic structure should not hastily be equated with a "Northwest European" model.

In Tuscany, daughters left their family of birth at their marriage and went to live with their husband; the son-in-law living under his father-in-law's roof is a figure practically nonexistent in this region. Sons, on the other hand, whether married or not, remained in their father's house, bringing their young bride there if they took a wife. Several generations of couples "co-residing" under the authority of a father frequently occur. Furthermore, after the death of the father the brothers do not always separate immediately but sometimes continue to live together, even for the rest of their lives. This sort of *affratellamento* often took place in Tuscany, proving the strength of family solidarity even unto two or three generations following that of the founding couple. Finally, relatives in the paternal lineage often remained attached to a family, which was thus broadened to include more distant blood relatives, something that seldom happened in northern France or in England in the early modern period. The originality of certain domestic forms in Tuscany is thus undeniable, and we should not be fooled by the statistical predominance of the conjugal family.

By examining the ages given for the heads of family we can reconstruct the history of an individual and his family from his birth onward—the developmental cycle of the domestic group and the succession of forms that a family takes as its head ages, its children marry, and the resources on which the domestic community lives increase or diminish.

The many varieties of family situation that our typology revealed can be reduced to two or three basic types. A *mezzadro* in the Florentine

9. P. Laslett, ed., *Household and Family in Past Time* (Cambridge, 1972).

countryside or his city-dwelling landlord have the best chance of living a good part of their lives in a household of complex structure in which several couples "co-reside." On the other hand, the households of the urban poor, of peasants who work several small, scattered parcels of land, and even those of artisans are rarely made up of several conjugal families gathered into a common household around *uno pane e uno vino;* and when they are, it is for brief periods.

These behavior patterns find their roots in the regulations governing the transmission of goods. At least from the thirteenth century onward, all the sons inherited an equal share of the paternal estate and excluded their "appropriately dowered" sisters from inheritance. If a man died without sons, his property would go to his blood relatives of the paternal line and not to his daughters. Thus, when provided with a dowry, the daughter, who had lost all of her rights to the paternal possessions, would leave the household into which she was born, while her brothers would remain there until the father's death, often staying together, with the estate undivided, long afterward. The eldest had no greater advantage, nor was primogeniture practiced: authority over the group was all that passed to the eldest brother. As soon as there was an estate to lay claim to and to transmit, this kind of household cycle could be found. But this model was also maintained in the sharecropped farms, where the peasant family had to provide sufficient manpower to exploit the holding.

Marriage, therefore dispersed the women to their husband's domicile or, rather, to that of their husband's father. To be sure, fathers were not always in a hurry to marry off their sons, who might take the earliest chance to contest their authority. Women went to their husbands at 18 or less, on the average, while young men remained unmarried until they were 26 in the country or 30 in the city. These trends are marked among the rich and among peasants settled on a family-owned holding; they are hazier among the poor, particularly in the cities, where crowded lodgings and the absence of goods to transmit or to share converged to disperse the sons as soon as they were old enough to work.

Can one speak, therefore, of two "models" of marriage and domestic structure? Among the poor, each new couple founded its own household, but many households were not based on a new union. Among the rich, the independent "establishment" of the children does not follow their marriage either, since the sons continued to live under the parental roof. Unlike families in northern Europe, marriage and the establishment of a household did not go hand in hand in Tuscany. Furthermore, the double model of marriage in Italy does not conform to the western model, as modern historians and demographers have defined it.[10] In Tuscany, there was no late marriage for daughters and there were few lifetime bachelors;

10. J. Hajnal, "European Marriage Patterns in Perspective," in D. Glass and D. Eversley, eds., *Population in History* (London, 1965).

on the other hand, the late marriage of sons was even more accentuated than in northern Europe. There was no privileged heir who continued to live on the land and who perpetuated the stem family, as was typical in many traditional rural societies in which the inheriting son lived by his parents' side and was the only one of the brothers to marry.

To what can we connect this Tuscan model, founded, as it seems, on agnatic solidarity? Does it provide evidence—happily preserved through Florentine documentation—of a medieval phase in the evolution of family and marriage of which we only know later forms in northern Europe? Or should we see it as a typically Mediterranean model, closer, in the last analysis, to central and eastern European structures than to those of north-western Europe? From what some studies—all too few of them—have told us about marriage and domestic structures in Tuscany in the modern period,[11] the second hypothesis seems preferable. Certainly the age at which women married rises slowly, beginning with the second half of the fifteenth century, to reach 20 or 21 years in Florence and in the surrounding countryside. It is true, moreover, that the practice of primogeniture evolved in the great Florentine families in the sixteenth century, reducing younger sons to celibacy and granting full rights of inheritance to the eldest.[12] Still, neither former matrimonial habits nor the typical cycle of family development would be turned upside down by these limited changes. In the monotony of its descriptions, the *catasto* brings to life a society that for centuries remained faithful to the portrait it traced, a society profoundly different from that of the area around Paris or of rural England.

The very large age gap between spouses—eight years on the average, but as much as fifteen among the rich—is a cultural trait that conditioned behavior in many ways and was to persist from the beginning of the fourteenth century to modern times. Characteristic especially of the upper classes, it is reflected in psychological relations that literature has often dramatized. It affected the relations between husband and wife, who were as far apart in age as a mother and her children. This overlapping of generations gave the woman the status of mediator between father and children, but it also exacerbated her marginality among her husband's kin, the demand for her submissiveness, and the lack of communication between spouses. That there was opportunity for real dialogue in the Tuscan household is an argument best supported by the speculations of a few well-intentioned humanists.

An administrative source like the *catasto* obviously cannot provide an answer to all the problems it elicits. So we are led to reread contemporary literary sources and to raise questions about the relations between con-

11. See, for example, E. Todd, "Mobilité géographique et cycle de vie en Artois et en Toscane au 18ᶜ s.," *Annales, E.S.C.* 30 (1975): 726–44.
12. See R. B. Litchfield, "Demographic Characteristics of Florentine Patrician Families, 16th to 19th Centuries," *Journal of Economic History* 29 (1969): 191–205.

science and social structure; between the ways in which contemporaries portrayed the familial and social fabric of which they were a part and their desire to act on that society, either to perpetuate it or to correct it.

The other limitation to a study of the family based on the analysis of the *catasto* consists in the very definition of the family that it permits us to observe. A descriptive document of this type, which takes the household as its unit of observation, does not cover the entire field of the family and even less that of kinship. The bonds that united related families, allies, neighbors, or business associates outside the walls of their dwellings are perceptible only very indirectly and partially through the data of a census. As the anthropologist Jack Goody so clearly puts it, "The fact that the 'family' or the 'household' is always small does not say anything about the importance attached to kinship ties in a more general sense."[13] This is true of the Tuscan domestic group, with its low average number of members and relative internal complexity. This very complexity informs us about certain characteristics common to the broader kinship ties and to domestic organization: both reveal a patrilineal inflection. The new couple's choice of residence normally reflects this patrilineal kinship structure, as does the recurrent presence, within the domestic group, of certain associations of blood kin and male descendants of the father's lineage. But what escapes the observer who limits himself to a single source like the *catasto* is, as Goody has also said, the value that people attach to these structures and the way they utilize the broader kinship networks that can theoretically follow from them.

Observation of the developmental cycle of a household at least permits us to cut short the false argument that the existence of lineage ties in kinship[14] is incompatible with the statistical predominance of narrower forms within the domestic group. Even in its numerically contracted form, the household of the fifteenth century continued to include individuals whose presence can be explained only by kinship ties; and this kinship structure is also the basis for the extradomestic solidarities of the lineage. Inversely, even in the fourteenth century the greater strength of lineage bonds did not proportionally increase the number of blood relatives who shared a household. It would be absurd to think that these families, or these related lineages, who during the age of the commune expressed their blood relationship by vendettas, private wars, and collective responsibility, also manifested it by crowding into a single dwelling. Lineage ties and domestic configurations evolved independently of one another, each according to its own logic, the latter much more sensitive, apparently, to the demographic conjuncture.

13. J. Goody, "The Evolution of the Family," in P. Laslett, ed., *Household and Family in Past Time* (Cambridge, 1972), 119.

14. Ties that are clearly demonstrated in F. W. Kent, *Household and Lineage in Renaissance Florence: The Family Life of the Capponi, Ginori and Rucellai* (Princeton, 1977.)

In clarifying the temporal, social, and geographical diversity of the Tuscan "hearth" and in revealing some of the elements that molded it, the *catasto* sends the problems involved in studying the family in the direction of purely demographic history, on the one hand and, on the other, toward a historical anthropology of the family and kinship freed of its conceptual confusions and more sensitive to symbolic structures. To formulate the articulation between these two research orientations will still be a delicate task; but Florence perhaps remains—by the enormous wealth of its archival resources—one of the best laboratories in which to attempt it. It is up to the imaginative historian—armed with private correspondence and family records, with scattered biographical data and serial demographic sources, with innumerable notarial acts and folk traditions, with representations in art and autobiographical accounts—to venture onto the dim byways that lie unlit by the wide boulevard of the *catasto*.

# 2

## Demographic Decline and Household Structure: The Example of Prato, Late Fourteenth to Late Fifteenth Centuries

Is it true that what has been called the "reconstitution of lineages" in the later Middle Ages[1] introduced a qualitative change in familial structures in western European tradition strong enough to have lasting results? I shall approach this problem here by studying the "minimal expression" of the family: the form and structure of the household, the everyday community of production and consumption.[2] My examples will be drawn from a region of Mediterranean Europe that up to this point seems to have been more sensitive—perhaps because it has been more fully studied—to the appearance, toward the end of the Middle Ages, of larger domestic groups.[3]

Originally published as "Déclin démographique et structure du ménage," in *Famille et parenté dans l'Occident médiéval,* ed. G. Duby and J. Le Goff (Rome: L'Ecole française de Rome, 1977), 255–68.

1. See E. Le Roy Ladurie, *Les paysans du Languedoc* (Paris, 1966), 160.

2. See P. Laslett, Introduction, in P. Laslett and R. Wall, eds., *Household and Family in Past Time* (Cambridge, 1972), 1–44.

3. In particular since the publication of the works of R. Aubenas: "Le contrat d'affrairamentum dans le droit provençal au Moyen-Age," *Revue d'histoire du droit* 1933: 478ff; "Tendances archaïsantes et famille artificielle en pays de droit écrit au Moyen-Age," *Annales du Midi* 1941:113ff; "Réflexions sur les 'fraternités artificielles' au Moyen-Age," in *Etudes historiques à la mèmoire de N. Didier* (Paris, 1960), 1 ff, and those of J. Hilaire: *Le régime des biens entre époux dans la région de Montpellier du début du XIII^e à la fin du XVI^e siècle* (Paris, 1957), 217ff; "Vie en commun, famille et esprit communautaire," *Revue d'histoire du droit français et étranger* 1973:8–53.

This region—Florentine Tuscany—boasts an exceptional wealth of documentation, and the various levels of family solidarity can be analyzed here by means of an entire network of sources: there are juridical sources (statutes, notarial acts, etc.); *ricordanze,* in which a family expresses the vision and the consciousness that it has of itself and that it wants to transmit; and tax surveys and administrative acts that describe households in completely original ways. Starting from the end of the fourteenth century, in fact, Florentine *estimi,* followed by the *catasti* in the fifteenth century, made an effort to define not only the economic situation of taxpayers but also the composition of their households and the age of each household member.[4]

The latter type of documentation prompts the historian to accent the domestic cell rather than the network of bonds that go beyond the day-to-day horizon of the household—a network that the census information touches on only indirectly or else ignores.[5] This sort of documentation may thus introduce a break between the approach to familial relations typical of the historian of the Late Middle Ages and the approach to which sources of a different type invite the historian of the Early Middle Ages —sources emphasizing the relations between domestic units rather than their individuality and internal composition. In particular, this documentation supports the presupposition of a "progressive nuclearization" of the family [6] and its simplification and reduction as time went by.

But what if the sources typical of the bureaucracy of the fourteenth and the fifteenth centuries present nothing but a documentary trap? What if the vision of the family to which the census documents lead us should be locked in a methodological ghetto of recognizing and pursuing a purely administrative frame of reference—that of the household—that was in-

---

4. These reflections arise from research carried out by David Herlihy and myself on the *catasto* of 1427, of which we prepared a computerized version. They were also developed in the book that resulted from that research, *Les Toscans et leur familles* (see chap. 1, n.1, above). For the Florentine *estimi* and the *catasti,* see also E. Conti, *I catasti agrari della repubblica fiorentina e il catasto particellare toscano (sec. XIV°–XIX°)* (Rome: Ist. stor. ital. per il Medio Evo, 1966). The Florentine *estimi* after 1370 describe the substance and the composition of taxpayer households, giving the age and the relationship of their members according to principles close to those of the *catasto* 55 years later. For a presentation and discussion of the information gathered in the *catasto,* see C. Klapisch, "Fiscalité et démographie en Toscane, 1427–1430," *Annales, E.S.C.* 24, No. 6 (1969): 1313–37.

5. Thus an important element in family consciousness, the family name—rarely fixed in the fifteenth century outside of the merchant bourgeoisie and the aristocracy—was frequently left out when the scribe copied the original taxpayer declaration onto the official register, even when the name appeared on the declaration. This indicates that the name served mainly to designate a circle of relations larger than the domestic group, without direct interest for fiscal administration.

6. See D. Herlihy, "Family Solidarity in Medieval Italian History," in D. Herlihy, R. S. Lopez, and V. Slessarev, eds., *Economy, Society and Government in Medieval Italy: Essays in memory of R. L. Reynolds* (Kent State University Press, 1969), 174–76.

capable of reflecting the totality of familial relationships?[7] In point of fact, thanks to the rich concept of the cycle of familial development,[8] analyzing the *estimi* and the *catasti* of the fourteenth and fifteenth centuries, which report the age and the relationships of people living under the same roof, can help us to reconstitute the *history* of this ephemeral domestic unit established by the marriage of two individuals; and to discover the *system* —on various levels of society—according to which the initial association is renewed or is transformed from one generation to another. Anyone interested in observing the household in the late Middle Ages thus finds himself in a privileged position as compared to the historian of other familial bonds, since it is from the family cell that he apprehends some of the mechanisms by which models of the family are reproduced.

Furthermore, the group that the Florentine surveys permit us to study with precision is more directly sensitive to demographic factors[9] than, for example, the *consorteria,* in which the bonds of defense, economics, patron-client relations, and so forth are woven between individual members of a family group, taken in the largest sense. "Demographic" sources of this type permit us to measure better than any other type of source the impact of upheavals of a demographic order, brought on by the epidemics of the fourteenth and fifteenth centuries, on familial structures. We start with the first "bomb" of the Black Death in 1347.[10]

The city of Prato, and to some extent its surrounding countryside, provide a particularly well-documented example from the end of the thirteenth century on.[11] Using late thirteenth-century and early fourteenth-century surveys (which are only partial and less detailed on the composition of households) and the *estimi* and the *catasti* of the last third of the fourteenth century and the whole of the fifteenth century, we can reconstitute

---

7. This is obviously the case if one is restricted to the hypothesis that the conjugal family is the basis of every society; under that hypothesis, the appearance of more complex forms, in the minority almost everywhere, and their implications for the history of family relations in the largest sense are apt to be systematically underestimated. See Laslett, Introduction, *Household and Family in Past Time,* 14–15.

8. M. Fortes, Introduction, in J. Goody, ed., *The Developmental Cycle in Domestic Groups,* Cambridge Papers in Social Anthropology, no. 1 (Cambridge, 1966).

9. See A. J. Coale, "Estimates of Average Size of Household," in A. J. Coale et al., *Aspects of the Analysis of Family Structure* (Princeton, 1965); T. K. Burch, "The Size and Structure of Families: A Comparative Analysis of Census Data," *American Sociological Review* 32 (1967): 347–63; T. K. Burch, "Some Demographic Determinants of Average Household Size: An Analytic Approach," *Demography* 7 (1970): 61ff; J. Dupâquier and M. Demonet, "Ce qui fait les familles nombreuses," *Annales, E.S.C.* 27 nos. 4–5 (1972): 1025–46.

10. See E. Carpentier, "Autour de la Peste Noire," *Annales, E.S.C.* 17 no.6 (1962): 1062–92; E. Le Roy Ladurie, "Un concept: l'unification microbienne du monde (XIV<sup>c</sup>– XVIII<sup>c</sup> siècles)," *Revue suisse d'histoire* 23, no. 4 (1973): 627–96.

11. Thanks largely to the work of E. Fiumi, in *Demografia, movimento urbanistico e classi sociali in Prato dall'età comunale ai tempi moderni* (Florence, 1968), whose figures we have taken for all that concerns the period preceding the Black Death.

changes in both the population as a whole and the forms taken by the household between the end of the thirteenth and the end of the fifteenth centuries. The surveys of 1371, 1427, and 1470[12] in particular (which I shall use here) have the enormous advantage of furnishing the material necessary to the study of the structure of population by ages and at the same time describing the makeup of the households.

The background to this picture is a large-scale demographic decline.[13] At the end of the thirteenth century and until about 1310, the city of Prato counted nearly 4,000 households, but a decline set in, as in other Tuscan cities, even before the Black Death.[14] In 1325, households were already reduced to about 3,400, and they fell another 18 percent by 1339. The Black Death hit Prato hard, but the "children's plague" of 1363–64, which did not diminish the number of households as strikingly, compromised the households of the next generation. The new attacks of plague between 1373 and 1394 reduced the population as a whole by annulling successively the effects of each of the periods of recuperation that followed the return of this scourge. Between 1365 and 1394 Prato had again lost nearly a quarter of its households within a thirty-year period; after the plague of 1400–1401 it counted no more than 1,178 households for a total decline of more than 21 percent during the previous eight years. After 1410, the population finally stabilized around 950 households, and this figure remained stable until around 1470–80. In short, within one century the population had dropped from 3,400 households to 950 for a total reduction of 72 percent. Decline in the surrounding countryside, also calculated in households, was only half as great, but it passed through approximately the same phases of acceleration. The *contado* of Prato, which counted some 1,630 families around 1300 and 1,430 in 1339, had no more than 943 families at the time of the *catasto* in 1427, or a loss of 35 percent within a century.

The age structure of the population revealed in the surveys of 1371, 1427, and 1470 shows how the population reacted to these blows. In 1371, the generations over 25 years of age, although already reduced in the aggregate by two waves of the plague, still show the regular structure, with balance between the sexes, of the generations born before the Black

12. This study is based for the most part on the *estimo* of 1371 (though one of the eight sections of the city, Capodimonte, does not give the age of adults), on the computer-coded edition of the *catasto* prepared for the research cited in note 4, and on a sampling of one-tenth of the families drawn from the *catasto* of 1470 (86 families).

13. For this demographic evolution, see Fiumi, *Prato,* chaps. 2, 3, 4, *passim.* The figures on households are as follows: 1325: 3,400; 1339: 2,760; 1357: 1,686; 1371: 1,806; 1384: 1,604; 1394: 1,478; 1402: 1,178; 1415: 988; 1427: 951.

14. Fiumi, *Prato,* 82–83. On the decline of population in Tuscany during the first half of the fourteenth century, see also E. Fiumi, "La popolazione del territorio volterrano-sangimignanese ed il problema demografico dell'età comunale," in *Studi in onore di A. Fanfani* (Milan, 1962), 251–90; E. Fiumi, "La demografia fiorentina nelle pagine di Giovanni Villani," *Archivio storico italiano* 108 (1950): 78–158.

Death. The discrepancy between the sparse ranks of those who had been under fifteen years old at the time of the 1363 plague and the infants who now gave a broad base to the population attests to its ability to recuperate. The age structure in 1427 is profoundly different. The *catasto* of that date presents a nearly vertical pyramid, in which the adult generations are crushed and youths and adolescents—children of the diminished age groups born between 1390 and 1410—are few. At the end of the stabilization period, the age structure that we can reconstruct from the 1470 *catasto* shows a population that has regained its impetus: the pyramid is pointed, its sides are concave, and it sits on a base of generations of numerous children, witness to the relative slackening of the epidemics.

After entering a long regressive phase starting in the first half of the fourteenth century, the population of our model city thus declined pro- digiously during the last third of the fourteenth century. This decline quickly became apparent in the aging of the population. The proportion of old people more than doubled between 1371 and 1427, and in 1470 it remained at a level twice as high as it had been a century earlier. De- mographic changes are also expressed in an inversion of the ratio between the sexes as the relative size of the female population showed a lasting decrease. Women, more numerous than men in 1371, were consistently fewer than men in the fifteenth century. To be sure, it is difficult to judge the reasons for this differential decline, but it is certain that it cannot be attributed only to the survey's failure to note women (see table 2.1).[15]

Population decline also brought appreciable changes in matrimonial practices. Our knowledge of the age at marriage at the end of the thirteenth century, at the time of the demographic peak, remains fragmentary and impressionistic. Some evidence from chronicles or from *ricordi*—obviously not fully representative—suggest that marriage was often delayed: men seem to have put off the time to take a wife until they were 40 or so; women until they were about 25.[16] Demographic pressure normally led

15. See chap. 5 below, "Childhood in Tuscany," for an examination of the abandonment and exposition of infants—even infanticide—as reasons for this. Many indications that cor- roborate the idea of a different treatment for female infants are provided by R. C. Trexler, "Infanticide in Florence: New Sources and First Results," and "The Foundlings of Florence, 1395–1455," *History of Childhood Quarterly* 1, nos. 1–2 (1973): 98–116 and 259–84 respectively.

16. Contemporaries occasionally had a strong sense of this recent drop in age at marriage; Giovanni di Pagolo Morelli, for example, in his *Ricordi* (V. Branca, ed., Florence, 1956), advises marrying between 20 and 25 years of age, perhaps putting off marriage until 30 years old, and choosing a girl "di poco tempo" (of young age), between 15 and 18 (207, 210, 223). He points out that men in the twelfth and thirteenth centuries married at 40 years old and women at 24–26 years (111–12). He returns several times to compare ages in that far-off time and at the beginning of the fifteenth century, when he was writing: 40 years old in previous times was like 26–30 years in his own day (111–13); he speaks of a "fanciullo" (boy) of 29, says "secondo l'età d'allora" (152), and he clarifies elsewhere "Nell'età d'anni venti, che a quel tempo era come oggi di dodici" (at the age of 20, which in that time was like 12 today) (110). See D. Herlihy, "Vieillir à Florence au Quattrocento," *Annales, E.S.C.* 24 no. 6 (1969): 1338–52.

Table 2.1

THE EVOLUTION OF STRUCTURES: POPULATION AND HOUSEHOLDS
OF PRATO—SOME POINTS OF REFERENCE

|  | 1371 | 1427 | 1470 |
|---|---|---|---|
| Structure of population by age |  |  |  |
| children 0–14 years | 39.7 % | 36.1 % | 38.7 % |
| adults 15–64 years | 56.5 % | 54.3 % | 54.2 % |
| old people 65 and over | 3.8 % | 9.5 % | 7.1 % |
| Ratio men/women | 97.9 % | 106.6 % | 107.3 % |
| Average age at marriage |  |  |  |
| males | 23.8 | 26.9 | 29.6 |
| females | 16.3 | 17.6 | 21.1 |
| average age gap | 7.5 | 9.3 | 8.5 |
| Average size of household | 3.44 | 3.73 | 4.26 |
| Households by size |  |  |  |
| 1–3 persons | 55.3 % | 52.1 % | 51.2 % |
| 4–5 persons | 25.9 % | 28.5 % | 23.2 % |
| 6–10 persons | 18.1 % | 17.9 % | 17.5 % |
| 11 or more persons | 0.7 % | 1.3 % | 8.1 % |
| Average number of children 0–14 years |  |  |  |
| by household | 1.38 | 1.34 | 1.65 |
| by family | 1.56 | 1.44 | 1.78 |
| Households headed by a female | 19.2 % | 16.7 % | 10.3 % |
| Households headed by a man 63 or over | 10.1 % | 23.3 % | 23.5 % |
| Households |  |  |  |
| without conjugal family | 20.3 % | 20.1 % | 22.1 % |
| with only one family | 62.8 % | 58.4 % | 54.7 % |
| with one extended family | 11.4 % | 9.9 % | 12.8 % |
| multiple families | 5.5 % | 11.6 % | 10.4 % |
| Households comprising |  |  |  |
| 1 generation | 36.2 % | 32.8 % | 32.5 % |
| 2 generations | 55.1 % | 51.4 % | 53.5 % |
| 3 generations | 8.7 % | 15.3 % | 14.0 % |
| 4 generations | 0.0 % | 0.5 % | 0.0 % |

to this most accessible Malthusian method for restricting population increase.[17] It is equally possible that the proportion of men and women who never took a spouse, even more that of widowers and widows who did not remarry, was higher toward the end of the thirteenth century than

17. On the age at marriage in western Europe, see J. Hajnal's extremely important article "European Marriage Patterns in Perspective," in D. V. Glass and D. E. C. Eversley, eds., *Population in History* (London, 1965), 101–43.

around 1400. We have an index of this in the oldest Prato surveys, which list a good number of autonomous women: in 1325, households headed by a woman make up 19.1 percent of the total; and in 1339, 23.8 percent.[18] The relaxing of demographic pressure had the immediate effect of permitting earlier marriage, especially in the poorer classes. In 1371, the proportion of bachelors in Prato allows us to estimate the average age for marriage at approximately 24 years for men and 16 for women.[19] As at the end of the thirteenth century (if we can trust the information concerning this period), a considerable age gap still separates the spouses, but around 1370 the age at marriage for both men and women seems to have fallen eight to ten years in response to the demographic decline. As to the proportion of unmarried men and women in 1371 who risked remaining unmarried, it seems low, for 96.5 percent of the girls in Prato were married at 25 years of age, and fewer than 6 percent of the men had not found a wife at age 45.[20]

When the population stabilized in the fifteenth century, the haste to find a conjugal partner abated somewhat. In comparison with 1371, female age at marriage rose in Prato in 1427 more than one year, and male age at marriage more than three years. The age gap typical of Tuscan spouses thus widened.[21] In 1470, at the end of this period of stabilization, the average age at marriage had risen still further, as elsewhere in Tuscany, by two or three years.[22] This evolution may have continued beyond 1500;

18. Fiumi, *Prato*, 80.

19. In 1371, 45 percent of 15-year-old girls were already married, as against 11 percent in 1427; 67 percent of 16-years-olds, against 15 percent in 1427; 95 percent of 18-years-olds, as against 89 percent in 1427. I have estimated the average age at marriage following the method proposed by J. Hajnal in "Age at Marriage and Proportions Marrying," *Population Studies* 7 (1953): 111–36. These average ages apply to the whole of the urban population, all social categories mixed. I have considered the unmarried female population under 40 rather than under 50 for two reasons. The *estimo* of 1371 does not note the matrimonial status of a large number of women alone, who become particularly numerous after the age of 40, and it is possible that many were widows (see below, note 27). Furthermore, the change that perhaps affected the age at marriage after 1348 may have considerably reduced the proportion of unmarried women under 40 years old, and the Hajnal method obliges us to consider a homogeneous population in which the rate of marriage remains stable.

20. Note that the unmarried religious population is excluded from these calculations. Before the middle of the fifteenth century, however, it carried relatively little weight in the population as a whole, so that the estimation of the proportion of definitive bachelors would not be modified to any great extent. See R. C. Trexler, "Le célibat à la fin du Moyen-Age, Les religieuses de Florence," *Annales, E.S.C.* 27 no. 6 (1972): 1329–50.

21. Herlihy, "Vieillir à Florence," 134–42.

22. The sampling of Prato in 1470 is too small to give very precise results. In the whole of the country areas of the Florentine *contado* the male age at marriage rises from 25.5 years in 1427 to 27.7 in 1470, and the female age from 18.4 to 21 years. This occurs in Florence as well, where, calculated by the same method, the male age at marriage rises from 30.3 years in 1427 to 30.5 in 1458 and 31.4 in 1480; the female age from 17.6 years to 19.5, then to 20.8 (results in 1458 and 1480 obtained from a sampling of one-tenth of Florentine households).

at least it is evident in the Florentine aristocracy.[23] Do these variations, linked closely to the demographic conjuncture, represent a mere episode? In point of fact, their influence on the structures of the household and their responsibility in the "reconstitution of lineages" were far from negligible; their effects were to abate only slowly and were for a long time to give the Tuscan family an original cast.

The form and structure of the domestic group in fact underwent a series of changes, certain of which directly reflect the modifications that had taken place in population structures. Thus the average size of household in the city of Prato was perceptibly reduced in 1371 as compared to its size before the waves of plague. In 1298 an urban household included 4.1 persons on the average, and in 1339, 3.9 persons. In 1371, it counted 3.4 persons.[24] This decline seems correlated to the fall in population, which proceeded slowly until 1347 and then accelerated under the effects of the first two great plagues. Later, however, the population continued to decline when the size of the household was already beginning to grow (3.7 persons in 1427). This increase continued in the fifteenth century (4.3 persons in 1470), when population stabilized at its lowest level.[25] The variations in household size therefore do not follow term by term the stages of demographic decline and renewal.

The number of households headed by a woman at first sight points to the same dependence on general demographic evolution; on further analysis it cannot be explained by that general evolution alone. The proportion of "female households" had already diminished in 1371 in comparison with 1339, returning to the 1325 level,[26] and it continued to sink further

23. R. B. Litchfield, "Demographic Characteristics of Florentine Patrician Families, Sixteenth to Nineteenth Centuries," *Journal of Economic History* 29 (1969): 191–205, particularly 198 and 199, table 3. The median male age at marriage in these patrician families moves from 29.3 years at the end of the fifteenth century to 29.4 years at the beginning of the sixteenth and to 33.6 years at the end of the sixteenth century; the median female age from 18.5 years to 18.2 and finally 19 years. Even in these rich families, in which women married earlier and men later than among poor families in the fifteenth century, the same tendency to a rise in the age at marriage is evident.

24. Fiumi, *Prato*, 47, 72, 89.

25. Ibid., 109–11, 151. In 1552 the population of Prato reached 5,800 persons in 1,095 households for an average of 5.3 persons per household, but these households include religious communities (ibid., 154); so it is more probable that the average of persons in lay households should be compared to the figures for the fourteenth or the fifteenth century, which would be less than 4.6.

26. Ibid., 80, 92. Fiumi arrives at a proportion of female-directed households lower than our figure (15.7 percent) because he retains the totals for the period that are not founded on the same criteria for "head of household" and count only aged widows living alone or with a family for which they were responsible. Proportions for 1371 and 1427 are as follows:

|                                                                 | 1371  | 1427  |
|-----------------------------------------------------------------|-------|-------|
| Female households                                               | 19.2% | 16.9% |
| Widows and women of unknown matrimonial status in relation to all women | 21.3% | 18.8% |
| Widows and women of unknown matrimonial status, heads of household | 49.5% | 46.5% |

(see table 2.1). This reduction of female heads of family is linked first to a decline in the relative weight of females in the population as a whole, as suggested by the rise in the proportion of males to females. It is also linked to the reduction in the number of women whose matrimonial status—widowhood or spinsterhood—could formerly have led to some sort of autonomy.[27] From this time onward, marriage or remarriage, facilitated by a demographic decompression, would make these women pass once more under male authority. In 1427, moreover, there was a smaller proportion of widowed women or women of unknown status who directed their own affairs or were responsible for their own households. Here we can see something like a tendency to reintegrate women into male-directed domestic group—a tendency independent of population structure by age and by sex—which thus adds to the general reduction of potential female heads of family to diminish the resulting proportion of female-headed households.

A third characteristic of the household, the age of its head, also evolves, at first sight, in perfect conformity with the population as a whole. When the population ages, the direction of the household passes to older generations and remains fixed there during the fifteenth century. Fewer young people in the population means fewer young at the head of households: the correspondence seems logical. But how can we explain that this aging is not reflected in the number of children per household? While the proportion of the generations under 15 years of age to the total population falls between 1371 and 1427, as does the average number of children per couple, the average per household remains stable. Along with the size of the household and the sex of its leader, this new characteristic, which does not vary in perfect agreement with the population structure by age and sex, raises questions about the changes that had taken place in the composition of the household.

In 1371, as in 1427 and in 1471, the cohesion of the domestic group rested fundamentally on the ties between male descendants of the paternal line. It was only in exceptional circumstances that ties of alliance introduced members of the wife's family under the husband's roof. In 1371, only one of some 1,800 households in the city of Prato included a son-in-law living with his parents-in-law, and sixteen others had taken in the daughter-in-law. Only one included a brother-in-law of the head of family (and/or his son). In 1427 there is not one son-in-law; mothers-in-law appear only in 8 households out of 950; and there are brothers or sisters of the wife in

27. If we consider only women characterized as widows in 1371, the group does not exceed 10.5 percent of the total female population at that date, against 16.9 percent in 1427, but in 1371 the proportion of women of unknown matrimonial status is much higher than fifty-five years later. A certain number of these women were probably widows, but it is possible that others born in the first half of the fourteenth century were survivors of the group that demographic pressures had constrained to spinsterhood (a category that had almost disappeared in 1427).

three other cases. These members of the wife's family are equally few in the households of 1470.[28] Consequently, it is evident that there was resistance to opening the basic family cell to relatives by alliance.[29] Normally the woman came to her husband's house and established herself there, remaining near her children when she was widowed: barely 3 percent of widows returned with their children to live with their own parents when they had lost their husband.[30]

What changes profoundly between 1371 and 1427 is neither the refusal to enlarge the family cell to members of allied families nor the attachment of a woman to her children and, eventually, to her new family, as represented by her brothers-in-law. It is the probability that a son who marries will live with his parents and, after the death of the father, with his widowed mother. This probability almost doubles in the span of a half century: the proportion of households including the family of a married child and the family of his parents (or the remaining parent) moves from nearly 11 percent to more than 19 percent in Prato.[31] At the same time, simple conjugal families decline, as table 2.1 shows. These changes modify the Pratese family in a lasting manner, for we find a configuration in 1470 analogous to that of 1427.[32]

---

28. In 1427, three widows with children described as *cognata* of the head of household must be added to this. Rather than sisters of his wife they may have been the widows of his brothers who had remained in their husband's house after his death.

29. This trait is not peculiar to Prato, but can be found all over the Tuscany of the *catasto*. On the Pisan countryside, see, for example, chapter 3 below, "A un pane e uno vino."

30. Here we can only consider the widows who appear with their children. Those who remarried immediately and left their children with their family-in-law, "leaving with their dowry," according to the expression of the times, obviously fall outside our calculations. Prato widows who appear with children (337 cases in 1371, 185 cases in 1427) can be divided as follows:

|  | 1371 | 1427 |
|---|---|---|
| Remaining in the family-in-law | 2.7% | 1.6% |
| Returning to their own family | 3.0% | 1.1% |
| Raising minor children independently | 25.5% | 25.4% |
| Living with unmarried adult children | 28.8% | 23.2% |
| Living with a married son | 40.2% | 48.7% |

31. These figures can be broken down as follows for 189 households in 1371 and 186 households in 1427:

|  | 1371 | 1427 |
|---|---|---|
| Nuclear family + widowed parent | 61.2% | 44.7% |
| Couples of parents and married son(s) | 25.2% | 43.5% |
| Married son(s) + what remained of parental family (widow + at least one child) | 9.4% | 8.6% |
| Married brothers + widowed parent | 4.2% | 3.2% |

On the household in the city of Florence in 1427, see D. Herlihy, "Mapping Households in Medieval Italy," *Catholic Historical Review* 58 (1972): 1–24.

32. The evolution of rural households around Prato followed the same trend: in three villages (151 households in 1371, reduced to 121 in 1427) the "great families" who lived "a uno pane e uno vino" move from 15 percent of the total in 1371 to 19 percent in 1427. The households with only one family plus a relative almost double, rising from 7.3 percent to 14.1 percent.

One peculiarity of the evolution that occurred around 1400 was the lesser position held by associations of married brothers, in the city at least. In 1371 and 1427, these fraternal associations accounted, in Prato, for only 2 percent of total households, but their relative importance among households comprising more than one family fell from 28 percent to 16 percent. They hardly ever continued after one of the brothers reached the age of 50. On the other hand, they appeared generally more solid in the countryside, and they occasionally ended up in the third generation in associations of "cousins," of uncles and nephews, of which the *catasto* gives some striking examples.[33]

What contributed to these structural changes? I shall not linger over the often and rightly invoked role of the economic conjuncture and economic insecurity. It is evident that the regrouping of fathers and sons answered a need to assure a minimal manpower to maintain the land or the shop in a period of demographic low tide and high salaries. But the "reconstitution of lineages" did not affect only those who had wealth to exploit: it also touched a notable proportion of the poor. In the city of Prato, multiple households that in 1371 and in 1427 belonged, respectively, to the 42 percent and 35 percent of the poorest households rose, between those dates, from representing 1.8 percent of their class of wealth to 9.3 percent, while among the 10–12 percent of the richest households, multiple households progressed only from 15.8 percent to 22 percent.[34] They thus passed from 1 to 5 among the poor in relative increase and only from 1 to 1.4 among the rich, although within both groups the absolute increase—about 6–7 percent—was comparable. This spectacular progression in multifamily households among the poorest of the population of Prato, who lived on wages and meager revenues, even on charity, still leaves those households very much in the minority, compared to conjugal families or to isolated individuals, who accounted for nine out

33. In 1371 it is rare to find households in the Prato countryside with more than a dozen persons. The largest we have found included 18 persons (Archivio di Stato di Firenze, henceforth abbreviated ASF, *Estimo* 215, fol. 395v gives 3 brothers and 2 of their married sons; fol. 458: 3 married brothers, bachelor brothers and a widowed father; fol. 461: 2 brothers; fol. 469: 2 brothers and 2 of their married sons) or 23 persons (ibid., fol. 484v, four brothers). For examples in the southwest of the Florentine territory, see chapter 3 below, note 34. The largest household of Florentine Tuscany in 1427 lived not far from Prato: 47 persons belonging to 10 families: 5 brothers and 5 of their married sons (ASF, *Castasto* 172, fol. 72). We should note that "artificial" households of brothers of the sort described by the works cited in note 3 rarely appear as such in our surveys: the cases of *affratellamento* that are mentioned concern isolated individuals and do not seem to give rise to large family groupings, which were founded instead on estates that remained undivided by the male descendants.

34. These categories of wealth represent, respectively, the 42 percent of taxpayers for whom the 1371 *estimo* notes zero payment or whom it qualifies as *miserabili*, and, in the 1427 *catasto*, the 35 percent of taxpayers who, after taking deductions, had not one taxable *fiorino*. The wealthiest 12 percent of households (215 households) declare over 100 *lire* in 1371, and in 1427 the highest 11 percent (100 households) had a taxable wealth of over 400 *fiorini*.

of ten poor households. This increase does show the limits of an economic explanation of the enlarging household, however. The need to feel secure to which the household responded can also be seen on another level, in temporary regroupings of relatives and close associates fleeing the epidemic, refugees together in a city judged to be safe.[35] More humbly but in more lasting fashion, the "great family" of 1400 manifests a defensive reaction of the same order, but the explanation is valid, particularly for the rural areas.

The cause of the "reconstitution" of the household that I would like to stress here is the drop in age at marriage and the enhanced possibilities for marriage that arose at the end of the fourteenth century. At first, the removal of the Malthusian barriers that had closed off entry into conjugal life rapidly reduced the proportion of long-term bachelors and lowered the age of marriage. With the reduction of the population in general and the appearance of troughs in the age scale during the last decades of the fourteenth century and the first decades of the fifteenth, the tendency to marry sons sooner was backed up by the possibility, indeed the economic necessity, of keeping them home with their wife and their children. Thus we can explain what the changes in population structure alone could not totally clarify in the aging and the masculinization of the direction of the household, in the rise in its average size when the population was still falling, in the stability in the average number of children per household (grandchildren mixing with the youngest of their aunts and uncles), in the integration of widows into their sons' households, and, finally, in the doubling of three- or four-generation households at a time when life expectancy must still have been quite low (see table 2.1).

The increased complexity of the household does not imply any revolution in the predominant familial system. The various aspects of the demographic decline simply revealed and exaggerated agnatic and patrilineal tendencies by giving them visible form and expression at the level of the domestic group, which seemed to call into question previous mechanisms based on the rapid fragmentation of the household. Along with the rules of kinship and of residence, which remained constant, the almost accidental upheaval in matrimonial practices considerably reinforced the paternal authority to which the conjugal life of sons and their wives was subjected. For young people in the Quattrocento, the price paid for a less delayed marriage was, more often than before, the acceptance of the parental or fraternal yoke, a source of tensions and conflicts. Widows too saw their autonomy diminish, but wives subjected to their husband's family were just as affected by this shrinkage in female independence, which went

---

35. Thus Morelli, in his *Ricordi,* 168, describes the refugee household in Bologna during one wave of plague: a widow with her children, her brother-in-law and his family, the nurse, the servants, etc. Similarly, B. Pitti, *Cronaca,* A. Bacchi della Lega, ed. (Bologna, 1905), 200.

along with an antifeminist juridical reaction that has been discussed by legal historians.[36]

Even in an urban setting—though the city was less sensitive than the peasant world to the virtues of undivided property and of tacitly accepted living in common—the domestic group thus underwent a relative "patriarchalization," which accelerated around 1400. The image drawn from the *catasto* of 1427, which otherwise remains incomprehensible in part, is put in perspective by the case of the small city of Prato, replacing that image within "phase B" of a cyclical history of the family. This case also shows the great variety of the forms that the household, the simplest expression of family relations, took on, within the same system and within a short period of time, in reaction to upheavals of various sorts—here for the most part demographic.

36. See Hilaire, *Le régime des biens* 356–61; P. Ourliac, "L'évolution de la condition de la femme en droit français," *Annales de la Faculté de droit de Toulouse* 14 (1966): 57ff; J. Lafon, *Les époux bordelais, 1450–1550* (Paris, 1972), esp. 52–58, 260ff; M. Bellomo, *Ricerche sui rapporti patrimoniali tra coniugi: Contributo alla storia della famiglia medievale* (Milan, 1961).

# 3

# *"A uno pane e uno vino"*: The Rural Tuscan Family at the Beginning of the Fifteenth Century

*by Christiane Klapisch and Michel Demonet*
*Translated by Patricia M. Ranum*

A *uno pane e uno vino*—sharing food and drink. Does this phrase express an unusual situation in the Tuscany of the early Quattrocento? Such does not appear to be the case, for these words are often used by the taxpayers and the scribes of the *catasto* of 1427 to describe families—"extended" in some cases to include an old mother, an uncle, a brother, or an isolated relative, and in others to include couples or entire families assembled under the same roof in large aggregates.

Originally published in *Annales, E.S.C.* 27 nos. 4–5 (1972): 873–901. This translation first appeared in a slightly different form in *Family and Society: Selections from the Annales: Economies, Sociétés, Civilisations,* ed. Robert Forster and Orest Ranum, trans. Elborg Forster and Patricia M. Ranum (Baltimore and London: The Johns Hopkins University Press), © 1976 by the Johns Hopkins University Press. Reproduced by permission.

This research was part of the series of projects involving the Florentine *catasto* carried out in close collaboration with David Herlihy, formerly professsor of history at the University of Wisconsin. We have worked together on this inquiry since 1967 and have been given financial support by the University of Wisconsin and the National Science Foundation on the American side, and by the Ecole pratique des hautes études, VIᵉ section, and the Centre national de la recherche scientifique (initially as part of the Recherches coopératives sur programme 181, headed by Professor P. Wolff) on the French side. Our study of the rural Tuscan family, based on the data in the *catasto* and programmed for the computer, complements Herlihy's work dealing with the same problems in urban Tuscany during the Quattrocento; cf. D. Herlihy, "Mapping Households in Medieval Italy," *Catholic Historical Review* 58 (April 1972). [For a summary of the results of research involving both the rural and the urban portions of the *Catasto* and also details concerning the compilation of this fifteenth-century census, see Christiane Klapisch, "Household and Family in Tuscany in 1427," in *Household and Family in Past Time,* ed. Peter Laslett (Cambridge, 1972), 267–81.—Trans.)

The answer to this question is not unimportant, since some scholars view the end of the Middle Ages as the moment in which Western Europe may have passed from a "medieval" model of marriage and family structures to a "European" model, with delayed marriages, a sizable amount of permanent celibacy, and small conjugal families.[1] In the following pages we intend to examine whether Tuscany, a southern province of that Europe in transformation, fits the model proposed for the regions situated farther to the north. A sort of chronological and geographical surveyor's staff, the Florentine census of 1427–30, called the *catasto,* is especially interesting since it permits us to avoid the sort of samplings taken from urban groups and from the upper levels of society which have been used in many of the best studies on the subject.[2] Such groups are not very representative of a population that is in the main essentially rural. On the other hand, of the 60,000 households described in the *catasto* of 1427–30, approximately 37,000, composed of some 175,000 persons, were rural.[3] In this census each individual was listed by name, sex, age, and relationship to the head of the household. Thus, this entire enormous rural population is available for use in studying the family, since certain of the variables that determine scope, structure, and duration are at our disposal—although we must keep in mind any distortions inherent in a census that is decided upon and organized by the tax authorities.[4] Compensating for the absence of literary works, journals, genealogies, and parish registers, which might have shed light on the structure of the medieval peasant family, this census permits us to elucidate the characteristics of the rural family group in Tuscany and the developmental cycle that it followed. In addition, beyond the limits of the province, this

1. Cf. especially J. Hajnal, "European Marriage Patterns in Perspective," in *Population in History,* ed. D.V. Glass and D. E. C. Eversley (London, 1965); and on the problem of family size, the studies of Peter Laslett, "Size and Structure of the Household in England over Three Centuries," *Population Studies* 23 (1969); "The Comparative History of Household and Family," *Journal of Social History* 4 (1970); and Laslett, ed., *Household and Family in Past Time,* Introduction.

2. Cf. L. Henry, *Anciennes familles genevoises: Etude démographique, XVIᵉ–XXᵉ siècles* (Paris, 1956); L. Henry and C. Lévy, "Ducs et pairs sous l'Ancien Régime, *Population* 15 (1960); J. C. Davis, *The Decline of the Venetian Nobility as a Ruling Class* (Baltimore, 1962); T. H. Hollingsworth, "The Demography of the British Peerage," *Population Studies* 18 (1964); L. Stone, *The Crisis of the Aristocracy, 1558–1641* (Oxford, 1965); R. B. Litchfield, "Demographic Characteristics of Florentine Patrician Families, Sixteenth to Nineteenth Centuries," *Journal of Economic History* 29 (1969).

3. Agglomerations of more than 1,000 inhabitants include a total of approximately 81,000 inhabitants, or 30.8 percent of the population. If to them we add the populations of those localities that comprised between 650 and 1,000 inhabitants and that seem to show "urban" characteristics—about 8,100 inhabitants in all—we find that a third of the total population described in the *catasto* lived in an urban setting.

4. On the fifteenth-century Florentine *catasti,* see E. Conti, *I catasti agrari della repubblica fiorentina e il catasto particellare toscano (secc. XIV—XIX),* Instituto storico italiano per il Medio Evo (Rome, 1966); see also the bibliography on the subject in Christiane Klapisch, "Fiscalité et démographie en Toscane, 1427–30," *Annales, E. S. C.* 24 (November–December 1969), and the discussion of the demographic value of certain aspects of the *catasto.*

census undoubtedly provides a few answers to the problems posed by
Western European population history as a whole.

At first glance, the peasant home as described by the *catasto* seems to
have been very small, although it was, on the average, larger than the
urban family in all regions. In the principal cities of Tuscany the family
was marked by an undeniable "urban" stamp.[5] It was very small (3.9
persons per household), and its predominant forms were the conjugal
family, an enormous mass of truncated families, and a crowd of isolated
individuals who had come to try their luck in the city.[6] The demand for
manpower, the mobility of individuals, and the high mortality rate undoubtedly explain the collapse of urban family groups and the breakdown
of solidarity among generations and relatives, at least among the lower
classes. The difference between the average sizes of urban and peasant
households is not excessive, however, since the average rural home included only 4.7 persons. Are these limited sizes compatible with a complex
family structure and a family group that has extended beyond that of the
simple conjugal family?

Here we will use as an example the *contado,* or countryside surrounding
the city of Pisa, an exclusively rural region in which 3,900 families lived
at the time of the *catasto.* This province was rather heterogeneous and
extended from the lower valleys of the Arno and the Serchio, through the
hills located to the south of this river basin, and as far as the region of
the Maremma, those low, almost deserted hills stretching along the shore
toward the south which served as pasture for transhumant herds.

The average rural family of this region included 4.7 persons, which was
a little larger than in a region of pure maremma such as the adjoining
*contado* of Volterra (4.4 persons) but clearly smaller than in other regions
of the Florentine territory such as the area southwest of the *contado* of
Florence itself—a region of hills and *mezzadria,* that is, sharecropper farms
—that adjoined the Pisan countryside and in which the peasant family
averaged 5.1 members. This average figure is higher than that for the
urban family of Pisa (4.2), and it is much greater than that of the small
Florentine family (3.8); but, although half the population lived in a household including 6 or more persons, houses with 3, 4, or 5 persons remained
the most common (15 percent of the total number of households for each
category) (see fig. 3.4[1] in the Appendix to this chapter).

This average has in itself only limited significance, as anthropological
and demographic research has shown.[7] One and the same statistic reveals

---

5. On "urban" characteristics, see W. J. Goode, *World Revolution and Family Patterns*
(New York, 1963).

6. Herlihy, "Mapping Households."

7. M. Fortes, in *The Developmental Cycle in Domestic Groups,* ed. J. Goody, Cambridge
Papers in Social Anthropology, no. 1 (Cambridge, 1966), introduction; L. K. Berkner, "The
Stem Family and the Developmental Cycle of the Peasant Household. An Eighteenth Century
Austrian Example," *American Historical Review 77* (April 1972).

very different demographic and social realities—for example, a high birth-rate in a society in which conjugal families dominate, or a preponderance of "extended" families where the mortality rate is high. A statistic showing the "average" family represents more than a typical household, for it masks households that have reached various stages in their development within societies that are characterized by very different family structures.

In order to determine the value of these data we can first relate them to the age of the head of the household. In the countryside about Pisa, until he was about forty years old a man directed a household whose size was smaller than the general average[8] (table 3.1). But a striking degree of stability is evident in the average size of households headed by a man over forty.[9] Until nearly the end of his life, a *capo di famiglia* presided over an approximately constant number of individuals. This was not the case for an urban Tuscan family, as we see in table 3.1;[10] the family generally reached a maximum size when its head was forty-five to fifty years old and then decreased until the end of his life. Is the developmental cycle of the

Table 3.1

SIZE OF HOUSEHOLD ACCORDING TO AGE OF THE HEAD

| Age of Head | Countryside around Pisa | | All Rural Areas | | | City of Pisa | | All Cities | | |
|---|---|---|---|---|---|---|---|---|---|---|
| | Male | Female | Male | Female | Total | Male | Female | Male | Female | Total |
| Under 18 | 2.1 | 1.5 | 2.5 | 1.7 | | 3.1 | | 2.6 | 1.7 | |
| 18–22 | 2.8 | | 3.1 | 3.1 | | 3.1 | 2.1 | 2.7 | 3.1 | |
| 23–27 | 3.4 | 4.5 | 3.7 | 2.8 | | 3.3 | | 3.1 | 2.4 | |
| 28–32 | 4.8 | 2.1 | 4.4 | 2.8 | | 3.7 | 2.7 | 3.7 | 2.8 | |
| 33–37 | 4.7 | 2.5 | 4.9 | 2.7 | | 4.4 | 2.8 | 4.2 | 2.7 | |
| 38–42 | 5.1 | 2.2 | 5.4 | 2.6 | | 5.3 | 2.7 | 4.8 | 2.6 | |
| 43–47 | 5.2 | 2.2 | 5.5 | 2.4 | | 5.6 | 3.4 | 5.2 | 2.4 | |
| 48–52 | 5.4 | 1.9 | 5.7 | 2.2 | | 5.3 | 2 | 4.9 | 1.9 | |
| 53–57 | 5.3 | 2.2 | 5.4 | 1.6 | | 5.3 | 2 | 4.9 | 1.8 | |
| 58–62 | 5.7 | 1.3 | 5.2 | 1.6 | | 5.1 | 1.6 | 4.6 | 1.7 | |
| 63–67 | 5.2 | 1.1 | 5.1 | 1.5 | | 4.7 | 1.5 | 4.5 | 1.4 | |
| 68 and over | 5.4 | 1.4 | 5.3 | 1.4 | | 5.1 | 1.7 | 4.5 | 1.4 | |
| Unknown | 2.7 | 1.2 | 2.5 | 1.2 | | 2.3 | 1.3 | 2.5 | 1.3 | |
| Total | 5 | 1.6 | 5 | 1.7 | 4.7 | 4.6 | 1.8 | 4.3 | 1.7 | 3.9 |

8. This involves 90.8 percent of the households; the percentage of homes headed by a woman remains low in the countryside and is generally less than 10 percent of the total.

9. As Herlihy emphasized in "Mapping Households," especially in table 3.2. The author does not find exactly the same characteristics in the second half of the fifteenth century in Florence.

10. Households headed by a woman remained on the average very small, more than three times smaller than those headed by a man. Their maxima are displaced toward the top, between twenty and fifty years, an age when widows were still raising children. But these large families have little effect on the total, since women reaching or passing their sixtieth birthday represent 62 percent of all female heads of households in this region.

urban family therefore a relatively short one, which stopped when its head died, although his counterpart's death did not interrupt the more slowly developing transformation occurring in the rural family?

The aggregate percentages of the various types of rural households confirm this first impression. The conjugal family, or what remained of it after the death of one of the partners, constituted only a little more than half (about 52 percent) of the 4,000 households in our study;[11] to which we add 12 percent for the households composed of isolated individuals, who were the residue of former conjugal families or who had been cast off by extant families. Therefore, a little more than a third of all households would belong in the broadest sense of the word to the category of "extended families," which were composed of several nuclear families living *"a uno pane e uno vino"* (22 percent), or which had added one or several individuals to the central nucleus as a result of either an agnatic [male kinship] or a collateral relationship (11 percent). This total percentage of extended families is markedly higher than the usual rates for Western Europe in the early modern period.[12] The rate for our rural Tuscan family comes close to that of the models for Eastern Europe, where nineteenth-century anthropologists thought they recognized, in reconstructing the *zadruga,* the archetype of the archaic European family community.[13]

These complex households bear the distinct stamp of the agnatic relationship through direct male descent since, in more than 70 percent of them, individuals or secondary groups were connected to the principal nucleus by the ascendant-descendant bond and since only 30 percent were cemented together by a purely lateral solidarity that prompted several brothers to live together after their parents' deaths.

This brief description reveals imperfectly a much more fluid reality that will no more allow itself to be embodied in a statistical summary than the household would allow itself to be reduced to an average size.[14] Can we go beyond this aggregate numerical evaluation and interpret the structural relationships among the various types of families?

A histogram combining the types of households, classified according to their structures for each age group of heads of households, permits us to project the probable cycle of family development by indicating the successive forms a household could take as its head aged (fig. 3.2 in Appendix).

11. This figure includes solitary couples or those living with unmarried children, and widowers or widows with unmarried children.

12. Cf. Laslett, *Household and Family*. By "nucleus" I mean the widower living with one unmarried child (or several children) who lives with another couple.

13. Cf. the work of E. A. Hammel, "Preliminary Notes on the Cycle of Lineage Fission in Southern and Eastern Yugoslavia"; P. Laslett and M. Clarke, "Household and Family Structure in Belgrade, 1733–34"; and J. Halpern, "The Zadruga," all in Laslett, ed., *Household and Family*.

14. Cf. Hammel, "Preliminary Notes."

Before the age of twenty, a young peasant male of this region had few chances of becoming his own master. If he succeeded, he rarely lived alone after both parents had died, for he usually had to provide for his brothers and sisters who were still minors. Most often he had a surviving parent with whom he lived, usually his mother.

The great majority of adolescents in rural areas, however, lived in a home in which the adolescent did not bear the responsibility as head, although twice as many children or adolescents were their own masters in the cities.[15]

By the age of twenty-five, not even a third of the young men in the countryside around Pisa had been able to set up a home of their own. Among those who were independent—be they bachelors or married men —a majority still had to support an aged mother or younger brothers and sisters.

After that, and until the head of the household was approximately forty-five or fifty years old—the point at which the household reached maturity —the development of the family was characterized by (1) a rapid increase, both in absolute and relative terms, in the number of families composed of couples with children; (2) a decrease in the number of families composed of a widower and his unmarried children, while those composed of a married couple with a widowed parent remained stationary; (3) an almost total disappearance of individuals living alone, while the number of child-less couples remained stationary; and (4) a steady increase of "multiple" households cemented by a horizontal or collateral relationship, which accounted for up to 15 precent of those households headed by a forty-year-old man.

After the head of the household had passed the age of fifty, there was a decrease in the number of couples with unmarried children, an increase in the number of solitary couples whose married children had left them, and an increase in the number of multiple families of the patriarchal sort in which sons and their families remained with the parents.

By the end of this cycle, when the old head of the household had reached or exceeded sixty-five years of age, more than 35 percent of the households were living under a patriarchal regime, with grandparents or even great-grandparents and the families of married sons living together year in and year out. Nearly 12 percent of the entire population lived in one of these "great families" ruled by an old man who was more than sixty-seven years old.[16]

---

15. Such children accounted for 1.4 percent in the entire rural region in the western half of the Florentine territory, a little more in the Pisan *contado* (1.9 percent), but less than 2.7 percent in the Tuscan cities as a whole.

16. In this region 23 percent of the households were directed by a head who was sixty-eight years or above (22 percent by a man of that age), and more than 24 percent of the total population lived there.

The distribution of households in this region of Tuscany according to the age and matrimonial status of their head confirms that the greatest chances of becoming the head of the family group occurred rather late, after one had reached approximately the age of forty. The position of *capo di famiglia*, as they described themselves with some degree of pride, could be claimed by 90 percent of all sixty-year-old men and 70 percent of all forty-year-olds, while only 45 precent of the men in the thirty-year-old group could do so, and only 30 percent of all twenty-five-year olds.

Marriage was surely not the means to authority. The ratio between males who were heads of households and the total number of men in their age group is similar to that between married or widowed heads of households and the total number of married men or widowers; and for each age group the chances of becoming the head of a household seem to have been totally independent of matrimonial status. Age, however, seems to have been a contributing factor to gaining control of the family rudder. In this region in which nearly half the men were already married at twenty-five, married or widowed heads of households constituted only 15 percent of the male population in this age group. At about forty years of age, when almost all men had married, a third still did not head the households in which they lived, and a sizeable number (about 10 percent) of old men, both married men and widowers, were still subject to another man's authority or at most were only able to share authority with him. It can be assumed that 87 percent of all male heads of households were married men or widowers;[17] yet this statistic actually conceals another that is more important for social history: of all married men or widowers, of all these aspiring "heads of families" who hoped for complete authority over a family cell that they had founded, only 72 percent were successful during their lifetime (see table 3.2, and fig. 3.3 in Appendix).

A factor analysis taking into consideration the sex, age, and matrimonial status of the head of the household by township, by wealth and profession, and by various indications of the size and structure of the household reveals that the percentages of the total population by large age groups or by matrimonial status remain approximately constant and consequently do not appear discriminative.[18] Male heads of households whether married

17. A woman's marital status evidently opened the way to authority, since 75 percent of the heads of households of this sex were widows. But this marital status was obviously a result of age: 31.5 percent of widows were more than sixty-seven years old. By the age of forty, 5 percent of the women were their own mistresses; at fifty, 8 percent; and after sixty, 15 percent.

18. The statistical technique of a factor analysis of relationships consists of seeking out in the whole at *n* dimensions the principal axes of inertia for the system. Its originality rests on the relationships existing between the two "clusters," that of characteristics and that of individuals. Only one analysis is necessary, while other methods would necessitate two; and the graphic comparison is much easier to interpret and "speaks" to the reader. In addition, this method takes *relative* frequencies into account and consequently analyzes profiles, while

Table 3.2
DISTRIBUTION OF MALE HEADS OF HOUSEHOLDS,
BOTH MARRIED AND WIDOWERS, BY AGE AND PERCENTAGE OF
TOTAL (CONTADO OF PISA, 1427–30)

| Age | % of All Heads of Households | | | % of Heads of Households, Married and Widowed | |
|---|---|---|---|---|---|
| | Heads of Households | Men of Same Age Group | % of Married Men and Widowers of All Men of Same Age Group | Of All Heads of Households of Same Age Group | Of All Married Men and Widowers of Same Age Group |
| Under 18 | 1.6 | 1.5 | 0.2 | 0 | 0 |
| 18–22 | 3 | 13.7 | 15.3 | 21.5 | 19.3 |
| 23–27 | 5 | 29.9 | 52.9 | 51.4 | 30 |
| 28–32 | 7.5 | 45.6 | 73.8 | 79.1 | 48.9 |
| 33–37 | 6.1 | 56.5 | 85 | 85.5 | 56.7 |
| 38–42 | 12 | 70.5 | 93.3 | 94.3 | 71.4 |
| 43–47 | 7 | 74.1 | 96 | 97.1 | 75 |
| 48–52 | 11.3 | 83.9 | 95.2 | 96.6 | 85.1 |
| 53–57 | 6.7 | 85.8 | 93.4 | 96.1 | 88.3 |
| 58–62 | 10.8 | 90 | 95.1 | 96 | 91.2 |
| 63–67 | 5.4 | 87.5 | 97.6 | 98.3 | 88.2 |
| 68 and over | 22 | 85.9 | 93.1 | 95.4 | 88 |
| Unknown | 1.5 | 54.1 | 28 | 40.2 | 77.7 |
| Total | 100 | 37.6 | 45.4 | 87.1 | 72.3 |

or widowed, adult or elderly (over forty-five and over sixty-five years of age), remain near the center of gravity for the whole. However, young unmarried heads of households or those whose status is undetermined are found to have been characteristic of certain large villages that stand apart from the central cluster. These same atypical localities also include a sizable number of households headed by women. Although the disparity between the number of married men or widowers who are heads of households and the number of married men or widowers as a whole remains only slightly noticeable and does not clearly indicate any one group of localities, the isolation of townships characterized by an unusual frequency of young heads of households reveals an atypical situation in these rural areas (see fig. 3.4[1] in Appendix). We shall return to this point later.

---

stressing the differences (cf. J. P. Benzecri, *Distance distributionelle et métrique du X² en analyse factorielle des correspondances,* Institut statistique de l'Université de Paris, 1969 [mimeographed] ).

Once the peasant of the region of Pisa—and this is undoubtedly valid for rural Tuscany as a whole—had reached a position of authority late in life, he did not loosen his grasp until the very end and gradually filled his house with his sons' children[19] as his own family let daughters marry and leave the family group.[20] Toward the middle of the long and slow cycle in the development of the household, there was a marked increase in the probability that several generations would overlap for an appreciable period of time, despite a high mortality rate, as we can see by the percentages of households comprising three generations in table 3.3[21]

Less than one rural household out of four, therefore, included a grand-father, or more often a grandmother, and grandchildren, but in the city the probability fell to a rate of one out of five. Although men were married at a relatively late age compared with girls, the sons of rural families do not appear to have postponed their marriages until they could "set up housekeeping" thanks to the retirement or death of the person holding the family inheritance or until they received a portion that would make them independent.[22] The father's voluntary renunciation of authority over his household was only on rare occasions recorded in the *catasto,* which

19. We obtain a very clear indication of this by comparing the distribution of children under fourteen years of age according to the age of the head of the household in which they lived, with that established on the basis of their own father's age. The first table involves a double maximum, the first point corresponding to the biological maximum reached at about forty or forty-five years of age, the age at which a man exerts his full power as father; this maximum, of course, is found in the second table as well. The second point, which only appears in the first table, represents the number of grandchildren living in a household comprising at least three generations and headed by an elderly man: 41 percent of the households directed by a head who was more than sixty-seven years old included between one and four children, and 7 percent had five children.

20. There was a very clear tendency for newlyweds to choose to live in the house of the groom's father. Sons-in-law are almost never mentioned in the *catasto;* I found only two in our 4,000 Pisan homes. The return of a widowed daughter and her children to her father's house was also rare in this region; she generally remained with her parents-in-law, who would reluctantly return her dowry; when she finally managed to obtain it, she would remain independent.

21. In this table, established on the basis of a computer program worked out by Herlihy, the percentages for the city of Pisa are used as a standard of comparison. Households including four generations, rare though they were, often sheltered a "centenarian." Thus, in the Pisan contado, Giovanni di Nardo, a sixty-nine-year-old head of a household, supported a father who was a hundred and three (Archivio di Stato, Pisa, Ufficio Fiumi e Fossi, 1542, fol. 143).

22. For this region the average marriage age for males, calculated by the method described by J. Hajnal in "Age at Marriage and Proportions Marrying," *Population Studies* 17 (1953): 111–36, was 26.3 years; in the *catasto* the average age of bridegrooms, fifteen in all and described as such, was slightly higher: 27.1 years. The average age for women at marriage was much lower, 17.3 years, both according to Hajnal's methods and according to a sample from the *catasto*. In the city of Pisa, the masculine age climbed to 28.8 years and the feminine age to 18.6. For Florence, see D. Herlihy, "Vieillir au Quattrocento," *Annales, E.S.C. 24* (November–December 1969).

Table 3.3
NUMBER OF GENERATIONS PER HOUSEHOLD
(CITY AND COUNTRYSIDE OF PISA, IN %)

| Number of Generations per Household | City of Pisa | Countryside around Pisa |
|---|---|---|
| One | 29  % | 23.3% |
| Two | 49.8 | 52 |
| Three | 20.4 | 23.5 |
| Four | 0.8 | 1.2 |
| Total | 100 | 100 |

lists an insignificant number of retired fathers who lived in the house of their son, who was officially considered to be the fiscally responsible individual.[23]

Did the death of the head of the household and the accession of the new heir therefore mean the beginning of a new family cycle? This event did not really break up a major number of households, and married brothers who continued to "live in common" formed a rather sizable proportion of the total number of homes (8.1 percent in the *contado* of Pisa). Equality among heirs was the general rule in rural Tuscany, as it was throughout Italy at that time;[24] and the chief recourse against breaking the peasant inheritance into pieces remained joint ownership, which generally went

23. Of almost 4,000 homes, 66, or 1.65 percent, included a retired father and 17 percent an elderly mother. In the city of Pisa, 8.5 percent of the households supported a retired father, 16.5 percent a widowed mother.

24. Cf. A. Pertile, *Storia del diritto italiano* (Turin, 1896); E. Besta, *La famiglia nella storia del diritto italiano,* 2d ed. (Milan, 1962); and Besta, *Le successioni nella storia del diritto italiano* (Padua, 1935). Primogeniture or ultimogeniture appeared later in the rural world, and during the Middle Ages the transfer of peasant possessions was rarely made exclusively in favor of a single son, who either excluded his other brothers by means of portions for minors established once they had agreed to renounce their inheritance, or who agreed to support them on the family property on condition that they remain unmarried. The "stem family" as it existed in the Pyrenees and the Alps (cf. Berkner, "The Stem Family") does not appear to have been a widespread system of family structure and inheritance in the region we are studying, nor, apparently, in the rest of the Florentine *contado.* The average age of adult, unmarried brothers living with a married head (twenty-nine to thirty years) shows that they still had the possibility of marrying and establishing an independent family or else of remaining on the paternal property. The ratio of adult brothers to heads of households is, moreover, lower in the Pisan countryside than in the chief towns. At Pisa, there were ten adult brothers per hundred heads of households; in the *contado* only seven. A stem family system would imply a higher percentage of permanent celibacy than the maximum of 6.5 percent that we have found in the rural population described by the *catasto* of this region.

hand in hand with co-residence and joint cultivation of the land.[25] An inheritance therefore did not automatically imply the division and fission of the family group.[26] Co-residence remained firmly entrenched as long as the replacement rate for families remained low (since a small number of sons reached adult age during their father's lifetime) and as the maximum size of the family group (beyond which coexistence became intolerable or impossible on a property that was too small) was as a result reached at a late date. At that point fission would eventually appear the only way to resolve the problems raised by divided authority and by shared means of subsistence among families that were too distantly related.[27]

Indeed, if we follow a group of families through the Quattrocento,[28] we note that the multiple families of 1427 tended to preserve their char-

25. But not always, and enough examples are found in the *catasto* to justify raising the question. "Division" generally involved the separation of families which until then had been welded together into a single home. Yet on many occasions division also followed upon the heels of a family separation, and in any case the *catasto* was slow to record this event, since it meant a revision of the fiscal rates for rural parishes. It was, however, the approval of the employees of the *catasto* and the recording of the event in their registers that rendered family schisms legal. Cf. C. Fumagalli, *Il diritto di fraterna nella giurisprudenza da Accursio alla codificazione* (Turin, 1912), 116, 127, 139. Cf. also examples of recent property and family divisions for this region in the Archivo di Stato, Pisa, Ufficio Fiumi e Fossi, 1540, fols. 350, 355, and 448; 1545, fol. 145; 1559, fol. 385 (in all three cases, the recorded division of property apparently followed an earlier separation of the families). According to jurists of the day, if two relatives were inscribed in the *catasto* under a common name, and if the fiscal burden was shared, they were presumed to hold the property in common. Thus, many factors come into play in an attempt to discover the actual situation within a certain number of extended families as they appear in the fiscal registers. Even though the persons are listed as co-residents, we encounter the problem of whether the individuals really lived in common; the phrase indicating such an arrangement assumes that the same table was shared (*a uno pane e uno vino*), but many large families nevertheless declared several distinct dwellings, though they might be very close to one another. (Cf. for example, Tommeo di Stefano, who lived with his three married nephews in "case due coniuncte insieme . . . le quale case elli habitano con la sua famiglia" [ibid., 1542, fol. 657].)

26. Less than in the city at any rate; in Pisa, only 4.4 percent of the households were formed by joint families of co-resident brothers.

27. For demographic factors influencing the size of the household, see the discussion of A. J. Coale et al., *Aspects of the Analysis of Family Structure* (Princeton, 1965, in T. K. Burch, "Some Demographic Determinants of Average Household Size: an Analytic Approach," *Demography* 7 (1970): 61 ff. This author stresses that in a regime of the extended family, a low mortality rate increases the probability that an adult son will remain in his father's household, thus increasing the size of that family. On the other hand, in a stem-family system, where a maximum of only two couples belonging to two successive generations can co-reside, and a greater number of sons survives until adulthood, only one will remain with the father once he has married, and the others will go off to increase the number of isolated households and will as a result decrease the average household size. In a system of extended families, a multiple household's increase in size depends essentially upon fertility and mortality rates or, in other words, on the number of children reaching adulthood. In Tuscany, the marriage age for women, although early, undoubtedly was not sufficient to increase fertility since the considerable difference in ages between husband and wife contributed to early widowhood (in this region at least 23.7 percent of women were widows by the age of fifty) and since women generally did not remarry.

28. In San Lorenzo al Corniolo, a parish of Mugello to the north of Florence, the fifteenth-century *catasti* compiled between 1428 and 1480 (the *catasto* of 1487 is missing

acteristics from one generation to another. It is clear that during the course of their development multiple families were more likely to form complex units in the years or decades to come, since two married brothers living together could each hope to see a son reach adulthood, marry, and found, on the same patrimony and under the same roof, a family that would live next to its cousins. The bursting point generally came during the third generation, between cousins or between an uncle and nephews too numerous to survive within the narrow framework provided by the family property. As in the Serbia described by Hammel, co-residence in family groups rarely continued after the marriage of the cousins—*fratelli cugini*, as they described themselves.[29] While the division that occurred at that time did not necessarily result in the appearance of simple conjugal families, we can nevertheless view this division as the point of departure for a new family cycle.[30]

Joint ownership among male heirs was the frequent solution to the threat of broken-up property inherent in the egalitarian customary law dealing with the transfer of property. Treatises by jurists of the day confirm this in their discussions of tacit, that is, unofficial joint ownership.[31] Canon lawyers of the fourteenth and fifteenth centuries devoted an abundant literature to the problems of "two brothers." Their chief concern was the urban family and the lawsuits resulting from the breakdown in family ties that had, until then, meant cohesion; but the large peasant family does not yet seem to have raised problems of this sort for the jurists of the period. In Tuscany, as in Venice or in Lombardy,[32] under certain con-

for this parish) indicate seventy-nine family groups, 17.7 percent of which were composed of lineages in which several co-resident fraternal couples were jointly responsible for taxes at one time or another during this period. Now, four of them continued this type of fraternal alliance over two generations at least, and perhaps even beyond 1480. Seven others remained stable units throughout the lifetime of the married brothers. In seven other lineages, one or several unmarried brothers joined the head and his wife; two later married and remained in the same house, thereby moving up into the first category.

29. Cf. Hammel, "Preliminary Notes." The proportion of cousins who were co-heads of adjoining households was at the most 1 percent of the total number of households. Taxpayers often insisted, in order to justify their claims, that joint ownership of this sort really existed, although it was unusual; thus Andrea di Puccio, who at sixty-seven was still living with his sixty-five-year-old cousin, declared, "Nostri padri non partitteno mai e chusi noi none abbiamo partito" (Archivio di Stato, Pisa, Ufficio Fiumi e Fossi, 1559, fol. 121). The bond between cousins seems to have been considered by these households of cousins as a fraternal one rather than one between distant relatives, and the term *fratello cugino*, which designated such households, was often replaced by the word *fratello* through a slip attributable either to the taxpayer or to the scribe.

30. Schisms occurring in the most complex families, those composed of brothers or cousins, occurred more frequently than among married sons and fathers. These schisms therefore gave rise to the appearance of more "multiple" households, although they were actually another type, since their predominant relationships were those between an ascendant and a descendant.

31. The study by Fumagalli, *Il diritto di fraterna*, is the most detailed; cf. also N. Tamassia, *La famiglia italiana nei secoli decimoquinto et decimosesto*, 2d. ed. (Milan, 1971).

32. Fumagalli, *Il diritto di fraterna*, pp. 89, 106.

ditions the male descendants of the deceased head of the household who still lived together in rural areas legally remained owners-in-common, or *fraterna compagnia;* and the principles established in the fourteenth and fifteenth centuries regarding the presumption and proof of jointly owned property would be repeated endlessly until the eighteenth century in the case of peasants, even though they had long since ceased to be applied to nobles or businessmen.

Was this cleavage, which lawyers of the period described, between occupational or social groups to be found in parishes and families in the region under study? First let us point out that artisans, small shopkeepers, and "services" comprised only a small minority (4.5 percent) of taxpayers in the large villages of the Pisan *contado,* a minority even smaller than in the Florentine rural areas as a whole (5.7 percent). Through factor analysis, using the township as a common unit, we have been able to draw a clear distinction between the families of these occupational groups and those of the peasants. In addition to the occupational pattern of families in those townships encompassing the greatest number of families from the "secondary" and "tertiary" sectors* (Livorno, Castiglione della Pescaia, and a major portion of the parishes in the *podesterie* of Campiglia and Palaia), we also encounter a greater number of very rich families (assessed on the basis of more than 400 florins), a greater than normal number of households directed by a woman or by an unmarried man, and an unusual number of small households composed of one person (see fig. 3.4[3] in Appendix).

If we then take the occupational groups themselves as units of analysis, we can verify that the distribution of family types is very different among artisans and tradesmen from that found among peasants[33] (see table 3.4 [2] and [3]). Everything seems to indicate that each generation of shopkeepers and artisans broke up the expanded solidarity so dear to the peasants, since they were incapable of expanding their means of production. Their family cycles, much shorter and more "individual" than those of the peasants, did not benefit from the conditions that helped the latter rebuild their families. Wealth being equal, townships predominantly composed of landowners working their land themselves are located along an axis of the factor analysis at the pole opposite that occupied by artisans. Their families are large (6–10 persons), extended to include several nuclear ones; their heads are firmly established men, either married or widowers. If we then look at those townships in which cultivators predominate (whatever the

*The French divide the economy into three "sectors"; the primary sector, which includes economic activities producing raw materials (chiefly agriculture); the secondary sector, which transforms these raw materials; and the tertiary sector, which includes all activities not directly involved in producing consumer goods.—Trans.

33. Respectively, 12 percent among isolated individuals as compared with 3 percent among peasants; 57 percent among conjugal families as compared with 53 percent; and 18 percent of multiple households compared with 30 percent (table 3.4[3] ).

manner by which they hold their land), we find them grouped about the variables that are characteristic of extended and large families, although they are all at very different levels of wealth (fig. 3.4[3] in Appendix).

Thus, rural taxpayers with a few fields appear to have maintained solid family structures. We see no fundamental difference between the family structures of the sharecropping *mezzadri* and those of small landowners

Table 3.4(1)
SIZE OF RURAL HOUSEHOLDS ON THE BASIS OF TAXABLE WEALTH
(WESTERN HALF OF FLORENTINE TERRITORY)
(IN % OF TOTAL HOUSEHOLDS IN EACH CATEGORY)

| Size of Household | Size of Fortune (in florins) | | | | | | | |
|---|---|---|---|---|---|---|---|---|
| | 0 | 1-25 | 26-50 | 51-100 | 101-200 | 201-400 | 401 and over | Total |
| 1-3 persons | 34.8 | 46.6 | 43.3 | 35.1 | 25.7 | 18 | 16.1 | 37.4 |
| 4-5 | 33.4 | 27.2 | 26.3 | 26.8 | 27.6 | 22.6 | 21.7 | 28.1 |
| 6-10 | 28.9 | 23.8 | 27.8 | 32.3 | 37.4 | 39.2 | 37.3 | 29.2 |
| 11 and over | 2.9 | 2.3 | 3.6 | 5.8 | 9.2 | 19.8 | 24.8 | 5.2 |
| Total | 100 | 99.9 | 100 | 100 | 99.9 | 99.7 | 99.9 | 99.9 |
| % of all households | 23.4 | 30.7 | 15.3 | 13.4 | 9.8 | 5.1 | 2.3 | 100 |

Note: The columns slightly less than 100% are due to the presence of declarations of patrimonies which have no dependent "mouths" to feed but which have nonetheless been included in the total.

Table 3.4(2)
SIZE OF HOUSEHOLDS ON THE BASIS OF OCCUPATIONAL CATEGORY
(SAME GEOGRAPHICAL REGION )
(IN % OF TOTAL HOUSEHOLDS IN EACH CATEGORY)

| Size of Household | Occupational Category | | | | |
|---|---|---|---|---|---|
| | Mezzadri (Share-croppers) | Affittuari (Persons Renting Land) | Small Landowners Operating Farm | Artisans, Tradesmen | Without Specified Occupation |
| 1-3 persons | 20.3 | 25.3 | 30.5 | 37.9 | 48.2 |
| 4-5 | 32.5 | 29.5 | 30.3 | 30.1 | 25.1 |
| 6-10 | 40.5 | 37.1 | 31.8 | 27 | 22.9 |
| 11 and over | 6.6 | 8.1 | 7.4 | 4.8 | 3.6 |
| Total | 99.9 | 100 | 100 | 99.8 | 99.8 |
| % of households | 21.2 | 4.7 | 18 | 5.8 | 50.2 |

Table 3.4(3)
TYPOLOGY OF RURAL HOUSEHOLDS ON THE BASIS OF OCCUPATION
(SAME GEOGRAPHICAL REGION)
(IN % OF TOTAL HOUSEHOLDS IN EACH CATEGORY)

| Type of Household | Occupational Category | | | | |
| | Mezzadri (Share-croppers) | Affittuari (Persons Renting Land) | Small Landowners Operating Farm | Artisans, Tradesmen | Without Specified Occupation |
|---|---|---|---|---|---|
| Isolated households | 1.4 | 2.8 | 4.6 | 12.2 | 19.9 |
| Conjugal families | | | | | |
| Not extended | 54.9 | 54.5 | 51.8 | 57.2 | 52.2 |
| With one ascendant member | 11 | 11.7 | 11.9 | 10.2 | 9.2 |
| With one collateral member | 1.3 | 1.1 | 2 | 2 | 1.3 |
| Multiple households With vertical principle | 22.6 | 21.3 | 21.1 | 13.4 | 11.7 |
| With horizontal principle | 8.8 | 8.5 | 8.5 | 4.8 | 5.5 |
| Total | 100 | 99.9 | 99.9 | 99.8 | 100 |

cultivating their own fields.[34] The abundance of land left vacant by the demographic decline and thus available for cultivation directly favored those attempting to gather together lands and indirectly favored "family regrouping." The bourgeois would piece together *poderi* ["small farms"] or sharecropping farms, while established peasant families would round

34. See above, table 3.4. At the most we can find more isolated households or nonconjugal ones in the second group than in the first (4.6 percent as compared with 1.4 percent), and as a result, slightly lower percentages of conjugal families (51.7 percent/55 percent) or of multiple households (29.6 percent/31.3 percent), while at the same time there is on the average a slight decrease in the families of small landowners cultivating their land. (These percentages are applicable to the western region of the Florentine territory and not specifically to the *contado* of Pisa.) The greatest family aggregates are found chiefly among small landowners and the *affittuari*, who took over *poderi* through a *mezzadria* when their homes became too crowded. Yet what sort of life-in-common and co-residence could this be, since the *mezzadro* was supposed to inhabit the peasant house on his landlord's property? Take

out their patrimony when a child was born or some member reached an age at which he could contribute new manpower. In the cases of both the *mezzadri,* who went from parish to parish in search of the best *podere,* and the families of small farmers, this "family regrouping" permitted the members to gather the strength needed to cultivate land that was more profitable for the owner and less risky for the cultivator. The "master" of the share-cropping farm asked that his *lavoratori* (laborers) form a complete unit of production, from small children up to grandmother, in order to assure the complete exploitation of his property. The small landowner found that the best protection of his inheritance lay in the cohesion of his family group, and he sought to delay the moment of fission as long as possible.

However, persons farming their land constituted a minority of the population described in the *catasto.* About half the households in the western portion of Florentine territory and three-quarters in the Pisan *contado* stated that they had no occupation or gave no indication that they personally worked the land. For the most part these taxpayers were humble people, many of whom worked as hired laborers, lived frugally on the income from a few fields, or were domestic servants elsewhere. The family structure of this group is related to that of rural artisans, though the characteristic traits are more accentuated, at least in the western sector of the Florentine state.[35] Within the Pisan contado those villages characterized by a major number of taxpayers with no declared occupation seem closer to other peasant townships than to the group of large villages conspicuous for the high percentage of artisans and "services."

On the whole, wealth appears to differentiate family structures more effectively than does occupational category. Family structures obviously varied enormously according to the household's wealth. Thus, the number of simple conjugal families and the number of multiple households differed considerably according to whether the household possessed from 1 to 25 florins, or had a capital of more than 400 florins—an enormous sum for

---

the example of the household of Antonio di Fanuccio, in the territory of the township of Colle, near the contado of Pisa. Antonio described himself as "de' fratelli della corte di Colle" and, indeed, he theoretically lived in a household composed of six families and twenty-seven persons; but one of his brothers lived in a separate house, and the head of the family also declared two residences "nella quale abitano i dette fratelli carnali et cugini stanno tutti insieme" (Archivio di Stato, Florence, *catasto,* 251, fol. 54). In the household of a neighbor, Bartolo di Nardo, which comprised five families and twenty-three mouths to feed, the eldest son was really a *mezzadro* in the region and probably lived on the *podere* (ibid., 251, fol. 156). Many examples are also found in the contado of S. Gimignano, where very large families rented *poderi* and were undoubtedly at least temporarily reduced in size as a result of settling a portion of the family on these lands (ibid., 266, fol. 453, with a theoretical household of thirty persons, and fol. 530, with twenty-two persons, fol. 534, etc.).

35. A high percentage of very small households (48.2 percent have from one to three persons) and of isolated individuals (20 percent; 17.8 percent were multiple households, in other words, far fewer than among small agricultural landowners or *mezzadri,* who averaged between 28 percent and 31 percent.

these rural areas, where the average fortune was about 55 florins.[36] The number of such families ranges respectively from 50 percent to 25 precent and from nearly 16 precent to 57 percent of the total number of households in the category, while the average size of the family increases noticeably with the wealth.[37] These contrasts are at least as clear in rural areas as in cities, and even in Florence, where multiple households and those adding an ascendant or a collateral member to the nuclear family (respectively 9.6 percent and 7.4 percent on the average) are found much more frequently among persons taxed on more than 400 florins (15.3 percent and 8.7 percent) than among poor or middle-income families (see fig. 3.6 in Appendix).

By factor analysis, we can clarify this link between wealth and the enlarging of the family group on the village level. The first axis, the horizontal axis of figure 3.4(2), is an axis indicating wealth; along the second axis, which is primarily an axis indicating the size of the households, we find associated with this variable other family characteristics, such as the number of nuclear families included in it, the type of association among these nuclear families, and the characteristics of the head of the family himself. Peasant townships show a tendency to increase in size and complexity of structure as their wealth increases; but the clusters linking wealth and large families split into two groups when we come to townships characterized by the presence of large fortunes. These same townships are also those which are set apart from the purely rural localities by the relative importance of the secondary and tertiary sectors.

These associations define certain regional groups that are representative of the diversity of functions and of wealth in villages. The poorest parishes of the Pisan province, situated in the low regions along the lower Arno (the *podesterie* of S. Maria al Trebbio and part of Cascina and Calci) show a connection between material poverty and family size, which is markedly below average. They form a very special group when compared with comfortable peasant townships to the north of Pisa (*podesteria* of Ripafratta), where extended families predominate, and with the villages of the "Pisan hills" south of the Arno, which, with their average-sized families and their moderate wealth, form the middle of the central cluster. In the large villages of the Maremma, we find smaller families, despite the presence of unusually large fortunes. More diversified employment, a greater degree of mobility within the population as a result of transhumance or of maritime activities, and perhaps malaria contributed to reduce the number of large families and to counteract the influence of their wealth (figs. 3.4[3] and 3.5 in Appendix).

36. In the *contado* of Pisa the average was 42 florins.
37. Cf. table 3.4 (1).

We must therefore qualify the idea that wealth and the extension of the family group always went hand in hand. In the townships of the Pisan *contado,* the nature of the occupational activities carried on and of the wealth possessed was a major discriminative factor that gave rise to considerable differences in behavior within social groups of equivalent wealth. The long cycle of family development is therefore characteristic exclusively of well-to-do and rich families but, rather, of those with lands to cultivate. Men who hired themselves out for the day obviously saw no advantage in maintaining co-residence and joint fiscal responsibility with persons other than members of their very close family. As soon as they were old enough to work, their sons went off as the labor market beckoned. These observations cast a light on the special role played by the sharecropping *mezzadria*. Although the families that worked a property through this sort of contract were stripped of any other source of income, the vast majority of them showed a strong tendency to form large and extended groups. Although the contract implied residence on the land of the *oste* (landlord) and frequently obliged families to move from one parish to another, this incessant transplanting did not destroy the cohesive bonds of these "family associations for production." The very instability of the *mezzadria* contract and the relative uncertainty about the future that consequently hung over the peasant's head did not prevent the extended family from persisting in a social stratum of peasants who had been stripped of any other resources, in contrast to the rest of the agricultural and industrial proletariat. Using taxable capital as our only criterion does not fully take into account the contrary trends that strengthened the extended structures of the family group among the sharecropping *mezzadri* and weakened them among the common laborers. In the diversified society of fifteenth-century Tuscany —a society that was in addition turned upside down by declining population and military conflicts—social hierarchies and class conflicts masked and distorted a family structure that varied according to the total social picture.

We might ask ourselves what implicit model of the family and of the authority exerted over it fits, as an ideal, the structures we have described and the demographic and economic constraints that influenced the family group. After all, it is not clear that the extended family was still considered the ideal family by the average peasant of this region, despite the great possibility that he would spend his entire life in such a family. But how can we discover the peasant's own view of the domestic group of which he was a part? An indirect method is to determine the hierarchies that peasants spontaneously introduced among members of the *famiglia,* by examining the place assigned to various members of the household on the list of the *catasto.* Such an attempt would be based on the assumption that the head of the household had personally dictated his family's composition to the scribe and that, in copies made subsequently, the order he had established was respected.[38] If we accept this premise, we can determine both the degree of respect due each individual and those internal relationships that were considered preeminent. A sampling of the first 1,000 families of the Pisan *contado* provides some interesting indications.

Assuming that the taxpayer whose name appears at the top of the declaration was indeed the head of the household,[39] we first discover that almost without exception his name appears at the top of the list of household members. If he was married, his wife was named immediately after him and before any other person in 87 percent of the cases in which the family also included children, ascendants, or collateral relatives. In the remaining 13 percent, she is listed after one or more of the latter, especially after her mother-in-law,[40] and on rare occasions—although apparently more frequently than in an urban setting—after her own children.[41]

In the rare cases (1.7 percent of all households) in which the father "has retired" and has ceded his authority to one son with whom he continues to live, the transfer of power was real. The old couple is listed before the son—who in such a case is always unmarried—only 12 percent of the time in this type of household. Otherwise, the elderly parents, always named together, are listed after the son and his family and even after the grandson's family or that of a second married son, if they exist. On the other hand, unmarried grandchildren are always listed after their grandparents.

38. With rare exceptions, the *campione,* or scribe copying the official register, was only recopying the list of household members as it appeared on the original declaration written or dictated by the taxpayer. On the other hand, it is possible that the peasant, without realizing it, had a certain hierarchical order imposed upon him as the result of the mental categories of the scribe, who by his questions influenced the order of the replies. (Likewise, the scribe would be following a traditional order in the general form of the declaration and in the description of the household property.) Our research therefore runs the risk of defining hierarchies within the peasant family as the scribe saw them rather than as the peasant himself lived them.

39. He is thus the head of the "fiscal household." The most striking discrepancies between fiction and reality in tax records appear in the families of minor orphans who had inherited paternal property that was now in their name and who declared their own mother as a dependent. In the list of *bocce* or dependent "mouths," to feed, the mother was often listed first, thus regaining the prestige commensurate with the authority she was actually exercising.

40. In two-thirds of the households that included an aged mother, the head's wife, her daughter-in-law, preceded her. In an urban setting, at Arezzo for example, it seems that the prestige of the head's wife paled before that of her mother-in-law, for in half the cases the latter was listed before her daughter-in-law. The brother-in-law allowed his sister-in-law to appear before him on the list in 56 percent of the cases in the region of Pisa, and half of those in our sample for Arezzo.

41. In households in the Pisan countryside composed of a couple and its unmarried children, the mother was listed after her children in only 3.4 percent of the cases; but the percentage was even lower in the city (1.5 percent). The husband-wife order was almost never reversed, but husband and wife were sometimes separated by the head's brother or, more rarely (in 4 cases out of 106), by a married son.

In multiple households in which several married brothers live together, the lists make a clear distinction between the various subgroups of the family in more than two cases out of three (70 percent). This is implicit evidence that distinct "families" were juxtaposed. In the very few cases in which a married son and a married brother live together with the head of a family, it is impossible to discern which of the latter is preeminent.[42] The hierarchies of age win out among ascendant or descendant couples and, secondarily, among collateral groups. There is no doubt that the fraternal bond that kept *affratellamenti* [married siblings in co-residence after the death or retirement of their elders] united was primarily considered a link between groups that had become slightly dissymmetrical through the difference in the ages of their respective heads. In any event, the eldest son of either family head was merely the chief among the children owing obedience to their father.

The place granted to women largely depended upon their matrimonial status. The wife of the old retired father met exactly the same fate as her husband and was either honored at the head of the list or relegated with him to the very end. But, once widowed, the woman found that the respect due her was greatly diminished, at least in rural families. In only one out of three occasions is she listed immediately after her son, the head of the family, and before her daughter-in-law, her grandchildren, and her own unmarried children.[43] The widowed sister-in-law of the head of the family would seem to have been considered the equal of her late husband while her children were still minors and she served as their spokeswoman before their uncle; but once they were of an age to claim their share of authority and their part of the inheritance, their mother was apt to be moved down, like the grandmother, to the end of the list. Even while married, women did not always share in the authority and prestige due their husbands. The married son rarely preceded his mother, but the married brother of the family head was listed before his sister-in-law in 30 percent of the cases, while unmarried sons were listed before their sister-in-law 25 percent of the time. We know that a patrilineal system often results in the disparagement of women and girls, by whom property is not transmitted. The *catasto* reflects this tendency to discriminate between the sexes to the degree that certain individuals described their children by listing boys first although they were younger than the girls, while the inverse never occurred. Using a sampling of 200 homes in which the presence of children of

42. Of these, 1,000 rural households, 10.6 percent included at least one married son of the head of the household, at least 1.6 percent included two sons, and at least 1 percent included a married brother and a married son. These percentages seem a little lower than those for the 4,000 families as a whole (12.8 percent of households included at least one married son, and 2.6 percent at least two).

43. Our sample shows that in the city of Arezzo, she would have one chance out of two to precede all these relatives.

different sexes permits us to discern this preference,[44] we find that only one of the twenty-four urban households considered the boys preeminent as compared with seven of the forty-two rural households. If a study of a larger proportion of the population were to confirm this tendency, we could consider it a secondary characteristic of patrilineal rural society.

The preceding remarks are only preliminary work in a more extensive and detailed research project we would like to carry out. At best these remarks permit us to discern within the family group the existence of subgroups hierarchically arranged according to the age of their respective head. In *affratellamenti* in which several *fathers* coexisted, the eldest seems to have been considered to a certain degree the head of the family community; but the threat that the property might be divided certainly must have tempered his authority in households of small landowners, if not among the *mezzadri,* and the younger son could attenuate his elder brother's authority over his own sons by evoking his title as coheir. The description in the *catasto,* therefore, generally makes a clear distinction between two parallel groups, subordinating sons to fathers and women to their husbands. In households of this sort, the entire younger generation is occasionally shown as submissive to the older generation as a whole, or all the women are listed after all the men. However, these tendencies are seen more often in the country than in our small urban sampling, and they indicate both an accentuation of the structural characteristics we have attempted to elucidate and a more deeply rooted sense of the agnatic bond of male descent.

On the other hand, these relatively rigid hierarchies of age operated fully in patriarchal households, and they made the sharing of authority by different generations impossible. If by chance authority was ceded, the direction of family affairs was no longer shared with the individual who had abdicated. This rapid decline of the old retired couple and, even more markedly, of the surviving grandparent or great-grandparent is striking in rural areas. As a general rule, the great majority of aged men made no concessions in exercising their authority; at times it was shared with a brother or a nephew, but never with a son.

We have described briefly the family structures in which the magnitude of the great, undivided, agnatic, partrilineal, and "patrivirilocal" family can unequivocally be seen. The fact that only a minority of the households studied represents such a family does not prevent the system from also

44. In addition to the families having only children of the same sex, we are excluding those in which children of both sexes are listed by age regardless of sex and in which it is therefore impossible or of no interest to try to determine the strength of the sexual criterion. In the contado of Pisa, where numerous corrections were made on the original list during the two years that followed the compilation of the register, during which time employees would add taxable sons who had been "forgotten" by their father, we have also eliminated such families since the list was not drawn up at one sitting (and since they are the only ones to list girls first before an older brother whose name was added later).

including the other types of families in a complex cycle in which this copy of the "medieval model" of the family remained sensitive to economic and demographic conditions. The predominant developmental cycle among landowning rural classes was one that continued over several generations, in the course of which these generations overlapped to the degree permitted by the mortality rate. But the family characteristics of the share-cropping *mezzadri* show that the economic criterion of the family patrimony was not the sole and absolute guiding force. Indeed, this type of contract preserved an extended-family system within a class of the rural population whose lack of possessions would more properly oblige it to limit the size of the domestic unit.

Within this rural society, in which the peasant family maintained a solid numerical base and an extended structure, the atypical families—as factor anaylsis shows—were those usually found in cities. In some places they were numerous enough to train a spotlight on a number of expecially wretched townships—or especially rich ones—that were not exclusively agricultural. Yet, as a whole, the population of the Pisan countryside follows the general model we have described.

The average size of the household, which remained rather low despite these structural characteristics, confirms empirically what demographers have been seeking to establish through their computations: a high mortality rate combined with a moderate or relatively low fertility rate effectively limits the average size of the family group, even in a regime where the extended family predominates.[45] Their theoretical calculations of average sizes roughly correspond to those we have found in rural Tuscany, where the great agnatic family based upon male descent was predominant, and in the cities of that province, especially in Florence, where the conjugal family and its remnants prevailed in the vast majority of the population and where more distinct and impermeable social categories prevented the "extended" model of the upper classes from spreading further down the social ladder.

Consequently, this rather low average size, observed within a society of the late Middle Ages, cannot lead us to conclude, in the absence of other data, that the "European" model of marriage and family structures had spread. The originality of Tuscany, when compared with Western Europe at the beginning of the early-modern period, lies in the fact that

---

45. Cf. Coale et. al., *Aspects of the Analysis of Family Structure,* commented upon by Burch, "Some Demographic Determinants." Since the life expectancy at birth was between twenty and forty years, under the same demographic conditions, the average size of households in a system of extended families would be 30 percent to 73 percent greater than that reached in the system of conjugal families. Thus, for $e_o = 20$, we can compute a theoretical average of 3.6 per household in a system of nuclear families, and of 4.7 in an extended system; with $e_o = 40$, we move to 4.2 and 7.2 respectively. The actual situation in Tuscany seems to have fallen between these two groups of figures at a level corresponding to an intermediate $e_o$.

a numerical decrease in the population and in families went hand in hand
with very low female marriage ages, reduced percentages of permanent
celibacy, and extended family structures—all characteristic traits of the
"non-European" model. Recent research has shown that certain sectors of
Tuscan society, the Florentine aristocracy in particular,[46] came close to the
"European" model during the sixteenth and seventeenth centuries. Did
identical tendencies also appear in the rural population, and at what period?
In any event, the *catasto* proves that the process had not yet started at the
beginning of the fifteenth century, with the exception, perhaps, of the
proletarianized rural classes or among those engaged in the process of
urbanization.

46. Cf. Litchfield, "Demographic Characteristics of Florentine Patrician Families."

# Appendix

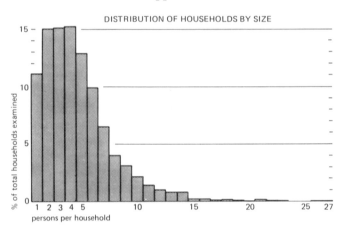

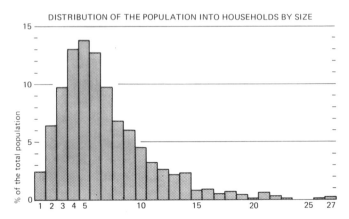

Figure 3.1 Size of Households (*contado* of Pisa, 1427–30).

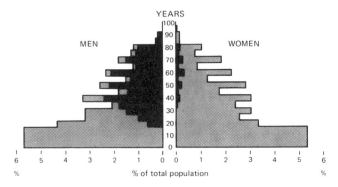

Figure 3.2 Proportion of Heads of Household by Age Group (*contado* of Pisa). Black denotes heads of household; gray, total population.

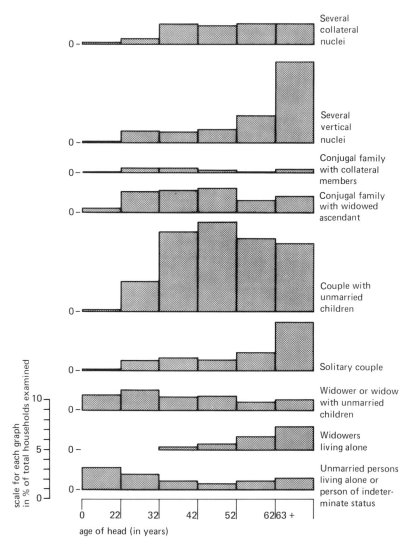

Figure 3.3 Typology of Households by Age of Head (*contado* of Pisa, 1427–30).

### 3.4(1). Clusters of characteristics and villages.

The two clusters, that of "characteristics" and that of "individuals"—in this case the 147 localities of the contado of Pisa—are arranged in relationship to one another according to the first three axes of gravity, which, combined, convey the inertia of 38 percent of the total data (20.8 percent, 10 percent, and 7.2 percent respectively).

(1) CLUSTERS OF CHARACTERISTICS AND VILLAGES

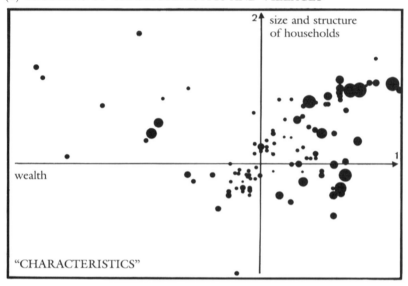

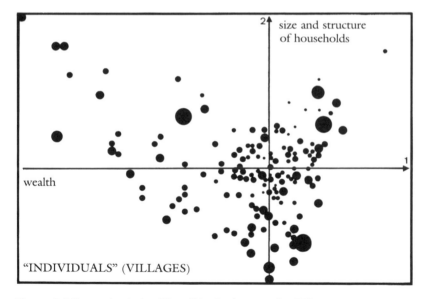

Figure 3.4 Factor Analysis of Localities in the *contado* of Pisa.

## (2) A FEW FAMILIES OF CHARACTERISTICS

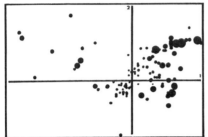

◄ THE CLUSTERS OF
CHARACTERISTICS


A FEW FAMILIES
OF CHARACTERISTICS
▼
(the line which joints the points indicates the
direction taken by each family of characteristics)

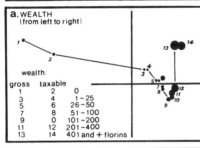

**a.** WEALTH
(from left to right)

wealth:

| gross | taxable | |
|---|---|---|
| 1 | 2 | 0 |
| 3 | 4 | 1 – 25 |
| 5 | 6 | 26 – 50 |
| 7 | 8 | 51 – 100 |
| 9 | 0 | 101 – 200 |
| 11 | 12 | 201 – 400 |
| 13 | 14 | 401 and + florins |

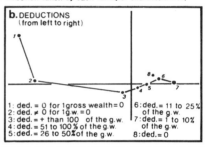

**b.** DEDUCTIONS
(from left to right)

1: ded. = 0 for 1gross wealth = 0
2: ded. ≠ 0 for 1g.w. = 0
3: ded. = + than 100  of the g.w.
4: ded. = 51 to 100 % of the g.w.
5: ded. = 26 to 50% of the g.w.
6: ded. = 11 to 25% of the g.w.
7: ded. = 1 to 10% of the g.w.
8: ded. = 0

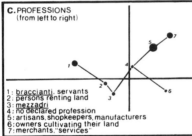

**c.** PROFESSIONS
(from left to right)

1: braccianti, servants
2: persons renting land
3: mezzadri
4: no declared profession
5: artisans, shopkeepers, manufacturers
6: owners cultivating their land
7: merchants, "services"

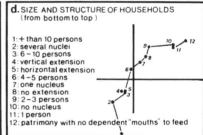

**d.** SIZE AND STRUCTURE OF HOUSEHOLDS
(from bottom to top )

1: + than 10 persons
2: several nuclei
3: 6 – 10 persons
4: vertical extension
5: horizontal extension
6: 4 – 5 persons
7: one nucleus
8: no extension
9: 2 – 3 persons
10: no nucleus
11: 1 person
12: patrimony with no dependent "mouths" to feed

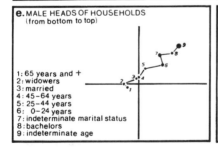

**e.** MALE HEADS OF HOUSEHOLDS
(from bottom to top)

1: 65 years and +
2: widowers
3: married
4: 45 – 64 years
5: 25 – 44 years
6: 0 – 24 years
7: indeterminate marital status
8: bachelors
9: indeterminate age

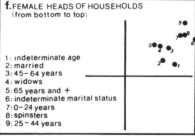

**f.** FEMALE HEADS OF HOUSEHOLDS
(from bottom to top)

1: indeterminate age
2: married
3: 45 – 64 years
4: widows
5: 65 years and +
6: indeterminate marital status
7: 0 – 24 years
8: spinsters
9: 25 – 44 years

## (3) REGIONAL GROUPS

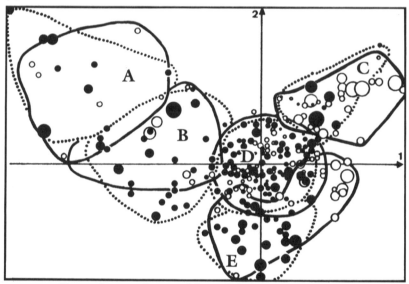

Above, the two clusters of figure 3.4 (1) are superimposed

**A** SANTA MARIA A TREBBIO
(in part)
Gross and taxable wealth nil
Mobile population
No houses belonging to occupants
Indebted households
Reduced sizes of households,
directed by men

**B** SANTA MARIA A TREBBIO
(in part)
CALCI (in part) + CASCINA
Taxable wealth nil, overburdened
household
No houses belonging to occupants,
or rented houses
Rented oxen
Salaried farm workers and small
farmers cultivating rented fields
Mobile households
Sick Persons

**C** PALAIA (in part), LARI (in part),
CAMPIGLIA (in part), LIVORNO:
CASTIGLIONE DELLA PESCAIA
Large fortunes
Secondary and tertiary professional
sectors
Households of reduced size and of
simple structure, headed by young
men, bachelors, persons of indeter-
minate status, or by women
Families bearing one name, mobile

groups of villages   groups of corresponding
characteristics

| **D** | | |
|---|---|---|
| CALCI | | PESCOLI |
| LARI | (in part) | VICO |
| RIPAFRATTA | + | ROSIGNANO |
| PALAIA | | MARTI |
| CAMPIGLIA | | VALLE DI BUTI |

Average or modest wealth
Indebted to an average or sizable
degree
Stable population
Agricultural workers, either small
landowners or sharecroppers, and
others, without declared occupation
Oxen and small livestock owned
House owned
Households of average or large size
(4–10 persons), extended either
vertically or horizontally, directed
by male heads who are mature or elderly, married or widowers

**E** RIPAFRATTA (in part)
LARI (in part)
Same socioprofessional characteristics
as D, but households large or of
complex structure

On both diagrams, the first axis, a horizontal one, indicates wealth; more specifically, it separates, on the left, the poorest individuals, those who possess no real estate and who are burdened with responsibilities, from all those on the right who possess something, however modest.

The second axis, indicated by a vertical arrow, goes from the largest and most complex households, at the bottom, to the smallest and simplest, at the top. Other characteristics are closely correlated to the size of the households: structure of household and social position of the head. They are therefore included in the same group of data symbolized by this second axis.

The third axis, represented here in perspective by the size of the dots (the largest are closest to the reader and the smallest are the most distant from the central point at which the three axes cross), is a sort of second axis indicating wealth and distinguishing property owners from one another according to the size of their fortune. It separates characteristics of unusual wealth within the rural setting (200 florins and over) from the common lot, i.e., the slender resources of small peasants and quit-rent holders grouped about the central point.

The first cluster therefore represents a selected group of 106 characteristics as related to the 147 rural localities in the region of Pisa that they describe; the second cluster represents these 147 localities as related to the cluster of characteristics. Although these two graphs can be superimposed, we have juxtaposed them to make them more readable. (In the following pages we have isolated a few of the "families" of characteristics whose arrangement permits us to define the "factors," and we have also indicated the regional groups of villages that can be set apart owing to a certain number of common characteristics.) In figure 3.4(1), the most general characteristics (and consequently the least discriminative ones) and the principal villages delineated by these characteristics are concentrated about the central point. The more eccentric characteristics are isolated, since the localities that are marked by their presence are located at some distance from the central cluster. As a result we can understand why the shapes of the two clusters are not identical: poverty, to the left, and the small size of households, at the top, mark a long, oblique trail of localities stretched out across the upper left portion of the village graph. On the other hand, characteristics unusual in these rural areas—such as fortunes greater than 400 florins, the presence of artisans and "services," major migratory exchanges, etc.—which are found grouped in the upper right quadrant of the cluster of characteristics, cause only a slight extension of the cluster of localities in that direction, while a single characteristic, such as households including more than ten persons, is sufficient to pull a large number of the villages down to the bottom of the graph.

### 3.4(2). *A few families of characteristics.*

In this figure we have isolated the most significant characteristics by presenting them in families.

In A and B we show two inverted representations of wealth. In A we show in increasing order the gross wealth (that is to say, before legal deductions) and the taxable wealth. The influence of the third axis, which makes a distinction between the rich and the less rich, is seen at the right, wheere the dots stand out clearly and stay away from the central point. The abrupt bend of the line joining these two points toward the top, on the side of the greatest wealth, reflects the socioprofessional differentiation among upper classes of the peasantry, which are pulled toward the bottom by the size of their households, and those even wealthier sectors of the population that have a more diversified economic activity and include smaller families.

In B we move, from left to right, from the heaviest responsibilities burdening the family to the lightest: this representation of the deductions authorized by the Florentine tax administration appears to be roughly the opposite of the preceding graph.

In C the spread of occupational categories moves from the poorest, the *braccianti* ("day laborers") and hired farm workers, to farmers and share-croppers (*mezzadri*) on their right. Toward the center of gravity of the whole are the numerous persons "with no declared occupation." In the right portion, close to the wealthiest individuals, we find landowners doing their own farming, who are clearly set apart near the bottom, and artisans, shopkeepers, and "services" at the top, although they are all on very similar levels of fortune (100 and 200 florins). This "fork" suggests, as in A, that these two occupational groups present very different family profiles.

In D the characteristics of the size and structure of households, indicated by the second axis, are strung along rather evenly from the bottom to the top until we reach households of two or three persons. But the very marked bend to the right and the horizontal line joining these points when we reach households with one person show in a remarkable manner how the presence of very small households, of solitary individuals, and of vacant patrimonies is clearly correlated with other "urban" characteristics (oc-cupational activities, economic independence of women and young per-sons, more accentuated concentration of wealth).

Graphs E and F isolate characteristics concerning heads of households in terms of their age and their marital status. In E mature men, either married or widowers, who are responsible for a *famiglia,* are grouped about the central point. This is where the authority resides in the great majority of households. Toward the top and to the right we find a separate

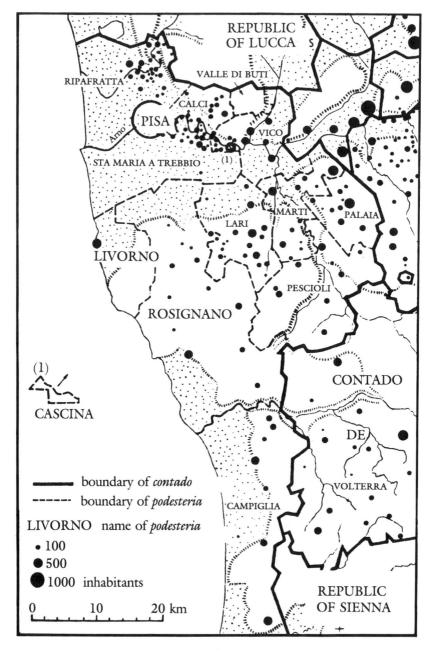

Figure 3.5 The *contado* of Pisa as seen in the *Catasto* of 1427–30. (Not shown on the map: Castiglione della Pescaia, an enclave along the coast, thirty kilometers to the south.)

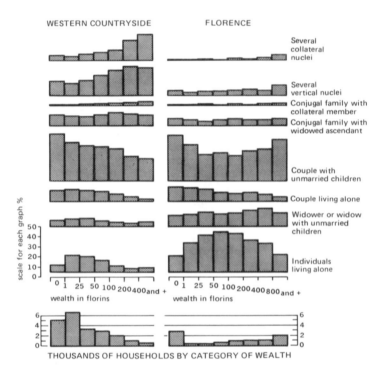

Figure 3.6 Proportion of Types of Households, According to Wealth, in Florence and the Western Rural Florentine Territory (in each percentage of total for each category of wealth).

group of young men who are already independent and who are associated with "urban" characteristics, both occupational and economic. Women appear in their turn in graph F in a very eccentric fashion; their presence at the head of a household can be indisputably observed in the less "rural" milieus of the Pisan contado but only in a completely marginal fashion within the agricultural population.

# 4

## "Kin, Friends, and Neighbors": The Urban Territory of a Merchant Family in 1400

*Parenti, amici, vicini*: these three words are constantly found closely associated in the thoughts of Tuscans of the fourteenth and fifteenth centuries. Around 1400 a man like Giovanni Morelli will often use them to express the many relatives and associates on which an individual could rely; to be betrayed or abandoned by them signified to him ruin and poverty.[1] With Morelli as with his contemporaries, kinship, friendship, and neighborliness are thus almost always evaluated in terms of their social utility. The same viewpoint will serve here to analyze the composition, the range, and the role of this "personal group" centered on a given individual; in particular, I shall try to determine whether the blood relationship is the dominant constituent of these ties. If we can define the criteria for the recruitment or exclusion of these persons—persons who permitted the individual to play his social role to the full—it should clarify the functions ideally assigned to kinship and to alliance, as well as the functions that these two sorts of ties (or their substitutes) really fulfilled. Some aspects of this problem may be clarified by examining one particular case.

Originally published as "Parenti, amici, vicini," *Quaderni storici* 33 (1976): 953–82.

1. Giovanni di Pagolo Morelli, *Ricordi*, ed. V. Branca (Florence, 1956), 232: "Così il povero pupillo è pelato da' parenti, dagli amici, da' vicini e dagli strani; e da oguno con chi s'impaccia egli è rubato, ingannato e tradito" (Thus the poor ward is skinned by his relatives, by his friends, by his neighbors, and by outsiders; and by all he encounters he is robbed, cheated, and betrayed). Similarly, ibid., 246–47.

A Florentine merchant, Lapo di Giovanni Niccolini dei Sirigatti, kept a *Libro degli affari proprii di casa* from 1379 to 1421.[2] Like other Florentine *ricordanze*, it evokes the pell-mell of daily life, notes the people Lapo encountered, and describes their dealings. In its conception and organization this book is by no means especially original; to the contrary, it is marked by the dryness of its observations and information. Lapo states his intention to record the "events of the house, . . . all notations and memoranda and every thing that pertains to me"[3]—all that regards him, then, and those close to him, members of his "chasa" (Lapo's spelling). As with so many other examples of this private literature, Lapo's book recounts day by day the events that affected the number or the status of the members of the household and the acquisitions, transfers, or exchanges of goods that influenced its wealth. In this way he records a great number of relatives, both consanguineal and affinal, and others connected with him in all sorts of ways.[4] A further interest of his book is that the author, like many of his contemporaries, indulges late in life in the preparation of an annotated genealogical introduction designed to prove the antiquity and reinforce the social status of his lineage.

The Niccolini were a family relatively new to Florence, distinguishing themselves, toward the beginning of the fourteenth century, from the older lineage of the Sirigatti from Passignano, certain members of which had already arrived in the city by that time. Lapo's immediate ancestors were soon honored with municipal offices. His grandfather, also named Lapo, was a prominent silk merchant (*grande mercatante*) and became a *priore* in 1334 and *gonfaloniere di justizia* in 1341—the highest civic magistracy in Florence. The father of our Lapo, Giovanni, was also active in city government, although he never became *gonfaloniere*. When Lapo wrote

2. *Il Libro degli affari proprii di casa di Lapo di Giovanni Niccolini de' Sirigatti,* ed. C. Bec (Paris: SEVPEN, 1969). The Niccolini have also been the object of a series of studies by one of their descendants, G. Niccolini da Camugliano: "A Medieval Florentine, His Family and his Possessions," *American Historical Review* 31 (1925): 1–19; "Libri di ricordanze dei Niccolini," *Rivista delle Biblioteche e degli Archivi* 2 (1924): 1–30, 88–91, 172–87, 243–52; *The Chronicles of a Florentine Family, 1200–1400* (London, 1933). The author has exploited and in part published the private archives of the Niccolini family, particularly a second book of Lapo's devoted to his landholdings and the books of his sons.

3. "Fatti proprii di chasa . . . tutte richordanze e memorie e [ognie] chose che s'appartenessono a me" (*Libro,* 55 ).

4. His *lavoratori* (peasant farmers) and his business relations, treated in his business account books, are almost totally absent. In order to verify the accuracy of the notes in his private *Libro,* I have checked the papers of one of his notaries and friends, ser Antonio dall'Ancisa, for the years 1408–13 (Archivio di Stato di Firenze, henceforth abbreviated ASF, *Notarile antecosmiano,* A 807). It is evident from this comparison that those absent from Lapo's secret book but present in the notarized acts recorded by his friend are, for the most part, witnesses, whom Lapo mentions very rarely. On the use of collections of notarial documents for the reconstitution of kinship networks, see Diane O. Hughes, "Toward Historical Ethnography: Notarial Records and Family History in the Middle Ages," *Historical Methods Newsletter* 7 (1974): 61–71.

his genealogical introduction (between 1417 and 1421),[5] he had already held that position himself at least three times and had played an important role in Florentine politics.[6] Why, in these circumstances, should he still feel the need to consolidate the political and social position of the family by evoking the Guelf loyalties of his ancestors and their admission into the circle of "good citizens"? Honors had been concentrated in one branch of the Niccolini family, and the lineage as a whole seems still relatively humble around 1400, whether we consider the number of its members and the influence of the entire group or the few individuals among them, notably our Lapo, who monopolized political command and material success. The interchangeable responsibilities and roles that assured the strength of the great Florentine families were less secure among the Niccolini. A man like Lapo, who had achieved personal success, sought to deflect onto all those he considered his kin the prestige that his grandfather, his father, his older brother, and he himself had acquired. Naturally, he expected personal benefits in exchange, but his first concern seems to have been dynastic. *Parenti, amici,* and *vicini* were to play an important role in this attempt at consolidation. When he conforms to the traditional strategies of his circle—and when he occasionally abandons these strategies in order to hasten their effects—Lapo ingenuously reveals the accepted functions of those contacts.

### "I nostri e quei di casa nostra"

The family was first and foremost those who shared a house, the domestic group that lived in common. It is significant that in his introduction Lapo emphasizes the geographical roots of his line. Two houses in via del Palagio del Podestà in the *quartiere* of Santa Croce, extending east along the Arno, gave tangible expression to the "Florentinity" of the Niccolini from the time they came to the city. Those who were admitted to or excluded from these houses provide some measure of who Lapo considered his intimates. But the "family," for a Florentine of the merchant aristocracy, also included the members of that spiritual *casa* that was the lineage—deceased family members whose last resting place the descendants provided and whose memory was kept alive by masses celebrated in the family chapel[7]—and

5. In his introduction to his edition of the *Libro*, C. Bec dates this addition between 1409 and 1413, basing his interpretation on the number of male children Lapo has at the time (*Libro*, 22, 58). In my opinion, Lapo's genealogy was composed either (as Bec suggests) before 1413, or between 1417 and 1421—that is, between the death of his first son and that of his last son, another moment in his life when Lapo had eight sons. I lean toward the second hypothesis, for he attributes an age to his brother Filippo (67) that is incompatible with the first date, and his remarks on the repossession of several houses could have been made only after 1417.

6. See *Libro,* C. Bec, Introduction, 11.

7. Lapo's father stipulates in his will that a *sepoltura nuova* (new tomb) be created in the church of Santa Croce. His descendants were to be buried there, and the tomb can still

living members scattered in different households, who by misfortune and awareness of their lineage were sometimes forced to unite under one roof. Lapo's book permits us to survey a great number of these persons, and even his reticences are in themselves significant.

First of all, the book offers a series of images, spread over forty years or so, that serve as points of reference to show how the composition and the size of the domestic group varied with the age of the head of household and with the tribulations undergone by the population as a whole.

At the time of his death in 1381, Lapo's father, Giovanni, was living with his wife, his married older son and the latter's wife and children, and two younger, unmarried sons. Two other children, both daughters, were married and living elsewhere. The elder, Monna, was already widowed and may have lived for some time under the paternal roof, with her daughter, before remarrying, as Florentine law and even her father's will permitted her to do.[8] By its size (nine to eleven persons) as well as by its vertical structure, the household was quite typical of the merchant families of Florence.[9]

After Giovanni's death, the brothers' alliance (made up of the family of the elder brother and the two younger brothers) did not long survive. Niccolaio, the eldest, separated from his brothers and received the house next to the principal dwelling of the family in the division of the estate that took place in 1382.[10] The two younger brothers, our Lapo and his younger brother Filippo, continued to live with their mother in the first house. At the beginning of 1384 they each took a wife simultaneously and celebrated their weddings with "a single festivity in our house on the via del Palagio."[11] Their behavior, once again, is quite typical of the young members of their class. The elder brother died soon after the father,[12] and to consolidate their situation our two young men[13] found it imperative to enter into alliances as soon as possible so that they could manage their own affairs and assure the guardianship of their nephews.[14] But—and this too is a typically Florentine trait—fraternal solidarity did not last long

---

be seen today. He also provided in his will for masses to be said for ten years in the parish church of San Simone, near his house (*Libro*, 60–61). The Niccolini in fact were to have a "chappella di Sancto Niccolaio, ch'è in San Simone, dov'è dipinta e intalgliata l'arme nostra" (chapel [in honor] of Saint Nicholas, in [the church of] San Simone, where our crest is painted and carved) (ibid., 90) and they also supported a priest at San Simone.

8. *Libro*, 61–62.

9. See D. Herlihy, "Mapping Households in Medieval Italy," *Catholic Historical Review* 58 (1972): 1–24; D. Herlihy and C. Klapisch-Zuber, *Les Toscans et leurs familles: Une analyse du catasto de 1427* (Paris, 1978), chap. 17.

10. *Libro*, 63–67.

11. "Una ffesta nella nostra chasa della via del Palagio" (ibid., 71–72).

12. His testament in *Libro*, 69–70.

13. Lapo must have been about 28 years old and Filippo about 26.

14. All the more so since their brother-in-law Pierozzo di Ruberto Ghetti, Fia's husband, had just died also, leaving two orphans, for whom Lapo took on the guardianship (February 1384; *Libro*, 71).

under a common roof. In September of 1385, less than one year after their marriages, the two couples moved apart and divided the goods that the 1382 agreement had left undivided. Since he was older, Lapo quite naturally became head of *casa* Niccolini and acquired the principal house on via del Palagio del Podestà, in which he was to live until his death in 1430.[15]

From this moment onward, births were to swell the household that occupied this dwelling. Lapo was prolific: he had seven children by his first wife, Ermellina da Mezzola, in less than sixteen years of marriage;[16] and six by the second, Caterina Melanesi, in the twelve first years of their union.[17] Around 1402 his roof sheltered ten persons, not counting the domestics, and around 1410, fifteen. He was at the time over 50. At the peak of his responsibilities as head of household, ten unmarried children lived at home, along with his old mother, who was at least 80, and his sister Monna, widowed for the second time and whom he had taken in with her daughter Nanna.[18] The plague of 1417 carried away his eldest son and his youngest daughter,[19] but these losses were made up for by taking in his three granddaughters—the daughters of his daughter Lena and his son-in-law Ugo Altoviti, orphaned when both parents also died of the plague[20]—and he was again responsible for at least twelve persons. According to his *catasto* declaration of 1427,[21] the household was at that time reduced to eight persons and one slave woman; Giovanni, now the eldest son, had married and left the house. At this point Lapo was living only with his wife, five children, and a grandnephew.

This reduction of his household late in life is also a characteristic that can be observed statistically in the households of city dwellers of his circle. Lapo's father had been able to continue to keep his married eldest son

15. *Libro*, 76–79. See his declaration to the *catasto* of 1427, ASF, *Catasto* 73, fol. 141.

16. *Libro*, 72. Ermellina was *menata* (brought to her husband's house) 11 May 1384 and died 28 February 1400. Only one of her children died in infancy, at one year.

17. Ibid., 92. She was *menata* 11 September 1401; Lapo's last son, Battista, was born 25 June 1413.

18. Nanna left his roof in January 1411 to go to her husband Berto da Filicaia (ibid., 113); Monna died before 1415 (ibid., 124). His mother, Bartolomea Bagnesi, died in 1416 (ibid., 134). Lapo had married two of his daughters, who left home in 1405 and 1409.

19. Niccolaio, 31 years old (ibid., 136); Ermellina, 14 years old, whose death is noted with her birth, not at the corresponding date (ibid., 94).

20. He took in their mother, who died in his house, for six months, and then kept her children (ibid., 137). Niccolaio, his nephew Francesco's son, was the sole survivor of a family of six persons (ibid., 135). The four children of his other nephew, Giovanni, were abandoned by their mother after the death of her husband (ibid., 137). The book does not say clearly if they continued to live in the house next to Lapo's own, which fell to their grandfather Niccolaio in the division in 1382 and which Lapo had bought back, or if they too were taken in by their great-uncle.

21. ASF, *Catasto* 73, fols. 141ff. The *uficiali* of the *catasto* decided to allow as *suo nipote* (his nephew) Bartolomeo di Giovanni di Niccolaio, "nine or ten years old," who was in fact his great-nephew.

with him, with his wife and children, because his household did not have too many mouths to feed; but Lapo, at the same age, had a *famiglia grandissima*. On several occasions he made an effort to make more room by getting his grown sons established elsewhere. His efforts were in vain: Niccolaio, the eldest, "too big a spender of his own money and others'," preferred to shelter "his appetites and desires" within the familial cocoon. The plague of 1417 swept him away, eliminating the problem of a congested house in radical fashion.[22] Giovanni, the next son, seems to have been in no greater hurry to submit to the holy laws of matrimony, even when Lapo paved the way with gold in 1418. While still seeking out a wife for him, Lapo offered him more than his share of his inheritance if he would leave the house.[23] His efforts were crowned with success before the *catasto* of 1427, since Giovanni is listed on its books on his own, with a wife at last.[24]

In the final analysis, Lapo owed the fairly simple structure of his household toward the end of his life to the fertility of his wives and to the fact that ten of his thirteen children survived to adulthood.[25] People of his rank in Florence were happy to marry one or two of their sons without having them leave the flock, as his own father had done. But the variations in the composition of Lapo's household reveal the flexibility of rules of residence in Florence, which bent to the practical conditions of cohabitation. If Lapo's progeny had suffered a higher mortality rate, he very probably would have been encouraged to keep his married son at home.

We can also see that his house was on several occasions saturated by an influx of close relatives who were widowed or in need owing to the

22. On Niccolaio: "Troppo grande gittatore del suo e dell'altrui." Lapo attempted an accounting with Niccolaio in October 1416 "perché io gli voleva dare molgle e dargli la sua parte e dividerlo da mme" (because I wanted to give him a wife and give him his inheritance and his independence from me). They were unable to reach a *compromesso*, he states, "perché ancora non eravamo venuti a perfetione di nostra intentione" (because we had not yet reached perfect agreement) (*Libro*, 134; for the death of Niccolaio, ibid., 136–37).

23. "E io Lapo volglendo dargli molgle, e io abbiendo la familgla grandissima, mi diliberai volerlo partire da mme e dargli delle mie sustanze quella parte gli tocchava e ancora molto più, e questo perch'era il magiore de' miei filgliuoli che m'erano rimasi" (and I, Lapo, desiring to give him a wife, and having a very large family, decided to emancipate him and give him of my substance the share he deserved and much more, and this because he was the eldest of my remaining sons) (ibid., 143, 7 November 1418).

24. ASF, *Catasto* 73, fols. 97ff. His wife Tita declares she is 28, and he himself 38, although he was born in 1395. On these exaggerations of age, see Herlihy and Klapisch-Zuber, *Les Toscans,* chap. 13. In 1427 Giovanni lived in a house his father had reacquired from a cousin; see below, notes 57–59. These long bachelorhoods found their solaces, which translated into additional crowding in merchant households. In this way, the slave Lucia, declared by Lapo as early as 1427, and aged 25 when Lapo died in 1430, gave three sons to Paolo di Lapo before 1434 and continued to live in the house with her children when Paolo brought in an official wife (see Niccolini, *The Chronicles,* 112ff).

25. His son Paolo was to have twenty children by two wives, a concubine, and a mistress. Of the sixteen legitimate children, only eight were to reach adulthood (ibid., 130–38).

plague. As head of *casa* Niccolini, Lapo opened his doors wide to these relatives in difficulty, as familial ethics required. The solidarity of these *congiunti stretti*—blood relatives—is never better expressed than in the momentary reunions brought about by a death or a low blow of fortune. To belong to the same *casa* also meant to be able to take refuge or to gather under the same roof when danger threatened.

We would have to exclude wives from among these intimates—the *prossimani* that Lapo finds himself taking in—as they are never completely considered full-fledged members of the lineage into which they entered by marriage. Nothing could better reflect their floating status than a comment of Lapo's at the time of his mother's death in 1416. He remarks that she "came to [her] husband in the year of our Lord 1349, the first day of October 1349, so that she remained in our house 67 years, 2 months, and 26 days."[26] The meticulousness of the reckoning reveals rather than masks the son's real feelings: this woman, who came of the Bagnesi family, remained all of her long life a transitory visitor in the Niccolini house.

The return of Monna and Lena Niccolini, when widowed, to their brother's or their father's house shows that they, in contrast, remained a part of the ideal *casa*, or "house."[27] Despite the intermittence of their appearances they continue to be considered blood kin, members of a family whose center remained the paternal or fraternal dwelling. An aged aunt of Lapo's, his father's sister Simona, widowed before the Black Death, may also have lived out her last years in the house of her nephew Niccolaio, Lapo's brother.[28] This woman thus returned to her family of birth after more than thirty years. The return of these widows (who, under the law, had the right of *tornata* to their family of birth) seems to have occurred because they were alone and, in particular, because they had no male descendant who could care for them—but who would also find it to his interest to avoid the loss of the mother's dowry should she leave his house.[29]

More surprising is the acceptance of relatives or descendants who were not born Niccolini. Thus in 1419 Lapo welcomes his three granddaughters, nées Altoviti, after the plague of 1417–18 had orphaned them. Their inclusion in the household seems contrary to the rule that dictates that the descendants of a couple belong to the father's lineage, whose name

26. "Ne venne a marito nelgli anni di Christo 1349, a dì primo d'ottobre 1349, sicchè venne a stare in casa nostra anni lxvii mesi due e dì 26" (*Libro*, 134).

27. His sister Monna, at least between 1406 and her death (1411–15?) (ibid., 104, 111–15, 124). Lena, her daughter, between February and July 1418 (ibid., 137).

28. Niccolini, "Libri di ricordanze dei Niccolini." Widowed in 1345, she and her two daughters were taken in, after the death of her father-in-law Gieri Delli, by her brothers. The daughters were married in 1349 and 1353. Her brother Giovanni's will, written in 1377, allowed her to live "sopra i suoi beni e delle sue herede a bastamento della sua vita" (on his holdings and on his inheritance, sufficient to her needs) (*Libro*, 61). The division between the three brothers gave this responsibility to the eldest, Niccolaio (ibid., 64).

29. See for example the case of Fia, Lapo's sister, cited in note 34.

they bear and within which they remain even if the widowed mother leaves this lineage to remarry. Here again, however, Lapo suggests that his grand-daughters' presence under his roof was somewhat exceptional: it was at the request of one of their Altoviti relatives and of the Ufficio de' Pupilli, the communal office responsible for wards, that he took them in (and was reimbursed for his trouble).[30] Similarly, he supported his niece Nanna Folchi when he took in her mother, his own sister Monna, because the Folchi family seems to have been undergoing financial difficulties, and his deceased brother-in-law had left his widow just enough to provide a dowry for the daughter.[31] In 1410 Nanna received her nuptial ring in the house of her uncle Lapo and brought her husband the 800 *fiorini* scraped together from her father's creditors and his movable goods. We should mention one final situation, just as exceptional, that linked *casa* Niccolini with a woman relative bearing another name. In the division of 1385, Lapo received, along with the dwelling on via del Palagio, the obligation of sheltering and maintaining a first cousin, Lena Aghinetti, the daughter of one of his father's sisters.[32] This woman was a *pinzochera*—a member of a third order and a noncloistered nun. When she retired from the world in 1396, perhaps under her cousin's roof, she bequeathed her estate (a farm in the Mugello) to the family chapel in the parish church, San Simone. She may have owed her welcome into the Niccolini house to her semi-cloistered state, which, in the best of cases,[33] would necessarily sanctify the roof under which her pious activities took place.

Aside from those to whom blood and the family name gave full rights of residence, the material house might shelter more distant blood relatives, forced by an extraordinary or temporary situation to turn to the head of family. Consciousness of the spiritual *casa* (what Lapo calls the "familglia") reaches beyond those living in the same dwelling, however, even consid-ering temporary additions to the household. Of blood relatives of all degrees mentioned in his *Libro*—those with whom he has dealings or whom he notes as among his contemporaries—only one-half (twenty-three persons) at one time or another share Lapo's roof. The rest break down into two groups of quite unequal size.

30. *Libro*, 137. In 1427, when his niece Ermellina took the veil, Lapo mentions another 70 *fiorini* owed to him "dalla redità d'Ugho Altoviti per abitamento della figliuola" (from the inheritance from Ugo Altoviti for the girl's lodging) (ASF, *Catasto* 73, fol. 142v).

31. For the recuperation of the dowry, *Libro* 104, 111–15. For the marriage of "Nanna" Folchi, ibid., 113: "E a dì vi [6] di lulglio 1410, il detto Berto le diede l'anello in casa di me Lapo, nella via del Palagio, dove io abito" (and on the sixth day of July, 1410, the said Berto gave her the ring in the house of myself, Lapo, in the via del Palagio, where I live).

32. Ibid., 77.

33. At least this was so in the best of cases, since many of these members of the third order—particularly the females—had a dreadful reputation as shameless bigots, "ispigolistri picchapetti, ipocriti che si cuoprono col mantello del religioso" (bigots, breast beaters, and hypocrites who hide under the friar's cloak) (Morelli, *Ricordi,* 227).

The first of these groups, and the largest, is made up of the families
descended from his elder brother, Niccolaio, who were hard hit by the
plague of 1417, and those of his sister Fia, whose four children remain
within the two lineages to which she was successively allied.[34] The second
group is made up of more distant cousins. Lapo calls them *nostri consorti*
(our consorts) and here they bear the name of Sirigatti alone. If we go
back to their common ancestor, Arrigo, surnamed Sirigatto, who lived
during the first half of the thirteenth century, these cousins are no less
than five canonical degrees removed from Lapo. Aside from them, Lapo
notes in his brief preliminary genealogy that his great-uncle Biagio Niccolini must have had at least six children, over whom, however, he casts
a modest veil: "[they] were all wicked men—one more than the other—
and [they] destroyed what their father had earned."[35] This "wretched
family" had only one descendant "about in the world" around 1420.[36] The
genealogy published by Passerini shows, furthermore, that Lapo passes
over certain branches of the family in total silence, as well as certain
individuals who bore the Niccolini name and lived not only during his
lifetime but even in his neighborhood.[37] Thus our author does not even
mention a paternal great-uncle, Giovanni, and all his descendants, long
settled in the *contado*. Men of war, businessmen who were unlucky or ran
through their fortunes, men who tilled the earth—Lapo considers them
marginal to society and better ignored.

When he cuts his ties with his cousins' descendants in this manner,
Lapo greatly reduces the number of his useful blood relatives. His contemporaries—Giovanni Morelli, for example, and later Leon Battista Alberti—saw in immediate kin the persons whom it is natural, and thus

34. Fia Magalotti, widowed in 1402, lived alone and *povera* (poor) in 1427 and made
out a declaration for the *catasto* in her own name (ASF, *Catasto* 80, fol. 342). She lived at
the time in the *quartiere* San Giovanni, while her son Guido lived in Santa Croce like Lapo
(ibid., 69, fol. 544).

35. "Che tutti furono huomini piu tristi [*l'uno*] che l'altro e distrussero ciò che il loro
padre avea ghadangniato" (*Libro*, 57).

36. Ibid. It may be the same Piero di Biagio, *commissario di guerra al Corniolo* in 1389
mentioned in the genealogy of L. Passerini, *Genealogia e storia della famiglia Niccolini* (Florence, 1870), table 1.

37. The branch of Giovanni di Niccolino, whose great-grandsons Antonio and Niccolò
di Piero were living at the time of Lapo's writing. In this connection see Passerini, *Genealogia;*
and J. Plesner, *L'émigration de la campagne à la ville libre de Florence au XIII^e siécle* (Copen-
hagen, 1934), 221, Généalogie G (ser Paganelli). In the *catasto* of 1427, as in other contemporary documents, *Tratte* or *Prestanze* (which I thank David Herlihy for having brought
to my attention) there appear a Niccolò d'Andrea Niccolini and a Giovanni d'Andrea Niccolini, *lanaiolo*, whose shop was on Lapo's street. They bear the name Niccolini, but never
"de' Niccolini" nor "de' Sirigatti" as do Lapo and his immediate family. Furthermore, toward
the middle of the fifteenth century, the descendants and heirs of Giovanni d'Andrea were
called Niccoli (ASF, *Catasto* 64, fol. 301v, marginal indications of transfers of goods occurring
between 1427 and 1457 or 1469). It is probable that this family was not related to Lapo's;
it attempts to emphasize its individuality after 1450 by using a name quite different from
that of the Niccolini de' Sirigatti (although the last part of that name disappears about the
same period).

logical, to trust in family or commercial affairs.[38] Lapo thus has only a few "natural" contacts—collaterals or adult cousins who could come to his aid.[39] In the family agreements noted in his *Libro*, few of the arbiters are recruited from among the Niccolini.[40] In contrast, ser Niccolò Sirigatti, a notary and the oldest of the three *consorti*, is called on to play this role on two occasions: in 1380 to settle a matter between Lapo and his sister Monna,[41] and in 1403 to draw up the accounts for the guardianship of Lapo's nephews.[42] This "savio huomo" (wise man), as Lapo calls him, enjoyed enormous prestige among the Niccolini and was certainly well informed of their affairs, since he acted as notary for Lapo's father from the mid-fourteenth century onward.[43] A respected man (and of respectable age around 1400), he held important communal offices.[44] His talents and his experience thus made him particularly well qualified to decide the affaires of his *consorti*. On the other hand, his nephew, also a notary, and his son seem never to have been called on to fulfill similar functions.

Lapo's book shows us what questions generally obstructed the solidarity and confidence normal among close kin. Paradoxically, the very means that their mutual confidence prompted relatives to employ in dealing with one another ended up working against them. Oral agreements that spared them the use of legal formulas and notarization were easily broken or reinterpreted, thus arousing the rancor of the other party. Lapo saves his bad humor and his scorn for those closest to him, in proportion to what he considers their betrayal: for his brother, who "per poco suo senno" (through his lack of good sense) failed to be grateful to Lapo for services rendered;[45] for a female cousin who acts as if he, Lapo, were not going to keep his word;[46] for his niece's husband, who was sticking his nose into

38. With numerous reservations and precautions, however, which Morelli recounts morosely (*Ricordi*, 218–23). On the choice of guardians, see ibid., 246–47.

39. His nephews Francesco and Giovanni arrived at adulthood and marriage in 1404 and 1405, probably at the age of 25 to 28 years. Their mature years were short, and twelve or thirteen years after their marriage they succumbed to the plague (*Libro*, 75 and 85).

40. This seems normal, since they were party to the problems concerning the estate. Filippo, Lapo's brother, was arbiter three times, however; his nephews Francesco and Nic-colaio once each, for a total of 5 occurrences out of the 44 accumulated by 27 different arbiters who appear in 22 family arbitrations and *compomessi* noted in the *Libro*.

41. Concerning a payment by the Buondelmonti of 352 *fiorini* to return Monna's dowry, a sum paid to "la cha nostra e in uso d'essa si spesono" (our house and spent for her) (*Libro*, 60).

42. Ibid., 96.

43. He drew up the marriage acts of Simona Delli's daughters in 1349 and 1353 (Niccolini, "Libri di ricordanze," 24–25). He may have had landholdings in common with the Niccolini in the region of Passignano, since in 1363 he countersigned an act concerning lands that the Niccolini owned in this region (Plesner, *L'émigration*, 143–44).

44. He was notary of the Signoria in 1390 and 1400; priore in 1383, gonfaloniere di compagnia in 1387, one of the twelve Buonomini in 1397, capitain of the Compagnia d'Orsanmichele in 1402 (Passerini, *Genealogia*, table 1).

45. *Libro*, 143.

46. Ibid., 146.

his mother-in-law's affairs;[47] also for his son, who had dragged him into a questionable affair and who died without amassing any fortune or showing any desire to perpetuate the family;[48] and for a nephew who went bankrupt and left a number of debts unpaid.[49] Because he had not taken the trouble to write things down (which, incidentally, characterized his daily behavior as a businessman), Lapo was forced on more than one occasion to admit his disappointment concerning his familial attachments.[50]

Traces of positive sentiments toward his close kin are hard to find in Lapo's book.[51] This does not mean to say that those sentiments did not exist, but simply that they are not expressed here. In fact, we can guess that the cohesion of this little group of blood kin is, minor accidents aside, so well maintained by its community of interests, by its shared sense of name and of spiritual patrimony, and by the authority and prestige of its uncontested chief, Lapo, that the expression of feelings could remain in the background. One thing that gives a clear indication of feelings within the lineage, however, is their attitude toward ancestral houses.

All his life, Lapo fought a centrifugal tendency for dwellings constructed by his ancestors to be removed from the control of the head of the "house" of Niccolini. The changing fortunes of the second of the houses situated on the via del Palagio are a good illustration of the need for geographical stability in order to maintain familial group identity. This house had fallen to the elder of the brothers, Niccolaio, in 1382. One of his sons, Giovanni, went bankrupt in 1409. To release him from prison, Lapo guaranteed a loan of 500 *fiorini* to satisfy his creditors, putting up the house as security. But when Giovanni died in 1417 without having been able to pay back his debts, Lapo found himself obligated, much against his will, to put the dowry of the deceased's widow before his own interests, and had to buy

---

47. Ibid., 124–25. Lapo does not keep a written account of the funds destined for his sister that pass through his hands, "che mmi faceva co'llei come con serocchia non pensando avere a renderne regione a Berto da Filicaia ne ad altri. . . . .E non avendo scritto alcuna cosa di ciò, ò fatta questa scrittura a ricordanza" (because I acted with her as with a sister, not thinking I owed any explanation to Berto da Filicaia [his niece's husband] or to others . . . and not anything written on this, I have made this notation and memorandum). He declares that he has rendered these services "perchè le donne non possono andare, né intendere, né essercitarsi come gli huomini" (because women cannot go about, nor comprehend, nor act as men do).

48. Ibid., 125 and 136–37: "mi diede assai fatiche" (It put me to a good deal of trouble).

49. Ibid., 135.

50. Similarly, Morelli, *Ricordi*, 243: "Non ti fidare mai di persona, fa le cose chiare e più col parente e coll'amico che cogli strani, come che con ognuno, fa con carte di notaio, con obbrighi liberi a un'arte, non ti affidare a scritta di libri, se non per terza persona" (Do not ever trust anyone; be clear in things and still more with a relative or friend than with outsiders, but [deal this way] with all, use notarial forms, with free obligations to a guild, do not trust what is written in books, except by third parties). See below, note 61.

51. Except with his mother, when she dies ("una valente e cara e buona donna"—a brave, dear, and good woman) (*Libro*, 134), as C. Bec rightly remarks in his introduction, ibid., 24.

back for 350 *fiorini* a house that he already considered his own.[52] Several years later, in writing the genealogical introduction to his book, he declares himself glad: "although in this way [the houses] were left to many institutions and to many persons and given by some people as a dowry, they have finally returned to us, and may it please God that it be so for long years to come."[53] These words speak to a desire for geographical roots, expressed by the urban family as forcefully as by the rural family.

On two occasions Lapo also exercised a right of repurchase of family houses granted him by relatives' wills. In 1403 a female first cousin bequeathed to the hospital of Santa Maria Novella a group of houses and shops that had belonged to Biagio Niccolini, Lapo's half-brother on his mother's side, which her husband had bought from Biagio's heirs—those "tristi huomini." She granted to Lapo and his heirs the right to buy back this group of buildings, which were situated a little further along the via del Palagio, at the price of 300 *fiorini*.[54] Lapo let eighteen years go by before he exercised his right and negotiated with the hospital for the transfer of his great-uncle's buildings.[55] Thus in spite of his scorn for Biagio's descendants, Lapo retained an evident attachment for the places where Biagio had been perhaps the first to lay the foundations of the Niccolini merchant fortune.[56] Reconstructing the original unity of the lineage by gathering its houses together appears here as one of the governing principles in Lapo's *affari proprii di casa*.

The second occasion on which he makes use of a similar right is offered by his *consorto*, ser Niccolò Sirigatti. Niccolò provided in his will for a circuitous destiny for the house in which he lived, contiguous to the two principal Niccolini houses on via del Palagio.[57] If his son and then his nephew were to die "without legitimate and natural heirs," Lapo and his own successors "in the male line" and, failing this, any other descendant of his own father, Giovanni di Lapo, could have the house on payment of 300 *fiorini* to compensate the other heirs.[58] The nephew died in 1417, ser Niccolò's son died in 1427. At that time, as Lapo notes with satisfac-

52. Ibid., 132 and 148.
53. "Bene che in questo mezzo si sono lasciate [le case] a molti luoghi e persone e date per alchuni in dote, alla fine sono tornate a nnoi, e chosì piaccia a Ddio che sia per lunghi tempi" (ibid., 156).
54. Ibid., 97–98. In 1427 one of these houses belonged to his great-nephew Niccolaio di Francesco, who rented it to Fruosino di Luca da Panzano (ASF, *Catasto* 73 fol. 334).
55. *Libro*, 143–45 (1421).
56. Ibid., 57: "E fu il primo di loro che chomincìò a fare merchatantie" (and was the first of them to go into business).
57. His testament in ibid., 101–2. This house was perhaps the first residential nucleus of the Sirigatti before the houses built by Lapo's direct ancestors. One ser Paganello Sirigatti, "judex et notarius populi sancti Simonis civ. Florentie" (judge and notary of the *gonfalone* of San Simone in the city of Florence) lived in the neighborhood around 1280–96 (Plesner, *L'émigration*, 221, Généalogie G).
58. "Sanza rede legittimi e naturali; per linea masculina" (*Libro*, 102).

tion, "we can carry out the testament of the afore-mentioned Niccolò Sirigatti according to our wishes, [concerning] our share."[59]

Ser Niccolò's nephew, ser Francesco Sirigatti, also owned a house in the neighborhood that he did not want to see leave the family.[60] Fearing for his life in the plague that was rampant in Florence in 1417, he entrusted Lapo with this house, which he had mortgaged to him several years earlier, asking him to transmit it to his cousin, ser Niccolò's son, and to keep it himself in the event of the latter's death.[61]

These parallel courses of action and our memorialist's efforts to gather his ancestors' houses into as homogeneous a group as possible clearly express their need to assure the physical cohesion and succession of *casa* Niccolini.[62] At the end of his life, Lapo obviously had not yet achieved the formation of a perfectly closed concentration of buildings grouped around a stronghold and its own church, like those that Florentine *consorterie* of a former age inhabited. His efforts, tinged with a certain archaism, at least must have afforded him the comforting sentiment that his family was as solidly planted as older lineages that were more secure in their rights and surer of their identity.[63]

## "Imparentarsi"

Because the material and political bases of his family were as yet not solid, Lapo could afford even less than some others to ignore the need for support from a powerful circle of relatives. His *Libro* shows how, in the span of thirty years, the Niccolini acquired them.

59. "Si può a nostra volontà accompiere il testamento del detto ser Niccolò Sirigatti, la parte toccha a noi" (ibid.).

60. "Non escha della nostra familglia" (should not leave our family) (ibid., 116–17 and 136–37). A register of this notary is preserved (ASF *Not. antecos.* S 813, a. 1406–14). He seems to have worked for the most part in the *contado*, and he died in December 1417 at Pescia, perhaps taken there by his business.

61. *Libro*, 136 and 149. In point of fact, as ser Francesco died intestate, Lapo was to have great difficulty in 1417 assuring that the wishes of the deceased, given orally before witnesses, were carried out. Ser Francesco's sister brought suit against him, and as Lapo considered himself the executor of the will of his *consorto*, he was irritated by the actions of this distant cousin, who was acting "a grandissimo torto . . . e danno della sua anima" (very wrongly . . . and at great harm to her soul). The house ended up back in his hands, since his son Giovanni was established in it and declares it in his name in the *catasto* of 1427 (ASF, *Catasto* 73, fol. 97).

62. Lapo also bought several houses to round off his real estate holdings, one to lodge "lo prete che uficerà la cappella nostra" (the priest who will serve our chapel). In *Libro*, 95–96; he records the purchase in 1402 from the company of Orsanmichele of a house in chiasso Riconte; in ibid., 98 and 147; the purchase of a house contiguous to the latter in 1403; and in ibid., 107; the purchase in 1408 of a house contiguous to those of Biagio Niccolini.

63. On the new tendencies that soon would arise in Florence, see R. A. Goldthwaite, "The Florentine Palace as Domestic Architecture," *American Historical Review* 77 (1972): 977–1012.

For a Florentine of 1400, a *parente* designated above all a *congiunto di parentado*, an affine. The term included maternal kin as well, however, and sometimes also close blood relatives. We have a sample of what the term represented for Lapo in the arbiters he chose in 1416 to supervise the liquidation of a debt. The five names he put forth "come miei tutti parenti e amici fidati" (all as my relatives and trusted friends) were those of his son-in-law, the husband of his niece (his sister's daughter), an ally through his daughter, a first cousin (son of a maternal uncle), and one other person whose possible kinship with the Niccolini I have been unable to establish.[64]

The matrimonial strategy that Giovanni Morelli recommended to his descendants when the possibility loomed that they might remain orphans and have to administer their own affairs is well known. In substance, Morelli advises them to acquire a substitute father, through friendship as long as they were too young to marry, or by alliance when that moment came.[65] The geographical area in which friends and particularly affines should be recruited is the *gonfalone*, a subdivision of the *quartiere*, and, failing that, the *quartiere*.[66] To look beyond the immediate neighborhood, a truly exceptional opportunity would have to present itself in the shape of "an excellent relative, able to give satisfaction in every way."[67] Lapo's book enables us to verify whether the Niccolini observed this neighborhood endogamy and whether, when they did not, they acted from conscious matrimonial policy.

When Giovanni, Lapo's father, married off his daughters, probably in the 1370s, he chose neighbors as their husbands. Lapo's eldest sister, Guiduccia, seems to have married a Magaldi, a family that included some members who lived in the *quartieri* of Santa Croce and San Giovanni in 1427.[68] Lapo's second sister, Monna, married Alessandro Buondelmonti, a family of prestigious name that had come from Passignano, like the Sirigatti (who had been their *clienti*—dependents—in the thirteenth century). The Buondelmonti lived in another *quartiere* of Florence, but their properties around Passignano bordered on more than one of the Niccolini's lands there. Monna's dowry, 975 *fiorini*—a large dowry for the end of the fourteenth century—shows that the Niccolini were paying for a good marriage, one that lent them some of the prestige enjoyed by this old, landed family.[69] Fia, the third of Lapo's sisters, married Pierozzo Ghetti

64. *Libro*, 129. On this last personage, see below, note 106.
65. Morelli, *Ricordi*, 253, 263, 283.
66. Ibid., 253. Florence was at that time divided into four *quartieri*, each of which was divided into four *gonfaloni*.
67. "D'uno parente che fusse ottimo e avesse tutte le parti da piacere" Morelli, *Ricordi*, 263.
68. This first sister died after eighteen months of marriage, according to her brother (*Libro*, 58). Passerini, *Genealogia*, table 1, gives her husband as a Magaldi, but her brother, who had cut all relations with that family, does not mention Magaldi's name.
69. On the Buondelmonti of that time, see L. Martines, *The Social World of the Florentine Humanists, 1390–1460* (Princeton, 1963), 210–14.

(who died in 1383) while her father was still alive. Lapo does not record the dowry, but it is probable that it did not reach the same heights as her sister's, since the Ghetti, a family from *quartiere* Santa Croce, like the Niccolini, were less prosperous than they.[70] Finally, Giovanni married his son Niccolaio to a Bardi, a family that held solid control of the *quartiere* of Santo Spirito, on the other side of the Arno, and that counted some family members who were landowners in the same region of Passignano.[71]

In these first marriages contracted by members of Lapo's generation, it seems that the father wanted to strengthen existing ties with families that had traditionally been their *padroni*, like the Buondelmonti, but at the same time to reinforce his ties with the land. In conformity with practices later recommended by Morelli, however, he clearly was also seeking to enlarge the circle of his relatives in the neighborhood by allying himself to relatively more modest families. The first marriages concluded after the death of Giovanni show that the two brothers, Lapo and Filippo, continued the same policy: their exogamous marriages are more numerous and seem somewhat more upwardly mobile than their local alliances.

Monna, widowed by Alessandro Buondelmonti before 1377,[72] was the first sister to remarry. She married a jurist, messer Jacopo Folchi, whose family lived in the *quartiere* of Santo Spirito.[73] Messer Jacopo was to die in Venice before 1406, leaving his wife a great many books and very few goods under the sun.[74] The dowry of 800 *fiorini* that Monna brought him reveals that this second marriage was less prestigious than the alliance with the Buondelmonti.

Lapo's sister Fia remarried as well, and into a fairly influential but less wealthy family in *quartiere* Santa Croce. The choice of Bese di Guido Magalotti, who later played a fairly active role in politics, is in the direct tradition of these local alliances: modest but solid and politically useful both on the level of the neighborhood and on that of communal institutions.[75] This marriage, however, was the last to take place in the Nic-

70. Another branch of the family figures among the 150 major contributors to the *prestanza* of 1403 (Martines, *The Social World*, 353–65), but not the branch to which Fia's husband belonged.

71. Niccolaio Niccolini's two brothers-in-law, Gerozzo and Andrea di Francesco di messere Gerozzo Bardi, have a *prestanza* in 1403 that amounts to less than Lapo's. They rank 130th in their *quartiere* while Lapo ranks 72d in his. Jacopo di messere Agnolo Bardi owned lands bordering on those of the Niccolini at Santa Maria di Monte Macerata and at San Fabbiano (*Libro*, 74 and 115). A Bardi, Vieri di Bartolo di messere Bindo, worked as *cassiere* (cashier) for Lapo in 1405.

72. According to his father's will, written in 1377 (*Libro*, 61).

73. He appears in 1382 as one of the three arbiters charged with settling the division of goods between Niccolaio, Lapo, and Filippo (ibid., 63). In 1427 the average wealth of the five Folchi was 817 *fiorini* (without deductions for *bocche*) at a time when the Niccolini's wealth reached 2,219 *fiorini*.

74. *Libro*, 104, 112.

75. On Bese Magalotti see ibid., Bec, Introduction, 13. The *catasto* of 1427 lists only four Magalotti households: three widows and Bese and Fia's son Guido, who declares only 809 *fiorini*. Lapo does not give the amount of Fia's dowry.

colini's own neighborhood. When Lapo and Filippo took a wife themselves, in 1384, they both allied themselves with Santo Spirito families. Ermellina da Mezzola, the daughter of an "honorabile chavaliere" (honorable knight) brought Lapo 700 *fiorini*, and Giletta Spini brought 800 *fiorini* to Filippo.[76] These dowries are not excessively high, somewhat lower, in fact, than the sums with which the Niccolini themselves dowered the women they gave in marriage. The imbalance suggests that they were seeking to marry upward; to *innalzarsi*, as Morelli recommends and as much contemporary evidence demonstrates.[77] The females of their family, on the contrary, had to have greater dowries to maintain their rank.[78]

In 1394, with the marriage of a niece, Agnoletta (the daughter of their elder brother), for whom they assumed guardianship in 1383,[79] the Niccolini entered a new period in their matrimonial activities. "As it pleased God, we married off Agnoletta," Lapo says, to a member of the great family of the Rucellai, giving her a dowry of 950 *fiorini*.[80] Like the Buondelmonti and the Bardi, the Rucellai family had many branches, some members of which (Agnoletta's husband, for example, Luca di Giovanni di Bingieri) were hardly shining lights in the firmament of Florentine fortunes.[81] Nevertheless, this new exogamous alliance—the Rucellai lived in the *quartiere* of Santa Maria Novella—undoubtedly appeared as advantageous to the Niccolini brothers, since they decided to greatly increase the dowry that her father had stipulated for Agnoletta in his will.[82] The marriage of their niece set the Niccolini's course firmly toward the merchant oligarchy.

Now a widower, Lapo took a second wife, Caterina Melanesi, who came from a family of *lanaiuoli* (wool merchants) from the other side of the Arno.[83] Lapo probably owed the 1,000 *fiorini* she brought him in dowry to the prestige he had already acquired in government service and to his professional success. In 1402 a niece, Checca Magalotti, born of the second marriage of his sister Fia, was given in marriage to Giovanni di Bernardo Ardinghelli, who belonged to a Santa Maria Novella family listed in 1403 as being as wealthy as Lapo's.[84] The wives that Lapo's nephews, Angoletta's brothers, took in the following years were not from

---

76. *Libro,* 71–72.
77. See Herlihy and Klapisch-Zuber, *Les Toscans,* chap. 14.
78. See below, note 93.
79. *Libro,* 70.
80. "Chome fu piacere d'Iddio, maritammo l'Angnioletta" (ibid., 88 89).
81. Martines, *The Social World,* 361. With his brother Jacopo he ranks only 121st in his *quartiere,* Santa Maria Novella.
82. Her father provided 600 *fiorini* (*Libro,* 69); her uncles and guardians gave her 950 *fiorini* (ibid., 89). On the practice of testators who reduced the dowries bequeathed to their marriageable daughters by one-quarter, leaving it to the guardians or to the brothers and the mother to increase them *insino in fiorini dugento più oltre alla dota* (by up to 200 florins more than the dowry [stipulated] ), see Morelli, *Ricordi,* 223.
83. *Libro.,* 92.
84. Ibid., 94. The dowry was 900 *fiorini*.

the *quartiere* of Santa Croce either. Lorenza Bischeri, whom Francesco married in 1404, came from a San Giovanni family much wealthier than Lapo and brought to her husband only *800 fiorini*[85] in the most unequal marriage that the Niccolini managed to conclude during this period. As for Giovanni, he married a Tosinghi, Tancia, dowered with 900 *fiorini*.[86] On the other hand, when Lapo's daughter Lena married Ugo Altoviti in 1405, father and husband were of equal wealth and the dowry Lapo paid him was no greater than 700 *fiorini*.[87] The dowry of Lapo's second daughter, Giovanna, married in 1409 to Giovanni Albizzi, rose to 1,000 *fiorini*.[88] It is difficult to grasp these differences between the amounts of the dowries accorded by the Niccolini otherwise than by a comparison of the fortune and the influence of the partners in the contract. Generally speaking, the Altoviti appear to be half as wealthy as the Albizzi.[89] A year later another of Lapo's nieces, Giovanna Folchi, Monna's daughter, married Berto da Filicaia, who came from a Santa Croce lineage that lived on its landholdings and had a favorable audience in political circles. The dowry, 800 *fiorini*, approaches the average for dowries given by the Niccolini.[90] The last union mentioned in Lapo's book, the second marriage of his son Filippo, brought Filippo only 500 *fiorini*, the smallest of all the dowries our family received during this period. Filippo married a Rucellai, Parte di Albizzo, taking a wife in the clan to which the Niccolini had given a wife in 1395 to the tune of many *fiorini*.[91] Another similar reinforcement of the chains of alliance can be seen some years later, when Lapo arranged the marriage of his son Giovanni to Tita Albizzi.[92]

The Niccolini's matrimonial strategy evidently depended on Lapo's personal achievement as the "strong man" of the lineage. Evidence of this can be seen by a comparison of the average sums given and received in dowry in the first period (until 1385) and in the second (1395–1410). While the dowries given by the Niccolini remain at the same level from the first to the second period (respectively 890 and 870 *fiorini* on the average), those they received increased notably, passing from 750 to 900 *fiorini* on the average.[93] This rise probably reflects the rise in Lapo's

85. Ibid., 98.
86. Ibid. It is unclear whether she was of the rich family of the Del Toso, *quartiere* Santa Maria Novella, or the Della Tosa, *quartiere* San Giovanni.
87. Ibid., 99–100. The rank of Ugo Altoviti in 1403 is 84th in *quartiere* Santa Maria Novella.
88. Ibid., 108. The Albizzi lived in *quartiere* San Giovanni.
89. In the *catasto* of 1427 the thirty Albizzi households have an average wealth of 2,514 *fiorini*; the twenty-four Altoviti households, 1,244 *fiorini*.
90. *Libro*, 113. On the De Filicaia, see Martines, *The Social World*, 176 and 218.
91. *Libro*, 139–40.
92. The amount of the dowry, unfortunately, is unknown. The marriage took place between 1421, when Lapo's book ends, and 1427, when Giovanni appears as married in the *catasto* (ASF, *Catasto*, 73 fol. 97).
93. A part of this increase was perhaps linked to the general upward movement of dowries at the time (see Herlihy and Klapisch-Zuber, *Les Toscans*, chap. 14).

own fortunes, for he now received more than he gave in matrimonial exchanges.

The strategy pursued by Lapo and those close to him becomes clearest if we look at its geographical dimensions. The alliances concluded plainly go beyond the borders of the *quartiere*; thus, if we remember Morelli's advice, they imply an abundance of exceptional opportunities offered to Lapo. Only one sister and the daughter of a sister were given in marriage (in 1385 and in 1410) to families in Santa Croce. But no Niccolini man took a wife within the *quartiere* during this period. On the other hand, there were many more exchanges with the families of Santa Maria Novella, in the west part of the city, since three Niccolini chose wives from that area and the family also gave three wives to it. The *quartiere* of Santa Spirito—across the Arno on the road to the family landholdings—and the *quartiere* of San Giovanni to the north gave two wives and took one each. The exchanges seem to be numerically equal with Santa Maria Novella, to show a profit with San Giovanni and Santo Spirito, and to show a debit with the home *quartiere* of Santa Croce. This balance suggests that the Niccolini were truly seeking out good matches outside their neighborhood and that they succeeded in making some major coups beyond its boundaries, to the detriment of local alliances. Alliance certainly appears to have contributed to their rise as it brought them closer, between 1400 and 1410, to the great commercial and banking families of the Ardinghelli, the Bischeri, Altoviti, the Rucellai, and the Albizzi.

Little appears of the practical relations involved in alliance in a book as schematic as Lapo's. Two-thirds of the fifty or so relatives by marriage who are mentioned—wives excluded—appear only once: they bring a dowry, witness or guarantee its payment, assure the guardianship of orphans born of the marriage that had allied their family to the Niccolini, or are named executors of the will of a deceased family member.[94] Some, however, were associated with the Niccolini in their commercial affairs.[95] One alone added spiritual relationship to affinal relationship by becoming godfather to one of Lapo's children.[96] A dozen of the affines appear to have the closest links to Lapo and his immediate family when they are chosen to settle family conflicts and problems by arbitration.

Blood relatives, as we have seen, are seldom seen as judges in the arbitration to which they are party. Affinal relatives, on the other hand,

---

94. The notarial protocols show that certain of these appear more often as witnesses to acts important in the life of the family. Research in this direction would thus be desirable.

95. This was the case for Niccolò di Gentile Albizzi and his brother Giovanni, Lapo's son-in-law, who were both Lapo's associates in his "bottega di San Martino" in 1415 (*Libro*, 119, 139) or for Andrea di Pierozzo Ghetti, associated with his first cousin Giovanni di Niccolaio Niccolini in 1409 (ibid., 73–74). Lapo's commercial books obviously would tell us much more about these familial business associations had they been preserved.

96. See below, note 127.

form the reserve troops from which Lapo calls up familial peacemakers: brothers-in-law first (his sisters' husbands[97] or his wife's brother[98]), then sons-in-law[99] or his nieces' husbands,[100] then relatives on the maternal side,[101] and finally somewhat more distant affines.[102] The frequent participation of his *parenti* shows that Lapo and his immediate family judged them knowledgeable enough concerning their family affairs to be able to take part, with the necessary discretion, in the resolution of thorny problems—as long as they were not directly involved. There are few of these family affairs, settled out of court—the appraisal of dowries, the division of estates, the settling of quarrels between a father and an independently established son, the repayment of non-interest loans conceded to friends, etc.—in which we do not see at least one of the arbiters drawn from this circle of in-laws. Their appearance was all the more welcome since a man of Lapo's age could not count on many of his close blood relatives. His paternal uncles were likely to be dead, like his father, whose contemporaries they were, while the maternal uncles, whose sister married young, were less distant from their nephew both in age and by their activity. In a society in which city men of this class married girls considerably younger than they, it is difficult to find a simple definition of the "generations" where affinal relatives are concerned. Thus, the husbands of sisters are contemporaries of the brother and can soon back him up in his affairs, while the wives' brothers, younger than the husband, will enter the picture later, and perhaps in a somewhat subordinate situation.[103] A man of fifty, contemplating his approaching death, would do well to provide for paternal

97. Bese Magalotti, Fia's husband, was called in October 1385 as arbiter in the division between Lapo and Filippo (*Libro*, 77–79); messer Jacopo Folchi, Monna's husband, was arbiter in 1382 in the division between the three brothers (ibid., 63).

98. Domenico Melanesi was called on at least three times as arbiter: to set the dowry for Nanna di Lapo in 1409 (ibid., 108), to supervise the application of an agreement between Lapo and his son Giovanni in 1411 (ASF, *Not. antecos.* A 807, 13 February 1411), and to supervise another agreement between Lapo and some bankrupt creditors in 1416 (*Libro*, 132).

99. Giovanni di Gentile Albizzi is arbiter in 1411 (ASF, *Not. antecos.* A 807, 13 February 1411) and twice in 1416 (*Libro*, 130 and 132). Ugo Altoviti also appears in the act of 13 February 1411.

100. Giovanni di Bernardo Ardinghelli was one of the five arbiters retained 8 May 1416 (ibid., 129).

101. Bardo di Filippo Bagnesi, Lapo's maternal uncle and the executor of Lapo's father's will (ibid., 63) was arbiter in arranging the settlement of a debt to Lapo in 1383 (ibid., 68); Rinieri di Bardo Bagnesi, Lapo's mother's nephew, served as arbiter twice in 1416 (ibid., 129 and 132).

102. Antonio di Tedice Albizzi, arbiter in 1405 (ibid., 100), 1416 (ibid., 134), 1418 (ibid., 143); Giovanni di Simone Altoviti in 1405 (ibid., 100), 1416 (ibid., 129, 132, 134); Jacopo di Berto da Filicaia in 1410 (ibid., 113). This "useful" kinship by affinity extended less far than kinship by consanguinity, however, since it does not seem to go beyond the second degree.

103. This can be observed in Lapo, whose brothers-in-law Jacopo Folchi and Bese Magalotti were called on around 1382–85, while Domenico Melanesi appears only in 1409 and 1416.

substitutes with sufficient life expectancy, choosing his wife's brothers rather than his own brothers or his sisters' husbands, who would be even older than he. Thus age gaps—one could almost say a generational gap—between spouses reinforced ties with the allied lineage from which the wife came, and also contributed to an early indifference toward the families into which the sisters had married.[104]

The least we can say is that these situations of unequal age wove a subtle network of relations spaced out in time, in which one man benefited from the experience and authority of his maternal relations and of persons allied to him through his sisters before he could offer his protection to his own affines—his wife's brothers and his brothers' affines—and obtain their services and their advice. This spacing of ages helps us to understand how affines changed place so rapidly in family councils and why their participation in Niccolini affairs remained for the most part episodic. But the number and the diversity of these instances undeniably reveal Lapo's need to rely on a circle of relations much broader than the nucleus of blood relatives.

## "Parentevolmente e amorevolmente"

In choosing his affines in other *quartiere*, Lapo created a sort of void between his blood relatives, crowded into their grouped houses, and *parenti* established farther away. This void was filled by the "allies of choice," the *amici* whose presence had the task of insuring the harmonious proximity of neighboring lineages.

In Florence, friendship or, as the Florentines of the fifteenth century said, *amore* is not to be confused with kinship. *Parenti* are often closely connected with *amici*, however. The text of 1416 cited at the head of this section strikingly juxtaposes the terms *parenti* and *amici fidati*.[105] The arbiters Lapo retained on the occasion described in the text included one man who seemed to be neither a close relative nor an ally of Lapo, although his father, a banker, had been active a quarter-century earlier in the affairs of the Niccolini family.[106] Still, this person does not permit us to say that

104. As we have seen, Lapo has no apparent relations with the Magaldi, into whose family he married his sister Guiduccia (see note 68 above). Nor did he maintain relations with the lineages with which his first cousins were allied (da Barberino, Villani, Panichi), or with the Delli, Vigorosi, Aghinetti families, into which his paternal aunts had entered by marriage.

105. *Libro*, 129. See above, note 64.

106. In 1416 "Simone di Bonarota Simoni," whose father "Bonarota," *tavoliere* (money changer), was arbiter in the division between the three brothers in 1382 (*Libro*, 63). A genealogy of the Niccolini family (founded essentially on Lapo's book and which appears in ASF, *Strozziane* 2d ser., 16, fol. 19 mod.) qualifies Bonarrota di Simone di Bonarota as a *cugino di serrochia* (a cousin of/through my sister), without explaining this appellation, however.

Lapo established the same confusion between kin and "friends" that can be easily found in France of the same epoch.[107] Who, then, were Lapo's friends?

Lapo presents an extremely small number of people as friends. Whereas he could rely on forty or so blood relatives and at least fifty affines, the number of his "friends" can be counted on the fingers on one hand. Excluding the five arbiters in 1416 who have been mentioned, those he declares as friends include, above all, a neighborhood notary, ser Antonio di ser Niccolaio di ser Pierozzo dall'Ancisa, and his entire family;[108] Antonio di Bertone Mannelli, the beneficiary of a non-interest loan in 1383;[109] and an intermediary at the time of the sale of a parcel of land.[110] Lapo's son Niccolaio had a bond of friendship with a certain Geppo di Bartolomeo.[111] Ser Antonio dall'Ancisa, the notary Lapo turned to from 1407 on,[112] also appears as his representative in delicate affairs,[113] which is probably what earned him the title of "intimo amico." Lapo and he were tied by the godparental relatationship, as were his son Niccolaio and his friend Geppo.[114] The *amore* that Lapo claims to bear this ser Antonio and his family is expressed in the desire to render him services, and the occasions for doing so reveal something of the nature of friendship in the fifteenth century.

In 1416, soon after ser Antonio had helped Lapo to untangle a complicated affair, the notary, his brother, and his mother attempted to buy back their paternal house, which had been sold.[115] Lapo guaranteed the 400 *fiorini* loan needed for this reacquisition, and he did so—"with no profit to myself, but for the love I bear that family." Thus *amore* permitted

107. See J. M. Turlan, "Amis et amis charnels d'après les actes du Parlement au XIVᵉ siècle," *Revue historique de droit français et étranger* 4th ser., 47 (1969): 645–98.

108. *Libro*, 129–31.

109. Ibid., 68.

110. Ibid., 121.

111. Ibid., 126.

112. Ibid., 105ff. Ser Antonio's mother was born a Castellani and remarried a Buondelmonti from Passignano (ibid., 129).

113. Lapo had given his guarantee "come semplice" (like a simpleton) for a loan of 500 *fiorini* given to a friend and *compare* of his son, Geppe di Bartolomeo, and his associate Luca da Panzano, both of whom "facevano i fatti de' soldati" (provided for soldiers.). The deal turned sour for Lapo when these two army supply men went bankrupt, and it was probably to the skill of ser Antonio that Lapo owed the compromise arrived at with the bankers who had made the loan (ibid., 125–29). Other arbitrations of ser Antonio: in 1418 (ibid., 140 and 141–42) and in 1421 (ibid., 144).

114. Ibid., 130: "Mio compare e intimo amicho e benivolo" (my associate as godparent and intimate and kind friend). Ser Antonio does not figure among the godparents of Lapo's children, so Lapo must have been godfather to one of his. On the *comparaggio* of his son Niccolaio, see ibid., 126.

115. Ibid., 129–31. The notary lived in 1427 with his mother, his brother, his wife and his ten children (two of them *nati d'amore*—love children) in this house on via del Palagio (ASF, *Catasto*, 73, fol. 1). The 2,015 taxable *fiorini* that he declares, before deductions for family responsibilities, make him a relative wealthy man.

him to understand a friend's pressing need to regain possession of an ancestral house and made him rise above his appropriate and natural love of gain and the custom that dictated that a *servigio*, a courtesy, must always be repaid. The exchange of free favors seems to characterize relations between "friends,"[116] and—in a society in which every penny was counted—*amore* introduced a certain freedom of action. Behind this exchange, when it was disinterested, we can divine a certain desire to leave accounts perpetually open between friends, not to hold friends to an exact accounting in the repayment of loans.

For Lapo, however, friendship usually involved important social functions.[117] Friends were a ready source of obliging intermediaries,[118] lenders or guarantors of non-interest loans, sometimes arbiters in amicable settlements, and godfathers to the children. These varied functions enable us to enlarge somewhat the circle of Lapo's "friends" to include persons who are not specifically designated as such.

It is, first of all, in the give and take of daily business that these privileged relations of *amore* and confidence, which contemporaries naturally associated with kinship but which also characterized friendship, seem to be initiated. One Cristofano del Bugliasso, for example, whose name appears constantly in the first pages of Lapo's book, was an associate of the Niccolini brothers, having been an associate of their father, in their wool, cloth, and wool products shop on the ground floor of the house.[119] The young Niccolini heirs often had recourse to his experience before 1407, and in drawing up several family agreements they cast him in the role of a *parente*.[120] The friendship born of doing business together, which sometimes relaxed the strict rules of the game, thus tended to take the place of kinship. Moreover, such feelings created bonds like those of kinship but on the spiritual plane. Morelli, once again, eloquently compares friendship

116. "Sanza niuno mio utile, ma per amore ch'i' ò a quella familglia." As early as 1383 Lapo lent 150 *fiorini*, without interest, to Antonio di Bertone Mannelli, "per amore chome fa l'uno amicho all'altro" (out of love, as is done between friends) (*Libro*, 68).

117. Morelli indicates in many passages how to acquire and keep friends: *Ricordi,* 150, 237, 241, 253, 260–61, 274, and particularly 279: "Ma sopra tutto, se vuoi avere degli amici e de' parenti, fa di non n'avere bisogno. Ingegnati d'avere de' contanti e sappigli tenere e guardare cautamente, e que' sono i migliori amici si truovino e i migliori parenti" (But above all, if you wish to have friends and relatives, try not to have need of them. Put your mind to having ready money and learn to keep it and treat it cautiously, and this will be the best friends and the best relatives that can be found).

118. Agnolo di ser Domenico Salvestri, *lanaiolo,* is *mezzano* (middleman) in the sale of a farmholding by Lapo to another wool merchant, for he is "amico dell'uno e dell'altro" (friend to both) (*Libro*, 121).

119. "Bottegha di lana, panni, istami (ibid., 65; September 1382).

120. He arbitrates the division between the three brothers (ibid., 63) and the settlement of a debt owed to Lapo (ibid., 68; 26 May 1383); he assures the guardianship and trusteeship for the orphans left by Niccolaio di Giovanni, (ibid., 70 and 96; 2 August 1383); he takes possession of a house bought from a priest for Lapo (ibid., 98; 20 November 1403); and he arbitrates between Lapo and his mother in 1407 (ibid., 105–6).

among fellow citizens to kinship;[121] he cites, among means of acquiring
or retaining friends, serving as godfather to children of "good men, [men]
of substance and power."[122] We have seen, in fact, that ser Antonio chose
Lapo as godfather to his children; in like fashion, the man who was so
obliged to Lapo and to his son Niccolaio served as the latter's *compare*
(associate through godparenting). The twenty-two godparents of Lapo's
thirteen children permit us to clarify somewhat better our author's network
of friends.

Of these persons who "make Christians" of Lapo's children, only six
carried out their mission *per l'amore di Dio* (for the love of God). The
others contract this spiritual alliance with Lapo at the cost of lavish gifts,
thus showing to how great an extent Florentine godparenting was an
opportunity to *far onore* to someone.[123] A good example of a godparent
chosen in this spirit of charity is Giovanni di Michele del Buono, who
sponsored three of Lapo's children at the baptismal font, and each time
*per l'amore di Dio*.[124] He enjoyed Lapo's trust, acted as purchasing agent
when Lapo bought a house next to his own,[125] and also seems to have
directed the first steps in the business world of Lapo's son Giovanni.[126] A

121. "Usa parentevolmente con ogni tuo cittadino, amagli tutti e porta loro amore; e
se puoi, usa verso di loro delle cortesie" (Treat all fellow citizens like relatives, love them all
and show them your love; and if you can, show them every courtesy) (Morelli, *Ricordi*, 237.
122. "Buoni homini e da bene e potenti." Ibid., 150: "Riteneasi con loro, mostrando
loro grande amore in servigli di quello avesse potuto, in consigliarsi con loro di suoi fatti,
dove e' dimostrava fede e speranza in loro; onoralli in dare loro mangiare e in tutte altre
cose; battezzare loro figliuoli, e simile cose e maggiori, come accaggiono tutto giorno nell'usare
e praticare con quelle persone a chi altri vuole bene" ( [His father] visited with them often,
showing them great love in serving them in all possible ways, in discussing his affairs with
them, whereby he showed faith and confidence in them; honoring them by giving them to
eat and in all other things, baptizing their children, and such and greater things as occur
every day in the frequentation and company of persons whom one esteems).
123. Besides Giovanni del Buono (see note 124), these included a priest of the Niccolini
chapel in 1403 (*Libro*, 93), Filippo di Niccolò Giugni in 1389 (ibid., 80), and Lapo's brother-
in-law Bernardo da Mezzola (ibid., 80), Simone Salviati in 1390 (ibid., 81), and the *speziale*
(druggist) Lionardo di Mannino in 1396 (ibid., 89). Later, in 1445, a granddaughter of
Lapo's, born to Paolo, who was at the time *priore*, had all of his fellow *priori* for godfather
*per l'amore di Dio* (Niccolini, *The Chronicles*, 129). The efforts of a friend in common often
permitted the arrangement of a desirable *comparaggio*. Francesco di Tommaso Giovanni
reports in his *ricordanze* that "intervenne per me Nichol mio fratello" (my brother Nichol
acted as intermediary for me) to ask Stoldo di Lionardo Frescobaldi if Francesco could stand
as godfather to one of Stoldo's children. It is probable that a godparental relationship of
this type was not *per l'amore di Dio*. On the other hand, Francesco himself insists that the
most frequent godparents of his children (monks, the midwife, or the nurse) act as such
"per l'amore di Dio, e così facciono" (for the love of God, and so shall it be) (ASF, *Strozz.*,
2d ser., 16, fols. 15, 20v; 3 December 1436 and 13 June 1440). See C. Klapisch-Zuber,
"Le *comparatico* à Florence: Parenté spirituelle et relations familiales avant la Contre-Réforme
(14e–16e siècles)," in preparation.
124. In 1409, 1410, and 1413 (*Libro*, 109).
125. Ibid., 107; 1 December 1408.
126. ASF, *Not. antecos.* A 807, 13 February 1411. He was an associate of Giovanni and
declares himself *lanifex* (wool merchant). In the 1427 *catasto* there is a *sensale* (broker) of

"friend" of this sort seems to occupy a position subordinate to Lapo's, like Cristofano del Bugliasso and even ser Antonio, or like the army supply man who was *compare* to Niccolaio di Lapo. Lapo and his immediate kin thus allow themselves to be bound by spiritual kinship to men who did not belong to their milieu and with whom the conclusion of a matrimonial alliance would have been going too far, even though they felt the necessity to express their closeness *parentevolmente* (like a relative). Thus spiritual alliances and matrimonial alliances coincided only exceptionally within the Niccolini clan: only one of Lapo's children had a maternal uncle for godfather.[127] None of the families from which Lapo's other *compari* were recruited were also his relatives.

The system of *compari* thus introduces us into a circle of relations of a much greater social heterogeneity than that of affines, since Lapo allied himself spiritually with persons with whom matrimonial exchanges were not possible. This circle consisted primarily of neighbors. The godfathers of Lapo's children are for the most part inhabitants of the *quartiere*: of the twenty Florentines[128] he chose as godfather, at least half lived in the neighboring streets of *quartiere* Santa Croce, and a third in the *Gonfalone delle Ruote* in which Lapo lived. Their tax rate in the *prestanza* of 1403 enables us to identify half of them as among the 150 most highly taxed in their quartiere, thus as belonging to the same social milieu as Lapo. Certain of them—the bankers in particular—were noticeably even richer than he.[129] The other half of these godfathers were of lower social status than Lapo. The fact that he chose them suggests that Lapo was using *comparaggio* to bolster his local sphere of influence.[130] Many of these *compari* disappear from Lapo's book after the one mention of the baptism to which they had been invited. The brevity of their appearance leaves the impression that the choice of a godfather was generally conceived as an opportunity to repay an obligation, to honor a debt, or to render on the spiritual plane a service received in the day-to-day business world. As the

---

the same name in the *quartiere* Santo Spirito (ASF, *Catasto* 67, fol. 295). He owed Lapo 23 *fiorini*.

127. Bernardo di messer Zanobi da Mezzola, Lapo's brother-in-law for five years, godfather of Luca Rinaldo "per l'amore di Dio" on 20 April 1389 (*Libro*, 81). Morelli's family often chose godmothers, either grandmothers or nurses, while Lapo chose only men.

128. His son, Jacopo e Miniato, was born when he was on official business in San Miniato Fiorentino. His godparents were the city government of that town (which accounts for his second name) and Bartolomeo Gambacorti, from a Pisan family (ibid., 89; 25 July 1398).

129. Thus Francesco di Agnolo Malatesti-Cavalcanti, *tavoliere*, (money changer) in 1386; Domenico di Domenico Giugni in 1395; Filippo di Niccolò Giugni in 1386 and 1389.

130. Among these less splendid godparents were ser Simone, the priest of the family chapel; Giovanni di Michele del Buono, *lanaiolo* (wool merchant); a *ritagliatore* (woolens cutter) and former business associate of Lapo, Matteo di Francesco di ser Orlandino (1410); a *speziale* (druggist), Lionardo di Mannino; an *approvatore* (appraiser), Niccolò di Monmigliore.

people chosen were for the most part neighbors, they entered into a whole network of exchanges that unfortunately is revealed in Lapo's book only in this familial aspect, but that other sources speak of with a wealth of detail.[131]

Friendship among the Niccolini tended toward kinship without ever— or hardly ever—reaching that point, except perhaps on the spiritual level. It appears as a geographically limited complement to marriage alliance, filling in gaps and for the most part exercising its role in situations where kinship did not operate. Friendship generally engaged individuals only. The godparent relationship, one of its best expressions, offered a tested means to reinforce the bonds between persons of the same geographical or business community without going so far as to ally their families. Thus "friends" were first of all privileged neighbors, encountered in the crush of the *bottega* or of the parish church, at the notary's down the street, or in the *loggia* of a neighboring house. These close encounters introduced a greater freedom in social relations. While blood relatives customarily ate together under the same roof and made this sharing into a right, and while affinally related families participated in the ritual feasting that sanctioned events important to their lineages, neighbors were invited to drop in for a glass of cool wine on a hot day or to stop for a snack outside the doorstep in simple gatherings that sealed neighborhood good feelings.[132] When he drinks wine with the baker, Cisti, messer Geri Spina becomes his "friend."[133] Thus Lapo must have drunk with the simple people among whom he chose certain of his *compari*. The goodwill of friends thus acquired or, more cynically, *comperati* (bought) (the expression is once again Morelli's)[134] satisfied a sociability that could not find complete expression in the constraining setting of the family and the lineage, or in the more formal relations of affinity, while at the same time it provided a complementary and locally-based support network.[135]

131. Thus Morelli, *Ricordi*, 260–61, for example, on how to drink with one's neighbors and maintain courteous relations with them.

132. "Arai una botte di vermiglio brusco, oloroso e buono, e simile il dì pe' gran caldi ritruovati co' tuoi vicini e con altri, e dà loro bere lietamente e proferra la botte e ciò che tu hai a ogni huomo" (You will have a barrel of tart red wine, with good taste and fragrance, and in this way on very hot days you will meet with your neighbors and others, and give them to drink merrily and offer the barrel and whatever you have to every man) (ibid., 261).

133. See Boccaccio, *Decamerone*, sixth day, second novella.

134. "Appresso, sia cortese: ingenati d'acquistare uno amico o più nel tuo gonfalone e per lui fa ciò che tu puoi di buono, e non ti curare per mettervi del tuo. Se se' ricco, sia contento comperare degli amici co' tuoi danari, se non puoi avere per altra via" (Next, be courteous: put your mind to acquiring one or more friends in your immediate neighborhood and do all the good you can for him, without stinting. If you are rich, be satisfied to buy friends with your money if you cannot have them by other means) (Morelli, *Ricordi*, 253).

135. See the observations of E. R. Wolf, "Kinship, Friendship and Patron/Client Relations in Complex Societies," in M. Banton, ed., *The Social Anthropology of Complex Societies*, 3d ed. (London and New York, 1966), 1–22.

It is difficult to say whether Lapo is representative of people of his class in his systematic search for exogamous relationships and his utilization of *comparaggio* (the godparent relationship) on the very local level. An analysis of his book leads us to think that the small number of blood relatives available to be called on and the personal prestige he enjoyed early in life placed him in the somewhat exceptional position of needing to strengthen his prestige by allying himself out of the neighborhood and to compensate this exogamy by spiritual alliance in a more restricted area. His recourse to different forms of kinship shows that, at least around 1400, a successful man's opportunities for action were still largely founded on kinship—but there were also occasions on which matrimonial strategy and choice of *compari* might violate his contemporaries' principles of action.

# 5

## Childhood in Tuscany at the Beginning of the Fifteenth Century

 "You treated him not as a son but as a stranger." A Florentine "merchant writer" of the beginning of the fifteenth century, Giovanni di Pagolo Morelli, addresses this reproach to himself as he recalls with pain how harsh his attitude had been toward his eldest son, dead at the age of ten.[1] Are we to take the image of family relationships that Morelli transmits to us, in which the child was a "stranger" to his own parents, as typical? Should we not rather emphasize the novelty of this introspection? Can we take this Quattrocento man's realization of the injustice of his severity toward a child that he nonetheless loved as indicative of a change in attitudes or of a new sensitivity widespread among his contemporaries? Morelli speaks directly, yet with great ambiguity (as so often with literary texts), to one aspect of the problem that Philippe Ariès has posed so vigorously:[2] that of the modern recognition of the individuality of childhood, and the appearance of feelings that were new, or at least less repressed, toward those who had traditionally been considered small-sized, less successful adults.

Indeed, Tuscan art and the iconographical themes that it developed or launched at the end of the Middle Ages have long attracted attention to

Originally published as "L'enfance en Toscane au début du XVᵉ siècle," *Annales de Démographie Historique* 1973: 99–122.

1. "Tu nollo trattavi come figliuolo ma come istrano," G. di P. Morelli, *Ricordi*, ed. V. Branca (Florence, 1956), 501.

2. P. Ariès, *L'enfant et la vie familiale sous l'Ancien Régime* (Paris, 1960); P. Ariès, *Histoire des populations françaises,* new ed. (Paris, 1971), 322–43.

the advent of the "modern" family in its urban settings.[3] But the plastic arts are not the only sources that throw light on attitudes toward childhood. For this period we have veritable family annals, in which the head of the family noted ordinary events on a day-to-day basis in journals or account books (*ricordi* or *ricordanze*), sometimes summarized in a family chronicle in which the life of the community and the life of the domestic group intermingled. The child has his place in this category of documents, and it is an easy task to look in them for a reflection of what those close to children said that they felt about them, or what they secretly did feel about them.[4] There are many other sources that also throw light on attitudes toward children: the practices and objects of daily life, toys and games, pedagogical treatises, notarial acts, the archives of religious foundations devoted to children, and so forth. Here I intend to use another sort of material, one that directly illustrates the real numerical importance of childhood and the pressures to which children were subjected and, indirectly, the place that the child occupied in contemporary sensibilities. The Florentine tax surveys (*catasti*) of the fifteenth century, and in particular the *catasto* of 1427–30, included the entire population of the territory governed by the commune of Florence. While they enable us to determine the number of children, they also permit a quantification of behavior that depends on unconscious judgments, such as the attitude of adults regarding the various "ages" of childhood, or sex discrimination. At the least, they allow us to evaluate the effects of these attitudes within specific social groups.[5] These preliminary observations are intended to clarify the weight of childhood, so to speak, in the body social at the end of the Middle Ages.

How did this society define the frontiers of childhood? At what age did it permit escape?

At the beginning of the fourteenth century, Dante gave expression to a traditional conception of the place of childhood in the system of the universe and in the uniquely human system of the "ages of life." In his

3. On Tuscan painting, see M. Meiss, *Painting in Florence and Siena after the Black Death* (Princeton, 1951). On the Italian family, see N. Tamassia, *La famiglia italiana nei secc. decimoquinto e decimosesto* (Milan, 1911); and V. Lugli, *I trattatisti della famiglia nel Quattrocento* (Bologna, 1909).

4. See V. Branca, "Fra Morelli e Sacchetti, vita pubblica e domestica nella Firenze del primo Quattrocento," in *Saggi e ricerche in memoria di E. Li Gotti* (Palermo, 1962), 1:274–78. Some of the many editions of Florentine family journals and *ricordi* are: G. Dati, *Il libro segreto, 1384–1434,* ed. C. Gargiolli (Bologna, 1869); *Libro di ricordanze dei Corsini (1362–1457),* ed. A. Petrucci (Rome, 1965); G. di P. Morelli, *Ricordi,* ed. V. Branca (Florence, 1956); *Il libro degli affari proprii di casa di Lapo di Giovanni Niccolini de' Sirigatti,* ed. C. Bec (Paris, 1969); Paolo da Certaldo, *Il libro di buoni costumi,* ed. A. Schiaffini (Florence, 1945). On this literature at the turn of the fifteenth century see C. Bec, *Les marchands écrivains à Florence, 1375–1434* (Paris and The Hague, 1967).

5. On the *catasti* of the fifteenth century, see E. Conti, *I catasti agrari della repubblica fiorentina e il catasto particellare toscano (secc. XIV–XIX)* (Rome, 1966). For an evaluation of the demographic data of the *catasto* of 1427–30, see C. Klapisch, "Fiscalité et démographie en Toscane (1427–1430)," *Annales, E. S. C.* 24, no. 6 (1969): 1313–37.

*Convivio*, and following Avicenna, he defines the first age, *adolescentia*, which reaches from birth to 25 full years of age, as the age of growth.[6] Previous tradition, however, particularly that of Isidore of Seville, transmitted in the thirteenth century by Vincent de Beauvais, distiguished three seven-year sub-ages within this vast segment of the lifespan: *infantia*, from birth to 7 years; *pueritia*, from 7 to 14; and *adolescentia*, strictly speaking, from 15 to 28 years. Dante totally disregards *infantia*: he states that adolescence really begins at the age of 8, but he gives no particular name to the childhood years immediately following infancy (*pueritia*). Between one age (8), which for us typically belongs to the different world of childhood, and another age (25), which seems to us situated well beyond the normal end of growth and to belong to the world of adulthood, only adolescents seem to exist in his eyes, growing beings striving toward human virtues. This is because for Dante the "increasing of life" does not refer merely to the adolescent's physical development and sexual maturation, and even less to his psychological maturity. Above all it describes a state of social and economic dependence characertistic of an age in which the chief virtue continued to be obedience. For this very reason I find it interesting that such a long and undifferentiated period could be attributed to the formation of an adult.

Imprecision and lack of differentiation among the periods of childhood—Dante does not even distinguish puberty as a milestone essential to physical development and to socialization—are reflected in the common vocabulary that designated childhood. In Tuscany in the later Middle Ages, common terminology describing childhood is relatively meager, and the notion of childhood blends with that of dependence. The word used most often in fourteenth- and fifteenth-century Tuscany, *fanciullo*, seems itself to be a diminutive of *fante*, a word with many derivations; its most common meaning at the time was valet or servant, but occasionally it was still used in the sense of child.[7] *Fanciullo* generally designated a child who had arrived at the age of reason and attained the age of speech but was nevertheless not yet a *adolescente* or *ragazzo* 16–20 years old. As for infancy, which Dante totally ignores, it was described by diminutives of *fanciullo* or by words such as *putto*, *bambolino* (baby, hence cherub, little doll). Does this relatively richer vocabulary for the earlier age indicate a more specific interest in the newborn and the infant than for the preadolescent child? Did children, led by the fragile avant-garde of the infants Dante did not even glance at, become visible to adults only at the time of the *castasto*?

How did one leave this dependent "state"? The corollary of the definition of adolescence, "first age [and] the gate and path whereby we enter

6. Dante, *Convivio*, IV:24–26, in *Opere*, ed. G. Barbero (Florence, 1964), 350–53 (*The Convivio of Dante Alighieri*, Temple Classics [London: J. M. Dent, 1903], 350).

7. *Fante*: the original meaning was a child capable of speech, by opposition to the classical *infans*.

upon a good life," as Dante describes it, is that adolescence prepares for all the responsibilities of the mature man, both those of marriage and those of the conduct of affairs. In the merchant oligarchy, however, as among the rural population, the married son who led his wife to his father's house had every chance of continuing to live for some years under paternal rule. Marriage, in these terms, was in no real sense the end of "adolescence" and often a son of a good family would put off marriage until that age of submission ended, at the death of his father. The Florentine adult was a head of family who had acquired his economic autonomy;[8] the child was someone still subjected to *patria potestas*, even if he had long been of adult age. The general conjuncture or the son's economic activity could hasten or delay his emancipation. Nevertheless, the division of the estate after the death of the father and the "separation" of families that up to that point had been united into a common household (a division that gave autonomy to family members until then joined into one domestic and economic unit) occurred in the fifteenth century more between brothers than it did between one generation and another.[9] We could say that childhood ended when the father died: a young man passed directly from the subordinate state of the *figliuolo* to the status of *padre di famiglia*.

There must, of course, have been a large part of the urban population that did not follow this model, and the sons of artisans or the industrial proletariat in Florence escaped paternal authority quite rapidly when they acquired the modest economic independence that a salary gave them. But in all cases, entry into adulthood was tied to the exercise of economic capacities, and this is perhaps the principal difference between the bourgeois or popular childhood typical of the Tuscany that interests us, and childhood under feudalism. Feudal ties, and the very notion of service rendered by an undifferentiated familial collectivity of vassals, maintained the cohesion of a whole in which the child was defined by his inability to give that service.[10] The end of childhood was marked by rites of passage into the full exercise of service. It was probably only where the lending of service was personal and excluded the other descendants to the benefit of one alone that the young lord would await the death of his father, who held the fief, before reaching autonomy and coming out of "childhood"— just like a bourgeois or peasant child.

The notion of dependence is all the more striking if we consider the numbers involved in these age classes.

A few figures taken from the Florentine *catasto* of 1427–30 will show that between 50 and 52 percent of the population were in a situation of

8. See chapter 3 above, "A uno pane e uno vino."
9. See C. Fumagalli, *Il diritto di fraterna nella giurisprudenza da Accursio alla codificazione* (Turin, 1912).
10. G. Duby, *La société aux XI^e et XII^e siècles dans la région mâconnaise* (Paris, 1953); G. Duby, "Dans la France du Nord-Ouest au XII^e siècle: Les 'jeunes' de la société aristocratique," *Annales, E. S. C.* 19 no. 5 (1964): 835–46.

"childhood" and of dependence, following Dante's definition and considering their age alone. In table 5.1, which shows the child population proportionally by age groups, we can see that children under 15 years of age formed more than one-third of the population, young people under 20 made up about 43 percent, and the group of children less than 8 years old account for something between one-fourth and one-fifth (perhaps more, for the younger members of this group were greatly underreported). These percentages show that Tuscany was comparable to other regions in Europe at that time for which we know age distribution. They show an imbalance between adults and young that is rather less striking, however, than that of many regions in our own day.[11] Still, we should note that the proportion of those whom Dante defined as "obedient" and subject to other age categories by the sole fact of their birth date is curiously paralleled by the proportion of young less than 20 years old in developing countries today.

Can these aggregate figures teach us something about attitudes toward childhood? It is clear that the two or three first years of life were the most underreported in the majority of the regions and towns of Tuscany. Exceptional cases aside,[12] the age pyramid shows a strong bulge at two or three years, and in all cases it shows a lower proportion of children under one year than of children two or three years old (see table 5.2). This phenomenon is well known to demographers of older or nonliterate so-

Table 5.1

PROPORTION OF TOTAL POPULATION IN AGE GROUPS UNDER 25, AND MALE/FEMALE RATIO (TUSCANY, *CATASTO* OF 1427–30)

| Age group | Country | | All Cities* | | Florence | | Total Pop. | |
|---|---|---|---|---|---|---|---|---|
| | % | M/F | % | M/F | % | M/F | % | M/F |
| Under 1 year | 2.5 | 130 | 2.85 | 127 | 2.95 | 114 | 2.6 | 129 |
| 1-7 years | 21.1 | 120 | 20.0 | 119 | 19.9 | 135 | 20.7 | 120 |
| 8-14 years | 12.8 | 114 | 13.0 | 122 | 14.7 | 121 | 12.9 | 116 |
| 15-19 years | 7.1 | 84 | 7.0 | 115 | 7.6 | 123 | 7.0 | 91 |
| 20-24 years | 7.0 | 110 | 7.0 | 122 | 7.2 | 135 | 7.0 | 114 |
| 0-7 years | 23.6 | | 22.8 | | 22.8 | | 23.3 | |
| 0-14 years | 36.4 | | 35.8 | | 37.5 | | 36.2 | |
| 0-19 years | 43.5 | | 42.9 | | 45.1 | | 43.2 | |
| 0-24 years | 50.5 | | 49.9 | | 52.3 | | 50.2 | |

*Towns and Cities of more than 800 inhabitants

11. See M. Reinhard, A. Armengaud, J. Dupâquier, *Histoire générale de la population mondiale* (Paris, 1968), 111 (Lombardy in the sixteenth century); 116 (Venice in the sixteenth century); 165 (Pavia and Venice in the seventeenth century); 654 (Maghreb in 1960).

12. In Pistoia and its *contado*, in Florence itself, and in the *contado* of Arezzo, only the first year of life lags behind the following years, while elsewhere the second year also counts fewer children than the third and fourth years.

Table 5.2

PROPORTION OF CHILDREN UNDER 5 IN THE TOTAL POPULATION,
AND MALE/FEMALE RATIO AT THOSE AGES (TUSCANY, 1427–30)

| Age | % Male | % Female | Total % | M/F Ratio |
|---|---|---|---|---|
| Under 1 | 1.47 | 1.15 | 2.63 | 129 |
| 1 year | 1.88 | 1.58 | 3.47 | 119 |
| 2 years | 1.97 | 1.69 | 3.67 | 116 |
| 3 years | 1.95 | 1.62 | 3.57 | 120 |
| 4 years | 1.55 | 1.32 | 2.87 | 118 |

cieties, and the underreporting of infants allows us to note the extent to which the taxpayers of the beginning of the fifteenth century unconsciously forgot their infant children. I say "taxpayer" quite purposely, though the term generally raises doubts concerning conclusions founded on fiscal documents. In this case the Florentine fiscal system accorded deductions by "mouth," or took family responsibilities into account to an extent great enough so that any father would seize the opportunity to declare all of his children under 14. To forget them he would have to have unconscious reasons more powerful than his immediate financial interest. Still, many heads of family did "forget" a portion of their "mouths"—those whose existence was the most fragile and the most uncertain. They did so even though they were immersed in a society that venerated written evidence and often based it on the accuracy of registered information concerning individuals and their essential characteristic, their given age. (The fiscal system, furthermore, was sufficiently constraining to give proportional aggregate figures for age groups within the population that seem totally reasonable.) Such is the case of one father who, several months after his first declaration to the fiscal authorities, adds mention of a two-year-old son who was, he says, sick at the time:[13] he had unconsciously given him up for lost and had renounced all thought of him, even when the child could have brought him a tax deduction. Or of another father who declares in good Christian fashion that, "as long as it pleases God," he has four children "between 0 and 22 years," but neglects to furnish their given names.[14]

This somewhat vague way of viewing small children can also be seen in the custom—which seems to have been fairly widespread in Tuscany—of reusing the given name of a dead child for a child born subsequently, sometimes even before the death of the older child, whose unhoped-for recovery might explain the occurrence of siblings with the same name. In

13. Archivio di Stato di Pisa (henceforth abbreviated ASP), *Catasto* 1540, fol. 115: Pasquino di Rinieri adds "uno mio figliuolo che era malato quando detti mio catasto" (one of my children who was sick when I made my declaration).

14. ASP, *Catasto* 1545, fol. 775: Guiduccio di Marco declares that he has "ifino che Dio vorrà figliuoli quattro."

1470 one Tuscan taxpayer took three words to express the notion that family continuity and the replenishment of generations were tasks full of unpredictable setbacks and necessary repetition: This poor sharecropper declares a three-year-old boy at the head of the list of five children older than he and two younger sisters. Perhaps for the benefit of the employees of the *catasto*, surprised to see so young a child listed under a name given in an earlier report to an older child, the father declares that the previous Antonio "died, and I remade him."[15] What better expression could be found for the notion that it might take several tries to achieve a new existence? And how could we possibly expect that one or another of the unsuccessful attempts not be forgotten now and then?

The variation in the numbers in each age group, as compared to the predicted mean (see figure 5.1), leads us to think that parents attached little importance to the exact tally of their children's ages or that they soon lost count. Rather than by precise age, they characterize their descendants by their respective place within the group, though even this rule permits exceptions and a younger child in one of the *catasti* can be found as the eldest in a subsequent *catasto*. The educated Florentine of the fourteenth and fifteenth centuries, however, was becoming conscious of the importance of knowing his own age or that of members of his family in many circumstances in public or private life. Some years after our *catasto*, Leon Battista Alberti recommended to the father of the family that he note in his *libro secreto* the exact day, month, year, and hour of a child's birth. Advice of this type was well heeded by the middle or higher classes of Florentine society, and not only because it responded to an obvious interest in astrology. Their exercise of political functions made knowledge of legal ages imperative, and this had long been the case, to judge from the family journals of the fourteenth and fifteenth centuries. The family documents of the "merchant writers" register births and deaths with some precision.[16] But these concerns were certainly not shared by less privileged classes. The rounding off of ages evident in the *catasto* is much more pronounced among the poor than among the rich, in the country than in the city, and in the part of the territory that was less well integrated into the Florentine political system and fiscal regime than in the city itself.

Still, it might be supposed that the ages declared by fathers for their very young children would, on all levels of culture, escape this phenomenon of rounding off. If this is almost true in Florence of children less than 8

15. Archivio di Stato, Florence (henceforth abbreviated ASF), *Catasto* 934, fol. 175, declaration of Bernardo di Andrea Lanciani: "Morì e refecilo." See chapter 13 below, "The Name Remade."

16. L. B. Alberti, *I libri della famiglia*, ed. R. Romano and A. Tenenti (Turin, 1969), 144; trans. by Renée Neu Watkins as *The Family in Renaissance Florence* (Columbus, S.C., University of South Carolina Press, 1969), 123. Many examples of the registration of births, deaths, and marriages can be found in the *ricordi* cited in note 4.

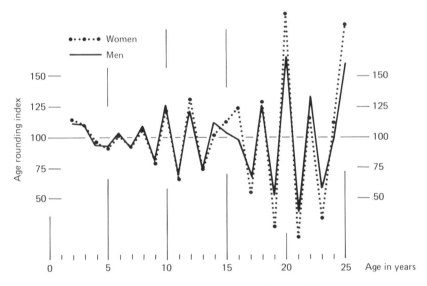

Figure 5.1 Age Rounding in Tuscany (*catasto* of 1427–30). The age-rounding index is the ratio between the actual and the predicted size for an average annual group.

years old, it is much less true as soon as one leaves the capital. The oscillations of the index of rounding off ages are pronounced at 3, 4, and 6 years of age in most of the secondary cities and even more so in the country; the population as a whole shows sharp peaks from 8 years on. The curves for boys and girls are exactly parallel until the age of 14, after which they branch: girls' ages are then strongly rounded off at 16, the modal age of marriage, as are boys' ages at 14, just before they come of age fiscally (see figure 5.1). Beginning at 17 years of age, the curves for males and females again run parallel, but young women can be seen rounding off their ages more than young men. Whatever might be the reason for these divergences, or for female rounding off, the inaccuracy of parents in the reporting of infant ages remains striking. From its very beginning, the existence of a child acquires an imprecision in its temporal evaluation that might seem more justified in adults or long-lived persons.

Does recognition of a child's existence vary with the sex of the child? Up to this point I have been considering children as an undifferentiated mass, but adults shifted their attitude toward the child in function of his or her sex. Disappointment at the birth of a girl was an extremely wide-spread phenomenon: the authors of familial memoirs or journals express this clearly, or at least let it be understood. The common opinion that a girl child was the fruit of a conjugal act stained by some impurity, sickness, debauchery, or broken taboo[17] translates, in the last analysis, into anomalies in the ratio of males to females.

The *catasto*, in fact, enables us to calculate the ratio of males to females in a large population of young people (approximately 133,000 of the persons reported are less than 25 years old). There is a clear imbalance between the sexes from early infancy on (see table 5.1 and figure 5.2). Up to the age of 7, girls are 16–17 percent less numerous than boys; in certain regions the male/female ratio shows extraordinary highs between 6 and 7 years and between 12 and 13, and in Pisa, Pistoia and its environs, and Arezzo we can count as many as two boys for every girl of 9 or 10 years old. This imbalance continues until the critical age at which males pay taxes (14 or 18 years). But could it be true that the superior number of males collapses at that point because a great many fathers manage to hide from the tax authorities adolescent boys who would bring them increased taxes? In reality, the simple fact of fraudulently reporting as younger some of the 14–15-year-old boys (in the country) or 18-year-olds (in the city of Florence)—at ages not yet liable to the head tax—probably is not enough to explain the relative scarcity of little girls. Indeed, the clerks and the employees of the Florentine fiscal administration gave proof of their vigilance, and if anything they were accused of unduly increasing the number of taxable boys. Furthermore, if the tax officials had an interest in locating taxable young men, the taxpayers, for their part, had no reason to forget their girls over 14. So one of the reasons why the male/female ratio under 14 shows boys at such a strong advantage might be that neither the parents nor the employees of the *catasto* attached any great importance to the sex of children, the number of whom counted more toward the determination of the "substance" to be taxed than their sex. Evident masculinizations are easy to spot, whether due to the carelessness of the father as he dictates his declaration or to that of the copyist when he enters the information in the registers: checking was not at all strict with respect to children. On the other hand, after 14 or after 18 the parents made sure that the sex of their daughters was noted scrupulously. But do these particular considerations entirely explain the disappearance of some pre-pubescent girls?

17. See L. Tamassia, *La famiglia italiana*, 266. Giovanni Morelli clearly asserts that these excesses played a role in sex determination: "Se tu tieni il contradio modo . . . tu non n'arai figliuoli se non a stento, tu l'arai femine, tu l'arai tisichi" (If you do the contrary . . . you will have children only with difficulty, you will have females, you will have them stunted) (212–13). In another passage Morelli recalls his joy at the birth of a child: "Tu l'avesti maschio per farti bene crepare il cuore" (You had a male, to make your heart burst) (501);". . . e di poi nato, e essendo maschio e intero e bene proporsionato, quanta allegrezza" (and when he was born, and being male, whole, and well proportioned, what joy!) (504–5). The disappointment of Lapo di Giovanni Niccolini at the birth of a daughter can be seen more discreetly in the absence of the usual formula of good wishes that generally greets the arrival of a boy (only two out of ten boys are not so greeted, and not one of his three girls are) (Bec ed., *Libro*, 24).

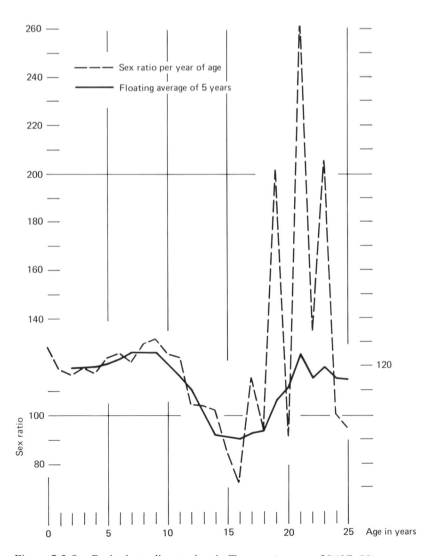

Figure 5.2 Sex Ratio According to Age in Tuscany (*catasto* of 1427–30)

At birth the male/female ratio can be set at about 104, to judge by the baptismal registers of San Giovanni in the second half of the fifteenth century.[18] This is a normal ratio, which immediately reflects one of the

18. This refers, in fact, to the male/female ratio at baptism, which usually occurred one or two days after birth. See M. Lastri, *Ricerche sull'antica e moderna populazione della città di Firenze per mezzo dei registri del battistero di S. Giovanni dal 1451 al 1774* (Florence, 1775); A. Zuccagni-Orlandini, *Ricerche statistiche sul Granducato di Toscana* (Florence, 1848–54), 1:413ff.

scourges of medieval Florence; abandonment, a sort of delayed-action infanticide that was widespread among the lower orders of society.[19] These babies—illegitimate children, even more the children of slaves, misery's children, unrecognized by the father, master, and seducer[20]—were abandoned immediately after birth and were usually taken in by one of the two or three religious institutions that specialized in their care. Two-thirds of these children were female. According to the *catasto* of 1427, Santa Maria della Scala, one of the hospices that took foundlings and abandoned children, sheltered 98 girls, as opposed to 41 boys. Between 1430 and 1439, a period of war and of terrible rural poverty, girls again made up two-thirds of the children taken in by San Gallo, another hospice that accepted foundlings (66.3 percent of admissions, as compared to 61.2 percent between 1404 and 1413, a decade of relative peace). Toward the middle of the century, the hospice of the Innocenti, devoted exclusively to newborn or very young *trovatelli*, was officially opened in Florence: girls accounted for 58.9 percent of its 708 admissions between 1445 and 1453.[21] It is noticeable that in troubled times the people of a countryside devastated by war brought an increased number of children of rural origin to the Florentine hospice, as well as a larger number of older children. A higher degree of sex discrimination can also be observed in crisis periods, although this increase is less marked than for the other two factors.

A terrible mortality rate reigned in these charitable institutions and among the charges of the outside nurses with whom the children were

19. On the abandonment of children in Italy see Tamassia, *La famiglia italiana*, 227–31. Furthermore, there is much evidence of real infanticide by the practice of "suffocation" mentioned, for example, in the episcopal constitutions of 1327 among the sins reserved to the absolution of the bishop of Florence (deaths of children of less than five years of age caused by the negligence of the parents, "a euphemism for infanticide by suffocation") or in the synodal constitutions of 1517, still in Florence, when keeping children younger than one year old in the parental bed was condemned. Although the crime of suffocation is not specifically mentioned in the latter instance, it is evident that the article refers to it. See R. C. Trexler, *Synodal law in Florence and Fiesole, 1306–1518*, Studi e Testi 268 (Vatican City, 1971), 64; R. C. Trexler, "Infanticide in Florence: New Sources and First Results," *History of Childhood Quarterly* 1, no. 1 (1973): 98–116.

20. See I. Origo, "The Domestic Enemy: Eastern Slaves in Tuscany in the 14th and 15th Centuries," *Speculum* 30 (1955): 321–66; G. Parenti, "Fonti per lo studio della demografia fiorentina: I Libri dei Morti," *Genus* 6–8 (1943–49): 281ff. According to I. Origo, 14 percent of the 7,534 children taken into the Innocenti and San Gallo in Florence between 1395 and 1485 were reputed to be born of slave mothers, and in Lucca, 33 percent of the abandoned children were so. R. Trexler counts 33 percent of the admissions to San Gallo between 1430 and 1439 as illegitimate (22 percent children of slaves) and 40 percent among the children who enter the Innocenti between 1445 and 1453 (34 percent children of slaves). It is clear that illegitimacy was not the reason for the abandoning of children in Florence except where children of slave women and members of the clergy were concerned. R. Trexler, "The Foundlings of Florence, 1395–1455, " *History of Childhood Quarterly* 1, no. 2 (1973): 259–84.

21. For the Scala see ASF, *Catasto*, 185, fols. 528ff; see Trexler, "The Foundlings," 263–64 for the figures on San Gallo and the Innocenti.

placed, and these children's chance of survival was probably even smaller than in the society at large.[22] Abandonment, which struck female babies twice as hard as males, thus contributed to the reduction of the number of little girls immediately after birth and baptism.[23] In the second third of the fifteenth century there were at least 300 abandoned children, infants for the most part, in the Florentine hospices.[24]

In families that had the means to put their children out to wet nurses, this practice may have represented more of a threat to girls than to boys. Florentine parents, in fact, left their babies of the fair sex with a nurse longer than their sons. Not only did the choice of a *balia* represent a serious decision in an epoch in which all were persuaded that the nurse transmitted her qualities and her hereditary constitution along with her milk; it also involved an increased threat to the health of the child. With a nurse, he would be less carefully watched over and less well cared for, he would live in hygienic conditions worse than those of the city, and his life would depend on the regularity of the family's payment to the nurse.[25] The fact that parents more willingly accepted the unknowns of putting their daughters out to distant nurses seems to me to indicate a lesser interest in girls. The girl's life and physical development was deemed of lesser importance. After 1445, the administration of the Innocenti adopted a behavior analogous to that of Florentine families, putting girls to outside nurses more frequently than the boys they took in.[26] The instructions that parents left with their abandoned male child—one more proof of a differential attachment to a child, even on the part of those who were aban-

22. Parenti, "Fonti per lo studio," 281ff. See Trexler, "The Foundlings," 276, on infant mortality among children who entered the Innocenti after 1445: 53.5 percent died in 1454. The death rate of children put out to nurse during their first year of life reached 23.8 percent of all children of that age group.

23. The *trovatelli* were usually baptized at the central baptistry of San Giovanni the day following their arrival at the hospice. Thus some of them are included in the baptismal records, with mention of the hospice responsible for them. The infants not so registered are those whose parents stated that they had been baptized before being abandoned.

24. According to Trexler, "The Foundlings," 263–64, this amounted to 160 children in San Gallo in 1448, to which we would have to add the 139 children of the Scala mentioned in the *catasto* of 1427, and after 1445 the many children in the Innocenti.

25. Two songs about nurses published in C. S. Singleton, *Canti carnascialeschi del Rinascimento* (Bari, 1936), nos. 29 (39–40) and 94 (125), describe the care that the child could expect from his country nurse: "Le pezze line e lane e fasce bianche/mutiam tre volte il giorno:/così di stargli intorno,/perchè non pianga, mai siam sazei o stanche" (The linen and wool diapers, and the white swaddling clothes we change three times a day: staying by him so he does not cry, we never weary or tire); or, "Sempre quando il bambin piagne/ci sentiàn tornar il latte/ . . . /Quand'e' sente di maldocchio,/sin a Poppi ce n'andiàno:/una donna sul ginocchio/se le pone e fàllo sano,/e po' vuol che no'l tegnàno/alle volte qualche giorno,/così 'gnudo driet'al forno/trastullando al solino" (Always when the baby cries, we feel the milk come . . . When he suffers from the evil eye, we go all the way to Poppi: a woman puts him on her knee and makes him healthy, and then she wants us to hold him, sometimes for days on end, so naked, behind the bake oven, playing in the sunshine).

26. See Trexler, "Infanticide," 101–2.

doning a newborn—may lie at the root of the hospital's better care of boys than of girls.

All of these facts show that a baby girl did not receive care equivalent to that shown her brothers, at least in difficult periods and among the poverty-stricken. It is possible that families hard pressed by famine may have allowed a higher mortality rate for females than for males, without going as far as abandonment, simply by unconsciously according an alimentary advantage to their boys. In this way, famine years could set off a rise in the male/female ratio and accentuate the disequilibrium between the sexes in the child population. Could that perhaps be one explanation for the anomalies in the male/female ratio between 7 and 12 years of age in certain regions particularly hard hit by plague, war, and famine in 1423–24?[27]

Other reasons, of a different nature, explain the imbalance between the sexes among children. The conditions in which their education took place or their entry into the labor market often made their parents forget to declare them. Undeniably, a precocious "vocation" for work was not exclusive to girls, nor to Tuscany. Like their sisters, boys were launched into economic activity at an early age, but the ties they maintained with their family and with its assets were more solid than a girl's, since she was headed for an early break with the family through marriage. It was the double separation of work and then of marriage that so brutally excluded young girls from the family circle and caused them to be forgotten.

The employment of children at an extraordinarily early age—a phenomenon striking to our current sensibilities—is certainly not characteristic of Italian society of the Middle Ages alone. The *catasto*, however, offers a great deal of astonishing information about it. Although the fiscal regulations excluded wage earners or the like (servants, apprentices, nurses) from the deductions authorized for each "mouth," even if they lived in the house of their employer, a large number of taxpayers mention obligations toward domestic employees among their expenses. And conversely, a majority of parents took care to cite those of their children who had been put out to service, even though they were no longer living at home. In this way, we know the age and occupation of a great number of children.

In the cities and among the middle classes, "little servants" often appear in the declaration of an employer who had agreed to give them a dowry when they reached marriageable age (usually 16). These *fantine* were often incredibly young: 8 years old or little more. The master owed them only the dowry—a "furnished" bed or sheets and some clothing—over and

27. In Pistoia the ratio was consistently well above 150 between 9 and 14 years of age, as it was in the *contado* of Pistoia between the ages of 6 and 12. On the effects of the plague in this region, see D. Herlihy, *Medieval and Renaissance Pistoia* (New Haven and London, 1967), 86–87. In Arezzo and surrounding area, which suffered much from the military operations during the preceding years, the ratio was also very high between 9 and 12 years of age, as it was in Pisa between 6 and 10.

above their daily keep. There are carnival songs that sing of these "little servants" who were "waiting for a husband" and who often had difficulty preserving their virture in the family in which they had only a few years to amass the dowry that would enable them to pass under a third and last authority, that of a husband:

> This one, who is a girl to be married,
> You will keep for your chamber maid,
> And a dowry in five years you will give her;
> But above all we want to beg of you
> That she not have to go
> To husband before the proper time,
> As is done to all of them today.[28]

The ties that these young girls were able to maintain with their families, often country people, must have soon slackened. To marry off a girl meant not only to provide a dowry but also to find her a husband. The family that gave up this essential task to an outsider could scarcely have felt responsibilities toward its daughter. Often the break was total and avowed. The master of these children, girls more often than not, declared that he "kept them for the love of God," and the formula covers a melancholy and somber reality of children orphaned, abandoned, or even sold. The expression implies that the patron took total charge of the child who shared his roof and that he could demand of the Florentine fiscal administration the legal deductions to which this new "mouth" gave him a right. For her family of origin, this implied the total loss of its rights and responsibilities. In 1428 a poverty-stricken sharecropper of the Pisan *contado* declares that he has in this manner "given for the love of God" his three daughters, 11, 12, and 14 years old, to three different citizens of the city. He may have received in exchange a small sum and the promise that they would later be married, as stipulated in certain notarial acts, veritable contracts of clandestine sale, as late as the middle of the fifteenth century.[29] Were those children, who from then on were part of the "family" of their master, considered as more than little scullions? Although their future dowry was assured, it is probable that their fate was less than enviable.

The boys placed in service or as apprentices more or less illegally before they were 14 may have sustained less brutal a break with their family setting. Not only did their working relieve their parents of their upkeep;

28. See Singleton, *Canti carnascialeschi,* 362, "Canzona degli acconciatori di fanti," by Niccolò Martelli: "Questa, ch'è una fanciulla a maritare,/per camera terrete,/e la dota in cinque anni le darete;/ma sopratutto vi vogliàn pregare/che' la non abbia andare/prima a marito che del tempo innante,/come oggi s'usa fare a tutte quante."

29. ASP, *Catasto* 1542, fol. 218, declaration of Marco di Nocco. On illegal contracts for the sale of little girls by their poverty-stricken parents and their subsequent rather shameful release *pro Dio* in exchange for maintenance and a dowry, see Tamassia, *La famiglia italiana,* 255 and 369–70.

sometimes it also produced a little income, no matter how modest the sum, or promised the parents future profit when the period of service or apprenticeship ended. Stepchildren or bastard children were sometimes charitably accepted by their family in exchange for a status of this type, and, like all young servants, they received a theoretical wage—one-fourth or one-third of an adult wage—which was just enough to cover their upkeep.[30] For many children of the poorer classes and the countless rural poor, years of service preceded those of apprenticeship, which began legally at 14 and very rarely went beyond the age of 25. At least apprenticeship did not force boys of urban origin to leave their family, as was the case in northern Europe.[31] Many artisans, in fact, refused to keep their "disciple" or their *garzone* in their house.[32] For these least favored of children in medieval society, who did not have the benefit of an educational infrastructure and, after they reached the "age of reason," had to furnish labor that was underpaid and little valued, we can speak of true economic exploitation at an age at which they had no recognized freedom of choice and no legal rights. But because they maintained ties with their families, this violent plunge into the economic world of adults probably affected them less than the employment of girls, which ended in marriage.

The middle classes and the richer families strove to assure their children an education capable of integrating them into the activities of the city, as service and apprenticeship did for their less fortunate peers. Giovanni Villani affirms, in an often-cited passage, that on the eve of the Black Death 60 percent of Florentine children between the ages of 6 and 13 went to school, regardless of their sex.[33] At the beginning of the fifteenth century, however, female education seems to have been dispensed less in the city's schools than in the bosom of the family or in convents specialized for the task. Cloistered even before they had come out of childhood, many little girls of the upper classes found themselves irreversibly removed from

30. Mancini, in *Cortona nel Medio Evo* (Florence, 1897), 127, cites a will that clearly places a bastard son under servitude to his brothers, in exchange for lifetime support.

31. A. Doren, *Le arti fiorentine* (Florence, 1940), 1:219–29 and 2:181–82. See also A. Fanfani, "La préparation intellectuelle à l'activité économique en Italie," *Le Moyen Age* 57: nos. 3–4 (1951): 327–46.

32. ASP, *Catasto* 1558, fol. 498: Giovanni di Aldobrandino Ciampolini keeps his son of 17 at home because he was unable to place him, "non volendo gli artefici garzoni in casa" ( [the masters] not wanting apprentice workers in their house).

33. G. Villani, *Cronica*, vol. 3, bk. 11, chap. 94: around 1338, 8,000 to 10,000 "fanciulli e fanciulle . . . stavano a leggere. . . . Fanciulli che stavano ad apparare l'abbaco e algorisimo in sei scuole, da 1000 in 1200. Et quelli che stavano ad apprendere grammatica e loica in quattro grandi scuole, da 550 in seicento" (boys and girls who were reading . . ., children who were learning calculation and mathematics in six schools, from 1,000 to 1,200 of them. And those who were learning grammar and logic in four great schools were from 550 to 600). See E. Fiumi, "Economia e vita privata dei Fiorentini nelle rilevazioni statistiche di G. Villani," *Archivio storico italiano* 91 (1953): 207–41. Fiumi estimates that the 8,000 to 10,000 children of both sexes who had the benefit of elementary schooling represented 60 percent of the age classes between 6 and 13 and about 10 percent of the total population of Florence.

their families, just like those who were put into service in the lower classes. As Richard Trexler has shown,[34] the father had to decide his daughter's destiny early. If he wanted to take advantage of public institutions like the Monte delle Doti to amass a dowry, he made the first deposit when his daughter was 6 in order to assure her a proper marriage ten years later. These girls, whose physical characteristics destined them at so early an age to marriage or to the convent, often went to a religious establishment around the age of 7. Those who were to return to secular society might remain in the convent until marriage, or their sojourn might continue uninterrupted if their father had promised them to a religious life. In the latter case, they would take the veil between 9 and 11 years of age and pronounce final vows after they were 12 or 13.

Boys, on the other hand, remained much more rooted in their family during their years of schooling. Secular schools were in good supply in Florence, and bourgeois fathers preferred a pragmatic education for their heirs and successors to the teaching dispensed by ecclesiastics. Schooling began at the age of 8 or 9 and continued to around 15 or 16 in the *scuola di grammatica*. After this, a boy might choose the university (between the ages of 15 and 31, according to those listed as students in the *catasto*) or he could learn the art of business, the *abaco*, either in specialized schools or behind the counter. The term that Florentines used for this school, the *botteghuzza*, is worthy of note. It gave a technical apprenticeship that substituted naturally for the one the young man might have found in the paternal shop, the *bottega*, from which the master was often absent on business. The term implies a conformity between family education and the education that this society of merchants assured in its public schools. Apprentices, schoolboys, or business associates, the young men of the urban middle classes thus passed from an early education at the hands of women in the familial gynaeceum to a life deeply involved with that of the community, without, however, breaking all ties as many of their cloistered sisters were obliged to do.

Separation during childhood seems to be all the more marked among girls because their marriage at a still tender age cut them off from their family definitively, while the course of the domestic cycle kept young men dependent longer on the household into which they were born.

There is more than one example in the *catasto* of a small minority of girls in the Tuscan countryside who were promised in marriage by their fathers even before the age of 7. Engagement was more frequent soon after a child was 10 years old, and the marriage was consummated at about

34. R. Trexler, "Les religieuses de Florence," *Annales, E.S.C.* 27, no. 6 (1972), also discussed by J. Kirshner and A. Molho, "The Dowry Fund and the Marriage Market in Early Quattrocento Florence," *Journal of Modern History* 50 (1978): 420–28. Little boys who were *frati* at 4, 8, or 11 years of age or *chierici* at 7 or 8 can also be seen occasionally in the *catasto*. A 4-year-old nevertheless would still live with his parents (B. Casini, *Il catasto di Pisa del 1428–1429* [Pisa, 1964) 246, no. 1008).

Table 5.3

PERCENTAGE OF MARRIED WOMEN ACCORDING TO AGE,
AND AVERAGE AGE AT MARRIAGE (TUSCANY, 1427–30)

| Age | Total Country | Total City | Total Population | Age | Total Country | Total City | Total Population |
|---|---|---|---|---|---|---|---|
| 10 and under | 0.1 | 0.5 | 0.2 | 17 | 38.1 | 43.3 | 40.0 |
| 11 | 0.1 | 0.0 | 0.1 | 18 | 65.0 | 71.1 | 66.8 |
| 12 | 0.5 | 0.3 | 0.4 | 19 | 68.2 | 72.4 | 70.1 |
| 13 | 1.2 | 0.5 | 0.9 | 20 | 89.8 | 87.7 | 89.2 |
| 14 | 3.5 | 4.1 | 3.7 | 25 | 96.1 | 91.6 | 94.8 |
| 15 | 12.0 | 14.5 | 12.7 | | | | |
| 16 | 26.0 | 31.1 | 27.5 | Average age at marriage (in years) | | | |
| | | | | | 18.1 | 17.5 | 17.9 |

12 in more than a negligible number of cases (see table 5.3).[35] What is
more, Saint Antoninus (Sant' Antonino), the bishop of Florence, allowed
a certain margin in the canonical age for marriage (six months), on the
condition that the child had reached puberty.[36] The average age at marriage
was around 17 1/2 for girls, however, and the most frequent age at marriage was 17–18.[37] For these child brides, who soon grew out of their
wedding dress,[38] coming under the rule of a family-in-law must have been
all the more traumatic because of the age difference (particularly notable
in urban settings)[39] between these tender young things and their husband—a difference that might make him a terrifying stranger. A girl's
childhood ended abruptly if this was the first time she had left her family,
and she was newly uprooted if she had been cloistered during her childhood or placed in service.

In contrast, moralists, pedagogues, poets, and jurists all recommended
that the marriage of a boy be put off until he was 25—the threshhold of
Dante's *gioventù*—or even beyond.[40] In the entire *catasto*, only seven boys

35. The most aberrant case of marriage before the canonical age is that of a girl given
as 8 married to a boy of 18 in the *contado* of Arezzo. Another half-dozen little girls can be
found married at the tender age of 10 or 11; married girls of 12 and 13 are more numerous
(fifteen for each age).

36. Saint Antoninus, *Tractatus de sponsalibus et matrimoniis* (original in the Vatican
Library). The good prelate mentions, without excessive surprise, a girl who conceived at 9
and gave birth at 10 (chap. 24).

37. These average ages are calculated by the method developed by J. Hajnal, "Age at
Marriage and Proportions Marrying," *Population Studies* 7: no. 2 (1953) and are confirmed
by the average ages that can be calculated using recently married couples listed in the *catasto*.

38. L. Simon, ed., *Les Quinze joies du mariage* (Paris, 1929), 8.

39. See D. Herlihy, "Vieillir au Quattrocento," *Annales, E.S.C.*, 24 no. 6 (1969): 1338ff.

40. Among very many others, Alberti, *I libri della famiglia*, 131: "A' nostri moderni
pare sia utile sposo ne' XXV anni" ("To our modern minds it seems to be practical for a
man to marry at twenty-five." Watkins trans., 144).

are reported as married before the age of 16;[41] the proportion of men already married at 20 is still only 14.8 percent; 48.5 percent of all men are married at 25, and only three-quarters of all men are married at 33. The age gap between spouses and the wife's automatic transfer under the roof of her husband (which, more than one time in four, was also that of her father- or mother-in-law) further isolated and estranged the transplanted young wife. A girl, who was often absent from her family in childhood and, what is more, could look forward to a childhood shorter than a boy's, was apt to be forgotten by her own family, who had seen little of her and were obsessed by the double onus of her virtue and her dowry. These reasons help explain the underreporting of females as well as the curious rounding off of ages as soon as the girls were old enough for marriage. Since the young woman was not responsible for reporting her age while residing either in her father's house or in her husband's, she left to her own family or to her family by marriage (whose imprecision was even greater) the task of situating her on the age scale.

This "childhood" that Dante presents as so uniform and so undifferentiated proves much more diversified in social and matrimonial practice. It varied greatly, first according to sex, then according to social rank. For many, the maternal education of the first years was followed (with a break that must have meant total upheaval for the child) by a brutal entry into the world of work and into a society of adults that exploited child labor with little tenderness or harshly taught the child to accept his social destiny. In spite of the counsels for moderation that pedagogues or religious orders had begun to offer, corporal punishment was a universal practice.[42] We could say that this second stage of childhood was devoted to clandestine work, to an unavowed apprenticeship, or, at best, to schooling, and that it ended for adolescent girls in marriage or the convent, and for young

41. Double this amount if newlyweds who bring home a wife in the months following the first declaration to the *catasto* are counted. The aberrant cases of very early male marriages are those of one boy of 11 married to a girl of 12 in the Arezzo *contado* and another 13-year-old who takes to wife a girl of 12 (Val d'Arno di Sotto). The *quartiere* of San Giovanni shows several cases of boys married at 14, the limit of the canonical age.

42. On corporal punishment, see Tamassia, *La famiglia italiana,* 257–58. There are many authors who protest not only against the barbaric treatment that heads of family had the right to inflict on their recalcitrant young, but even against the many daily physical dressings down that the father, the employer, the tutor, or the pedagogue distributed for the edification of the younger generation. The traditional attitude is represented, around the time of the *catasto*, by the Dominican Giovanni Dominici, who wanted to have children subjected to *spesse non furiose battiture* (frequent, yet not severe whippings) until they were 25 years old. See Dominici, *Regola del governo di cura familiare,* ed. D. Salvi (Florence 1860), 156: trans. by Arthur Basil Coté as *On the Education of Children* (Washington D. C.: Catholic University of America, 1927) 48. From the end of the fourteenth century on, many reacted against this harshness toward children, among them Paolo da Certaldo, Giovanni Morelli—who regrets the *molte ispesse e aspre battiture* (many severe beatings) that he had formerly inflicted on his oldest son (*Ricordi,* 501), though it is unclear whether his other children profited from his belated remorse—and, later, Alberti. See Bec, *Les marchands écrivains,* 288–89; E. Garin, *Educazione in Europa, 1400–1600* 2d ed. (Bari, 1966) chap. 2.

men by their entry into active life, though in a subordinate position until they were over 25 years old.

All the children of 8, 11, or 15 who followed the mercenary soldiers, the 10- or 12-year-old vagabonds in search of adventure, *iti con Dio*, the runaways who had broken with their father or their patron, the orphans who supported a family at 7 or 12 years old, the prisoners of war of 4 or 6 years old, the wanderers, the beggars, the little girls sold by their parents and nourished "for the love of God"—all this sad childhood that a document like the *catasto* reveals in profusion is scandalous in our eyes. The tender age of these unfortunate creatures, however, did not particularly shock the society in which they lived. Even in the old saw of the abandoned and exploited orphan we often feel that contemporaries had more sympathy for the estate that was frittered away by the unscrupulous guardians than for the victim. If childish innocence constantly evoked reference to the Gospels, this was far from implying the conclusions concerning child psychology that we are quick to draw. Such reference was much more likely to express admiration for little men who, like Jesus among the doctors, reason, act, and express themselves better than adults.[43] Integration into the adult world began early and was carried on energetically: a father took great pride in a girl's early marriage or willing entry into a convent. A good upbringing was one that enabled a father to obtain from his children all the formal marks of respect and submission.[44]

The humanist movement, however, set off a renewal in pedagogical thought around the time of the *catasto*.[45] Like the merchant pedagogy, humanist pedagogy encouraged the young to reason and to seek pragmatic knowledge founded on facts or on texts, but always linked to direct experience. This humanistic approach had ties with the monastic pedagogy of the very early Middle Ages, which had tried to adapt apprenticeship in knowledge to the faculties and the "passions of childhood."[46] The new thought concerning childhood behavior in the fifteenth century reflects a fundamental optimism that softened the repressive attitudes of medieval pedagogy. The notion of authority was indeed present in both approaches, but its application now took into consideration the psychological and intellectual autonomy of children.[47] The knowledge, the morality, and the behavior inculcated in children by the new pedagogy were those of adults, and the aim of education was still to lead the child to conduct himself

43. One example of this is in novella 67 of Franco Sacchetti, *Il trecentonovelle,* ed. E. Faccioli (Turin, 1970), 170–73, where a *fanciullo* of 14 outtalks a *messere* and has the last word.

44. On outward conformity, which both Morelli and Paolo da Certaldo seek to inculcate in the child, see Bec, *Les marchands écrivains,* 59, 106–8, and 279ff.

45. E. Garin, *Educazione,* and E. Garin, *Il pensiero pedagogico nell'Umanesimo* (Florence, 1958).

46. P. Riché, *Education et culture dans l'Occident barbare, VI^c–VIII^c siècles* (Paris, 1962); Garin, *Educazione.*

47. Bec, *Les marchands écrivains* 279–99; Garin, *Educazione.,* chap. 2.

outwardly like an adult, but the means now differed. Interest in child psychology even reached those who reacted to counter the new pedagogical tendencies: thus the Dominican, Giovanni Dominici, reflects on the educational and moral value of games and the encouragement of Christian behavior through pictures or toys.[48] In a society that valued the exercise of manual or commercial professions, schooling attempted to put such exercise within the reach of children's understanding.

This interest extended back to the newborn child, to this little person so fragile that no one had dared consider him before or, at least, judged him worthy of attention. It was not just the choice of a nurse that interested moralists. The feelings a father might legitimately experience in relation to an infant became matter for literature and reflection. The interlocutors who take the stage in Alberti's treatise on the family discuss the subject at length. Can one take joy in the least actions and gestures of a little child when he knows, like Adovardo, that he is risking great unhappiness if the child should die? (And more do indeed die, he continues, during this first age than during all the other ages.) Or is it better to take advantage of the child's presence, of his first advances and his first attempts at speech like Lionardo, who prefers to trust the robustness hidden under apparent fragility, but resigns himself in Christian fashion to the idea of the child's death?[49] These contrasting attitudes display a rather surprising interplay of traditional sentiments (refusal of the emotional burden and resignation)

48. Dominici, *Regola del governo* ed. D. Salvi, 145–46 and 150ff. See chapter 14 below, "Holy Dolls." The author makes a Pascalian wager, saying that the imitation of piety should assure the birth of true religious sentiment in children. He advises children to amuse themselves by the erecting and decorating of little altars and imitating priests. If that were not enough, he advises that they "sieno menati alcune volte alla chiesa e loro mostrato quel che fanno e' veri sacerdoti acciò imparino a contraffargli" ("be brought to the church sometimes and shown how real priests do it, that they may imitate them," Coté trans., 42–43).

49. Alberti, *I libri della famiglia* 42, 46. Adovardo:"Stima tu a chi duole vederli piangere se forse cadendo un poco si li percuotono le mani, quanto gli sarà molesto pensare che più fanciulli di quella età che d'ogni altra periscono. Pensa quanto gli sia acerbità aspettare d'ora in ora essere privato di tanta voluttà. Anzi mi pare questa età prima esser quella che da ogni parte sparge le molte e grandissime maninconie" ("Consider, you who hate to see them cry when they have fallen and hurt their hands, how much anguish it is to a father to think that more children perish at this age than at any other. Imagine the painful waiting from hour to hour in expectation of losing so great a happiness. In fact this first period of life seems to me the one that particularly causes many and great sorrows." Watkins trans., 52). Lionardo replies: Ma ben sai, stare in paura come tu me parevi e dubitare di quella prima età periscano molti, a me questo non pare da lodare. E' si vuole, mentre che ne' fanciulli si sente spirare qualche anima, più tosto sperarne meglio che dubitarne. . . . E quando a Dio fusse in qualche età piaciuto che a' figliuoli tuoi el corso de' giorni suoi fusse finito, stimo sia officio de' padri più tosto ramentarsi e rendere grazia de' molti piaceri e sollazzi, quali e' figliuoli hanno loro dati, che dolersi se chi te gli prestò se gli ha in tempo rivoluti" ("But you know, to be as anxious as you seemed to be, and worried because so many children die in those first years, does not seem commendable to me. As long as there is breath in a child, one should hope for the best rather than fear the worst. . . . And if at some point in the course of childhood it pleases God to end your child's days, I think it is the father's duty rather to recall and to render thanks for the many joys and delights which the children have given him than to sorrow because the one who lent them to you has in his own time claimed them again." Watkins trans., 54).

and "modern" reactions (being touched by and passionately interested in the child, observing his nascent "individuality"). What Alberti expresses here is something like the indecision of the educated man of the Quattrocento, caught between old and new attitudes toward the child.

Or should we say, toward the very young child? This interest in the newborn and the infant reflects a "feminization" of thought patterns, at least in cultivated urban settings and perhaps, by means of imagery, even into the popular strata of society. For although the pedagogues were more interested—for obvious reasons—in the second stage of childhood, iconography in Tuscany at the end of the Middle Ages put more and more emphasis on the very young child. The origins of this phenomenon are well known. During the thirteenth century the cult of Mary, having stressed the mother, turned its interest to the child she presents for adoration. Later the baby Jesus turns once more toward his mother and begins to behave like a real baby—playful, laughing, and hungry. Even later his relationship with the worshiping spectator becomes more animated, when the baby Jesus invites participation in his games and in his interests.[50] But what is most striking in Tuscan art of the fourteenth and fifteenth centuries is not only the reinterpretation of the traditional themes of the mother and the child, but even more the wealth of new themes tied to the family and to the child. There was the theme of the family, exalted in the life of the Virgin, in the Holy Families, and even in the representation of Saint John founding a new family when Christ entrusts him with his mother. There was the theme of marriages, including those mentioned in holy Scripture, those of the donors, and the spiritual marriages of saints male and female (the most revealing of new sensitivities among the latter is that of Saint Catherine to the infant Jesus, a motif that joins together several deep currents of family devotion). There were the themes, finally, of childhood—that of the Christ child appearing miraculously to Saint Agnes of Montepulciano or to Saint Humiliana (Santa Umiliana dei Cerchi); in its tragic form, the slaughter of the Innocents; in its profane form, the transition from Amor or the adult angel to the beautiful adolescent, then to the *putto* that invades Quattrocento canvases.[51] The appearance of the *putti*, like that of the slaughtered Innocents, is probably a sign of an increased sensitivity to the death of children. Since these little angels were identified with the souls of children who had died in infancy,[52] the *putti* testify to

50. See P. du Colombier, *L'enfant au Moyen Age* (Paris, 1951): M. Meiss, *Painting in Florence* 60–61; 106–13 (on Saint Catherine and her mystic marriage); 132–56 (on the maternal theme of the Madonna of Humility).

51. We should note that *putti* are male—and that fifteenth-century artists thus settled the age-old question of the sex of angels. On Amor, see E. Panofsky, *Studies in Iconology* (Oxford, 1939), chap. 4.

52. In contemporary *danses macabres* in northern Europe, the child seldom figures as such among those that death comes to cut down. The theme of equality before death is first of all a social theme, while the Massacre of the Innocents gives symbolic form to the recognition of a demographic scandal.

a consciousness of the fragility of childhood and all that threatened it that is just as poignant as the reflections of Alberti's Adovardo. The irruption of these little children pushing around their saintly elders reflects for us a recently discovered early childhood.

The relations between this art of intimate, human, familial devotion and the place of the child in the domestic group will perhaps be clarified by Dominici's advice on painting and its usefulness for young children. This "reactionary" pedagogue tells the mother:

> Have pictures of saintly children or young virgins in the home, in which your child, still in swaddling clothes, [i.e., under two years old] may take delight and thereby may be gladdened by acts and signs pleasing to childhood. And what I say of pictures applies also to statues. It is well to have the Virgin Mary with the Child in her arms, with a little bird or apple in His hand. There should be a good representation of Jesus nursing, sleeping in His Mother's lap or standing courteously before Her, drawing while His Mother embroiders according to His drawing. So let the child see himself mirrored in the Holy Baptist clothed in camel's skin, a little child (*fanciullino*) who enters the desert, plays with the birds, sucks the honeyed flowers and sleeps on the ground. It will not be amiss if he should see Jesus and the Baptist, Jesus and the boy Evangelist pictured together; the slaughtered Innocents, so that he may learn the fear of weapons and of armed men. Thus it is desirable to bring up little girls in the contemplation of the eleven thousand Virgins as they discourse, pray, and suffer. I should like them to see Agnes with her little fat lamb, Cecilia crowned with roses, Elizabeth with roses on her cloak, Catherine and her wheel with other such representations as may give them, with their milk, love of virginity. . .[53]

After its feminist growing pains, western art was invited to appeal to children by means of a sugary and touching iconography that reflected, first of all, the adult's new vision of the child and the pleasure that the adult took in *looking at* children.

In the middle class family of the modern period, the child, at least the male child, had become the goal of his parents' undertakings, even if he did not bear a "name." (In Tuscany, family names were not fixed before the sixteenth century outside of the urban oligarchy.) It was the child who was to profit from the moral and material acquisitions of the parents, from their worldly goods as well as from the accumulation of their spiritual merits, and society exalted this transfer of powers from father to son. When the child became the living nucleus of the family cell, charity and social expectations reflected these changes in attitude. Just as art, having

53. Dominici, *Regola*, 131ff. (Coté trans., 34).

portrayed the mother, quickly turned to represent the child, so Florentine society became conscious almost simultaneously of the need to preserve its female capital (which held the promise of its marriages) and the need to protect the children who were the aim of those marriages. The foundation of the Monte delle Doti and the decision to create a hospice reserved exclusively to foundling infants were contemporary events: the Monte was created in 1425; the decision to construct the Innocenti, superbly decorated at a later date with swaddled babies, was taken in 1421. Traditionally compared to the weak, the humble, and the dispossessed and mingled in the hospitals with the miserable horde of society's rejects, the child was gradually separated out from the wretched. At least in his first years he became the object of a special kind of social attention, while in Florentine families the father, who showed such severity toward his older children, was touched by the babblings of his newborn child.

With their homes for newborn *trovatelli*, designed to combat open infanticide and, later, to hide the scandal of illegitimate births, the cities of Tuscany seemed at the beginning of the fifteenth century to be in advance of most of the other Italian communes, and Florence and Siena were expressly cited as examples for Lombard institutions.[54] In a society that valued productive capacities and the success of the entrepreneur, the adult beggar yielded his place to the young child as the object of traditional Christian compassion. Iconography translates this fundamental difference in charitable behavior with a clear symbol: the image of *Caritas*, formerly shown accompanied by a lame beggar, was supplanted by an image in which she gives her breast and her protection to young children.

This new solicitude, widespread at the turn of the fifteenth century, was still limited to the very young child, the *trovatello*, or the very young orphan. The age of reason—that is, the age of reasonable, quasi-adult speech—closed a period of fragility that people had begun to find touching. Crossing this frontier made the *infante* pass to the state of the *fante*, the subservient or the servant. The age of reason opened onto an age of economic subordination in which the psychological differences and individuality of childhood were misunderstood. In iconography as in vocabulary or in daily life, the child was no longer, after 7 years of age, any more than a second-class individual, often passed over in silence or brutally thrown into the world of adults.

54. B. Pullan, *Rich and Poor in Renaissance Venice* (Oxford, 1971), 197–206. On the ancient Florentine institutions, see L. Passerini, *Storia degli stabilimenti di beneficenza della città di Firenze* (Florence, 1853); Trexler, "The Foundlings."

# 6

# The "Cruel Mother": Maternity, Widowhood, and Dowry in Florence in the Fourteenth and Fifteenth Centuries

In Florence, men *were* and *made* the "houses." The word *casa* designates, in the fourteenth and fifteenth centuries, the material house, the lodging of a domestic unit, and it is in this sense that many documents of a fiscal, legal, or private nature use the term. But it also stands for an entire agnatic kinship group. The *casa* in this case designates all ancestors and living members of a lineage, all those in whose veins the same blood ran, who bore the same name, and who claimed a common ancestor—an eponymic hero whose identity the group had inherited.[1]

"Houses" were made by men. Kinship was determined by men, and the male branching of genealogies drawn up by contemporaries shows how little importance was given, after one or two generations, to kinship through women. Estates also passed from one generation to another through men. Among the goods that men transmitted jealously, excluding women from ownership as far as they could, was the material house, which they "made" also, in the sense that they built it, enlarged it, and filled it with children who

Originally published as "Maternité, veuvage et dot à Florence," *Annales, E.S.C.* 38, no. 5 (1983): 1097–1109. A first version of this essay was presented at the colloquy at Sénanque organized by Georges Duby in July 1981 on the topic "Maisons et sociétés domestiques au Moyen Age"; it was later revised for the workshop "La femme seule," held 1980–82 at the Centre de Recherches Historiques.

1. D. Herlihy and C. Klapisch-Zuber, *Les Toscans et leurs familles* (see chap. 1, n. 1 above), 532ff.

bore their name. The Florence of the early Renaissance, the Florence of
the great merchants and the first humanists, was not a tenderly feminine
city. Family structures and the framework of economic, legal, and political
life remained under the control of level-headed males, bastions of solidarity, and family values were inspired by a severely masculine ideal.[2]

In these *case*, in the sense of both physical and the symbolic house,
women were passing guests. To contemporary eyes, their movements in
relation to the *case* determined their social personality more truly than the
lineage group from which they came. It was by means of their physical
"entrances" and "exits" into and out of the "house" that their families of
origin or of alliance evaluated the contribution of women to the greatness
of the *casa*.[3] The marriage that brought a woman out of the paternal house
and lineage, the widowhood that often led to her return, these incessant
comings and goings of wives between *case* introduced a truly indeterminate
quality in the ways they were designated: since reference to a male was
necessary, a woman was spoken of in relation to her father or her husband,
even when they were dead.[4] It is clear that the mere reference to the name
of the lineage into which she was born or into which she married situated
a woman much more clearly than the place where she was living at the
moment. Women, then, were not permanent elements in the lineage.
Memory of them was short. An important woman, a benefactress for her
kin, for example, would eventually be known under her own name and
brought to people's attention; but the family chronicler or the amateur
genealogist would feel obliged to explain *why*, since the process fit so
poorly within their definition of kinship. Thus Paolo Sassetti, noting in
his journal the death of a female relative in 1371, writes, "Let special
mention be made here, for we considered her to be like a beloved mother,
and in all of her works she has been and was among the beloved women
who have gone forth from our house."[5] As one who had both "come into"
and "gone out of" the house, this exceptional "mother" must have stood
out for her fidelity to the family into which she was born. Equally worthy
of "special mention" but marked with the seal of the lineage's disapproval
were the women who usurped an inheritance and persuaded a husband
on his deathbed to disinherit his own kin.[6] More often, the family chroniclers keep the memory of an alliance with a certain lineage, but forget, a

2. See R. C. Trexler, *Public Life in Renaissance Florence* (New York: Academic Press,
1980).

3. Thus several tables drawn up by genealogists of the fifteenth and sixteenth centuries
categorize women under *uscite* and *entrate* according to lineage.

4. See chap. 13, below "The Name Remade."

5. Archivio di Stato, Florence (henceforth abbreviated ASF), *Strozziane*, 2d ser., 4,
Ricordanze di Paolo Sassetti (1365–1400), fol. 34 (11 February 1371). Dates are given in
modern style.

6. Ibid., fol. 68v (24 September 1383); ASF, *Strozz.*, 2d ser., 13, Ricordanze di Doffo
di Nepo Spini, fol. 83 (7 July 1434).

few generations after the marriage, the given name of the woman on whom the alliance was built.

The determination of a woman's identity thus depended on her movements in relation to the "houses" of men. The corollary was that upper-class Florentines found females who remained in their house of birth just as intolerable as females who lived independently. "Honorable" marriages were what regulated the entries and exits of the wives, and the normal state, the state that guaranteed the honor of the women and the "houses," could be no other than the married state. Any woman alone was suspect. An unmarried woman was considered incapable of living alone or in the absence of masculine protection without falling into sin.[7] Even if she were a recluse and lived a holy life,[8] even if she retired to a room on the upper floor of the paternal house,[9] she placed the family honor in jeopardy by the mere fact of her celibacy. The convent was the only way out, although terrible doubts about the security of the cloister continued to torment her parents.[10] Among the "best people," therefore, families did not include females over twenty years of age who were not married.[11]

The widow's solitude was hardly less suspect. Although the Church advised the widow with a penchant for chastity not to remarry and to practice the related virtues of *mater et virgo*, secular society did not set much store by her chances of remaining chaste.[12] The problem of where

7. In the *catasto* of 1427 there are only 70 unmarried women among the 1,536 female heads of household in Florence.

8. On the suspicion that greeted *pinzochere* (women who took the habit of third order nuns to live in communities or, worse, alone), see below, note 22, and R. Davidsohn, *Storia di Firenze* (Italian trans., Florence, 1965), 6:66ff. On Church attitudes concerning *pinzochere*, see R. C. Trexler, *Synodal Law in Florence and Fiesole 1306–1518* Studi e Testi no. 268 (Vatican City, 1971), 121–22, 142. On the various forms of religious life for women, in community or in seclusion, see the works of A. Benvenuti-Papi, esp. "Penitenza e penitenti in Toscana: Stato della questione e prospettive della ricerca," *Ricerche di storia sociale e religiosa* nos. 17–18 (1980): 107–20; R. Pazzelli and L. Temperini, eds., *Prime manifestazioni di vita comunitaria maschile e femminile nel movimento francescano della penitenza* (Rome, 1982), 389–450.

9. On women who were nuns *in casa*, see Herlihy and Klapisch-Zuber, *Les Toscans*, 153–55 and 580. In Florence, thirty such women made a declaration to the *catasto* in their own name, but many more were part of a family. (In Arezzo, four out of eleven *suore in casa* or *pinzochere* declared their wealth independently.) See below, note 40, on Umiliana dei Cerchi.

10. R. C. Trexler, "Le célibat à la fin du Moyen-Age. Les religieuses de Florence," *Annales, E.S.C.* 27 no. 6 (1972): 1329–50.

11. Among Florentine women who belonged to the age group of 20–24 years of age, 92 percent were married; the proportion is even higher among the wealthier classes.

12. See J. Kirshner, *Pursuing Honor while Avoiding Sin: The Monte delle Doti of Florence*, Quaderni di *Studi Senesi* 41 (Milan, 1978), 7, n. 22; A. Burguière, "Réticences théoriques et intégration pratique du remariage dans la France d'Ancien Régime, XVIIᵉ-XVIIIᵉ s.," in J. Dupâquier et al., eds., *Marriage and Remarriage in Populations in the Past* (London, 1981), 43. On popular treatment of remarriage, see J. Le Goff and J. -C. Schmitt, eds., *Le charivari* (Paris and The Hague, 1981). See also "De la vie des veuves," in E. C. Bayonne, ed. and trans., *Oeuvres spirituelles de J. Savonarole* (Paris, 1879–80), 5–51.

the widow was to live became crucial in such a case, for she was a threat to the honor not only of one family but of two. Given that a wife must live where her father or her husband lived (since they were the guarantors of her good conduct and her social identity), where should a wife be when she lost her husband?

### On the Dwelling Place and the Virtue of Dowered Widows

Theoretically, a widow had some choice in the matter. She could live in her husband's family, by her children's side; she could live independently without remarrying, but near her children; or, finally, she could remarry and leave the first family that had received her. But in practice a widow, if young, was barred from the second option and found herself subjected to contradictory pressures that prevented her from quietly choosing between the other two possibilities. Young widows were in fact the target of a whole set of forces struggling fiercely for control of their bodies and their fortunes.

The statistics of the *catasto* show that widows in 1427 were much more numerous in the general population than widowers (13.6 percent and 2.4 percent, respectively). In Florence these percentages doubled (25 percent and 4 percent).[13] Widowers tended to be older men (14 percent of the age classes of 70 years old and older were widowers), for men remarried promptly up to a late age. Definitive widowhood came much earlier for women: at 40—that is, at an age at which they might still give children to their new husband—18 percent of Florentine women appear in the census as widows, and at 50, nearly 45 percent do so. Furthermore, according to the statistics on couples drawn from family diaries, two-thirds of the women who became widows before 20 found a new husband, one-third of those widowed between 20 and 29, but only 11 percent of those widowed between 30 and 39—when their numbers grow. We might conclude that after 40 they no longer had much chance of remarrying, while from 75 to 100 percent of all men up to 60 years of age took another wife.[14] Even if they hoped for remarriage, then, widows' liberty of choice was singularly limited by their age.

The social group to which they belonged added other constraints. According to the statistics on households, it was easier, in 1427, for a widow to live independently in the city than in the country. In Florence itself, nearly 14 percent of the heads of household were at that time widows, as opposed to 4 percent who were widowers. The difference between the

---

13. Herlihy and Klapisch-Zuber, *Les Toscans*, appendix V, tables 1 and 2.
14. For comparative data on the problem of remarriage and its implications for fertility, see Dupâquier et al., eds., *Marriage and Remarriage*.

two was smaller in rural areas: 7.6 percent widows and 4.4 percent widowers. What is more, among wealthy Florentines the probability of a widow's living alone collapses: 2 percent of the 472 wealthiest households (which represent less than 5 percent of all Florentine households) were headed by a woman (an even lower percentage than in the country), and rich widows who lived really autonomously were the exception at the upper levels of urban society.[15]

Since it is strikingly obvious that a widow's ability to live alone or simply to head the household of her minor children was correlated to her wealth, we need to raise questions concerning the processes that tied her fate to that of the family estate. By processes I mean legal mechanisms as well as individual and collective behavior that affected the widow or motivated her decisions.

It was of course the dowry that tangled the threads of a woman's fate. In principle, the dowered goods that a wife brought her husband were attached to her for life: they had the double function of providing for the expenses of the household and, when the household dissolved at the husband's death, of providing for the surviving wife.[16] Since she could not inherit her father's estate, which went to her brothers,[17] a woman looked to her dowry to assure her subsistence: she could "keep her estate and her honor" before transmitting to her children, male and female, the dowry she had received at marriage. This lovely scheme was unfortunately often belied by the facts. Every widowhood threatened the economic equilibrium the domestic group had achieved during the father's lifetime. If the widow was 40 years old or older, the difficulty of finding her a new husband discouraged her own parents from intervening. It was up to her husband's heirs to persuade her to remain with them and not to "leave with her dowry" to live independently. What is more, her husband would do his utmost, on his deathbed, to encourage her to give up any such idea. He would agree to assure her a lifetime income and supplementary advantages, over and above the income from her own estate, if she would remain under his roof, and he would make his heirs swear to show her all consideration and to consult her in the management of the holdings in which her dowry

15. Many widows who made independent declarations of their worth to the *catasto* of 1427 in reality lived in their children's household but took this opportunity to have their rights to their personal estate recognized (see Herlihy and Klapisch-Zuber, *Les Toscans*, 61).

16. M. Bellomo, *Ricerche sui rapporti patrimoniali tra coniugi* (Milan, 1961), 61ff.

17. And, in the absence of brothers, to the agnates of the intestate father, up to three-quarters of the total estate. A daughter could inherit only in the absence of agnates to a stipulated degree of consanguinity. (For examples of how this right was put into effect and how it affected lineage ties, see R. Bizzocchi, "La dissoluzione di un clan familiare: I Buondelmonti di Firenze nei secoli XV e XVI," *Archivio storico italiano* 140, no. 511 [1982]: 3–45.) See *Statuta populi et communis Florentiae (1415)*, (Fribourg, 1778–81), 1:223ff. A father could, of course, leave more to his daughters in his will; for example, ser Alberto Masi left one-third of his estate to his two brothers and the other two-thirds to his two daughters (ASF, *Manoscritti,* 89, fol. 15).

would continue to be sunk.[18] All of this was not unique to Florence, or to Italy.[19] Clearly, well-off Florentines did succeed in dissuading their wives from flying with their own wings, since there were very few rich and elderly widows who lived independently. If a widow, however, did not get along with her husband's heirs and preferred her freedom, she had no claims other than to her dowry. The suits initiated by widows to regain their dowry show that the heirs did not always see matters her way. In the fifteenth century, however, widows had the law and judicial institutions on their side: if they were not discouraged from the start, they ended up by taking back what they had brought to their marriage.

Finally, if the heirs—who were not always her own children—did not want to keep her under their roof or give her back her dowry, the Florentine widow could fall back on the *tornata*, a right of refuge in her family of birth. It was the obligation of her close kin or their heirs to receive her and assure her board and lodging.[20] In the fifteenth century, some Florentines, anxious to assure shelter to the widows of their blood after the extinction of their male descendants, provided in their will that one of their houses be devoted to "taking in, in the future, all of our women 'gone out' [of the house] and widowed, and assuring them the *tornata*." Thus, veritable old people's homes for family members were created, in which women rejected by their family by marriage could end their days honorably, knowing they could count on the solidarity of those of their blood even unto the next generation.[21]

These arrangements attest to an anxiety among men—who were deeply committed to maintaining the honor of their "house"—at the thought that a woman of their kin might not be included in a familial group. Even when old, a widow represented a threat to the reputation of good families.

18. See the example cited in Herlihy and Klapisch-Zuber, *Les Toscans*, 557, n. 21 (year 1312). For another example: Barna Ciurianni stipulates that his widow share in all of the revenue of the family and that she "be in all things honored as it is appropriate, and [that she be] trustee, with Valorino [her son], without having to give accounts" (ASF, *Manoscr.* 77, fol. 19, 1380). Giovanni Niccolini, who died in 1381, left his wife a share in the administration of his estate, with his children, as long as she lived with them, and, after ten years, if she wanted independent widowhood without taking back her dowry, he left her the profits from a farm, or half of the latter if she preferred to take back her dowry—the choice that the widow seems to have preferred after 1382 (C. Bec, ed., *Il libro degli affari proprii di casa de Lapo Niccolini de' Sirigatti,* Paris, 1969, 62ff.). See also the case of Matteo Strozzi in 1429 (ASF, *Strozz.*, 5th ser., 12, fol. 25).

19. See M. T. Lorcin, "Retraite des veuves et filles au couvent: Quelques aspects de la condition féminine à la fin du Moyen-Age," *Annales de Démographie historique* (1975), 187–204; Lorcin, *Vivre et mourir en Lyonnais à la fin du Moyen Age* (Paris, 1981), 65–73.

20. On the right to support and on the *tornata* see *Statuta,* 1:135, 223–25.

21. Conflict with the male heirs could result from the *tornata*: see ASF, *Strozz.*, 5th ser., 1750, Ricordanze di Bartolomeo di Tommaso Sassetti, fols. 181 and 154v. For examples of these houses for retirement within the family, see ASF *Strozz.*, 5th ser., 12, Ricordanze di Matteo di Simone Strozzi, fol. 25 (1429), and *Strozz.*, 5th ser., 15, fol. 96 (the will of Matteo's widow in 1455) and fol. 97 (1464); ASF, *Conventi soppressi*, 83, 131, fol. 100 (1548). See also Biblioteca Centrale Nazionale, Florence (henceforth abbreviated BNF), Magliab. VIII, 1282, fol. 122v (1367).

Since she had tasted the pleasures of the flesh, she was considered prone, like the hideous merry widow portrayed in Boccaccio's *Corbaccio*, to fall into debauchery.[22] If the heirs let their material interests pass before defense of their honor, the widow's kin, their allied family, felt sufficient responsibility toward her to take her back under their charge—not always without recriminations. Piero di Bernardo Masi, a coppersmith, gave solemn instructions to his progeny, in 1512, to take all precautions to avoid what had happened to his own father and to get guarantees for the dowries they gave their daughters. For fifteen years—until she died—his father had had to maintain at his own expense a sister whose husband had left her penniless.[23]

In this game, a married woman embodied stakes that were fully revealed only if she was widowed young. Early widowhood revived the claims of the widow's family of birth on the goods brought as a dowry. As these were irrevocably attached, by law, to the physical person of the woman for the duration of her life, widowhood forced her own kin to use her as a pawn by making her "come out" of her husband's family. When she remarried, her family could join a new circle of affines. By the remarriage of a widow of their blood, Florentines affirmed that they had never totally relinquished control over the dowries that they had given their daughters or their sisters.[24] At the same time, they claimed a perpetual right to the women's bodies and their fertility. Marriage alliance did not obliterate blood kinship; it did not signify a definitive break between the wife and her family of origin. When the widow returned to her family of birth and once again became part of its matrimonial strategies, the family took back cards it had already played, with every intention of making the most of a second deal of social prestige bought by the conclusion of a new alliance.

As soon as the husband had been buried and the funeral ceremonies had ended, the wife's kin came to claim her if she was young. They brought her back to their own house: such is "the custom of Florence," Paolo Sassetti says in 1395,[25] and a contemporary asserts that it was less than honorable for the widow to leave before the ceremony, but that it was understood as proper and accepted by all that she do so immediately afterward.[26] The right of families of birth to take back their widows was

22. A debauchery that was all the more repugnant because it was hidden behind the state of *pinzochera* and because the widow opened her door to mendicant friars, "great consolers of widows" (Giovanni Boccaccio, *Corbaccio*. ed. P. G. Ricci, Classici Ricciardi, 44, [Turin, 1977], 71–72).

23. ASF, *Manoscr.* 88, fol. 160v.

24. On the remarriage of widows and the recycling of their dowry or their dower, see G. Duby, *Le chevalier, la femme et le prêtre* (Paris, 1981), 88, 96, 283.

25. ASF, *Strozz.*, 2d ser., 4, fols. 74ff.

26. BNF, *Panciatichi*, 120, fol. 156 (1377). Here the widow leaves "although she had four children and she was pregnant and she failed to pay him honor in the church." In the same manner the Bolognese mason, Gasparre Nadi, notes that the neighborhood gossiped a good deal when a widow went to a second husband too quickly (*Diario bolognese*, ed. C. Ricci and A. Bacchi della Lega, Bologna, 1886, 47).

stronger than the desires the deceased had expressed in his will. The Sassetti "extracted" (the verb *trarre* is used) a sister in 1389, a niece of this same Paolo, and they remarried her promptly, even though she had "three little boys of very young age," for whom her husband had named her guardian and of whose inheritance she had been named coadministrator. But, Paolo Sassetti says, "as we had to remarry M[adonn]a Isabetta, she could not, and we did not want her to, take on this guardianship, and she renounced it 7 December 1389." The maternal uncles then took over responsibility for their sister's sons.[27]

### The Widow's Defection and the Abandonment of Children

A departure like Madonna Isabetta's constituted a double threat: to the children of the couple broken up by the death of the father, and to the children of a previous marriage. If their mother or their stepmother left them abruptly for a second marriage, their economic situation underwent a much more brutal shock than when an aged widow demanded her dowry in order to retire where it suited her. The heirs could put many an obstacle in the way of an older widow, for she would find less support from her own kin than if they had decided to remarry her. Remarriage was an honorable objective—so honorable, in fact, that long delays in the restitution of the dowry were frowned upon. For this reason testators who left minor children and a young widow made every effort to stave off the danger by including many dissuasive stipulations. Giovanni Morelli, in devoting many pages of his *Ricordi* (around 1400) to the fate of the widow after her husband's death, testifies to his own dread of leaving his heirs and their guardians the frightening obligation of a sudden restitution of a dowry.[28] That possibility also explains the recurring advice in Florentine writings that the sums demanded for dowries be kept within reasonable limits. Otherwise their restitution would jeopardize the children's future.[29] Since an inflationary movement inexorably carried urban dowries upward in the fourteenth and fifteenth centuries, these repeated appeals have an almost desperate tone. Nothing could be done about it, however; contemporaries saw the size of a dowry as an indicator of their social status, and they were little inclined to receive a dowry that was less than "honorable."[30] Testators set up barriers to keep a dowry from ebbing from their house toward the house that had given and was taking back the

27. ASF, *Strozz.*, 2d ser., 4, fols. 74, 103.

28. Giovanni di Pagolo Morelli, *Ricordi*, ed. V. Branca, (2d ed. (Florence, 1969), 213–23.

29. Ibid., 211. L. B. Alberti, *I Libri della famiglia*, ed. R. Romano and A. Tenenti (Turin Einaudi, 1969), 135–36. A study by Julius Kirshner, to be published, clarifies changes in attitudes regarding the remarriage of widows, which eventually, in 1415, introduced a notable change in the statutes.

30. See Kirshner, *Pursuing Honor*.

widow, but they could do little to counter the perverse effects of the dotal system in a society in which patrilineal transmission of estates tended to dominate.[31]

"Give a thought, reader," writes one hard-pressed guardian, "of the expenses that have fallen to me in order to satisfy the widows so that they will not abandon their children, especially Neri's widow, who was 25 years old."[32] The remarriage of a widow cast the shadow of a second threat: the abandonment of the children. In fact, the children belonged to the lineage of their father.[33] Thus, boys all their life and girls until their marriage resided with their agnatic kin. Statistics on households, like the daily events chronicled in family journals, show that children rarely stayed for long periods with their maternal kin. If the latter did take them in, they were paid for the children's keep, or they took on management of the children's estates, since children had no rights to goods that belonged to a lineage not their own. Children who followed their remarried mother were even rarer.[34] The documentation shows that arrangements permitting a widow to establish the children of her first marriage (also with payment of their keep) under the roof of the second husband were usually provisional.[35] Although the stepmother was a very familiar figure in Florentine households, the stepfather was practically unknown.

When a widow left a house in order to remarry, she left with her dowry but without her children. In 1427, many of the tax declarations deplore the abandonment of orphans whose mother had "left the family, taking away her dowry," leaving her husband's heirs in the charge of guardians and of paternal kin.[36] The Florentine family journals, too, overflow in the

31. See chapter 10 below, "The Griselda Complex."

32. Bonaccorso Pitti, *Cronica*, ed. A. Bacchi della Lega (Bologna, 1905), 200.

33. There is one case that is a tragicomic example of belonging to the father's lineage: a pregnant woman is widowed, her family "retracts" her after the husband's burial but sends her back to the husband's lineage until the child is born. When this happens, the family takes her back to remarry her (ASF, *Acquisti e Doni*, 8, Ricordanze di Jacopo di Niccolò Melocchi fol. 56 [1517] ). See also the squabbles of the Minerbetti family: one of them quarrels with his brothers to marry a woman whom he leaves pregnant when he dies. The mother sees her newborn baby whisked off by her brothers-in-law; then her own family has the baby snatched from his nurse. It takes a court decision to get him restored to his paternal uncles, who, when all is said and done, return him to his mother (Biblioteca Laurenziana, Florence, *Acquisti*, 229, fol. 69 (1508).

34. One exception, notable because it is so well known, is that of Giovanni Morelli and his young brothers and sisters, who lived with their maternal grandparents for seven or eight years after their mother's remarriage (see below, note 49).

35. Antonio Rustichi remarried his widowed sister in 1418, and he reached an agreement with his new brother-in-law that the children of the first marriage who accompanied their mother, would renounce all claim to the dowry, probably in compensation for the expenses of their upbringing, assumed by the stepfather (ASF, *Strozz.*, 2d ser., 11, fols. 12v, 13v).

36. As examples: in the Pisan countryside the three heirs of Giovanni di Biagio, ranging from 1 to 7 years of age, were abandoned by their mother (Archivio di Stato, Pisa, *Ufficio dei Fiumi e Fossi*, henceforth abbreviated UFF, 1542, fol. 400); so were the two daughters, aged 9 and 12 years old, of Giovanni di Corsetto (UFF, 1559, fol. 580), and the two children of Battista di Giovanni Guideglia, 3 and 10 years old (UFF 1538, fol 479).

fourteenth and fifteenth centuries with such situations, brutally initiated by the departure of a widow. The paternal kin had to take charge of orphans "of whom it can be said that they are orphaned on both the father's and the mother's side," one Florentine orphan reiterates, "since it can well be said of those who still have a mother that they have none, given the way she has treated them and abandoned them."[37] Giovanni di Niccolaio Niccolini left four orphaned children in 1417, and his uncle Lapo notes bitterly that the widow "left the house [with her dowry of 900 *fiorini*] and left her children on the straw, with nothing."[38] When Bartolo di Strozza Rucellai's mother remarried, he threw himself, with his brothers, on the mercy of the tax officials, declaring, "See what a state we are in, without a father and, one could also say, without a mother, having no one else on earth, abandoned by everyone."[39]

Young widows would certainly have to have had singular tenacity and a good deal of courage to resist the contradictory pressures of their two families. Umiliana dei Cerchi, at the beginning of the thirteenth century, who hoped to live out her life in holy seclusion,[40] and Tancia, the daughter of the notary ser Giovanni Bandini, who wanted to enter a convent in 1450,[41] came into conflict with the desires and the maneuvers of relatives eager to bed them down with new husbands. Umiliana had her way (she was subsequently beatified), but Tancia failed (she was to remain an anonymous housewife). Some women—extraordinarily few—seem to have succeeded in their desire for independence, though there is no way of knowing how widespread this desire might have been.[42] Often, widows really did want to remarry.[43] Nevertheless, what contemporary reports emphasize above all is the irresolution of widows, and they leave an impression of widows' abject submission to the demands of their kin. Widows had few

37. ASF, *Strozz.*, 2d ser., 15, Ricordanze di Cambio di Tano and di Manno di Cambio Petrucci, fol. 64v (1430).

38. Bec, ed., *Il libro degli affari proprii*, 135.

39. Cited in F. W. Kent, *Household and Lineage in Renaissance Florence* (Princeton, 1977), 36. We might also cite the case of Bernardo di Stoldo Rinieri, who lost his father in 1431 and whose mother remarried eight months later, leaving him with his two young sisters when he was 3 years old (ASF, *Conventi soppressi*, 95, 212, fol. 150).

40. "Vita S. Humiliane de Cerchis," by Vito da Cortona, *Acta sanctorum*, May, IV, col. 388. For Umiliana's life, see also A. Benvenuti-Papi, "Umiliana dei Cerchi: Nascita di un culto nella Firenze del Dugento," *Studi francescani* 77 (1980): 87–117.

41. ASF, *Conv. soppr.*, 102, 82, fol. 15.

42. D. Herlihy has focused on widows' desire for independence and on the role that the new autonomy brought by their widowhood allowed them to assume in urban society. See his "Mapping Households in Medieval Italy," *Catholic Historical Review* 58 (1972): 14; "Vieillir à Florence au Quattrocento," *Annales, E.S.C.* 24 no. 6 (1969): 1342ff. For a discussion of these positions, see Kirshner, *Pursuing Honor*, 8 and n. 23.

43. This is the case with the anonymous widow cited by Vespasiano da Bisticci in his *Vite di uomini illustri del sec. XV*, ed. L. Frati (Bologna, 1892), 3:261, who, "desiring to remarry and take back her dowry, which was great," left her four young children with their paternal grandmother. See also below, note 47.

legal weapons, their whole upbringing had inculcated docility in them, and only in exceptional circumstances could they avoid remarriage if their relatives had decided in favor of it.[44] The widow of Barna di Valorino Ciurianni, to the immense displeasure of her stepsons, "leaves the house with her dowry" the minute her husband was in the ground, probably with remarriage in mind, since she was young. In spite of her promises to Barna and the advantages assured her in his will, she left her twelve-year-old son in the charge of his half brothers.[45]

Manno di Cambio Petrucci's narration, in 1430, of the days following the death of his father, who was carried off by the plague, offers a striking example of the anguish to which a widow could be subjected when her brothers wanted her to remarry.[46] We see her here at the age of thirty-four torn between her aunt—probably sent by her family—and her children and stepchildren, who beg her to remain with them. "Madonna Simona," Manno, the eldest of her stepchildren implores her, "your own children are here. We will treat them as our brothers and you, Madonna Simona, as our mother. Alas! our mother, I beg of you and throw myself at your mercy, for you know our situation. Left without father or mother, if you do not come to our aid we will go headlong into ruin." The widow, however, bowed to her family's wishes: "I will do what my family decides," she says, and Manno adds, "for Madonna Pipa, her aunt, had done her job well overnight." It is a poignant tale, and one in which the children's dismay at the threat of being abandoned is expressed in protestations of respect and fidelity. The children avoid frankly broaching the question of what was most at stake in the conflict, however: the dowry that they might have to give back. Manno admits as much once the break was irreversible: "If Madonna Simona had agreed to remain with us, we would not have had to sell our things at half their price, wasting our substance so that we could give her back some of her dowry."[46]

## "Good Mothers" and "Cruel Mothers"

When one famous orphan, Giovanni Morelli, became an adult, he accused his mother (who remarried when he was three years old) of having been "cruel" to him and to his brothers, though he does say the epithet was

44. Some mothers must have ended up by regaining the children from whom they had been separated, like the widow Minerbetti cited in note 32, but for one case of this sort, how many scenarios must there have been in which the mother seems to fall in line without the slightest complaint—or at least, with no complaint that succeeds in piercing the thick cloak of male narration of their behavior.

45. ASF, *Manoscr.* 77, fol. 19. She had married Barna in 1365, when he was 43 years old, and had been widowed less than three years before.

46. ASF, *Strozz.*, 2d ser., 15, fols. 61v–65.

prompted by the Evil One in a moment of doubt and despair.[47] But what did a man of the fifteenth century mean by this accusation? Did it perhaps signify an affective abandonment, a case in which a mother would leave young children who needed her "love" and her "maternal" care? This is the way we spontaneously understand the situation today.[48] The texts of the time suggest this meaning, but they emphasize, perhaps even more strongly, the financial debacle, the ruin that the remarried widow left behind her. The "cruel mother" was the woman who left her young children, but it was above all the mother who "left with her dowry." There is no better evidence of this than this same Giovanni Morelli, who lived a good part of his childhood and adolescence in his stepfather's house, brought up by the very mother whom he nevertheless accuses of having "abandoned" him.[49] The abandonment was economic as much as affective, and what abandoned children complained of explicitly was the financial implications of their mother's remarriage. The mother who deserted the roof under which her children lived placed the interests of her own lineage and her own family above her children's interests, and that is why she was stigmatized. The clearest reproaches on the part of children or children's guardians rarely dwell on anything other than this consequence of remarriage.

The positive image, that of the "good mother," shows *a contrario*, the range of functions that the "cruel mother" who left to remarry failed to fulfill. There is truly no "good mother" who is not "both mother and father." This is the widow who refuses to remarry, no matter how young she might be, "in spite of the objurgations of her entire family," "so as not to abandon her children," "in order not to lead them to ruin," and who is both "a father and a mother for her children."[50] Just like the father, she assured, by her stability, a transmission that was first and foremost a transmission of material goods, without which there was no family. "Remaining," "staying," "living with" her children, bequeathing them the

47. Morelli, *Ricordi,* 495. See especially L. Pandimiglio, "Giovanni di Pagolo Morelli e le strutture familiari," *Archivio storico italiano* 136, nos. 1–2 (1978): 6. R. C. Trexler, in *Public Life in Renaissance Florence*, chap. 5, gives a long analysis of the case of Morelli and (particularly p. 165, n. 27) sees one of the reasons for the abandoning of children by their mother in her desire "to establish her *persona*." The fact that the wife's kin in most cases take the initiative in encouraging her departure seems to me to contradict this hypothesis.

48. See the debate about maternal love prompted by E. Badinter's book, *L'amour en plus* (Paris, 1980) and the colloquy of the Société de Démographie historique in November 1981 devoted to the theme "Mothers and Wet Nurses."

49. As noted by Pandimiglio, "Giovanni Morelli e le strutture familiari," 6. For relations with the maternal grandmother, see also the *ricordanze* of Morello Morelli, Giovanni's brother, in ASF, *Carte Gherardi,* Morelli, 163.

50. Giovanni Rucellai, cited in Kent, *Household and Lineage,* 40, n. 64, and in G. Marcotti, *Un mercante fiorentino e la sua famiglia nel sec. XV* (Florence, 1881), 49, 59–60. "Memorie di Ser Cristofano di Galgano Guidini da Siena," ed. C. Milanesi, *Archivio storico italiano* 4 (1843): 25–30. BNF, *Panciatichi,* 134, Memorie Valori, fol. 4 (1438).

wealth that was theirs—such was the primary paternal obligation in a system of residence and transmission of patrimony organized by patrilineal filiation. The virtues of an exceptional mother are from this point of view all manly virtues.

The widow qualified as a "good mother" was also one who devoted herself to the upbringing of her children with firmness and discipline.[51] Perhaps she could not compete with the father on the terrain of pedagogy. She could not offer a boy all the models of behavior that a father offered his sons, and her inexperience in public and political life constituted a vexing handicap. Her culture was often limited, and worse yet, she was unable to transmit to her sons the values and the spiritual heritage of the lineage, to talk to them of "what happened to their ancestors and of their actions, of those from whom they had received gifts and services and those by whom they had been badly used, of who was their friend in need and, conversely, the vendettas they had engaged in and of recompenses given to those to whom they were obliged."[52] A uniquely maternal upbringing had lacunae and was necessarily incomplete. Nevertheless, if undertaken with constancy and rigor, it could be comparable to the education administered by a father. When widowhood precluded other choices, the "good mother" was an acceptable substitute for the father. The "love" she bore her orphaned children took its full value from its masculine connotations.

Conversely, the bad mother, the "cruel mother," violated the values and the interests of her children's lineage when she showed too much docility toward her family of birth. In this she demonstrated the traditional vices of woman in exaggerated form. "Inconstant," "light," "flighty," she swings from one family to the other, she "forgets" her children and the husband she has just buried to seek pleasure in the bed of a second husband; she shifts shamelessly between the rigid structures of the contending masculine lineages. There is no doubt that the growing misogyny and mistrust of women at the dawn of the Renaissance were reinforced by structural contradictions that made it difficult to combine dotal system with patrilinearity. Among jurists, moralists, and those who reflected on the family, stereotypes presented woman as avid and capricious, eager to appropriate male inheritances for herself or other women, without pity for her children, whom she abandoned the moment she was widowed; a creature inconstant

51. Donato Velluti found in his mother the equivalent of a father, since his father was "nearly continually absent" on business (*Cronica domestica*, ed. I. Del Lungo and G. Volpi, Florence, 1914, 119–20).
52. Such are some of the merits of a paternal upbringing, as enumerated by G. Morelli, *Ricordi*, esp. p. 269. Conversely, the wife who harangues her husband continually about the great actions of her own lineage is a stock figure in contemporary literature (as in Boccaccio, *Corbaccio*, 46, 61)—a figure perhaps linked to the social hypergamy of men common at the time.

in her family loyalties, of immoderate attachments and inordinate sexuality, insatiable, and a menace to the peace and honor of families.[53] In short, a creature intent on destroying the "houses" that men had constructed.

The tensions caused by the problem of the autonomy or the remarriage of widows did not simply blacken the image of woman in the collective consciousness. They also generated positive but contradictory images of women to serve the opposing interests of the lineage that gave and the lineage that received the wife. The image of the mother loyal to her children countered that of the sister or the daughter faithful to her blood relatives; the wife attentive to the interests of her household contrasted with the woman who remembered her own lineage; the good mother who nearly equaled a father was the counterpart of the good daughter, nearly as good as a son. Even more than the somber image of the concupiscent widow or the "cruel mother," this ambivalence, this double and deep-rooted source of qualities appreciated in women provoked masculine resentment of them for their "inconstancy." No woman was perfect: a man attached to only one woman would be perpetually disappointed with her. Only the male sex, backed up by the law and by the structure of society and the family, could boast of perfection that was seen primarily as fixity and permanence.

Few contemporaries grasped the reasons for these tensions and tried to look beyond their lineage-inspired and antifeminist prejudices. One, however, puts a fine defense of remarried widows into the mouth of a young Florentine. In the *Paradiso degli Alberti*, written around 1425 by Giovanni Gherardi of Prato,[54] a courtly discussion arises among a group of people of polite society.[55] The problem posed is whether paternal love or maternal love is the better. One young man argues heatedly that mothers are not worth much since, contrary to fathers, they abandon their children. In any event, as they are inferior beings, their love could not possibly be as "perfect" as that of men. One young woman "of great wit and of most noble manners" is then charged by the women to respond to him. She cleverly turns his arguments against him by placing herself in his logic: since women are less "perfect" than men, they must obey men and follow

53. The statutes of the city of Pisa in the middle of the twelfth century accuse mothers of manifesting an "impietatem novercalem" (stepmotherly impiety) toward their children rather than their "maternum affectum" (maternal affection) when they take back their dowry and their *antefactum*, and the female sex is frequently qualified by jurists as "genus mulierum avarissimum atque tenacissimum promptius . . . ad accipiendum quam ad dandum" (most avaricious female sex, much more tenacious. . . in receiving than in giving) (texts cited by D. Herlihy in "The Medieval Marriage Market," *Medieval and Renaissance Studies* 6 (1976):27, nn. 58–59). Let me note once more Boccaccio's *Corbaccio* as the most complete broadside on the vices and misdeeds of women, the root of which is sensuality and greed.

54. Giovanni Gherardi da Prato, *Il Paradiso degli Alberti*, ed. A. Lanza (Rome, 1975), 179–84.

55. The debate on the preeminence of paternal love is a commonplace that runs from the preachers to Alberti, who classes it among scholastic stylistic exercises (see L. B. Alberti, *I libri della famiglia*, 349).

them; and "since [women] cannot take their children, nor keep them with them, and they cannot remain alone without harm, especially if they are young, nor remain without masculine protection, it is almost perforce that mothers see themselves constrained to choose the best compromise. But it is not to be doubted that they think constantly of their children and remain strongly attached to them in spite of this separation."[56]

In this demonstration the young woman throws back to her male interlocutor the very contradictions in which he—along with the whole society of his time—let himself be trapped. For how could the "honor" and the "status" of a lineage be increased by taking back a woman and her dowry in order to give them elsewhere, without offending the honor and the standing of the family to which she had given children? How could such a family reassert its rights over the person and the wealth of a woman without depriving another family of those rights? How could the separation of mother and child be avoided when the mother's identity was always borrowed and the child could belong only to his paternal kin? How could a woman be reproached for her docility before men when society denied her economic and legal autonomy?

But the young woman's words go farther. When she evokes the mother's attachment to her children—an attachment that the males of her time either failed to express, rejected, or sublimated into "paternal love," according to whether they stood on one side or the other of the dowry fence—our clever Florentine exposes the mechanisms by which a society that manipulated woman and the wealth attached to her attempted to prove its own innocence by reinforcing the image of the insensitive and destructive female.

---

56. For the masculine argument, see Herlihy and Klapisch-Zuber, *Les Toscans*, 558 n. 22. What the young woman has to say—which occupies three times the space of the young man's argument—astonishes the master of ceremonies: "Per nostra donna, per nostra donna vergine Maria, che io non mi credea che le donne fiorentine fossono filosofe morali e naturali né che avvessono la rettorica e la loica così pronta come mi pare ch'abbino!" (By our Lady, by our Lady the Virgin Mary, I had no idea that Florentine women were moral and natural philosophers, nor that they had such ready rhetoric and logic as it seems to me they have!). He then gives the victory to the ladies (*Il Paradiso degli Alberti*, 183–84).

# 7

## Blood Parents and Milk Parents: Wet Nursing in Florence, 1300–1530

*Oh! What joy the Virgin had in suckling!*
*Surely it is impossible that in nursing such a*
*son she not have felt delights unknown to*
*other women!*

Meditationes vitae domini nostri Jesu Christi,
*attributed to Giovanni da Calvoli (thirteenth*
*century)*

Several studies in recent years have examined the abandonment of children in Mediterranean societies. Florence and Siena, which had hospices that specialized in the care of *trovatelli*,[1] have been the object of particularly thorough studies.[2] We are beginning to learn a great deal about the circumstances surrounding the abandonment of foundlings and their life expectancy from the late fourteenth century on, but also about the appointment of nurses by these charitable institutions and about changes in their salary scale. The elements missing from this picture are, of course, the child's parents: a hazy outline of the parents appears only in the note sometimes found pinned to a baby's blanket or, occasionally, in their subsequent attempts to regain the child. The fact remains, however, that the history of paid breast feeding in these establishments—important as it might have been socially—is not the history of

Originally published as "Parents de sang, parents de lait: La mise en nourrice à Florence (1300–1530)," *Annales de Démographie Historique* 1983:33–64. That study was an enlarged version, based on many more data, of an article on the same theme that appeared in Italian, "Genitori naturali e genitori di latte nella Firenze del Quattrocento," *Quaderni Storici* 44 (1980): 543–63.

1. San Gallo took in *trovatelli* from the end of the thirteenth century; la Scala, founded in 1306, from 1316 on; the Innocenti, founded in 1419, from 1445 on.

2. On the abandonment of children in Tuscany, see R. C. Trexler, "The Foundlings of Florence, 1395–1455," *History of Childhood Quarterly* 1 (1973): 259–84; G. Pinto, "Personale, balie e salariati dell'ospedale di San Gallo," *Ricerche storiche* 2 (1974): 113–68; C. A. Corsini, "Materiali per lo Studio della Famiglia in Toscana nei secoii XVII–XIX: Gli esposti," *Quaderni storici* 33 (1976): 998–1052; L. Sandri, *L'ospedale di S. Maria della Scala di San Gimignano nel Quattrocento: Contributo alla storia dell' infanzia abbandonata* (Florence, 1982).

the average baby in the big cities: it obviously leaves out the triangular relationship that bound two sets of parents—the natural parents and the nursing parents—and the child who moved from one set to the other.

The practice of putting children out to nurse was widespread among middle class Florentines as early as the mid-fourteenth century. How widespread it was can be judged by the extraordinary blossoming of the *ricordanze*, domestic journals that related, usually on a day-to-day basis, how a newborn child was received and what happened to it in the years following. To be sure, it may take patience to pick these jottings out of the hodgepodge noted daily by heads of families in these journals. They are invaluable, however, not only to throw light on the history of the infant and on attitudes toward him, but also because, by spotlighting the two parental couples, they give a good idea of their relations and clarify the place that the nurse and her husband occupied in the life of the family.

It might be objected that the Florentine *ricordanze* do not present all levels of society, and that the paid breast feeding they speak of is still typical only of a rather narrow stratum of urban society. It is true that the great majority of the 318 infants studied here, who were born of 84 couples and suckled the milk of 462 different wet nurses, belonged by right of birth to the established middle class in Florence. However, between one-third and 40 percent[3] of the fathers in this group were artisans or skilled craftsmen, small merchants or landholders, notaries, doctors, and jurists, who did not belong to the governing circles in the city. Moreover, I have counted among the city's leaders some fathers who bore an illustrious family name—Strozzi, for example—but who were poor relations with a fortune unequal to the fame of their lineage.[4] I might add that nearly 8 percent of the fathers considered here did not live in Florence: three were Sienese or Bolognese, and four others lived in a secondary city in the Florentine domain (Prato, Pistoia, Poggibonsi).

The *ricordanze* reveal the spread in society of the practice of putting an infant out to nurse—at least in the fifteenth century, for before 1360 this is more difficult to judge.[5] Out of fifteen fathers whose children we know

3. Depending on whether or not the people of the *distretto*—the cities subject to Florence—are included. On the *ricordanze*, see D. Herlihy and C. Klapisch-Zuber, *Les Toscans et leurs familles* (Paris, 1978), 190, n. 3. On this literature see the recent studies of F. Pezzarossa, "La memorialistica fiorentina tra Medioevo e Rinascimento: Rassegna di studi e testi," *Lettere italiane* 1979: 96–138; Pezzarossa, "La tradizione fiorentina della memorialistica," in *La memoria dei mercatores* (Bologna, 1980), 39–149. J. B. Ross, "The Middle-Class Child in Urban Italy, 14th to early 16th Centuries" in L. De Mause, ed., *The History of Childhood* (New York, 1975), 183–228, has used these family journals for a first picture of childhood in Tuscany (see esp. pp. 184–96 for early infancy).

4. Thus Tribaldo dei Rossi (see note 44 ), Doffo Spini (Archivio di Stato, Florence, henceforth abbreviated ASF, *Strozziane*, 2d ser., 13, 1415–36), and Giovanni di Jacopo d'Ubertino Strozzi (ASF, *Strozz.*, 3d ser., 275, 1443–77).

5. Approximately 19 percent of these 84 fathers lived in the fourteenth century, 68 percent in the fifteenth, and 13 percent in the first third of the sixteenth century. The distribution of children, in like manner, is, respectively 16 percent, 70.4 percent, and 13.5 percent, and that of the nurses 19.8 percent, 67.7 percent, and 12.5 percent.

to have been put out to nurse between 1302 and 1399, only two did not come from prominent families,[6] whereas after 1450 half of the families concerned were of modest social rank. Does this change show an evolution in behavior and the extension of paid breast feeding, or does it simply reflect a more widespread keeping of account books and journals—or, even, better conservation of such records—in levels of urban society that had made little use of them before? If the first hypothesis proves correct, it implies that paid breast feeding and the keeping of domestic journals progressed in strictly parallel manner. Indeed, all the account books,[7] from of all levels of society, mention salaried nurses when they speak of births in the family. Conversely, the *ricordanze* never note, except in truly exceptional circumstances,[8] that Florentine mothers nursed their children themselves.[9] We would probably have to look to a still lower social level; in particular we would have to leave Florence and delve into the smaller towns of the territory that is administered[10] to get back to a world in

6. Francesco di Giovanni di Durante (Biblioteca Nazionale Centrale, Florence, henceforth abbreviated BNF, 2, 3, 280, 1342–48) and Paliano di Falco Paliani (ASF, *Strozz.*, 2d ser., 7, 1382–1406).

7. The *ricordanze* that concentrate on recapitulating the great events of one lineage obviously do not report on putting infants out to nurse. For others that do not mention the practice, on might assume the presence of a slave woman permanently charged with the job, as, for example, in the book of Francesco di Tommaso Giovanni, ASF, *Strozz.*, 2d ser., 16, 16 bis (1422–58), fol. 11; Francesco, who does not mention nurses for his children, does mention in passing the *schiava e balia* (slave and nurse) of his grandson.

8. It was often a feeling of insecurity that justified the mother's breast feeding: see the Sienese Cristoforo Guidini's 1384 "Ricordi," ed. G. Milanesi, *Archivio storico italiana* 4 (1843): 25–48. On Guidini, see G. Cherubini, *Signori, contadini, borghesi* (Florence, 1974), 373–425, esp. pp. 410–12. Some taxpayers, conversely, invoked their wife's inability to nurse in order to get their taxes eased, in particular a notary from San Gimignano, ser Nazario di Lorenzo, whose wife "has no nipples on her breast and cannot nurse" (ASF, *Catasto*, 266, fol. 513, 1428).

9. A priest in Pistoia, Jacopo Melocchi, living with a concubine—a certain Cicilia da Mantova, whom he seems to have cherished in spite of her social status, obviously much inferior to his own—permitted her to nurse all the children she bore him (ASF, *Acquisti e Doni*, 8, 1497–1517). Her simple origin and breast feeding are not incompatible. The arrival of twins also explains why the parents of Catherine of Siena, the next-to-last of twenty-five children, put out her twin sister to nurse. The twin soon died, while the future saint was nursed by her mother until she was weaned. None of her older siblings were so treated, for "propter frequentes conceptiones, nullum ex filiis potuerat [mater] proprio lacte nutrire" (because of frequent conceptions, the mother was unable to nourish any of her children with her own milk) (*Acta sanctorum*, Aprilis III, 859). In the *catasto* of 1427, the less wealthy taxpayers occasionally complain that their wife was obliged to put one twin out to nurse and to the nurse the other herself, or worse yet, that poverty obliged her to nurse both of them. See Archivio di stato, Pisa, *Ufficio dei Fiumi e Fossi* (1540), fol. 75: twins are nursed by their mother, "ch'è grande faticha e affanno e mizeria" (which is a great effort, worry, and hardship). On salaried nursing, see J. Heers, *Esclaves et domestiques au Moyen-Age dans le monde méditerranéen* (Paris, 1981), 199–204.

10. Paradoxically, the *catasto* of 1427–30 describes the nursing children of the countryside or of the subject cities better than those in Florence: obviously the Florentine taxpayers were aware how slight their chances were of touching the hearts of the tax collectors. (Out of the 234 infants put out to nurse mentioned in the *catasto*, only 34 are in Florence. Rural taxpayers who speak of their nurses always give the reason for a situation that they consider

which the mother took on the function of nursing. We can state that in the large city of Florence, nursing by a salaried nurse or by a slave woman became the dominant practice, at least from the middle of the fifteenth century onward, even if we cannot for the moment trace the exact limits of the practice.

Furthermore, a Florentine who put one of his children out to nurse would put out the others as well, both girls and boys.[11] Discrimination does not enter the picture on the level of a decision as to whom the mother would or would not nurse. It might do so in the choice of a nurse, on the other hand, according to both the sex and the birth order of the child. The *ricordanze* tell us much about the criteria, both individual and contingent, that were respected in the selection of these substitute mothers, about their supervision, and about the terms and conditions of wet nursing.

## The Choice of a Nurse

In Florence, putting a child out to nurse implied, for the overwhelming majority of parents, separation from the child. Among the more than 400 nurses for whom we have sufficient documentation, we can count, from 1300 to 1530, one nurse *in casa*, who was part of the household of the child's parents, for more than four who take the baby to their own house.[12] The general tendency throughout the period is toward a somewhat lower proportion of nurses living under the master's roof. The shrinkage is noticeable particularly during the first two-thirds of the fifteenth century. (It is perhaps linked to our greater knowledge of the customs of middle-class families from this period onward.) A similar and even more insistent pattern may be observed in the relative likelihood of a child's departure for the country or remaining in the city of Florence near its parents: in

---

exceptional (the mother's pregnancy, the birth of a younger child, the mother's inability to nurse). Giorgio di Piero di ser Galletto, from Poggibonsi, permitted his wife to nurse all their children except for his son Piero, whom he placed with a nurse in 1528 because his wife was pregnant. His second wife took an aversion to one of the twins she bore in 1538, and "this aversion lasted from when he was with his nurse." The child died of the "poor care" of his mother in 1540 (Biblioteca Laurenziana, *Acquisti,* 203, fol. 51).

11. This can be verified every time it is possible to follow the destiny of a complete set of siblings. Unfortunately, many of the *ricordanze* permit only a partial reconstruction of the history of the descendants of one couple because they cover only a limited period. Antonio di ser Tommaso Masi reports that when his wife died in 1459 at the age of 57, she had given him 36 children (*sic*) "28 of whom were put out to nurse and, at her death, she still had 9 male children." It is probable that the 8 babies who were not sent out to nurse died soon after their birth (ASF, *Manoscritti,* 89, 1455–59, fol. 18).

12. On the *in casa* nurses, see Heers, *Esclaves et domestiques,* 200–201, which cites data from the Pisa *catasto:* three families employ such a nurse, but twenty-eight other families send their babies out. On more general aspects of putting babies out to nurse, as seen in the *catasto* as a whole, see Herlihy and Klapisch-Zuber, *Les Toscans,* esp. pp. 340, 507, 555–61.

the latter case, the parents naturally followed the child's development more carefully. Although there was, on the average, one nurse caring for a small Florentine in the city for 2.4 in the country, rural nurses show constant gains from 1300 to 1530 (see table 7.1).

Whether these changes should be interpreted as indicative of a real diffusion of paid breast feeding in this society, or whether we are simply better informed by the *ricordanze* of the middle class, the fact remains that the increasing predominance of outside nurses, particularly rural nurses, gives a glimpse of parental strategies—both those of the natural parents of the infant and those of the nursing parents.

We learn from the communal statutes of 1415[13] and from descriptions of practice in our family journals that a nurse's salary varied greatly with her residence. A nurse *in casa* was a luxury that demanded a higher price than a peasant woman living on her sharecropped farm. When she lived in her master's house, the woman generally received 18–20 *fiorini* a year between 1400 and 1480—more than any other category of paid domestics. According to how far her farm was from Florence, a country nurse could hope for the equivalent of 9–15 *fiorini* a year[14]—in common coin, subject to depreciation, and not in good *fiorini d'oro*. The pay of a nurse whose own home was in Florence was close to that of a woman living under the master's roof, discounting the latter's living expenses, which she was expected to pay.[15]

Table 7.1
NURSES *IN CASA* AND OUTSIDE NURSES

| Nurses's residence | 1300–1399 | 1400–1469 | 1470–1530 | 1300–1530 |
|---|---|---|---|---|
| a. Employer's household | 16 | 32 | 23 | 71 |
| b. In Florence | 12 | 22 | 9 | 43 |
| c. In the country | 51 | 131 | 90 | 272 |
| Total | 79 | 185 | 122 | 386 |
| Ratio a/b + c | 3.9 | 4.8 | 4.3 | 4.4 |
| Ratio a + b/c | 1.8 | 2.4 | 2.8 | 2.4 |

13. *Statuta populi et communis Florentiae* (1415), bk. 4, 148 (Fribourg, 1778–80), 2:267–70. See M. Roberti, "Il contratto di lavoro negli statuti medievali," *Rivista internazionale di scienze sociali* 40 (1932): 166.

14. Around 1500, salaries for city domestics were counted in *fiorini da serva* at 4 *lire* to a *fiorino*. This made them compatible with rural salaries, which were always paid in *lire*. The *fiorini d'oro* was worth a good deal more.

15. Nurses in Florence were paid 6 or 7 *lire* per month. During the final third of the fourteenth century the monthly salary for a nurse *in casa* was about 100 *soldi*, at a time when a peasant nurse's pay averaged 62 *soldi* (with considerable variation). A century later they were, respectively, 111 and 72 *soldi*.

A map of nurses' residences would show that Florentines were not at all reluctant to send their nursing infants quite far from home. A good 42 percent of the outside nurses lived beyond the suburbs of the city, within a radius of fifteen kilometers; 45 percent lived even farther out, particularly in the Mugello, to the north of Florence, where many Florentine families had their roots and owned farm lands,[16] in the countryside around Prato, or, less frequently, in the more mountainous Casentino, all of which were regions known for their nurses.[17] Florentines vied with one another to celebrate the salubrity of these parts—perhaps with the secret thought of justifying the exile of their progeny.[18] The "goodness of the air" is a less logical explanation for the departure of Florentine babies to peasant houses on the Florentine plain, between Florence and Prato, where the climate was more suspect. One Florentine baby out of six was raised there, however. As for nurses within the city of Florence, whose high salary was beyond the reach of many purses, they seem to have been called on for shorter periods, such as the first days, before the arrival of the permanent nurse, or a gap between two nurses.[19] The effects of a diversity of salaries as great as this need to be examined from two points of view—the nurses' and the parents'.

There was one parental demand that anyone who proposed to nurse a tiny Florentine had to take into account: the parents took it for granted that a nurse could breast-feed no more than one baby—their baby—at a time. "Milk brothers" are never spoken of in Florentine texts, and this absence seems to me to be explained by the customs connected with breast feeding. Either the Florentine's baby followed a child of the nurse who had been weaned early, or the nurse's child has died, "liberating" its mother's milk, or the child was itself put out to nurse so that its mother could be hired by a Florentine. This last solution is attested in the *ricordanze,* and never does a nurse arrive under her employer's roof with her own

16. See, for example, the Morelli children, who were sent to the Mugello, from which the family came (Giovanni di Pagolo Morelli, *Ricordi,* ed. V. Branca [Florence, 1956], 87–104) or the Minerbetti children (Biblioteca Laurenziana, Florence, *Acquisti e Doni,* 229, 1492–1551), where eleven of the sixteen nurses employed by Andrea di Tommaso lived in the Mugello.

17. See the carnival songs about nurses: *Canti Carnascialeschi del Rinascimento,* ed. C. Singleton (Bari, 1936), no. 29 (pp. 39–40); no. 39 (p. 51), no. 94 (p. 125).

18. Morelli thus sings the praises of the Mugello of his ancestors. On "la buona tenperanza de l'aria molta generativa" (the excellent temperance of the highly productive air) of the Florence region, see the "Diario fiorentino d'anonimo," BNF, *Panciatichi,* 158, fol. 188v.

19. See Appendix to this chapter. The mother was not supposed to nurse immediately after the birth, as colostrum was reputed to be harmful to the child. See Francesco da Barberino, *Del reggimento e costume di donne,* ed. G. E. Sansone (Turin, 1957), lines 275–76: "It is true that in the beginning it is better to give the milk of another than the mother." Giovanni Michele Savonarola, *Il trattato ginecologico-pediatrico in volgare,* ed. L. Belloni, (Milan, 1952), 149–50 also states that the first milk is "serale, non buono come il sequente" (thin, not as good as the subsequent) (my thanks to Linda Duchamp for this reference).

child,[20] whereas we can often see her paying her own child's nurse with her own wages.[21] The example of Piero Puro,[22] cited in the Appendix to this chapter, shows that he found it advantageous to send his own children out to nurse, and rather far from Florence, so that his wife could offer her services to Florentine families. When the country nurse's pay had been deducted from her own, their net gain was exactly equal.[23]

It is probable that the demand for nurses among proper Florentines motivated the *popolo minuto*—particularly those who, like this Piero Puro, had professional dealings with the merchants and the families of the highest society—to dispatch their children to the country as soon as they were born so that they could offer the wife's milk to the burghers who found it unthinkable that their own wives be allowed to breast-feed. This behavior enables us to understand how the mechanisms of a model that had originated in the dominant classes spread to other classes during the Fifteenth century.

One thing we need to ask is whether natural parents gave preference to certain of their children according to their birth order or their sex, and whether they agreed to a greater financial sacrifice for their breast feeding. An examination of all the nurses studied reveals that Florentines were more apt to keep their boys at home than their girls: for the whole of the period scrutinized (1300–1530), 23 percent of boys were entrusted for a relatively long period to a nurse who lived in the house, as opposed to only 12 percent of the girls.[24] Conversely, 68.5 percent of girls and 55 percent of boys were sent to the country. Florentine nurses who took the child into their own houses are in comparable proportion for the two sexes. In the aggregate, then, the parents' preferences, without being systematic, are beyond doubt: it was easier for them, generally speaking, to separate themselves from a female baby than from a little boy and future heir (table 7.2).

20. One exception occurred in the house of Manno di Cambio Petrucci (ASF, *Strozz.*, 2d ser., 17, fol. 99v, January 1441), but the child brought along by the *balia* was six years old.

21. The *balie* of Matteo Strozzi (ASF, *Strozz.*, 5th ser., 10, fols. 19v–20, 1425–26; fol. 74, 1427) received advances on their wages to pay the nurses of their children. The same was true of the nurses of Niccolò Busini in 1395 (ASF, *Strozz.*, 4th ser., 563, fol. 6), of Recco Capponi in 1452 (ASF, *Conventi soppressi*, S. Piero a Monticelli, 153, fol. 14) and of Marco Parenti in 1450 (ASF, *Strozz.*, 2d ser., 17 bis, fol. 18v). Heers, *Esclaves et domestiques*, 200, states somewhat hastily that the nurses *in casa* had lost their own children.

22. This humble person lived off his salary as a servant for a Castellani in 1422; he was later employed by the Ufficio del Banco until 1428, then by the Arte di Calimala in 1428, finally by the Parte Guelfa from 1430 to 1457. His social position was the lowest of all the cases of *ricordanze* studied. (Archivio degli Innocenti, Florence, *Estranei*, 714, 1413–65).

23. See Appendix to this chapter. She received two *fiorini* per months and gave one to her own nurse.

24. If we add to these figures the 9 percent of nurses (of boys) and 6 percent of nurses (of girls) who seem to have lived in Florence, either with the child's parents or with their own families, the percentages for urban nurses change from 36 to 45 percent for boys and from 25.5 to 31.5 percent for girls.

Table 7.2
CHOICE OF NURSE AND SEX OF THE CHILD

| Nurse's residence | Males | | Females | | Males and Females | |
|---|---|---|---|---|---|---|
| Employer's household | 53 | 22.8% | 29 | 12.3% | 82 | 17.6% |
| In Florence | 30 | 12.9 | 31 | 13.2 | 61 | 13.0 |
| Employer's household or in Florence | 21 | 9.1 | 14 | 6.0 | 35 | 7.5 |
| Outside Florence | 128 | 55.2 | 161 | 68.5 | 289 | 61.9 |
| Total | 232 | 100.0% | 235 | 100.0% | 467 | 100.0% |

If we look at just the twenty most numerous sibling groups for which we have data on the whole series of nurses, we arrive at the same conclusion. Approximately one family out of three shows a tendency to keep its male infants closer at hand, to keep them nursing longer, and pay for more expensive nurses for them, sending their girls, on the other hand, to some more distant farm at lower cost. Birth order also plays a role in these parental strategies: in one family out of four, the eldest child or children, both male and female, have a certain advantage over younger siblings and are more likely to remain at home.

It would be difficult to state that this was conscious policy on the part of parents—that they deliberately sent away females to the advantage of their brothers, or treated their younger children worse once the elder ones were raised. However, what the child represented and the place that its sex conferred on it in its family's expectations naturally affected the nature and the strength of the bonds that were formed between a child and its family at a very early age. These data seem to be strong confirmation of information taken from other sources that also points to an antifeminine tendency in Florentines' attitudes toward the child.[25]

How was the ideal nurse to be found? In Florence, the father in search of a nurse alerted the entire network of his clients and friends. If he himself held lands in the countryside, he could count on his knowledge of the area and keep track of promising pregnancies or nursing mothers, and in like manner he would get his acquaintances to survey the villages and farms they were familiar with in order to locate potential nurses. Many writers of *ricordanze* mention the intermediary who had helped them to find the woman who eventually took in their infant: one such writer, one month before the expected birth, even notes several possible names, which share space in his notebook with the address of a weaver reputed to cure pox scars.[26] If all else failed, the father could turn to one of the "placers of

25. See Herlihy and Klapisch-Zuber, *Les Toscans*, 338–40; R. C. Trexler, "Infanticide in Florence; New Sources and First Results," *History of Childhood Quarterly* 1 (1973): 96–116.

26. Biblioteca Laurenziana, *Buonarroti*, 27, no. 3 (ricordanze di Buonrroto di Lodovico Simoni Buonarroti, 1517–22), fols. 8 and 41.

nurses and servant women," women who made a profession of finding an
employer for other women newly arrived from their region, in exchange
for just retribution of their services.[27]

What was this ideal nurse like—not as doctors or moralists had described
her from antiquity on,[28] but, in balder terms, as Florentine families dreamed
of her? The first criterion for their choice was the abundance[29] and the
"youth" of her milk. The nurse they dreamed of was a woman fresh from
childbirth whose child had died. This was the opinion, about 1400, of
Margherita Datini, the wife of the merchant of Prato, whose Florentine
acquaintances often charged her with finding a nurse for them.[30] For her,
a good nurse has the use of both eyes and her milk should have started
within the last two months or less. Preferably, she will have lost her own
baby, for "never shall I believe that when they have a one-year-old child
of their own, they give not some [milk] to it." Margherita writes with
disappointment that, alas, the child of one potential nurse recovered from
his illness; and later, full of hope, she reports that she made another woman
promise to come as soon as her child was buried. Thus anyone prospecting
for a nurse was watching out for death as much as for the life to come.
Florentines were insensitive to the moral handicap that weighed on their
nurses—women who had had to give up raising their own children.

As a matter of fact, it is difficult to eliminate a more serious suspicion:
did not a good number of Florentine fathers accept or even hasten the
death of certain socially condemned infants (the children of slaves or of
servant women) when they abandoned such infants in order to have the
benefit of the mother's milk, and gave the milk to their own newborns or
sold it at a good price to other fathers in search of a nurse? At the end of
the fourteenth century and still during the fifteenth, domestic slaves were
part of the belongings of most of the wealthy urban households.[31] Their
presence, however, was not constant. They were acquired, sold, or rented

27. ASF, *Acquisti e Doni*, 21, fols. 39v–40 (1526) (ricordanze di ser Piero Bonaccorsi).
ASF, *Strozz.*, 2d ser., 10, fol. 77v (1422) (ricordi di Cambio di Tano Petrucci). Ibid., 2d
ser., 15, fol. 12 (1426). Archivio Innocenti, *Estranei*, 300 (1463) fols. 53v, 60v, 68 (ricordi
di Battista Vernacci).

28. On this advice (which was always addressed to men), see Ross, "The Middle-Class
Child," 185–86; Herlihy and Klapisch-Zuber, *Les Toscans*, 555–56; the famous pages of
L. B. Alberti, *I Libri della famiglia* (Turin: Einaudi, 1969), 102; Paolo da Certaldo, *Il libro
di buoni costumi*, ed., A. Schiaffini (Florence, 1945), 233–34.

29. Cambio Petrucci congratulates himself that the nurse he had engaged for his child
"did not take him away, for she did not want to stay the evening, whereas we wanted to
see if she had milk. I am glad not to have given him to her. I think it is for the best" (ASF,
*Strozz.*, 2d ser., 10, fol. 10v, 12 March 1411).

30. I. Origo, *The Merchant of Prato: Francesco di Marco Datini* (London, 1957), 200–
201. See also Luca da Panzano, who rejoices in 1423 that his nurse had "milk fifteen days
old" (ASF *Strozz.*, 2d ser., 9, fol. 22).

31. Domestic slaves appear in the 1427 *catasto* in 323 households in Tuscany, 261 of
them in Florence. See Heers, *Esclaves et domestiques*, 135ff. Origo, *The Merchant of Prato*,192ff.;
Origo, "The Domestic Enemy: the Eastern Slaves in Tuscany in the 14th and 15th Centuries,"
*Speculum* 30 (1955): 321–66.

out according to the household's needs. Two of the functions to which they were destined, in perfectly good conscience, were the satisfaction of the master's sexual needs, those of his sons, who married late, or of family friends, and the nursing of their newborn children.[32] The pregnancy of a slave, of course, did have a drawback: there was obviously a risk involved in the deterioration of a valuable capital. But if childbirth went well, her child could be abandoned in all haste to one of the city homes,[33] and the slave, in two or three years of loyal service, would enable her owner to amortize his investment by sparing him the expense of a salaried nurse *in casa*. Or else she would earn a solid income for him when he rented her, *cum lacte*, to another household.[34] Even free servant women, whose condition was not profoundly different from that of the domestic slave women,[35] were perhaps not fully shielded from this sort of calculation, which was also, after all, just like the thinking of fathers who came to the city to find employment for their daughter, the mother of an illegitimate child to be brought up in some remote country area or destined to the foundling home.[36] The correlation that Peter Laslett has observed in various societies between the statistics for the abandonment of children and those for paid breast feeding is evident here.[37] Florence permits direct observation of the mechanism that makes these two phenomena work together.

This suggests that the first criteria in the choice of a nurse were not her moral qualities. Girls who had been seduced, "bestial" Tartar slave women, or mothers who had abandoned their children all made good nurses if their milk was "young" and abundant. In fact, the social identity of the nurse often seems of little importance to parents. Of the nurses

32. Thus in 1447 Giovanni Strozzi spent 47 *fiorini* on a slave woman "with her fresh milk" to nurse his son Piero (ASF, *Strozz.*, 3d ser., 275, fols. 14v–16). On these sales of slave women *cum lacte*, see Heers, *Esclaves et domestiques*, 203.

33. Trexler, "Foundlings," 266–68; Trexler, "Infanticide," 101–2. Nearly one-fourth of the admissions to San Gallo from 1430 to 1439 were the children of slave women, and more than one-third of those to the Innocenti in 1445. Pinto, "Personale, balie," 126, n. 55 also mentions seven children of slaves among the admissions to San Gallo around 1400.

34. On the rental of slaves *cum lacte* see Heers, *Esclaves et domestiques*, 203–4. Giovanni Strozzi (see above, note 32) found a position as a nurse for a slave he had bought in 1447 and no longer needed, after which he took her back, then rented her out again as a servant. He did the same in 1453–54 with another slave woman bought in 1453 for 35 *fiorini*, rented out, then resold, then taken back and placed as a servant with someone else (ASF, *Strozz.*, 3d ser., 275, fols. 16v, 19, 31v, 43, and 45v).

35. As Heers, *Esclaves et domestiques*, 204–4 rightly emphasizes. Servant women were also sometimes rented out by their employer to a third party. See also the affair of the servant woman of one of the Baldovinetti, whose liason with Jacopo Niccolini resulted 20 February 1474 in the birth of a boy, given to a country nurse through an intermediary and in secret, "to avoid scandal"—Jacopo had married in September 1473—and later abandoned to the Innocenti (ASF *Acquisti e Doni*, 190, 3, Memorie diverse Baldovinetti, fol. 28v).

36. This was perhaps the case of one Maddalena, daughter of an inhabitant of the Valdigreve who came to nurse one of Lorenzo Morelli's sons in 1477 and received an advance of 5 *lire* 15 *soldi* "to send to her father so he could pay the nurse of her son" (ASF, *Carte Gherardi*, Morelli, 137, fols. 150v–151).

37. According to the lectures given by P. Laslett at the Collège de France, June 1982.

employed, 22 percent seem to manage their own affairs and produce no
male guarantors;[38] some of them come from far, having wandered along
God knows what routes before they end up in a Florentine household.
Their employer seldom seems particular about the legitimacy of the liaison
that made their breasts swell (see table 7.3).

The great majority of women who offer their milk have an irreproachable conjugal identity, to be sure. One time out of four, however, the
Florentine journals give only the anthroponymic mention of the *balio,* the
husband of the *balia,* and simply omit the given name of the woman.
Behind her rustic husband, the nurse remains a vague silhouette, and it is

Table 7.3

MATRIMONIAL STATUS OF NURSE BY NAME GIVEN

| Nurse Name Given | Nurse First Name Known | | | Nurse First Name Unknown | | | Totals | | |
|---|---|---|---|---|---|---|---|---|---|
| | a | b+c | a+b+c | a | b+c | a+b+c | a | b+c | a+b+c |
| N. wife of X | 14 | 160 | 174 | — | 15 | 15 | 14 | 175 | 189 |
| % of total | 2.9 | 33.8 | 36.7 | — | 3.2 | 3.2 | 2.9 | 36.9 | 39.9 |
| N. widow of X | — | 10 | 10 | — | — | — | — | 10 | 10 |
| % of total | — | 2.1 | 2.1 | — | — | — | — | 2.1 | 2.1 |
| N. daughter of X | 1 | 2 | 3 | — | — | — | 1 | 2 | 3 |
| % of total | 0.2 | 0.4 | 0.6 | — | — | — | 0.2 | 0.4 | 0.6 |
| N. *di* X (father? husband?) | 10 | 84 | 94 | — | — | — | 10 | 84 | 94 |
| % of total | 2.1 | 17.7 | 19.8 | — | — | — | 2.1 | 17.7 | 19.8 |
| N. or N. *da* (place of origin) | 45 | 32 | 77 | — | — | — | 45 | 32 | 77 |
| % of total | 9.5 | 6.7 | 16.2 | — | — | — | 9.5 | 6.7 | 16.2 |
| Slaves | 8 | — | 8 | — | — | — | 8 | — | 8 |
| % of total | 1.7 | — | 1.7 | — | — | — | 1.7 | — | 1.7 |
| Only man's name known | — | — | — | — | 93 | 93 | — | 93 | 93 |
| % of total | — | — | — | — | 19.6 | 19.6 | — | 19.6 | 19.6 |
| Total | 78 | 288 | 366 | — | 108 | 108 | 78 | 396 | 474 |
| % | 16.5 | 60.7 | 77.2 | — | 22.8 | 22.8 | 16.5 | 83.5 | 100.0 |

a = servant woman in employer's household
b = living in Florence
c = living in the country

38. See table 7.3 for anthroponymic references. This point is developed further in C.
Klapisch-Zuber, "Genitori naturali e genitori di latte nella Firenze del Quattrocento," *Quaderni storici* 44 (1980): 549–50.

to her husband that the father gives the infant to be raised—and breast-fed.[39] We can see here a first characteristic of the paradoxical "masculinity" of the function of the wet nurse. The nurse's personality mattered infinitely less to our Florentine burghers than all the good authors of books in their libraries told them that it should.

## Wet Nursing: Men's Business

When the parents intervened in any of the arrangements for the *baliatico*, the period of nursing, it was the father who acted. The agreement was usually reached by the natural father and the *balio* "alone,"[40] sometimes between the father and the couple of the nursing parents, and sometimes between the father and the nurse alone. Hardly ever is the mother mentioned,[41] and it was generally the father who later discussed salary adjustments with the nurse *in casa*, who paid out advances or full pay to the nurse or to one of her kin, and, above all, who seemed to supervise all aspects of the progress of the breast feeding and to determine when it should end.

If they had chosen to take the nurse into their household, Florentines seem to have installed her in the upper portions of the house, near the kitchen, "in the servant women's room." In this way it was easier for them to check on the movements of the women of their domestic staff and to supervise their visitors. Indeed, keeping the nurse in the house offered the theoretical advantage—which was dearly paid—of avoiding a pregnancy that might interrupt breast feeding. There was, unfortunately, no total guarantee of this: the *balio* occasionally came to "visit" his wife, and the charms of an unmarried nurse might tempt other men. Virgilio Adriani learned this in 1470, to his loss, when a woman from Ragusa in service in his house for more than a year had to admit that she was two months

39. Certain texts push the masculinity of the formulas to absurd extremes. In 1468 Vergilio Adriani put a daughter out to nurse with the daughter-in-law of one of his share-croppers, monna Cosa. Twenty months later he writes: "I agreed with Giovanni di Benozzo and his sons Benozzo [the husband] and Meo that they would no longer give the breast to Alessandra, I mean Monna Cosa" (ASF, *Strozz.*, 2d ser., 21, fol. 59v). Luca da Panzano says, when he put an illegitimate son out to nurse: "I gave him to nurse 7 February 1423 to Nencio di Martino from Torri in the Valdipesa in exchange for 4 *lire* 5 *soldi* per month." The description of the trousseau follows, then the report of the child's death and the following clarification: "Given to Nencio di Nanni from Torri in Valdipesa whose milk was fifteen days old" (ASF, *Strozz.*, 2d ser., 9, fols. 22–22v).

40. As one Bolognese father, ser Eliseo Mamelini, says frankly ("Cronaca e storia bolognese del primo Cinquecento nel Memoriale di ser E. M. [1480–1531]," ed. V. Montanari, *Quaderni culturali bolognesi*, 3, 9 [1979], fols. 10–11).

41. It seems exceptional for a mother to reach an agreement on a contract with the nurse couple (see the text cited in Appendix to this chapter and the *ricordi* of Marco Parenti, ASF *Strozz.*, 2d ser., 17 bis, fol. 28v, 1451).

pregnant.[42] Such accidents were rare, however, and it is easy to see why nurses taken into the household could breast-feed for much longer periods than women who stayed with their husbands.[43]

When the child was carried away from the paternal house in the arms of his new mother or "in a basket on the donkey," guided by the *balio* or by a servant,[44] the family's control over what subsequently happened was relaxed, except when nursing parents were also family sharecroppers. Although one author advises families, around 1370, to "visit [children put out to nurse] often, so as to see how they are, and if they are not well, to change them on the spot to another nurse, without leaving them there for monetary reasons,"[45] the father in question does not seem to have made the trip for the express purpose of checking on the progress of his child. The nursing couple occasionally brought the child to Florence "to show it." But news, good and bad, did circulate, above all by means of the bailiffs and servants who were in constant movement back and forth from the Florentine's city residence to his country holdings and from farm to farm. They alerted the Florentine father in case of need, as when the nurse failed in her duties or the child fell sick.

### Broken Contracts

If the nurse became pregnant or if the child was not progressing properly, the father had to look for another nurse, breaking the contract that bound him to the nursing parents. It was his task to recognize changes in the quality of the milk, to force the admission of a hidden pregnancy, and to take necessary decisions without delay.

The nurse's contract often specified that the salary was due only "as long as the *balia* furnishes good and healthy milk" and that "if she becomes pregnant or loses her milk she must respect all of the parents' rights, as custom reasonably demands."[46] As soon as she herself became aware of her condition, an honest nurse who became pregnant was expected to bring the child back to its parents.[47] The *ricordanze* show that more often

42. ASF, *Strozz.*, 2d ser., 21, fols. 3 and 70. The same sense of honor being held up to ridicule by the behavior of a servant woman can be found in G. Brucker, *The Society of Renaissance Florence: A Documentary Study* (Harper Torchbooks, 1971), 218, document 105.

43. The average is eighteen months, as against ten months for the total group of nurses.

44. Tribaldo dei Rossi, BNF, 2, 2, 357, fol. 173v (1500).

45. Paolo da Certaldo, *Il libro di buoni costumi*, 233.

46. Francesco di Matteo Castellani, ASF, *Conventi soppressi*, 90, 84, no. 2, fols. 34 and 45 (1448). None of the agreements mentioned in the *ricordanze* states that it was drawn up before a notary, contrary to the affirmation in J. Heers, *Esclaves et domestiques*, 201 for Genoa (citing, inappropriately, Ross, "The Middle-Class Child," 190).

47. And even before, if we can believe Francesco da Barberino, who authorizes nurses to return to relations with their husbands on condition that they take the infant back to his parents immediately and look for another nurse for him (*Del reggimento*, 192).

than not she did so. Out of thirty pregnancies mentioned in our sampling that necessitated the search for a new nurse or the weaning of the infant, twenty-two provoked no recriminations on the part of the parents. The pregnancy had been declared in good faith, and the *balii,* judging that the child was ready, sometimes took this opportunity to wean it.[48] In eight cases, however, the suspicions expressed by the father of the child show that he was not fooled by their allegations, and he accuses them of having given the child bad milk longer than they say.[49] In that event, the father keeps track of the date at which the nurse gives birth in order to deduct from the sum owed her payment for the months during which she was pregnant but continued to nurse.[50]

In all, 36 percent of the changes of nurse for which reasons are given are justified by the nurse's pregnancy, and 15 percent by her sickness. Milk that gave out or that was "too old" are the cause of another 16 percent of the broken contracts. One time out of ten, the accusation of having cared poorly for the child, of having behaved badly, of being addicted to drink is the pretext the father gives for withdrawing his baby, and in another 10 percent of the cases the child is taken from the wet nurse because the child is sick (table 7.4).

These momentary obstacles resulted in some infants being tossed from nurse to nurse. Children remained only ten months, on the average, with the same nurse. Out of 100 infants, we can estimate that 33 went on to a second nurse, 8 to a third, 3 to a fourth, and nearly 2 to a fifth. This mobility is particularly marked in the fourteenth century but becomes noticeably attenuated in the fifteenth century and even more so after 1500 (table 7.5). Is this because parents realized that a degree of stability is more favorable to the development of a child? Did they choose the nurse with more care? Were they, on the other hand, less attentive to the baby's well-being or more inclined to leave him in the hands of a mediocre nurse? We would do well to avoid premature judgments.

48. As for a child of V. Adriani, ASF, *Strozz.,* 2d ser., 21, fol. 70 (1471).
49. "She gave him 'sullied' milk, for she was long pregnant, as we shall see. . . . She has been paid, but I got bad merchandise for it since she was pregnant" (Cipriano Guiducci, ASF, *Acquisti* e *Doni,* 83, Prov. ign., 2, fol. 52, 13 May 1429). "She became pregnant before the time foreseen and gave a 'pregnant' milk to the child for more than a month" (Matteo Strozzi, ASF, *Strozz.,* 5th ser., 11, fols. 58–59, March 1428). "It is true that it seems to me that she has given him 'pregnant' milk" (Antonio Rustchi, ASF, *Strozz.,* 2d ser., 11, fol. 48, 1428). "As she was pregnant, so it seems, by several months," the nurse was to be paid at the rate of 3 *lire* per month "for the time during which she was not pregnant" (Tribaldo dei Rossi, BNF, 2, 2, 357, fol. 111, 1494).
50. See the reactions of Antonio Rustichi when he thought that his *balii* "had given him bad services"; he writes, 18 January 1427: "She gave 'pregnant' milk to my daughter for a month and a half, and [the baby] nearly died of it; I do not want to pay her. We will verify carefully when the nurse comes to term" (ASF, *Strozz.,* 2d ser., A11, fol. 42). The same reactions can be seen in Neri di Bicci, *Le ricordanze, 1453–1475,* ed. B. Santi (Pisa, 1976), 271–72, year 1466). See also above, note 49.

Table 7.4

CAUSES FOR TERMINATION OF CONTRACT FOR WET NURSING

| *A. Change of nurse* | | | | |
|---|---|---|---|---|
| Without explicit reason | 88 | 24.7% | 56.1% | |
| Because of weaning | 3 | 0.8 | 1.9 | 4.4% |
| Lack of milk, "old" milk | 11 | 3.1 | 7.0 | 15.9 |
| Nurse's pregnancy | 25 | 7.0 | 15.9 | 36.2 |
| Nurse's illness | 10 | 2.8 | 6.4 | 14.5 |
| Bad care, bad conduct of nurse | 7 | 2.0 | 4.5 | 10.1 |
| Illness of the child | 7 | 2.0 | 4.5 | 10.1 |
| Nursing couple's refusal to continue | 3 | 0.8 | 1.9 | 4.4 |
| Child sent to foundling home | 1 | 0.3 | 0.6 | 1.4 |
| Death of an older sibling | 1 | 0.3 | 0.6 | 1.4 |
| Return to the mother (for breast feeding?) | 1 | 0.3 | 0.6 | 1.4 |
| | 157 | 44.1% | 100.0% | 100.0% |
| *B. Definitive end of breast feeding* | | | | |
| Weaning and return to parental household | 126 | 35.4% | 92.0% | |
| Weaning justified by: | | | | |
|    birth of a younger sibling | 5 | 1.4 | 3.7 | |
|    death of the nurse | 1 | 0.3 | 0.7 | |
|    nurse's pregnancy | 5 | 1.4 | 3.7 | |
| | 137 | 38.5% | 100.0% | |
| Death of the child | | | | |
|    by sickness, accident, or without given | | | | |
|       reason | 53 | 14.9% | 85.5% | |
|    by suffocation | 9 | 2.5 | 14.5 | |
| | 62 | 17.4% | 100.0% | |
| Total explained terminations of contract | 356 | 100.0% | | |
| | (77.1%) | | | |
| *C. Outcome or conditions of the ending of* | | | | |
| *breast feeding unknown or unclear* | 106 | | | |
| | (22.9%) | | | |
|    General Total | 462 | | | |
| | (100.0%) | | | |

## When the Child Dies

A Florentine could fear the worst if the *balio* came knocking at his door. In 17.4 percent of the cases, putting a child out to nurse ended in the death of the child. In 85 percent of these cases, "sickness" carried him off; in the other cases the nursing parents had to confess that they caused his death directly and that they "suffocated" him in their sleep.[51] According to the fathers of the children, only once in the nine cases studied here, in

51. Or 62 out of the 356 *baliatici* the outcome of which is known. On the smothering of children during the Middle Ages, see Trexler, "Infanticide," and the bibliography cited

Table 7.5

DISTRIBUTION OF CHILDREN BY NUMBER OF THEIR NURSES

| | Nurse | | | | | | Total number of nurses |
|---|---|---|---|---|---|---|---|
| | 1st | 2d | 3d | 4th | 5th | 6th | |
| **Males** | | | | | | | |
| 1300–1399 | 27 (100) | 17 (63) | 4 (15) | 1 (4) | 1 (4) | 1 (4) | 51 |
| 1400–1449 | 60 (100) | 14 (23) | 5 (8) | 3 (5) | 1 (2) | — | 83 |
| 1450–1499 | 48 (100) | 15 (31) | 3 (6) | — | — | — | 66 |
| 1500–1530 | 24 (100) | 7 (29) | 1 (4) | — | — | — | 32 |
| 1300–1530 | 159 (100) | 53 (33) | 13 (8) | 4 (3) | 2 (1) | 1 (0.6) | 232 |
| **Females** | | | | | | | |
| 1300–1399 | 24 (100) | 10 (42) | 3 (12) | 2 (8) | 1 (4) | — | 40 |
| 1400–1449 | 58 (100) | 16 (28) | 2 (4) | 1 (2) | — | — | 77 |
| 1450–1499 | 58 (100) | 19 (33) | 5 (9) | 3 (5) | 2 (3) | — | 87 |
| 1500–1530 | 19 (100) | 6 (32) | 1 (5) | — | — | — | 26 |
| 1300–1530 | 159 (100) | 51 (32) | 11 (7) | 6 (4) | 3 (2) | — | 230 |
| **Both Sexes** | | | | | | | |
| 1300–1399 | 51 (100) | 27 (53) | 7 (14) | 3 (6) | 2 (4) | 1 (2) | 91 |
| 1400–1449 | 118 (100) | 30 (25) | 7 (6) | 4 (3) | 1 (1) | — | 160 |
| 1450–1499 | 106 (100) | 34 (32) | 8 (8) | 3 (3) | 2 (2) | — | 153 |
| 1500–1530 | 43 (100) | 13 (30) | 2 (5) | — | — | — | 58 |
| 1300–1530 | 318 (100) | 104 (33) | 24 (8) | 10 (3) | 5 (2) | 1 (0.3) | 462 |

The figures in parentheses give the number of children, on a basis of 100 children, who had a second, third nurse, etc. during each period.

which the nurse's husband was formally accused of rolling over on the baby in his sleep, was the *balio* held responsible for the accident. In all the other cases, it was the nurse who was blamed for her negligence.[52]

Several aspects of these smotherings of children in Tuscany should be noted. In the first place, the father never calls on any justice other than

there. R. C. Trexler, *Synodal Law in Florence and Fiesole, 1306–1518* (Vatican City, 1971), 64 (1327), 126–27 (1517) for the ecclesiastical texts concerning this problem.

52. Biagio Buonaccorsi lost two children by suffocation. The second daughter of his second marriage, at the age of eight days, in 1517, "having been suffocated by this Bernardo" (the *balio*), and the first son of his fourth marriage in 1524, at less than one month: "He was suffocated by the nurse as she was giving him the breast" (BNF, *Panciatichi*, 101, fols. 31 and 36). A *balio* of Andrea Minerbetti refused to be paid for the eight months due him after the baby girl entrusted to him was *affoghata* by his wife (Biblioteca Laurenziana, *Acquisti*, 229, 2, fol. 95v., 1515).

the divine. Even when he suspects that the accident could have been avoided, he seems resigned, and he expresses no doubt that the act was unintentional.[53] A deliberate suffocation would be difficult to explain, what is more, since nurses were paid at regular intervals. (This was not true of nurses employed by the foundling homes, which were not always able to pay what they owed the nurses, nor among the poor women in the country, overburdened with children.)[54]

Does this mean that Florentines made no effort to prevent the 15 percent of infant deaths that occurred before the age of six months? We should note that it seemed normal to all, in the fourteenth century, that the child should sleep at his nurse's side: Donato Velluti states, around 1368, that his eldest son, who was born in 1342, made all of the nurses with whom he slept fall ill.[55] This accident, then, could take place even under the gaze of the parents, under their own roof.[56] It is interesting that children who were *affogati, schiacciati,* or *stretti* (smothered, crushed, squeezed) in our sampling appear explicitly in the family journals only in the fifteenth century, and that they become more frequent at the beginning of the sixteenth century.[57] Some degree of sensitization to this avoidable cause of infant mortality came from the Church, which specifically *named* it a crime and insistently called the attention of parents and nurses to their responsibility for it.[58]

53. The only somewhat lively reproach comes in 1506 from Carlo di Niccolò Strozzi: "May God forgive her if she deserves it!" (ASF, *Strozz.*, 4th ser., 75, fol. 138). Battista Vernacci strikes out the word *disavedutamente* (negligently), which he had first written concerning his nurse's suffocation of one of his children (Innocenti, *Estranei*, 300, fol. 23v, 1461).

54. Trexler, "Infanticide," 108–10.

55. D. Velluti, *Cronica domestica*, ed. I. Del Lungo and G. Volpi (Florence, 1914), 310–11.

56. One example is in the *ricordanze* of Terrino di Niccolò Manovelli (ASF, *Strozz.*, 2d ser., 14, fol. 19, 22 November, 1433). A temporary nurse with the best of intentions finds the child she had charitably taken on for a few days, "until his mother had milk," dead in her bed beside her, killed *disavedutamente* (by negligence) (*Ricordanze di Bartolomeo Masi calderaio fiorentino dal 1478 al 1526*, ed. G. O. Corazzini [Florence, 1906], 140). Filippo Strozzi has nurses *in casa*, one of whom suffocates his daugther Lionora "in the bed" in 1474 (ASF, *Strozz.*, 5th ser., 22, fol. 90, 1474).

57. The dates of the nine cases of suffocation in our group of infants put out to nurse are: 1423, 1433, 1461, 1473, 1476, 1506, 1514, 1517, 1524. See Trexler, "Infanticide," on the increase in such cases in the beginning of the sixteenth century. Other cases, all from the fifteenth and sixteenth centuries, are known by various texts or *ricordanze* that are not part of the corpus analyzed here. Thus Benvenuto Cellini tells in his *Vita* (Rizzoli edition, 343–44), vol. 2, chap. 66, how the nurse of his illegitimate son, the wife of one of his sharecroppers and his *comare* (godmother of his child) suffocated the child three days after he had been to see him. Giovanni Morelli (*Ricordi*, 452) expresses the suspicion that his nephew had been suffocated in 1405. Matteo di Giovanni Corsini accuses the nurse of his son Orlando of having "killed" him in 1457. (*Libro di ricordanze dei Corsini (1362–1457*, ed. A. Petrucci, [Rome, 1965], 147).

58. See Trexler, *Synodal Law* and "Infanticide." As early as the first half of the fourteenth century, however, Francesco da Barberino, citing Soranus, warns of the danger (*Del reggimento* 195). A religious painting of the Judgment of Solomon could be taken as an object

Along with this increased consciousness came a search for ways to remedy the problem by avoiding suffocation, even when a child was warmly tucked in next to his nurse. Many of the *ricordanze* list the trousseau that accompanied the baby.[59] Out of twenty-five families, thirteen send a cradle, which in ten instances was equipped with a frame of arched ribs to prevent the covers from stifling the baby.[60] Were these frames also supposed to protect the child from being smothered? If so, we would have to suppose that the nurse placed all this equipment in her own bed. In any event, the frame evidently did not prevent all accidents, and in at least two of the cases of suffocation studied here the child's trousseau included a cradle with a frame.[61] Thus, either the nurse took the baby in with her at night, removing him from his protective frame, or the frame was insufficient protection against the couple's heavy sleep. "Little boxes to put in the bed," more specifically aimed at avoiding the suffocation of the child, are mentioned in two of the trousseau lists. These may have brought a better answer to the problem at a time when the Church's campaign against what it characterized as a crime was in full swing.[62]

There were other ways to avoid having a small, livid body sent home that were just as important in the parent's eyes. The babies left home covered with talismans: little crosses or "Agnusdei," pious medals,[63] but also the coral branch or coral bouquet that were always present in a baby's trousseau, or the "wolf's teeth set in silver" that served both as a good luck charm and a teething toy.[64] This arsenal of more or less magical objects

---

lesson to warn mothers not to keep their child in bed with her while nursing. See Diane Cole Ahl, "Renaissance Birth Salvers and the Richmond 'Judgment of Solomon,'" *Studies in Iconography* 7–8 (1981–82): 157–74.

59. The infant's trousseau is discussed in Ross, "The Middle-Class Child," 191.

60. These bent wood frames were called variously *archetto* or *arcuccio*. There were also *arcioni*, used to rock the child: see the "zana nuova con uno arcione da ongni testa da chullare" (new, rocking basketware cradle with a frame at each end) that figures, with mattress and blankets, in the trousseau of one of Luca da Panzano's children in 1423 (ASF, *Strozz.*, 2d ser., 9, fol. 22). The oldest example of a cradle of this type that I have found dates from 1403 (Ricordi di Rossello d'Ubertino Strozzi, ASF, *Strozz.*, 3d ser., 271, fol. 20v). Trexler, "Infanticide," 116, n. 66 cites a latter depiction of the frame.

61. Andrea Minerbetti (see above note 52 and also Biblioteca Laurenziana, *Acquisti*, 229, 2, fol. 43v).

62. "Una chassetta da tenere nel letto" (a box to keep in bed) (*Ricordi C di Filippo di Neri Rinuccini*, Archivio Corsini, fol. 17v, 1509); "Una cassetta" (a box) (Ricordi di ser Piero Bonaccorsi, ASF, *Acquisti e Doni*, 18, 2d notebook, fol. 50, 1509).

63. These are the *brevi di tenere a collo* (amulets, charms to wear around the neck) that appear so often in an infant's trousseau (see, for example, Filippo di Neri Rinuccini, as cited in the previous note).

64. Dog teeth or wolf teeth figure in the trousseau of Rossello Strozzi in 1404 (see above, note 60), Antonio Rustichi, Filippo di Neri Rinuccini, and Luca da Panzano. The *Madonna della Pergola*, a painting by Bernardino di Antonio Detti (1498–1554), now in the collection of the Museo Civico of Pistoia, shows a small John the Baptist offering the infant Jesus a wolf's tooth, a coral branch, a cross, and a small round reliquary with the inscription "Ecce Agnus Dei" (my thanks to Caroline Elam for calling this curious painting to my attention).

Plate 7.1 Bernardino di Antonio Detti, called del Signoraccio, *Madonna della Pergola* (talisman offered the infant Jesus by John the Baptist). Museo Civico, Pistoia. (Photo Caroline Elam).

was supposed to fend off evil, particularly the *malocchio,* the evil eye, to which nurses attributed their failures and which they conjured away by carrying the infant promptly to the village healing women.[65] This was how the city infant was armed to confront life.

65. See the *Canti Carnascialeschi*, no. 29 (pp. 39–49). See chap. 5 above, "Childhood in Tuscany," n. 25.

We can estimate the infant mortality rate for children put out to nurse at 17.9 percent. It was notably higher for boys than for girls.[66] These rates need to be checked against larger population samplings; furthermore, they are probably understated, since they do not include mortality during the first days or the first weeks of life, before the child left with his nurse. To be sure, the nurse who took the child to her house did so, in the majority of cases, during the first two weeks of his life,[67] but more than a negligible proportion of these departures took place in the succeeding weeks, as table 7.6 shows. This preliminary estimate of infant mortality will have to be reconsidered, then, on the basis of all children from birth on—which the *ricordanze* will indeed allow us to do.

It seems to me important to stress, even before these figures can be ascertained more accurately, that breast feeding, albeit for money, gave these children of Florentine merchants and middle-class families a decent chance of survival—a chance that was in any event superior, in ordinary times, to those of abandoned children. Richard C. Trexler has calculated an infant mortality rate of 26.6 percent in the hospice of the Innocenti in Florence for the years 1445–47, which were relatively good years from the point of view of the home's directors. In the following years, however, the combination of famine, epidemics, and military operations made the rate rise to 50.6 percent. The average for the period 1445–51, given these conditions, can be established at 40.3 percent.[68] Giuliano Pinto, who has studied the mortality rate of children in the hospital of San Gallo during the period 1395–1406, which included a violent wave of the plague in 1399–1400, confirms these frightening statistics, setting the death rate for abandoned children at 50 percent.[69] Obviously, it remains to be seen whether the estimate based on the *ricordanze* and the one for foundling mortality represent the outside limits of average infant mortality—that of the population as a whole. Between these two extremes—the group of tiny privileged creatures of the best families and the miserable children rejected by their families, both of which we know thanks to meticulous accounting of their breast feeding—we are forced to admit that we know practically nothing about the conditions in which the offspring of the rural and popular masses survived their first year of life.

66. Out of 283 children (144 boys and 139 girls) put out to nurse soon after their birth and whom we can trace through their first year of life, 48 died before their first birthday (26 boys and 22 girls, respectively, or a rate of 18.1 percent for boys and 15.8 percent for girls).

67. And often very soon after their birth. Ser Piero Bonaccorsi had a fifth son 24 April 1515; the 25th "the nurse and her husband came to my house," and 1 June the *baliatico* officially began and the child left his family (ASF, *Acquisti e Doni*, 19, fol. 36v).

68. Trexler, "Foundlings," 275.

69. Pinto, "Personale, balie," 127: out of 168 infants (62 boys, 106 girls), the mortality rate is 20 percent for the first month. The other deaths were during the next eleven months.

## Table 7.6
### LENGTH OF TIME BETWEEN BIRTH AND NURSE'S TAKING CHARGE OF CHILD

| Period | First months (in days) | | | | | | Following months | | | Total |
|---|---|---|---|---|---|---|---|---|---|---|
| | 1st | 2d | 3d–5th | 6th–14th | 15th–30th | Total | 2d | 3d–6th | 7th–12th | |
| 1320–1429 | 5 | 6 | 14 | 22 | 14 | 61 | 4 | 3 | 1 | 69 |
| % | 15.9 | | 52.2 | | 20.3 | 88.4 | | | | 100.0 |
| 1430–1469 | 3 | 4 | 17 | 18 | 4 | 46 | 3 | 1 | 1 | 51 |
| % | 13.7 | | 68.6 | | 7.8 | 90.2 | | | | 100.0 |
| 1470–1530 | 7 | 6 | 21 | 18 | 8 | 60 | — | — | — | 60 |
| % | 21.7 | | 65.0 | | 13.3 | 100.0 | — | — | — | 100.0 |
| 1320–1530 | 15 | 16 | 53 | 58 | 26 | 167 | 7 | 4 | 2 | 180 |
| % | 17.2 | | 61.7 | | 14.5 | 92.8 | 3.9 | 2.2 | 1.1 | 100.0 |

What did these children die of when "sickness" carried them off? Unfortunately, the father's diagnoses are infrequent and, naturally, imprecise.[70] Certain characteristics of death by illness can be seen, however, in the seasonal distribution of deaths. One time out of six, Florentine babies died in August.[71] The next most deadly months were July, November, and March, followed by April and, farther down the list, June, then September, October, and February. January, December, and May—a month that smiled at infants as at lovers—closed the list. If we compare this distribution to that of deaths in the population as a whole (excluding deaths from the plague), we can see that Florentine infants had less resistance to the rainy months of spring and autumn than their elders.[72] Children under five months old were hardest hit in summer and autumn, while spring carried off more of the newborn and infants over five months of age. Here also, the data permit only a brief exploration of an almost unknown area.[73]

## Weaning

With weaning, the child arrived at an important moment in his short life. If he overcame its dangers, weaning soon brought him separation from the woman who had nourished him up to that point if he had been taken outside the home, and reunion with his family. Until recently little has been known of this event except what a very few authors had to say about the subject.[74] Fortunately, if we take the *ricordanze* as a serial source, they tell us much about both the moment of weaning and the conditions under which it was carried out.

Let me once again stress the place that men—the father and the *balio*—occupied in this decision. Three-quarters of the authors of *ricordanze* pres-

70. Illnesses that are explained in some detail are a *male di chanchero e bole nela bocha* (cankers and boils in the mouth) (1444), *rosolie* (German measles) (1497), *febbre e lattime* (fever and milk crust), a *mal di tossa* (coughing illness), a *certo zitomore saldo* (a bad case of milk fever) in 1509, and an *uscita ghrande* (serious diarrhea) in 1507.

71. August accounted for 16.7 percent of infant deaths. The large number of summer illnesses (plague excluded) suggests intestinal disorders and diarrhea. The same conclusions are suggested in J.-L. Biget and J. Tricard, "Livres de raison et démographie familiale en Limousin au XVᵉ siècle," *Annales de démographie historique* (1981): 345–46.

72. The comparison can be made using the data from table 76 in Herlihy and Klapisch-Zuber, *Les Toscans*, 465, and subtracting deaths due to plague during the years 1424–30. These data concern all ages and can be compared with the seasonal distribution of deaths of children less than two years old in our sampling: January: 5.0% of infant deaths, 5.2% of all deaths; February: 6.7% and 4.4%, respectively; March: 11.7% and 5.7%; April: 10.0% and 5.7%; May: 1.7% and 7.2%; June: 8.3% and 8.9%; July: 11.7% and 14.1%; August: 16.7% and 17.9%; September: 6.7% and 12.7%; October: 6.7% and 7.3%; November: 11.7% and 5.7%; December: 3.3% and 5.2%.

73. See Herlihy and Klapisch-Zuber, *Les Toscans*, 191–93, 456–66.

74. Ross, "The Middle-Class Child," 195; Herlihy and Klapisch-Zuber, *Les Toscans*, 559–60. Cherubini, "Un notaio senese," in *Signori, contadini, borghesi,* 411.

ent themselves as responsible for, or at least the principal partner in, the decision to wean the child.[75] Never does the *balia*—even less the mother—appear as an expert in this affair.

According to table 7.4, deaths in category B accounted for 31.2 percent of the definitive terminations of breast feeding contracts. But some of the children from category C, whose destiny is unknown or unclear, should probably be added to the group of children for whom we know the date of weaning.[76] If we correct the figures in this manner, the death rate drops to 25.6 percent and, conversely, successful weanings rise from 68.8 percent to 74.4 percent. Thus, three out of four of the children given over to a nurse were brought back, weaned, to their parents.

A more restricted sampling of 131 well-documented contracts that ran to term[77] enables us to calculate the age at which weaning took place. An even more restricted group of 53 contracts specify the exact modalities of the weaning, permitting us to ascertain whether its beginning coincides with the child's return home. As might be expected, the child's age at the start of weaning is markedly younger than the age at which he is returned to his parents. Weanings in this well-documented group begin on the average at about 18.7 months, while the children return definitively to the family at 20.4 months. If these ages do not coincide, it is because in one-third of the cases the child is left with the nurse who breast fed-him, or is transferred to another woman, perhaps one who specialized in weaning. When this happened, he remained there for a transitional period, during which the nurse was paid less and the child was gradually shifted to a more solid diet. This period could last one or two months or could continue for up to six months. When it went beyond this time, it is clear that the nurse had become guardian and governess, and she was paid not even half as much for this work and for the more varied diet that she now gave the child.[78]

75. One time out of three the first person plural used by the father seems to refer to the natural parents or the nursing parents, but in nearly 30 percent of the cases, the decision seems to have been taken by the *balio*, and the rest of the time the father and family head takes exclusive responsibility: "I have weaned Vettorio, and Monna Apollonia, his nurse, has left for home with her husband," Bonaccorso di Vettorio Ghiberti says in 1503 (Archivio Innocenti, *Estranei*, 546, fol. 74); and, in 1419, Antonio Rustichi writes: "I have weaned the said Lionardo and I have given the nurse Stefano in exchange" (ASF, *Strozz.*, 2d ser., 11, fol. 11).

76. We can distinguish among them some children for whose breast feeding we have some subsequent information (the payment of the nurse, for example) or about whom we have biographical data that allow us to conclude that this part of their early childhood had a happy ending.

77. Thus they make up 41 percent of the 318 infants under examination. We know the precise date of their birth and that of their definitive return to the parents' household.

78. The cut in salary that often strikes a nurse after fifteen or eighteen months of service indicates either lower pay for a milk judged to be "old" or a change in the child's diet that involves less milk. It is rare that these cuts in salary are noted in the original contract. Most of the adjustments observed occur in connection with the weaning of the child.

Florentines clearly agreed to and paid for this supplementary period of one to six months, which permitted unhurried weaning,[79] more readily for their sons than for their daughters. Although we have seen that, for both sexes, two-thirds of the children appear to have been weaned abruptly, without transition,[80] the practice was accentuated for females, 74 percent of whom (as opposed to 59 percent of their brothers) were taken from the breast and from the nurse with no interim step. Generally speaking, a girl returned home earlier than her brother. In the cases for which we know the exact date at which weaning began, the same gap of about a month and a half attests that a girl's stay with a nurse—an index to the real length of the breast-feeding period, which is somewhat exaggerated but nevertheless dependable—was shorter than a boy's (18 months and 19.4 months, respectively; see table 7.7).

I know of no contemporary medical or pedagogical text that puts forth scientific arguments authorizing parents to cut short the breast feeding of their daughters for constitutional reasons.[81] The statutes of the city also made no difference between the sexes. As late as 1415, probably repeating older dispositions, they prescribed the legal length of the contract for a

Table 7.7
DURATION OF BREAST FEEDING BY SEX

|  | 1340–1399 | 1400–1469 | 1470–1530 | Total 1340–1530 |
|---|---|---|---|---|
| Males | | | | |
| number | 13 | 35 | 19 | 67 |
| age* | 23.2 | 21.6 | 18.5 | 21.0 |
| Females | | | | |
| number | 12 | 39 | 13 | 64 |
| age* | 20.8 | 20.4 | 16.5 | 19.6 |
| Both sexes | | | | |
| number | 25 | 74 | 32 | 131 |
| age* | 22.0 | 21.0 | 17.7 | 20.4 |

*Child's age in months at the time of his return from the nurse or of the nurse's departure from the household.

79. See Paolo da Certaldo, *Il libro di buoni costumi,* 126, which advises (around 1370) "not to give anything but the breast during the first year; you will then begin to give, aside from the breast, other things to eat, little by little." This is confirmed in Francesco da Barberino, *Del reggimento,* 192. See Herlihy and Klapisch-Zuber, *Les Toscans,* 560.

80. We can see evidence of this brutality in formulas like Francesco di Giovanni di Durante's in 1343: "che si spopò questo dì" (who was weaned this day) (BNF, 2, 3, 280, fol. 18).

81. For older girls, Paolo da Certaldo, *Il Libro di buoni costumi,* 126–27, recommends a diet that is simply sufficient, whereas the diet for boys should be richer and more varied. But he is not speaking of nursing infants, in contrast to the statements that Joubert (see below, note 94) puts in the mouths of the women of Languedoc.

wet nurse to be thirty months, a duration only the parents were authorized to cut short.[82] The distribution of ages at the termination of the nursing period shows that they did not hesitate to do so (table 7.8). What is more, parents adapted legal or medical recommendations to the sex of the child. Parents continued to enjoy a good deal of autonomy in their decisions, and this autonomy probably increased during the period studied. Table 7.7 summarizes children's ages at the moment of their separation from the nurse over a period of two centuries around 1500, weaning generally took place, a good four months earlier than a century before. The shortening of the nursing period affects boys more than girls, thus reducing slightly the gap between boys' and girls' length of stay.

These figures speak of a phenomenon that continued from previous times, and which unfortunately we can perceive only through the normative texts. Statutes in Tuscany of the end of the thirteenth century recommend a three-year period for putting children out to nurse and, as we have seen, these norms were repeated well into the fifteenth century, whereas pedagogues or doctors attest, beginning in the fourteenth century, that the duration of the nursing period was really shorter.[83] This shorter duration may perhaps be the price paid for a certain popularization of the practice—whether this be a true popularization or the effect of better documentation, as we have pointed out. In any event, the latest dates of weaning can be found in the fifteenth century among the richest families.[84]

Unforeseen circumstances sometimes hastened the moment of weaning,[85] but, generally speaking, the father decided the matter, taking into account the state of the child and that of his own finances. The first of

82. *Statuta,* bk. 4, sec. 148 (2:269). On the duration of breast feeding see J.-L. Flandrin, "L'attitude à l'égard du petit enfant et les conduites sexuelles dans la civilisation occidentale: Structures anciennes et évolution," *Annales de démographie historique* 1973: 143–210, esp. 179–81. There are in fact few instances in the *ricordanze* of contracts broken by the nursing couple. We can even find *balii* who did not want to give back or wean the child (*Libro A di richordi, 1459–1498* of Antonio Rospigliosi, ed. G. C. Rospigliosi [Pisa, 1909], 47–48 for the year 1481).

83. *Statutum potestatis comunis Pistorii anni 1296,* ed. L. Zdekauer (Milan, 1888), and Francesco da Barberino, *Del reggimento,* 192, indicate a duration of two years. The rental of slave women *cum lacte* was set at a period of three years (Heer, *Esclaves et domestiques,* 203). In the sixteenth and seventeenth centuries the recommended duration was still three years, although practice did not respect this norm (Flandrin, "L'attitude à l'égard du petit enfant," 180).

84. One member of the great Bardi lineage left his children out to nurse between 27 and 32 months (Ilarione di Lipaccio Bardi, ASF, *Conventi soppressi,* 79, 119, passim, 1420–55), while Filippo Strozzi's brother-in-law, Marco Parenti, went as far as 24 months (ASF, *Strozz.,* 2d ser., 17 bis, passim, 1447–94), and the needier Manno Petrucci took his children back from their nurses at about 15–17 months (ASF, *Strozz.,* 2d ser., 17, passim., 1441–50).

85. See table 7.4: out of 137 contracts terminated because of weaning, 5 were linked to the birth of a younger child whom the nurse was asked to take on, 7 to the nurse's pregnancy, one to her death. The insecurity of the countryside also prompted fathers to call their infants home (Tribaldo dei Rossi, BNF, 2, 2, 357, fol. 112, 1494).

## Table 7.8
### Age Distribution at Termination of Breast Feeding

| | 12–19 months | 20–24 months | 25–32 months | Total | Average Age | Median Age |
|---|---|---|---|---|---|---|
| **Males** | | | | | | |
| 1300–1399 | 4 | 4 | 5 | 13 | 23.2 | 23 |
| 1400–1469 | 12 | 17 | 6 | 35 | 21.6 | 22 |
| 1470–1530 | 13 | 6 | 0 | 19 | 18.5 | 18 |
| 1300–1530 | 29 | 27 | 11 | 67 | 20.4 | 20 |
| **Females** | | | | | | |
| 1300–1399 | 7 | 3 | 2 | 12 | 20.8 | 18 |
| 1400–1469 | 15 | 16 | 8 | 39 | 20.4 | 21 |
| 1470–1530 | 10 | 2 | 1 | 13 | 16.5 | 16 |
| 1300–1530 | 32 | 21 | 11 | 64 | 19.6 | 17 |
| **Both sexes** | | | | | | |
| 1300–1399 | 11 (44.0%) | 7 (28.0%) | 7 (28.0%) | 25 (100%) | 22.0 | 22 |
| 1400–1469 | 27 (36.5%) | 33 (44.6%) | 14 (18.9%) | 74 (100%) | 21.0 | 21 |
| 1470–1530 | 23 (71.9%) | 8 (25.0%) | 1 ( 3.1%) | 32 (100%) | 17.7 | 17 |
| 1300–1530 | 61 | 48 | 22 | 131 | 20.4 | 20 |

these criteria is rarely expressed as explicitly as in one rather late text (1534), in which a father deplores the June departure of the nurse, "when she had promised us to remain with us until September, so that we could avoid having Cecchina weaned during the great heat and before she has all her teeth."[86] Financial considerations are usually more evident. The study of twenty well documented sibling groups has already shown us that subsequent children generally enjoyed shorter stays, with more distant nurses, and the sum involved was less than for their elders. There is one Tribaldo dei Rossi, for example, member of an ancient lineage that had fallen on evil days around 1500, who complains that his poverty forces him to break off the breast feeding of his last daughter, Maddalena, at one year old, whereas her older siblings had returned home between 17 and 20 months.[87] Poor Maddalena here suffers the accumulated disadvantages of her birth order and her sex. When the household had its fill of children, and when, what is more, the child was a girl, the financial burden represented by the nurse's wages became unbearable. So, contrary to general usage, Maddalena was weaned at one year.

For most children, however, weaning around 19 or 20 months—a late weaning—offered them a good chance of coming through this trial successfully. Weaning seems responsible for only a very small number of deaths, and they occurred as weaning was started.[88] Tiny Florentines thus found compensation for the handicap they suffered in their start in life, when maternal milk with its precious antibodies was refused them, in a breast feeding that was fairly prolonged and a weaning gradual enough to enable them to shift easily to a more solid diet, whether they were armed with "all their teeth" or just with a wolf's tooth.

The mother also derived some benefits from putting her children out to nurse. In a society in which daughters were married before they were 18 years of age[89] and in which fertility was highly valued, it may have been easier for a woman to agree to more closely spaced childbirths than to the demands of incessant breast feeding. In 701 births, occurring in 115 couples, the intergenetic interval was 20.8 months, and the median falls to 17.8 months. Between two childbirths, the Florentine woman of these well-off circles could hope for a real respite, freed of all obligation to breast-feed, and lasting from 8 to 12 months, according to the length of time the child was put out to nurse. If she breast-fed her child, on the other hand, she would have a very good chance of doing so until the next pregnancy, thus devoting all of her energies to the two female "functions"

86. Bartolomeo di Lorenzo *banderaio* (banner maker), ASF, *San Paolo*, 129, fol. 71v. The contract with the nurse stipulated that she would leave only in the case of her husband's death.

87. BNF, 2, 2, 357, fols. 173v and 59v, 112, for an older son and an older daughter.

88. Two cases, both of which occurred in April.

89. On age at marriage, see Herlihy and Klapisch-Zuber, *Les Toscans*, 394–400.

of procreation and suckling. The engagement of a wet nurse liberated her from the second of these burdens, and although it contributed to the closer spacing of the births of her children, it at least permitted her to enjoy complete liberty during half of her life as a fertile woman. It seems more than likely that Florentine women were sensitive to such advantages and therefore all the more willing to consent to separation from their children. Paid breast feeding was a distinctive sign of the urban elites; it flattered the vanity of the husbands, to be sure, but it also enhanced the woman's status as a fertile and prolific wife.

### Blood and Milk

From the beginning of the contract to its end, the father of the child presents himself as the principal actor in this quintet that paid breast feeding puts onto the stage. Of course, he casts himself as leading man: he holds the script and he speaks in the first person. But even though he plays a double role and exaggerates its importance, he is still the leading actor. His male voice dominates, echoed and amplified by the solo voice of the *balio,* who, one time out of four, sells him "his" milk and negotiates with him. The mother, on the other hand, cuts an uncertain figure and appears even less important than the nurse. What is exchanged here— money, child, or milk—seems out of her grasp. The relationship between the four adult actors is thus asymmetrical, an imbalance which, above and beyond the context of the contract, raises problems.

As we have seen, the reason cited by the nursing couple or by the father for breaking a contract was very often the nurse's pregnancy. Furthermore, when Florentines complain of their nurse, it is not so much because they are afraid that her milk will dry up as because they fear that it will be "denatured" or "perverted." It may have been the medical tradition that came down from Galen that taught educated Florentines to fear that pregnancy might send poorer, baser milk to the woman's breasts.[90] But in the *ricordanze,* milk that is *pregno* (pregnant) is also called *sozzo*—repugnant and somewhat sickening. Permitting the child to drink it amounted to insidious poisoning, which explains the anger of the nurse's employer when she conceals her pregnancy too long.[91] The employer's resentment seems out of proportion with the teaching of antiquity, for this sullied milk provokes a reaction of horror. Behind the violence of the father's

90. In reaction to this attitude, however, one of the characters in Leon Battista Alberti's *I Libri della famiglia* (Einaudi, 1969), 44, contradicts the ancient doctors, Favorinus and Aulus Gellius, according to whom "milk makes mothers weak and sometimes makes them sterile." For Alberti's character, nature provides equally well for procreation and the child's survival, and "pregnancy multiplies milk."

91. See the citation from Antonio Rustichi in note 49 above, to which he adds, "and she nearly died of it."

rejection, should we not read, if not the infraction of a true taboo, at least ambiguous sentiments and feelings of guilt?

When a pregnant nurse "fouls" her milk and it becomes such a threat to the baby's well-being that the baby must be removed from it as quickly as possible, her behavior obliges Florentine parents to consider all the contradictions of the choice that they have made. J. T. Noonan and J. L. Flandrin have shown how the consciousness of risk to the child imposed continence on parents or recourse to contraceptive methods incompatible with their eternal salvation.[92] The payment of a salaried nurse resolved this contradiction, but it created others.

When parents bought milk from the *balii* to the tune of good hard *fiorini*, they bought their own right to pursue conjugal relations without worrying about the fruit that might be born of their actions and without threatening the older child with maternal milk that might dry up or become "perverted." In the logic that J. L. Flandrin has outlined, such behavior reflects a degree of concern for the welfare of the child, for his health, and for his survival. Whether or not this is so, the compromise represented by putting a child out to nurse allayed two fears: that of sinning in the flesh and that of acting in opposition to beliefs or violating prohibitions concerning lactation. But this agreeable compromise rested on a fundamental hypocrisy. Parents preferred not to think of the sin that their actions might impose on the nurse couple: when threatened with withdrawal of the child, a source of profit for them, they too might refuse their conjugal obligations or have recourse to disapproved means in order to avoid a new pregnancy. The anger expressed in the *ricordanze* when a nurse became pregnant was undoubtedly born of the feeling of having to some extent been cheated in a contract that stated implicitly that the nursing couple curb, if not totally interrupt,[93] conjugal relations. But might not their denunciations of the nurse couple's irresponsibility also stir up in the parents a certain bad conscience regarding their egotistic initial decision? All things considered, they had preferred acts of the flesh and the exclusion of their child over what the doctors of the period unanimously presented as a natural duty, one that even the most ferocious animals did not shirk. And, as it usually happened among Florentine men, the accounts they rendered to God and to their own conscience took them back to their account books.

The *balii* most probably did not share their employers' fears regarding the quality of a pregnant woman's milk. As Laurent Joubert was to observe

92. J. T. Noonan, *Contraception: A History of Its Treatment by the Catholic Theologians and Canonists* (Cambridge, Mass., 1969). Flandrin, "L'attitude à l'égard du petit enfant." On older condemnations based on the sinfulness of pleasure (Council of Paris, 823), see G. Duby, *Le chevalier, la femme et le prêtre* (Paris, 1981), 35.

93. The text of Francesco da Barberino cited in note 47 demonstrates that Florentines were conscious of the promises that they made nurses make in this regard, at least when the woman was taken in to the household of the child's father.

a good century later in Languedoc, peasants did not believe that pregnancy corrupted maternal milk, and they let their children drink it, thin as it was, to the last available drop. The children, Joubert adds, were none the worse for it.[94] It must have been fear of sanction if they broke a law in force that led the Tuscan sharecroppers to declare pregnancies promptly and to return the child, thus submitting, willy-nilly, to the cultural models of the dominant classes. In this fashion, the "negligence" in delaying the declaration of a pregnancy was perhaps not intentional: we can credit these peasants with a certain fidelity to their own cultural traditions—a fidelity misunderstood by the city people, who saw in it only rustics' treason.

There is a further contradiction that explains the parents' malaise vis-à-vis the nursing couple. The moralists in the family, the medical authorities they read, and the preachers they listened to tirelessly repeated the warnings of ancient authors who opposed the very idea of breast feeding by any woman other than the mother. For them, the pregnant mother, then the nursing mother, rose above the passive role imposed on her at the time of conception: she nourished the child she carried with her blood and, after his birth, with her milk, which was presented as directly derived from menstrual blood (a notion to which an anatomical drawing by Leonardo da Vinci, dated about 1492, testifies).[95] The nursing mother thus continued to shape the child in her own image; according to these theories, she ceaselessly rooted her own qualities in him. The seed planted in the womb by the father matured through the administration of maternal milk, and this idea prompted doctors to recommend—if the mother was out of the question—the choice of a nurse who resembled the mother. This was obviously considered a lesser evil, preferable in any event to animal milk—goat's milk or cow's milk—which might degrade the little man-to-be and push him in the direction of the brutes. These respected authors add that the intimacy born of nursing would forge indestructible ties between mother and child.[96]

These literary spokesmen for our bourgeois families repeat such ideas ad nauseam.[97] They also draw the consequence that the choice of a wife and future mother is extremely difficult and important, since she will nourish her child with her blood and her milk and will transmit to him

94. L. Joubert, *La première et la seconde partie des erreurs populaires touchant la médecine et le régime de la santé* (Paris, 1587), 226–28, cited in Flandrin, "L'attitude à l'égard du petit enfant," 208–10. In the chapter he devotes to weaning, Joubert incidentally compares Tuscany and Montpellier for the similarity of their climates (242). He also notes that pregnant nurses are said to *enganar* (fool, cheat) the child "d'un mot italien pour dire ingannare" (228).

95. This drawing shows veins that lead from the upper part of the uterus to take menstrual blood to the breast (*Disegni anatomici dalla Biblioteca reale di Windsor,*, exposition in Palazzo Vecchio, Florence, 1979, no. 16A).

96. Ross, "The Middle-Class Child," 185–87; Herlihy and Klapisch-Zuber, *Les Toscans*, 555.

97. See the texts of Alberti, Palmieri, Ruccellai, Vegio already cited.

qualities complementary to those transmitted by the father. However, our Florentines contravened these handsome precepts merrily and consistently by putting their children out to nurse; and in order to have done so they must have been governed by infinitely stronger and more dynamic values than this medico-moral literary heritage. The values were those of lineage: according to them, the children born of a couple belonged to the father and to his kinship group. Such values minimized female roles and female contributions to the family group; the only valid anchors for personal and collective identity lay in the various kinds of patrimony received from the male line.[98]

Such an ideology in no way contradicts the behavior of Florentines as we have observed it. To send away one's child to be cared for by another woman—chosen with as much care as a wife—promised him successful maturation of the virtues inherited from the father and from his lineage. Basically, the qualities inherent in the wife did not count. To forbid the mother this share in the nurture of her children, this complicity that many authors had found of capital importance, did not at all contradict the idea of the continuity of the lineage, which was satisfied when the wife was fertile. Thus we can explain the remarkable absence of the mother in all that pertains to her children's nurses: the father took responsibility, both material and spiritual, for assuring the development of his seed. This was how Florentines proclaimed the superiority of the paternal "blood," transmitted in the act of generation, over the blood and the milk with which the mother, then the nurse, would nourish the child. Lastly, a "pregnant" milk was considered the final move in a feminine plot, widely denounced at the time, to destroy or dilapidate the wealth created or transmitted by men.

Our Tuscan *balii* were thus often taken as scapegoats in a conflict greater than they. Were their relations with the child entrusted to them any less burdened with ambiguity? The most human touches in the *ricordanze* concern them rather than the natural parents. We perceive this when we listen to one nurse, who refused further payment to prolong the pleasure of breast-feeding and enjoying the child she had raised—a pleasure worthy of the Virgin, if our epigraph is to be believed.[99] Or when we listen again to Piero Puro from Vicchio, *balio* for a Florentine family, according to whom "by the grace of God and of my wife" a child was occasionally saved.[100]

98. On lineage in Tuscany, see F. Kent, *Household and Lineage in Renaissance Florence* (Princeton, 1977); Herlihy and Klapisch-Zuber, *Les Toscans*, 532–50; C. Klapisch-Zuber, "L'invention du passé familial à Florence (XIVᶜ–XVᶜ s.)," in *Temps, mémoire, tradition au Moyen Age,* Actes du Congrès des Médiévistes de l'enseignement supérieur d'Aix-en-Provence, June 1982 (Aix-en-Provence, 1983), 95–118.

99. Ricordi d'Andrea Minerbetti, Biblioteca Laurenziana, *Acquisti*, 229, fol. 45: "She said she wanted to suckle Maria until March for her pleasure, without other salary and with only her salary [as a servant] noted above."

100. See Appendix to this chapter.

Appendix
Extracts from the journal of a Florentine *balio,*
Piero di Francesco Puro da Vicchio

(Archivio degli Innocenti, *Estranei,* 714, Ricordanze A e memoriale G. di
Piero, etc., 1413–60)
. . . [fol. 2v] I gave a child to nurse 20 October 1422 to Jacomino di
Bartolo di Bianco da San Benedetto at the salary of 4 *lire* per month.
[Payments continued until 9 August 1424 for a total of 51 *lire,* 17 *soldi.*]
. . . [fol. 4r] 20 October 1424, I received from Niccolò dei Ricci a child
of his to be put to nurse; he will give me two *fiorini* per month; thus we
agreed for the two years to come, or [a total of] 48 *fiorini.* I shall note
below what he gives me. [Notations of payments follow until 18 September 1425, for one of which, 17 March 1425, for 5 *lire,* he notes "which
my *balio* at Poppi received."] The above mentioned Niccolò has paid 46
*fiorini* for the 23 months during which my wife gave the breast to San-
miniato his son.
. . . [fol. 12r] 7 April 1428, I received from monna Leonarda, wife of
Piero son of messire Vanni Castellani, her daughter, whom my wife is to
raise; the said wife and nurse shall receive each year for her trouble and
for the breast feeding of the said little girl seven *lire* per month paid by
the said monna Leonarda, who is bound to pay for the whole year 21
*fiorini* to Piero Puro and to his said wife.
Thursday 6 May 1428, I have returned to monna Leonarda her daughter, whom my wife had taken to nurse, and I have also returned 20 linen
swaddling cloths [diapers], 7 bands, 6 woolen swaddling cloths, one mattress, one sheet, one cradle. She still owes me 6 *lire,* 15 *soldi,* 8 *denari,* and
I must return to her one linen cloth. [On 14 May he is paid 6 *lire.*]
Friday 7 May (1428), I have received from Santa Maria della Scala[101]
a child named Valoriano; I kept him until the 31st of this month when,
for a servant woman of Giovannozzo Pitti,[102] I returned him to the superior
of S. Maria della Scala.
Tuesday 31 May, I have received from Giovannozzo Pitti a child to
put to nurse for several days at the price of 6 *lire* and a half per month.
He has sent me with the child 12 linen swaddling cloths, 3 red cloths,[103]
5 bands, and the cradle. Sunday 13 June, I have returned the son of
Giovannozzo Pitti and all the cloths, woolen and linen, the bands, the

---

101. Santa Maria della Scala was one of the two institutions that accepted foundlings
in Florence at that time. It had been opened in 1316. In 1389 it had 130 infants out to
nurse, and about 1435, nearly 200 (see Trexler, "Foundlings," 261, 263–64).
102. The sense is not quite clear. Is this child of G. Pitti's the son of the servant woman?
103. Nursing infants often seem to have been wrapped in red cloth; see ASF *Strozz.,*
2d ser., 7, Ricordanze di Paliano di Falco Paliani da Firenze (1382–1404), fol. 2v, where
the father gives three *fiorini* to the nurse "for red cloth for the swaddling cloths."

cradle, and the blanket, at the same time as the child. And I have received
from him 3 *lire* for the time I kept him.

. . . [fol. 12v] Thursday 15 April 1428, I have given to Meo di Cucio
da San Tomato my daughter to nurse at the salary of 3 *lire* per month.
He has taken with the child 4 woolen swaddling cloths, two red ones,
two linens (?), as well as four bands (two new, two used), twelve linen
swaddling cloths, old or new, and a new cradle to put the little one in, as
well as a mattress and a small quilt. [The child was returned 17 June.]

13 June 1428, the [medical] nurse of Francesco di . . . , a grocer in
the Old Market at the sign of the keys, gave me his son to be nursed. He
was so sick that he could not suckle. They had let him get so weak that
we very nearly lost him. With the grace of God and of my wife, we saved
him, so that this day, 16 June, I have decided to keep him until the time
when the wife of Francesco di Benedetto di Caroccio brings her child into
the world;[104] until then, my wife is to receive for her trouble with the
child 7 *lire* for one month, or more, if she sees fit. [They kept the child
seventeen days and were paid 3 *lire* 10 *soldi* 6 July.]

---

104. That is, until the time at which Piero's wife was to take on this child, having agreed
with the mother to do so. It is clear that she neither breast-feeds her own child at the same
time as a child under contract, nor two children under contract.

# 8

## Female Celibacy and Service in Florence in the Fifteenth Century

"I engaged Caterina, who tells me that it was forever, with the consent of her father, and also with that of her mother. . . . She has done this because she does not in any manner want a husband. All, quite in agreement, have therefore given her to me. I must clothe her and shoe her as one does for servant women, and this they leave to my discretion. When God decides my death, I shall leave her what I shall judge, with my wife, to be her deserts, considering the time spent with us, and, since she refuses a husband, we shall make sure that she has something in her old age, that is, the clothes she wears, as it will seem proper to us and not otherwise."[1]

A contract of this sort, let me hasten to note, was an exception to the rule.[2] Does it nevertheless betray one important function of domestic service, analogous, in the popular classes, to the entry into a convent among rich girls? Was a surplus of girls for whom the lack of a dowry, an unfortunate physical appearance, or a lopsided marriage market made a nor-

---

Originally published as "Célibat et service féminins dans la Florence du XVᵉ siècle, " *Annales de Démographie Historique* 1981: 289–302.

1. Archivio di Stato, Florence (henceforth abbreviated ASF), *Manoscritti* 96, fol. 24 (27 March 1492) (*Ricordanze di Bartolomeo Salvetti*).

2. There is only one other example, in the *ricordanze* of Andrea di Tommaso Minerbetti, dated 1 November 1499: "and the said Marietta says that she wants no husband and that she wants to remain with us always; and thus it shall be if she behaves well and does not change" (Biblioteca Laurenziana, Florence, *Acquisti e doni* 229 bis, fol. 27v).

mal conjugal career impossible absorbed into domestic service? The fate of girls in older societies who willy-nilly remained unmarried constituted a crucial problem for them and for their families, from both the financial and the legal points of view. If a husband failed to come and take her over from her parents, or if marriage, as is the case here, proved sufficiently repugnant to make a girl prefer the uncertainties of a "solitary" life, the question of her material survival became a pressing one. In practice, the legal obligation to dower a girl was observed in Florence only if she married or entered a convent. On the other hand, the corollary of this obligation, exclusion from the paternal inheritance, pertained whatever her destiny might be—wife, nun, or old maid. Giving up hope of a marriage or refusing it led the woman and her guardians to search with all haste for a substitute solution to assure her shelter and board—and to assure her virtue.[3] Entry into domestic service might solve the problem for girls of humble origins, a solution parallel to entry into a convent for the wealthy. Recent works suggest that such was the case in Florence of the fifteenth century.[4] But since it is easier to define the behavior and the motivations of the ruling classes (which are much better documented) than that of the lower classes, it may be worthwhile to reexamine this fairly explicit hypothesis in the light of what we are beginning to learn about the demographic structures and the demographic history of Tuscany, looking closely at the conditions of female employment in Florentine families.

The present examination is based on some 132 agreements reached between a middle-class head of family and a woman entering his service I gleaned from the *ricordanze* (account books and family journals) kept daily by many Florentines.[5] The conditions of engagement, which seldom were notarized, are carefully set down here. The *ricordanze* often enable us to follow a servant's career, ascertain the length of her stay, and sense the atmosphere in the household when she left. We need first to determine the extent of female celibacy in Florence between the end of the fourteenth and the beginning of the fifteenth centuries. Then I shall examine the conditions of domestic employment of women, using the *ricordanze* as a point of departure, in an effort to determine whether service and the celibate state were indeed interconnected.

    3. See J. Kirshner, *Pursuing Honor while Avoiding Sin: The Monte delle Doti of Florence*, Quaderni di *Studi Senesi*, 41 (Milan, 1978).
    4. D. Herlihy, "Mapping Households in Medieval Italy," *Catholic Historical Review* 58 (1972): 8–9; D. Herlihy and C. Klapisch-Zuber, *Les Toscans et leurs familles* (Paris, 1978), 208; D. Herlihy, "The Population of Verona in the First Century of Venetian Rule," in J. Hale, ed., *Renaissance Venice* (London, 1973), 111–12, 113, 115; J. Kirshner and A. Molho, "The Dowry Fund and the Marriage Market in early *Quattrocento* Florence," *Journal of Modern History* 50 (1978): 420.
    5. On Florentine *ricordanze*, see C. de la Roncière, *Un changeur florentin du Trecento: Lippo di Fede del Sega (1285 env.–1363 env.)* (Paris, 1973); see esp. pp. 11–15 for a brief description.

If the *catasto* of 1427 is to be believed, the age structure of the Florentine population was marked by striking social contrasts. To establish this we need only compare the age pyramid of the two groups, of equivalent size, at either end of the scale of wealth: the taxpayers who didn't have a *fiorino* to their name, whom I will call the "poor," to simplify things (4,563 persons, including 2,199 women); and the "rich," who declared more than 3,200 *fiorini* (4,248 persons, including 1,802 women). To generalize, we could say that the population increased in youth as it increased in wealth. The pyramid of the poor (see figure 8.1) shows a narrow base and vertical sides, while that of the rich spreads out noticeably at the base and shrinks in marked but regular manner after adolescence. Young girls 8–12 years of age make up 10 percent of the female population among the poor, as against 16 percent among the rich; adolescent girls of marriageable age—those in the next higher group—are 7.4 percent of the former and 10.3 percent of the latter.

In the aggregate, the difference is particularly accentuated on the female side: the median age, in the two categories of wealth we are considering, is 24 years old for men and 25 for women among the poor, while it falls to 17 and 15, respectively, among the rich.[6]

This is not the only contrast between "rich" and "poor," however. If we examine the male/female ratio by age groups of ten years, we can see that the rich show a movement exactly contrary to that of the poor. The ratio is quite comparable in the two wealth categories before the age of 10, but men diminish continually among the poor until the ratio falls under 100 after 40 years of age, and it rises again only after 65 years of age. Among the most impoverished of Florentine taxpayers, women exceeded men in number between 40 years of age and 65. To the contrary, the male/female ratio increases consistently among the rich until it reaches fantastic heights after 30 years of age and during all of the mature years, after which it collapses in old age, coming closer to that of the poor. Three adult men for two women, on the average, lived under the roof of rich Florentines (figure 8.2).

These contrasts can be found in attenuated form on the broader scale of the population of all Tuscany[7] (where, to be sure, the category of superior wealth includes few who are not Florentine patricians and, consequently, reproduces their demographic characteristics). We might suppose that migration increased the population of Florence as well as the natural movement of the population. Yet inward migration had a much greater influence on the number and the structure of the poor and the working population of Florence than on that of the businessmen, bankers, merchants, manufacturers, and landowners who made up the greater part

6. Herlihy and Klapisch-Zuber, *Les Toscans*, 384–85.
7. Ibid., 328, 343.

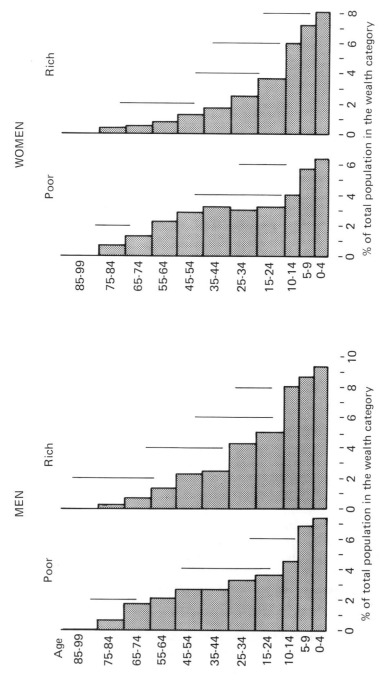

Figure 8.1 Ages among the Poor and the Rich in Florence (1427)

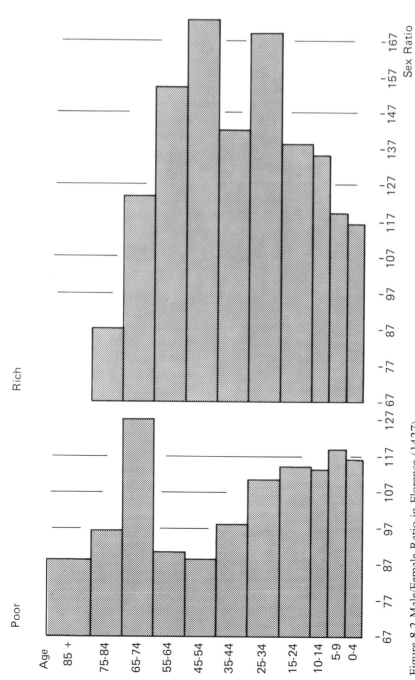

Figure 8.2 Male/Female Ratio in Florence (1427)

of the upper category. The population of the rich was much more closed than that of the destitute. It is probable that the sudden increase in the poorest females 40–60 years of age signals an afflux of women, widows in particular, newly arrived from the countryside to seek work or succor in the city.[8] In the three wealth categories immediately above the lowest (1–100 *fiorini*), adult or elderly women are even better represented than among women living in absolute poverty. And these same wealth categories include a much higher proportion of widows living alone than any other class—women who declare to the tax authorities the income from some small field, obviously insufficient to live on. We might suspect that many retired to the city to make ends meet.

Matrimonial status, in fact, introduces another cause of social discrimination in the female population. This can be evaluated on the basis of the average age at marriage, which we can calculate by looking at the percentage of unmarried people.[9] For the population of Florence in 1427 as a whole, the average age at marriage is near 18 for women and 30 for men. But among the rich, who had every interest in keeping account of the changes that occurred in their households and who noted carefully the departures of their married daughters, this age falls to 17.6 years for women.[10] Figure 8.3, which represents the percentages of unmarried women and widows according to their age, does in fact show poor girls who marry lagging slightly behind rich girls: at 20 years of age 91 percent of the girls of the upper classes who are mentioned in the books of the *catasto,* which registered laypeople, have found a husband, as against 87 percent of the poor girls. The difference is small. It does not contradict the existence of a Florentine model of marriage according to which girls married between 15 and 20 years of age. Material difficulties merely delayed the moment at which a poor girl could marry.

More curious is the fact that after 25 years of age the number of unmarried daughters of the lower classes reaches a remarkably low level (about 3 percent, a percentage we can consider that of definitive old maids, in spite of the random variations involved in population data taken from a census). The percentage of girls of good family who remained unmarried, on the other hand, stays at a higher level—around 10 percent—in the various age categories. Marriage or remarriage thus absorbed almost the entire group of girls belonging to the least privileged classes (albeit more slowly), while the numbers of unmarried women of the ruling class, although singularly reduced, continue to include three to four times more

8. The chronicler Giovanni Cavalcanti describes how the region of the Casentino was emptied of its women between 1430 and 1439. The uncertainty of conditions there and plague pushed them to Florence, where they were "welcomed with open arms and paternally" (*Istorie fiorentine*, ed. G. Di Pino, Milan, 1944, 397).

9. Herlihy and Klapisch-Zuber, *Les Toscans,* 399–400.

10. The ages at first marriage noted in the *ricordanze* confirm this figure for the period 1400–1469, with an average of 17.85 years of age.

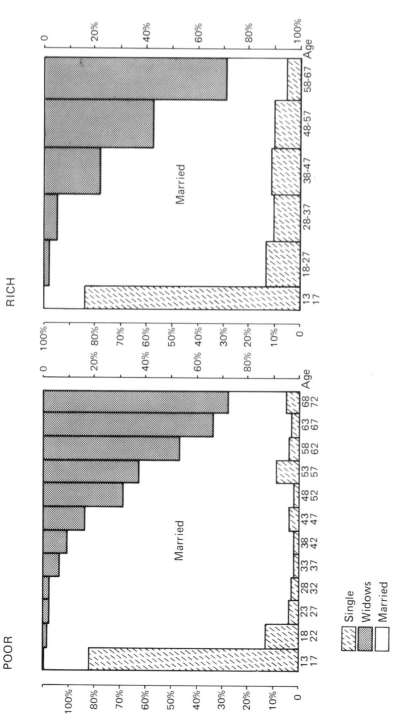

Figure 8.3 Percentages of Unmarried, Married, and Widowed Women by Age, Poor and Rich, in Florence (1427)

old maids up to and beyond 50 years of age. Without entering further here into the particularities of marriage and widowhood in the upper levels of Florentine society,[11] I would like to stress how difficult it was for rich Florentines to marry or remarry their daughters after 20 years of age, as is evident in figure 8.3. The full dimensions of the problem of marriage affecting this social class become clearer if we add to the women who remained at home husbandless the many nuns who had entered a convent—during childhood if their father so decided, or later, if necessity or vocation pushed them to it.[12] Cloistered nuns came for the most part from the "best families" of the city—to those very families included in the category of superior wealth. Thus the convent failed to offer a solution perfectly adapted to girls of all social levels, since it could not absorb all women reduced to celibacy.

On the other hand, only a small minority of adult unmarried women from the lower echelons of society (relatively, if not absolutely speaking) faced a life of solitude in Florence. The greater part of the troop of "women alone" was not recruited from among the unmarried; much more common, as could be guessed, were mature women who lived alone, widows or abandoned wives, bereft of family support, and who often had children to feed. In these conditions it seems doubtful that domestic service could have played the role I presented as a supposition at the beginning of this essay. Do the *ricordanze* confirm that the recruitment of women servants more often remedied the distress of widows or married women than of husbandless girls?

The Florentine who records the entry into his service of a new servant woman specifically notes her civil status in only very few cases. Very exceptionally he indicates the presence of a husband or a father at the drawing up of the agreement. One time out of six, however, the woman's name[13] permits us to say whether she was unmarried, married, or widowed. But in 60 percent of the cases the servant is designated by her given name alone, perhaps followed by the place she came from. How can we judge her matrimonial status? One index is the term of respect, *monna,* generally reserved to wives, widows, or at least to middle-aged women. Unmarried girls, whose name is given followed by their father's name, are never qualified as *monna* in the fifteenth century. The relative ceremoniousness in citing the name of a servant thus allows us to classify the 111 women without a male guarantor into two groups—those presumed unmarried

11. Herlihy and Klapisch-Zuber, *Les Toscans*, 414–18, 578–80.
12. R. C. Trexler, "Le célibat à la fin du Moyen-Age: Les religieuses de Florence," *Annales, E.S.C.* 27, no. 6 (1972): 1329–50; Herlihy and Klapisch-Zuber, *Les Toscans*, 157, 402; Kirshner and Molho, "The Dowry Fund," 424–28.
13. A woman in Tuscany was designated by her given name followed by that of her husband, living or dead, or that of her own father if she was still unmarried. The relation to the man whose name follows her own is not always specified by such qualifiers as "daughter of . . . ," "wife of . . . ," or "widow of . . ."

and those presumed married or widowed. This gives us 52 unmarried women and 80 married or widowed women, for a ratio of close to 2 to 3. It is interesting to note that the ratio of the unmarried and the widowed among the highest wealth class is exactly the same in 1427.[14] This would seem to support the hypothesis that domestic service drew from the stock of available women without particular preference for the unmarried.

The indications of place of origin that accompany the name of the servant women we presume to have been unmarried (in 44 percent of the cases) and that of widows or married women (56 percent) further clarify this recruitment of domestic help. Percentages in both categories demonstrate the greater mobility of older women. Close to 15 percent of women of this age group were born outside of the territory of Florence, and more than half (52.5 percent) were born in the "subject" territories—this is, those more recently acquired by Florence (41.5 percent and 11 percent respectively).[15] This recruitment over a widespread area is not found among the servants we presume to have been unmarried, 56.4 percent of which, as we have seen, were probably Florentine in origin. Fewer than one-third of the latter came from the *contado* or the subject cities, and 12.7 percent were foreigners (nearly all former slaves). In fact, the women who came from the lands farthest from Florence ("subject" territories and foreign lands) are particularly numerous among the group of servants qualified as *monna;* by contrast, girls placed into service are typically of more local origin. In both groups, about 60 percent of the servants for whom a place of origin is noted came from rural areas near the city. Domestic service, therefore, was not limited to absorbing the surplus of unmarried women in Florence alone; it recruited widely outside the unmarried class and outside Florence.

Let me add that the conditions of the agreement drawn up between the master and the servant or her guardians show that ancillary celibacy was often seen as a provisional state and domestic service as offering a way to marriage. In ten contracts or acts concerning servant women whom I presume to have been unmarried (they are more numerous after 1450), the stipulations include the eventual or immediate dowering of the girl by her employer. The servant girls engaged under such conditions are often children of 8 or 9 years of age,[16] whose wages earned in ten years or so of service were to be paid to them when the contract ran out—that

14. Or 676 unmarried women for 433 widows (a ratio of 1.56, as opposed to 1.54 among servant women).

15. A degree of uncertainty is introduced by the 27 women presumed to be married or widowed for whom provenance and residence are not given; there are also 31 women presumed unmarried whose place of origin is unknown. The chances are good, however, that they were Florentines or had come from country areas close to the city.

16. More than one-third of the female servants for whom their masters give an age in the *catasto* of 1427 are 8–17 years old, as opposed to 41.5 percent of the male servants (Herlihy and Klapisch-Zuber, *Les Toscans*, 331).

is, when the girl married. The employer was guarantor to the virtue of his child-maid, he was truly responsible for her upbringing, and he was the guardian of her savings as well. She would not get her wages until her employer, like a true father, judged that the time had come for her to marry and that a good match was available.[17] Far from prolonging their unmarried state endlessly by creating conditions that made it impossible to marry, the time spent in domestic service brought poor girls the hope of finding an appropriate husband.

This ancillary celibacy that ended at the normal marriage age of 17 or 18 years of age attached the servant girl to her master longer than any other form of agreement. Out of 100 women servants whose real term of service can be known from the *ricordanze,* we know that exactly 60 remained only one year or even less in their employer's house, 19 of them leaving within the month. There are only seven loyal-hearted domestics who stay in the same house more than five years. A longer term of service, on the other hand, is particularly characteristic of the servant girls presumed unmarried. More than one-half of them remain over one year, as against one-third of the older women. This speaks to the more episodic nature of the employment of women who were not tied to their employer by the constraints of a dowry or by the semiservitude that marked the fate of former slave women, who were never totally freed. Leaving one's employer, furthermore, was often the only way that a servant could get the pay owed her: the master was then obliged to close her account. Wage earners were incapable of conceiving of their pay as something due them periodically and regularly—and the employers were apt to put off payment as long as possible[18]—which meant that wages were paid in fits and starts, according to the servant's needs. These characteristics of medieval wage earners also explain why servant women chose to force the payment of back wages with a precipitous departure.

When widows (or women who left their families for a while) entered the service of a middle-class Florentine, they seemed to be responding to a momentary problem or a pressing necessity: a debt or the rent to pay, famine, the need of a pair of shoes or a new petticoat, the urgent need to pay a nurse. Two times out of three they returned home or looked for a better place when they had earned the needed amount. Domestic service thus permitted a good number of women either to gather a little nest egg or to cope with a momentarily difficult situation. But it also assured some old women, usually hired without wages for their upkeep alone, a sort of

17. Marriages sponsored by the master, often taking place in his house, with total or partial dowering by him: 1414, 1428, 1470, 1502, 1511; hiring contracts that specify dowering at the end of the service: 1454, 1465, 1509, 1530. On the dowry of servant girls and poor girls see Herlihy and Klapisch-Zuber, *Les Toscans,* 322, 331, 416.

18. These characteristics of salaried workers are discussed in G. Pinto, "Personale, balie e salariati dell'Ospedale di San Gallo," *Ricerche Storiche* 2 (1974): 124.

retirement and the assurance that they need not end their days miserably in the street or in the hospital. One instance of this is a certain monna Margherita who, on her way to serve a priest in the back country, stopped to rest, one fine day in 1446, before the house of Manno Petrucci. Without further ado, we find her declaring before witnesses that she "wants to live and die in our house, without pay; I, Manno Petrucci, will nourish her as it pleases me, without owing her anything for clothing, shoes, or stockings. The other servant in the house will leave."[19] This was charity that quickly turned sour: the master soon accused the old woman of stealing, and Monna Margherita set off again for the hills.

The scarcity of manual workers for hire in the fifteenth century allowed these women to take their leave without waiting for their master to dismiss them or for their contract to run out (in the rare cases in which a term is specified.[20] To keep his servant, a master sometimes dangled the promise of something extra before her eyes if she would stay a full year: a blouse, occasionally a wimple, or a pair of shoes.[21] Usually, however, the master only covered expenses for board and lodging over and above a servant's wages, but he often advanced money to her as her needs arose, devoting whole pages of his account books to transactions with women who remained in his service. The freedom of movement of servant women, who were always sure of being able to find work, can also be seen in the frequency of their absences, a few days at a time, to care for a sick relative, help with a childbirth, or go home to lend a hand with the harvest.[22] At this point, the master floundered among complicated calculations to deduct the lost time from their pay. He was also quick to deduct for periods during which they were immobilized because of sickness—even for a work accident in his own service[23]—and he often dispatched them at the first signs of failing health to have their illness treated or to end their days in

19. ASF, *Strozziane* 2d ser., 17, fol. 60v (*ricordanze* di Manno di Cambio Petrucci).

20. Only one of the contracts I have seen specifies a fifteen-day notice if the servant woman wants to leave (ASF *Conventi sopppressi*, San Piero a Monticelli 153, fol. 8, 20 July 1440, *ricordanze* d'Uguccione di Mico Capponi). The contract was generally more flexible. Thus the notary Piero Bonaccorsi reaches an agreement with a woman from Pontormo, and he "engages her for the time that it will be convenient to me and to her, so that every year, if we no longer please one another, any day may be considered as the first of the year" (ASF, *Acquisti e doni*, 21, fol. 98v, 10 January 1529).

21. See for example ASF, *Strozz.* 2d ser., 15, fol. 43 (16 January 1431): the servant thus bated by Cambio di Tano Petrucci did in fact remain sixteen months.

22. Thus a servant woman of Bernardo Strozzi took care of women in childbirth six times (ASF, *Strozz.* 3d ser., 347, fol. 113, 1430 31).

23. Out of the four years and five months of salary that he owed one servant woman, Bernardo Strozzi deducted six months' wages "because she fell sick and broke her arm" (11 January 1407). The poor woman broke an arm again 15 May 1409, and her master paid one *fiorino* for the doctor and for medication. She fell sick in October 1415 and was again cared for, and twelve days later she was buried at the expense of her master—who in any event owed her an impressive sum in back wages (ASF, *Strozz.* 3d ser., 346, fols. 15v, 16, 22v).

the hospital.[24] That real affective ties occasionally existed between masters and servants—bequests in wills on both sides give evidence of this—does not belie the episodic and temporary nature of female domestic employment.

The amount of the wages themselves was fixed, in theory, by the communal statutes, which were revised in 1415.[25] In practice, however, the spread was greater than the statutes provide for. Servant women in the fifteenth century earned an average of 8.5 *fiorini* a year, a wage that approaches the 9 *fiorini* that the statutes consented to the *famula foemina* or the 10 *fiorini* granted to the *cameraria*. But nearly one half (46.4 percent) of the wages stipulated in our contracts are situated between 5 and 8 *fiorini*, and only 27.5 percent are for sums greater than the 9 *fiorini* admitted as the norm. Thus in her negotiations with her employer the servant woman was not necessarily the winner. The situation of her male colleagues, furthermore, was no better. Male servants were scarce among Florentine families before the end of the fifteenth century, and I have little information (eighteen cases) on their annual salaries, expressed in *fiorini*. Their remuneration, fixed at 12 *fiorini* a year by the statutes of 1415, was 10 *fiorini*, on the average. Half of the male servants were paid less than this sum, and the pay was never higher than 12 *fiorini*.[26]

The stability of these pay scales before 1480 is even more remarkable. The annual wages for servant women comes up to their mean maximum level in the decade 1410–20 (9.4 *fiorini*), becomes stable until about 1440 just under this level, then decreases extremely slowly until about 1475, only to drop much more quickly after 1485 and particularly after 1500. As the price in *fiorini* of a *staio* of wheat rose noticeably in Florence after 1470,[27] the shift of the average wages of the servant woman from 8.5 *fiorini* per year in the decade 1450–59 to 8.33 *fiorini* in 1470–79, then to 7 *fiorini* in 1490–99, implies a real lowering of purchasing power.

The conditions of female domestic service seem therefore to have grown harsher after 1480–90, and, at first sight, we might be tempted to relate the stages of this decline to population change. Sparse in the first third of the century and stable in the second, the population of Florence grew rapidly after 1470. Even wet nurses—a woman's job if there ever was one—saw a similar deterioration in their status at the beginning of the sixteenth century.[28] But the arrival on the labor market of more numerous

24. Bartolomeo Sassetti in 1473 (ASF, *Strozz.* 5th ser., 1751, fol 162) and Bartolomeo Salvetti in 1485 (ASF, *Manoscritti*, 96, fol. 14v) quickly dispatch their sick servants to the hospital. Was this solicitude? Discharge of responsibilities? Abandonment? Three servant women of Marco Strozzi (ASF *Strozz.* 4th ser., 353, fol. 9v, 1509) and Francesco Gaddi (Biblioteca Laurenziana, *Acquisti* 213, fol. 95, 1496, a plague year) died in the hospital.

25. *Statuta populi e communis Florentiae* . . . (1415) (Fribourg, 1778–81), 2:267–68.

26. The salaries paid by the hospital of San Gallo to its male workers between 1396 and 1415 ranged from 4.5 *fiorini* to 12 *fiorini* a year (see Pinto, "Personale" 121, table 1).

27. R. A. Goldthwaite, "I prezzi del grano a Firenze dal XIV al XVI secolo," *Quaderni storici* 10 (1975): 11.

28. See chapter 7 above, "Blood Parents and Milk Parents."

female generations after 1490 does not account for the whole phenomenon. For the women who sought employment now had to deal with more aggressive male competition. Domestic service, typically a women's activity during the whole period of demographic penury, made more and more room for male servants after 1490–1500. Of the data on men gathered from the years 1370–1510, 39 percent of the cases concern the last period (1480–1500), as against 14 percent for that period in the data on servant women. The search for employment certainly made a number of men who would otherwise have been absorbed into the flourishing Florentine industries turn toward this little-respected type of work. The imbalance in the ratio of men to women, even more accentuated in 1480 than in 1427,[29] and the rise in the female marriage age from the end of the century,[30] are two beacons that signal women's difficulties in finding a place in the Florentine labor market.[31] Around 1500, female employment seems to be paying for the new demographic growth, as seen in worsening terms of employment and in the hiring of proportionally fewer women.

In the fifteenth century, domestic service does not seem to have depended on either temporary or definitive female celibacy, to some extent restricted to the lower strata of society. The same can no longer be said after the turn of the century, when many girls were forced into a preconjugal purgatory as harsh as before the great demographic upswing in the beginning of the fourteenth century. To judge by the number of Florentine servant girls toward the middle of the sixteenth century, the wait for a husband would henceforth take place under the roof of a master. Domestic service and celibacy were to work hand in hand, whereas a century or a century and a half earlier they had evolved relatively autonomously.

29. This ratio shifts in Florence from 118.9 in 1427 to 123.8 in 1458 and to 126.7 in 1480 (Herlihy and Klapisch-Zuber, *Les Toscans*, 341).

30. Ibid., 207. Age estimated on the basis of the percentages of the unmarried in the Florentine population as a whole shifts from 17.6 percent (1427) to 19.5 percent (1458) and to 20.8 percent (1480) among women. For men it shifts in the same period from 30.3 percent to 30.5 percent and then to 31.4 percent.

31. In 1552, 16.7 percent of the Florentine population was composed of servants, of whom 70 percent were women. At that later date 42 percent of households employed at least one servant (ibid., 520).

# 9

## Zacharias, or the Ousted Father: Nuptial Rites in Tuscany between Giotto and the Council of Trent

Between 1300 and 1500, one iconographic theme—the Marriage of the Virgin, or *Sposalizio*—was surprisingly popular in central and northern Italian art. It was of course not alone in presenting an image of marriage. Millard Meiss has demonstrated the appearance in Tuscan painting of the fourteenth century of several quite new themes centering on the family, the couple, and the child.[1] Should the *Sposalizio* be considered, then, simply as one example of a new sensitivity to family and domestic life among the Italian middle classes?[2] The insistent blossoming of this theme on the walls of the churches of Tuscany—and subsequently those of Umbria and other parts of Italy—also suggests that the Church found it an instrument for the edification of the faithful. But to what ends? The object of this study is to examine what was original in the iconography of the *Sposalizio*

Originally published as "Zacharie ou le père évincé: Les rituels nuptiaux toscans entre Giotto et le Concile de Trente," *Annales, E.S.C.* 34 no. 6 (1979): 1216–43. This study is the most recent offshoot of those that the *Annales* devoted to rituals of kinship in 1978 (pp. 623–76). The various topics treated were put together during a seminar held in 1975–76 on this subject, and the papers were submitted to the discussion of American colleagues on the occasion of a series of lectures in January 1979. Special thanks for suggestions and criticisms go to M. Becker, G. Brucker, S. Chojnacki, S. Cohn, R. Goldthwaite, D. Herlihy, R. Lopez, E. Muir, R.Starn, and R. C. Trexler.

1. M. Meiss, *Painting in Florence and Siena after the Black Death. The Arts, Religion and Society in the Mid-Fourteenth Century* (1951, Harper Torchbook, 1964), 60–61, 109–17.

2. Ibid., 61.

by comparing its component elements with contemporary practice in rituals of engagement and marriage. I shall use the *Sposalizio* to reveal the evolution of nuptial rites—already thoroughly analyzed with respect to other regions—and the progressive appropriation of those rites by the Church.[3] The present study is thus frankly historical in point of view: it aims to clear the way for a thoroughgoing study of the place of ritual in Tuscan society.

Before the Council of Trent, the Church's efforts to gain control over the ceremonies accompanying marriage were applied to widely different situations in western Europe. To a great extent, rituals of alliance had evolved autonomously in the various parts of Europe since the later Roman Empire, even though borrowings and harmonizations had at times seemed to bring similarity to rites observed in provinces quite far apart from one another. From the fourth century, however, *matrimonium justum*, in the western empire, was primarily based on the couple's intention to wed. Nuptial rites and customs were supposed to demonstrate this intention, although the validity of the marriage was not tied to particular forms. The Church went further in this direction and soon permitted its flock to observe the "custom of the place," insisting only that both spouses must express consent freely. A couple's expression of consent thus became the foundation of Christian marriage, and this choice tended to force into the background other criteria of "just marriage," such as the validation of the union by recognition of conjugal cohabitation alone, or the conclusion of an alliance founded in law and guaranteed by written acts, gifts, and donations.[4]

One of the three ways of expressing an intent to marry thus became privileged as time went on, although obligatory forms were not imposed on the gestures, words, or acts involved in the conclusion of an alliance. Until the Council of Trent, the form of matrimonial rituals was typically extremely free in western Christendom. In 866, Pope Nicholas I addressed the Bulgarians, who had already been instructed in the Greco-Byzantine rite, in a declaration that has remained famous. This document clarifies the conception of nuptial rites prevalent in the West—rites that were subject to the "consent of those who contract the ties of marriage and of those who have authority over them." In the West, as opposed to the

3. See the summary given in A. Burguière, "Le rituel du mariage en France: pratiques ecclésiastiques et pratiques populaires (XVIᵉ XVIIIᵉ siècles)," *Annales, E. S .C.* no. 3 (1978): 637–49. J. Bossy, "The Counter-Reformation and the People of Catholic Europe," *Past and Present* 47 (1970): 51–70.

4. L. Beauchet, "Etude historique sur les formes de la célébration du mariage dans l'ancien droit français," *Nouvelle revue historique de droit français et étranger* 6 (1882), 351–93. J. Dauvillier, *Le mariage dans le droit classique de l'Eglise depuis le décret de Gratien (1140) jusqu'à la mort de Clément V (1340)* (Paris, 1933). A. Esmein and R. Génestal, *Le mariage en droit canonique* (Paris, 1929–35). G. Le Bras, *Dictionnaire de théologie catholique* (Paris, 1927), s. v. "mariage," 9:2:2044–335. P. Vaccari, "Il matrimonio canonico, corso di diritto ecclesiastico" (Milan, 1950, mimeographed).

eastern Churches, the absence of the *iura nuptiarum*—for example, if the couple were too poor—did not stigmatize as illegitimate any marriage to which the parties had freely consented.[5]

The clear affirmation of the consent of the spouses "and of those having authority over them" as the principal obligation for the founding and validation of a marriage thus permitted the retention and autonomous development of former popular rituals and of the wedding liturgy in the western provinces of Christendom. To limit our comparison to France and Italy, this autonomy of ritual forms of alliance in respect to the doctrinal positions of the Church allowed these lands, and their various provinces, to give an individual and original stamp to actors, gestures, words, and objects, putting them into a framework and organizing them into a ritual scenario that varied enormously from one region to another.

In France, however, the churches made an effort to establish norms, beginning in the eleventh and particularly in the twelfth centuries, as concern for tighter control developed. Their aim was threefold: to make the parties to the contract aware of the sacramental nature of the bond that was to unite them, to make sure that the projected alliance was not illicit, and to ensure that the consent expressed was freely given.[6] In certain regions there were changes in ritual that corresponded to these aims, or ritual was invested with totally new meanings. The place in which the ceremonies took place was changed, roles were transferred from one participant to another, or the symbolic value explicitly attributed to the gestures, words, or objects involved in the liturgy were modified.[7] In Italy, the Church succeeded in these ends with greater difficulty than in France and at a later date. Might this have been because the ecclesiastical model for marriage (as Georges Duby has defined it for twelfth-century France) remained less clearly defined in Italy and because the clergy there showed less determination to impose it?[8] By the study of the nuptial scenario, of its shifts and its internal substitutions, and by the study of the ideal model presented by the *Sposalizio,* I hope to ascertain the distinctive features of the historical development of ritual in Italy, as compared to France and northern Europe.

5. J. Dauvillier and C. De Clercq, *Le mariage en droit canonique oriental* (Paris, 1936).

6. Esmein and Génestal, *Le mariage en droit canonique,* 1:68ff.

7. K. Ritzer, *Le mariage dans les Eglises chrétiennes du I<sup>er</sup> au XI<sup>e</sup> siècle* (1962; French trans., Paris, 1970). R. Metz, *La consécration des vierges dans l'Eglise romaine* (Paris, 1954), 363–410. J.-P. Moulin and P. Mutembé, *Le rituel du mariage en France du XII<sup>e</sup> au XVI<sup>e</sup> siécle (Paris, 1974)*.

8. G. Duby, *Medieval Marriage: Two Models from Twelfth-Century France* (Baltimore and London, 1978). R. H. Helmholz, *Marriage Litigation in Medieval England* (Cambridge, 1974). P. Toubert, *Les structures du Latium médiéval* (Rome, 1973), 1:743–49.

Wedding Procedure in Florence in the Fourteenth and
Fifteenth Centuries

What sources have we for such an investigation? Historians of marriage
such as Emile Chénon for France[9] or Francesco Brandileone for Italy [10]
have made wide use of normative or proscriptive legal documents and of
notarial documents. Brandileone, however, to his credit, has also analyzed
a lengthy description of the weddings of the Roman aristocracy written
not long after 1500 by a humanist, Marco Antonio Altieri. This fascinating
and highly important text[11] is perhaps the first attempt on the part of a
European at systematic reflection concerning the rituals of alliance, marriage, and the weddings of his contemporaries and immediate ancestors.
Altieri was not a member of the clergy, and his vision of Roman matrimonial rites was permeated by two cultures—Christianity and classical
antiquity—which led him to more than one "transcultural" interpretation.
Thus his description of nuptial customs of the fifteenth century is just as
valuable for the mass of information he gives us as for the symbolic reelaboration to which he subjects the elements of ritual that he analyzes.
To be sure, we can discern a normative or pedagogical tone underlying
his discourse: Altieri makes no secret of hoping to instruct the other
characters in his dialogue on the nature of the aristocratic weddings of
yesteryear, a model corrupted after 1500 by the spirit of money-grubbing.
But it is from a lay point of view that he condemns many of the civil
customs of his times. His criticisms thus escape the limitations of ecclesiastical denunciations of popular "superstitions," while his description of
nuptial rituals goes far beyond the strictly liturgical setting of diocesan
rituals.

Texts of civil origin—generally linked to the sumptuary legislation drawn
up by Italian communes on the uses and abuses of times of rejoicing[12]—
escape such reproaches as well. The field of inquiry becomes considerably
wider when documentation of juridical origin can be compared, if not to
documents revealing practice (about which little is as yet known for Italy),
at least to the many reports written (some succinctly, some less so) by the
actors in the nuptial drama themselves—both the marriers and the mar-

9. E. Chénon, "Recherches historiques sur quelques rites nuptiaux." *Nouvelle revue
historique de droit français et étranger* 16 (1912): 573–660.
10. F. Brandileone, *Saggi sulla storia della celebrazione del matrimonio in Italia* (Bologna,
1906).
11. M. A. Altieri, *Li nuptiali*, ed. E. Narducci (Rome, 1873). See below, chapter 11,
"An Ethnology of Marriage."
12. P. Toubert, "Les statuts communaux et l'histoire des campagnes lombardes au XIVe
s.," in *Mélanges d'archéologie et d'histoire* (1960), 468ff. On Florence, see R. Caggese, ed.,
*Statuti della Repubblica fiorentina* (Florence, 1910–21); *Statuta populi et communis Florentia*
(1415) (Fribourg, 1778–81).

rying. We can find such texts in great abundance in the *ricordanze* or *ricordi* that so many Florentines kept between 1300 and 1550.[13] This Florentine corpus[14] underlies the present study, but the same investigation could certainly be carried out on the basis of analogous documents from other Italian cities.

When our "merchant writers" report on the marriages of those close to them and note the expenses incurred in the festivities, they give an excellent idea of how those ceremonies were linked together and what were their most important moments. They show us the actors in these festivities and the gestures expected of them, the gifts and objects that exchanged hands, and certain of the words the actors had to pronounce to turn the projected marriage into a reality. The domestic chroniclers undeniably had a sense of the coherence of the marriage ritual and of the necessarily complementary nature of its various episodes.[15] Thus the system that the phases of this ritual went to make up comes to their pen as a whole; they try to summarize it on one page, even if its various elements were scattered through a certain lapse of time, so that reports of alliance and marriage are generally lumped together in the notations that these Florentines made doggedly, day after day. To be sure, their reports all too often condensed and stereotyped;[16] furthermore, they describe the customs observed by only a very limited social circle—the middle echelons of the bourgeoisie and the families of the merchant oligarchy or the city aristocracy. In spite of these reservations, we can consider the information they bring us as extremely revealing of the distinctive characteristics of marriage in Italy (for Tuscany underwent profound Lombard influences), and we can compare them with ceremonies in France that had long been guided by the Church.

Two traits in particular show what we might call the archaic quality of traditional rituals in Italy, which remained under the influence of the Roman and the Lombard heritage and were by and large insensitive to Church action.

13. P. J. Jones, "Florentine Families and Florentine Diaries in the Fourteenth Century," *Papers of the British School at Rome* 24 (1956), 183–205. C. Bec, *Les marchands écrivains à Florence, 1375–1434* (Paris and The Hague, 1967).

14. Scrutiny of about 120 unpublished family journals, conserved in the Archivio di Stato of Florence and in the Biblioteca Nazionale Centrale of Florence, plus thirty or so published journals (for a list see D. Herlihy and C. Klapisch-Zuber, *Les Toscans et leurs familles: Une étude du catasto florentin de 1427* [Paris, 1978], 190, n. 3 ) gave a sampling of about 140 marriages.

15. See J. Le Goff's remarks in "Le rituel symbolique de la vassalité" republished in his *Pour un autre Moyen Age* (Paris, 1977), 348–420, esp. p. 365 (Trans. by Arthur Goldhammer as *Work, Time, and Cultures in the Middle Ages* [Chicago, 1980] ).

16. Examples are published in: J. Del Badia, "Fidanzamento e matrimonio nel sec. XV," *Misellanea fiorentina di erudizione* 1 (1886); 189–92. G. Biagi, *Due corredi nuziali fiorentini, 1320 e 1493* (Florence, 1899). Descriptions of the proceedings of weddings in Italy can be found in: N. Tamassia, *La famiglia italiana nei sec. XV e XVI* (Milan, 1911), 188–93; G. Pampaloni, "Le nozze," in *Vita privata a Firenze nei sec. XIV e XV* (Florence, 1966), 31–52; D. Herlihy and C. Klapisch-Zuber, *Les Toscans,* 588–94.

In the first place, the group of ceremonies that made up the nuptial ritual was organized around several focal points, and it is difficult initially to say which was dominant.

The structure of the nuptial scenario might be compared to a triptych. Its predella would be the initial negotiations and the preliminary agreement between the two parties who form the subject of the ensemble. These first negotiations—well described by Altieri[17] and by many of the Florentine *ricordanze*—are initiated by a *sensale*, a marriage broker specializing in such work, or by some relatively disinterested kind soul, who comes to the family to propose a profitable match. Negotiations continue through the efforts of one or several intermediaries: *mezzani*, friends of the family, and buffers to their contrasting interests. They culminate in a first meeting between the parties—that is, between the parents of the future spouses, accompanied by three or four of their close kin. Together they seal the alliance (*fermare il parentado*). In the fifteenth century the conditions of the agreement are noted in writing, and this *scritta*, a private act, is kept by the accredited intermediaries.[18] Indeed, the agreement very often remained confidential; many domestic chroniclers stress that the two parties had promised not to reveal it before a certain lapse of time, either because the betrothed couple were still too young or because they had to wait for a dispensation to marry, for the preparation of the dowry agreement, and so forth. Symbolic gestures sanction the agreement. In Rome, where the ceremony is called the *abboccamento*,[19] much importance is given to a kiss on the mouth exchanged by the partners in the agreement, who undoubtedly exchange many a handclasp as well. Florentines put more emphasis on the immemorial gesture of the handclasp, the customary sanction of the contract, in their *impalmamento* or *toccamano*.[20] A father will say in his journal that he has *impalmato* his daughter. After this agreement, the groom-to-be goes in all haste to the house of this betrothed, to whom he usually brings a present—rings or jewels—and whose family customarily treat him to a good dinner.

The first panel of the triptych consists in a solemn and public meeting between the parties, accompanied by the greatest possible number of their kin and friends. Only the male members of the families to be allied or already related appear. Even the bride-to-be is not invited to this masculine festivity, and it is the person who "has authority" over her who promises her future husband to give her as a bride and promises to obtain her

17. Altieri, *Li nuptiali*, 50–51.

18. Around 1500, Florentines carefully recopied some of these in their *ricordanze*. See one example from 1509 published in D. Fachard: *Biagio Buonaccorsi, sa vie, son temps, son œuvre* (Bologna, 1976), Appendix.

19. Altieri, *Li nuptiali*, 51.

20. E. Westermarck, *History of Human Marriage* (London, 1891), vol. 4, chap. 24, pp. 183–86. R. Corso, *Patti d'amore e pegni di promessa* (Santa Maria Capua Vetere, 1924); R. Corso, "Gli sponsali popolari," *Revue des études ethnographiques et sociologiques* 1 (1908): 487–99.

consent. As for the future groom, he promises to take her as wife within the time period and according to the conditions agreed upon, and, in Rome, another *baso de bocca* (kiss on the mouth) ritually expresses the validity of the agreement, as publicly proclaimed.[21] This time, however, a notary has written the *instrumento delli futuri sponsalitii*, as Altieri calls it, in which the dowry and the other financial conditions of the marriage are noted.[22] Guarantors and arbiters are chosen, whose role will be to specify the terms of the contract and to supervise its execution—the payments of the dowry, in particular, but they also set the dates of the festivities to follow. This sequence of events, which bears various names—in Florence, the *giure* in general parlance, or *giuramento grande, sponsalia,* or *sponsalitium* in notarial language; *fidanze* in Rome—can be found in all of central and northern Italy. It constitutes the act of alliance par excellence, in which the exchanges involved—of a woman and of goods—are spelled out and guaranteed.

This engagement was highly binding and could not be broken without grave consequences. We can see in it a variant of the ancient Germanic *bewedding*.[23] Florentines kept these *sponsalia* strictly contractual, and the woman, the object of their negotiation, does not appear at them. Thus the *giure* of the better Florentine families only vaguely resemble the more intimate ceremony of *fiançailles* that the Church tried to substitute for it in certain regions of France.[24] In Florence, where the promised bride-to-be (who in some of the older texts is not even mentioned by name among all the daughters of the family)[25] was absent, no real banns were proclaimed. Antoninus, archbishop of Florence and subsequently canonized (for Florentines, Sant' Antonino), emphasizes the role that public *sponsalia* played among the city's *grandi*, taking the place of banns in due form "in certain places where they are celebrated publicly long before the marriage."[26] It was therefore the public character of the alliance agreement

21. Altieri, *Li nuptiali*, 51.
22. This is the term that Tuscan notaries use to designate the notarial act drawn up at the *giure*.
23. See the controversy on the place of this engagement in medieval law in E. Friedberg, *Ehe und Eheschliessung im deutschen Mittelalter* (Berlin, 1864); E. Friedberg, *Das Recht der Eheschliessung in seiner geschichtlichen Entwicklung* (Leipzig, 1865); R. Sohn, *Das Recht der Eheschliessung aus dem deutschen und kanonischen Recht geschichtlich entwickelt* (Weimar, 1875); R. Sohn, *Trauung und Verlobung; Eine Entgegnung auf Friedbergs Verlobung und Trauung* (Weimar, 1876).
24. A. Burguière, "Le rituel du mariage," 645; K. Ritzer, *Le mariage dans les Eglises chrétiennes*, 373–402. See the ritual for engagement from the second half of the thirteenth century published in Molin and Mutembé, *Le rituel du mariage en France*, 299, Ordo XI.
25. Even Antonius, citing Hostiensis, admits this procedure in the *sponsalia*.. The choice in this case falls to the father, who must then propose one of his daughters, but who is freed of his promise if she is refused (*Summa*, 3:1:18, Venice edition, 1582, fol. 18).
26. Ibid., 3:1:16, fols. 16v and 17r. The dispensation of banns was common "cum magnatibus quia eorum matrimonia cum magna deliberatione solent tractari per amicos" (among magnates because their matrimonies are usually contracted through friends with

that, in theory, permitted the contracting parties to raise any objections to a possibly illicit union well before the marriage ceremony.[27] But at this stage of the alliance procedure, any move to question it without "good reason" ran an excellent risk of setting off a civil war (in the fourteenth century) or a long feud between offended families (in the fifteenth). The waiting period usually observed between the *impalmamento,* the first direct but not public agreement, and the solemn *giure* was generally much too short to permit any serious outside investigation. The application of the Lateran IV rules on the impediments to marriage necessarily remained rather vague under such conditions. It was above all their own knowledge of genealogy that helped Florentines to avoid errors that would threaten collective peace or offend the honor of the engaged families.

The setting of the second panel of our altarpiece is the house of the girl. Her kin and her family's allies, men and women, are gathered there, invited by her father, her brother, or her guardian, who has also sent for a notary. The groom, his kin, and his friends are also present. The notary then poses the questions prescribed by the Church in order to elicit the express acquiescence of the newlyweds to the union negotiated by their families. After this, he takes the right hand of the woman and draws it toward the husband, who places the nuptial ring on her finger. The notary sets down this whole sequence of events in the *instrumentum matrimonii.*[28] Often, according to Altieri,[29] gifts brought by the husband and his retinue were then offered to his family-in-law, and a supper or a feast offered by the family of the bride followed. In Florence this ceremony was generally called the "ring day" from the symbolic object, solemnly given and received, that most obviously strikes the imagination. The notaries and canonists called it *matrimonium,* but the words *sponsalia, sposalizio, despon-*

---

great deliberation). The oldest synodal constitutions of Fiesole (1306) or Florence (1310 and 1327) intimate that priests were obliged to announce the coming marriage only once, to permit eventual opposition to be heard (R. C. Trexler, *Synodal Law in Florence and Fiesole, 1306–1518* [Vatican City, 1971], 68–69). On the other hand, the synodal statutes of 1517 were to state firmly that banns must be proclaimed by the parish priest or no notary could celebrate the *sponsali de praesenti* (*Sacrorum Conciliorum nova et Amplissima Collectio,* ed. Mansi [Florence and Venice, 1758–98], 35, col. 248).

27. One example of a rupture between the *giure* and the *annello:* "per ligiptime e buone chagioni e chon bolla di Chorte di Roma" (for legitimate and good reasons and with a bull from the Court of Rome), dated 1449, in the *ricordanze* of Uguccione Capponi, Archivio di Stato, Florence (henceforth abbreviated ASF), *Conventi soppressi,* S. Piero a Monticelli, 153, fol. 12v.

28. These are numerous in the notarial registers: see S. K. Cohn, *The Laboring Classes in Renaissance Florence* (New York: Academic Press, 1980). Cohn has drawn up two samples, one for the fourteenth century, containing 523 *acta matrimonii,* the other for the period 1450–1530, containing 2,244 acts. F. Brandileone, *Saggi,* 213–16, publishes a Florentine notarial formulary of the fifteenth century and, p. 476, the text of Rainerius of Perugia on these marriage procedures.

29. Altieri, *Li nuptiali,* 51. See the regulations concerning festivities and gifts in Florence in the *Statuta* of 1415, 3:366–69. On gifts, see chapter 10 below, "The Griselda Complex."

*satio,* all of which more frequently designate the *giure* in the fourteenth century,[30] were all commonly applied in the fifteenth to the ceremony of the exchange of consent and the *anellamento.*[31] These marriage ceremonies were also called the *arraglia* in Rome, a term in which Altieri discerns, somewhat tortuously, the old meaning of *arra sponsalicia,* a down payment on the marriage, and which he attributes, with some embarrassment, to the dowry itself as "a pledge for the future marriage."[32] In Florence the Latin expression *subarratio per anulum* referred to the same root, and in the Tuscan countryside, well into the fifteenth century, brides were called, after this ceremony, *subarrate, anellate,* or *waidiate*—that is, "pledged."[33]

At the end of this day, the betrothed couple were considered man and wife.[34] But, in order to be *perfetto* (completed), public signs of the celebration of the marriage still had to be given to the entire community, after which the marriage needed to be consummated. The third panel of our triptych is devoted to this "publicizing" ceremony, during which the young bride was transported to the house of her husband, whose kin and friends welcomed her with feasting and festivities that sometimes spread over several days. Traditionally it was at the end of this day of the *nozze* that the union was actually consummated. This sequence of events, among Florentines and Romans alike, reflects the classical characteristics of the rites of passage described by Arnold van Gennep.[35] The bride, in tears, took leave of her parents and went with all solemnity to the home of her husband, led by his friends. She crossed the city in the evening and by the light of torches, crowned and beautifully dressed, riding a white palfrey,

30. Antoninus, *Summa* 3:1:18. This chapter, *De sponsalibus,* still reserves this term for the "promises of future weddings."

31. There is some confusion in the Florentine statutes of 1415, caused by compiling texts of different dates, concerning the meaning given to the term *sponsalia.* A shift in sense is clear in Lapo Niccolini, for example, when he writes in 1402 in his *ricordanze:* "E del decto matrimonio e sponsalitio è charta fatta" (And of the said matrimony and *sponsalitio* there was made a notarized document) (*Il Libro degli affari proprii di casa di Lapo di Giovanni Niccolini de' Sirigatti,* ed. C. Bec [Paris, 1969], 94). Lapo reserves the word *giuramento* for the ceremony that precedes the engagement. Similarly, Recco Capponi says: "Fu roghato delo isponsalizio e voglianno dire dell'anello" (There was notarized an *isponsalizio,* that is, the ring) (ASF, *Conventi soppressi,* San Piero Monticelli 153, fol. 27, 1475). The French word *épousailles* had a similar evolution.

32. Altieri, *Li nuptiali,* 53.

33. F. Brandileone, "Die Subarrhatio cum anulo. Ein Beitrag zur Geschichte des mittelalterlichen Eheschliessungsrechtes," *Deutsche Zeitschrift für Kirchenrecht,* 3d ser., 10 (1901): 311–40. L. Zdekauer, "Usi popolani della Valdelsa," *Miscellanea storica della Valdelsa* 4 (1896): 64–66, 205–12.

34. The Church considered marriage as indissoluble, and Antoninus proves at length in his *Summa* 4:15:7, *De desponsatione Mariae,* fols. 299–301, that Joseph and Mary were united in a *verum matrimonium* since the first perfection of marriage is to consent "in copulam conjugalem, non autem expresse in copulam carnalem," and the second perfection is to raise the child.

35. A. van Gennep, *Manuel de folklore français contemporain,* new ed. (Paris, 1976), 1:2:4:373–648 (on marriage). N. Belmont, "La fonction symbolique du cortège dans les rituels populaires de mariage," *Annales, E. S. C.* 33, no. 3 (1978): 650–55.

and escorted by her spouse's "friends."[36] According to Altieri, Roman couples met on Sunday morning at a church, where they heard mass, at the end of which they were blessed by the priest.[37] In Rome of the fourteenth and fifteenth centuries, then, liturgy had a secure place in this marginal phase of the lengthy nuptial ritual. We shall see that the same is not true of Florence: the bride's route on her way to her new home did not involve a stop at a sanctuary. The *nozze*, then, spelled out for the entire community the agreement and the consent that had united the new couple. They permitted her new kin to honor the bride, and they led the couple to the nuptial bed, thus putting the finishing touches to a union that had been brought about gradually.

To summarize this description of the principal episodes of marriage in Florence, I would like to stress the careful distinction maintained between the contractual phase, which regulated the legal transfer of the woman to another group within society, and the highly ritualized festive phase, which organized her physical transfer to her husband, in full sight of the entire community, and her passage into the class of married and adult women. But, in Tuscany as elsewhere, the *desponsatio* was split in two: certain of its contractual aspects were shifted into the public *giure*, a ceremony that cannot easily be compared to *fiançailles*, at which future spouses would exchange the *verba de futuro* that the Church recommended. The consensual nature of marriage, on the other hand, found expression in the "ring day," which also included the legal formalities of the giving of the bride to her spouse and the payment of the dowry. In the fifteenth century the last phase, that of the *nozze*, or the wedding proper, was something of anticlimax after the previous ceremonies. We can judge this better if we examine the days chosen for these various ceremonies.

To understand the inner workings of the nuptial scenario and to judge the hold that the Church was able to exercise on it at the time, we need to situate these ceremonies in time, to attach them to a specific day of the week. Altieri gives a few chronological references. In Rome at the end of the fourteenth century, the Rome of the forebears whose rites he believed he was describing, Sunday (the day on which the greatest number of people, thus of witnesses, could be expected to attend such solemnities) was always the day of the public transfer that signaled to society as a whole a new union. Altieri also places the blessing of the bride on her way to her new home on that Sunday. But although he indicates the periods of time that separated the first three events in the proceedings (from eight to fifteen days between the *abboccamento* and the *fidanze*, another eight

---

36. S. Bernardino da Siena (Saint Bernardine), *Prediche volgari*, ed. L. Banchi (Siena, 1880–88), 2:359. See the advice to the young wife on how she should act during her wedding, in Francesco da Barberino, *Del reggimento e constume di donne*, ed. G. E. Sansoni (Turin, 1957), 59–61.

37. Altieri, *Li nuptiali*, 66–67.

days between the latter and the *verba de praesenti,* and up to a year before the *nozze*), and although he describes the chronological framework of the immediate preparations for the wedding in great detail, he says very little about the days chosen for the first three ceremonies.[38] Fortunately, the Florentine narrators, whose domestic journals give the various phases in scrupulous detail, make this temporal outline clearer. Their habit of noting, day by day, every single family event, even the least of them, gives their reports a precision in dating that permits us to analyze the stages of the process by which a woman entered into a new family. When they fail to note the day of the week, it can easily be calculated with the help of other chronological indications.

Sunday was chosen the most often for the three principal ceremonies around which the ritual was organized, but Thursday and Wednesday, separately or together, appear to have been almost as attractive. Out of 126 "ring days" mentioned in these Florentine texts between 1300 and 1530, one-fourth took place on a Thursday and another good fourth on Sunday. Florentines thus were divided between the day of *Juno pronuba* and the day of the Lord as to the most appropriate day to lend solemnity to the exchange of consent on which marriage was founded. A more detailed breakdown by periods shows that the tendency to put the "ring day" on a Thursday may have come later. One out of six or seven of the ring-giving ceremonies took place on Thursday before 1430, but nearly one out of three did so after that date. The attraction of Sunday for the *nozze* is undeniable, though not exclusive: between 1300 and 1530, 45 percent of a group of 122 new brides were "led" to their husband on a Sunday. The concentration on Sunday seems, here again, to show a recent increase: before 1430, Wednesday and Thursday account for as great a number of these solemn transfers as does Sunday (40 percent for the two days together, 40 percent for Sunday)[39]; whereas, during the second period, about the time to which Altieri refers when he speaks of the habits of his forebears, Sunday was chosen for the celebration of Florentine weddings in nearly half of all cases.

What conclusions can we draw from this set of facts and this first attempt to draw up statistics? First, the predominance of Sunday as the day for the celebration of certain of the more important nuptial ceremonies probably reveals a desire to give them wide publicity rather than a desire to integrate them into Sunday religious ceremonies. I shall return to this point in examining the participation of the clergy in these rites. Second, might not the flexibility in the place and relative importance of the different phases of the nuptial drama reveal profound changes in the entire ritual? The moment chosen by the new couple to consummate their marriage

---

38. Ibid., 51, 53, 55.

39. See for example Luca da Panzano, who celebrates the *nozze* of his son Antonio Thursday 21 December 1458, "e fu giovedì che ssi dicie essere buono dì" (and it was Thursday that was said to be a good day) (ASF, *Strozz.,* 2d ser., 9, fol. 194v).

should help to clarify the value attached to these various ceremonial points of focus.

Altieri attributes to his Roman ancestors a wise self-control that made them wait until the evening of the *nozze* to bring the bride to the conjugal bed, no matter how long a time—a year and sometimes even more— separated the *matrimonium* from the wife's departure for the house of her husband.[40] It seems this was also the most common practice in Florence in the fourteenth century and at the beginning of the fifteenth. The texts considered here are unfortunately seldom explicit, and in the Florentine *ricordanze* for that earlier age I have found only five mentions of the date on which the couple consummated the marriage. In all cases, this took place the evening of the *nozze*, after the woman, first "sworn," then "es-poused" or "ringed," had been "led" to her husband's house. In the four-teenth century and still at the beginning of the fifteenth, the expression *menare donna* had the unequivocal significance of "bringing one's wife under one's roof": it implied that the consummation of the marriage followed this transfer. In one city of Lombardy, witnesses could infer from the nuptial cortege they had seen passing that the union had been con-summated soon afterward.[41] It was therefore the *ductio uxoris in viri domum* that, in the last analysis, opened the way to union of the flesh.

In the domestic *ricordi* of the end of the fifteenth and the beginning of the sixteenth centuries, explicit notation of the moment of the consum-mation becomes more frequent. Out of some fifty precise indications of the consummation of a marriage, sixteen place it on the "ring day," after the exchange of consent, and nineteen on one of the days that separated this ceremony from the bride's transfer to her husband's house. In both cases it is evident that the union was consummated at the home of the parents of the young woman. Only ten date the consummation on the evening of the bride's introduction into the husband's house. In five cases, the ring day and the wedding day seem one and the same, and the marriage is consummated that very day. Do these data permit us to conclude that the exchange of consents gradually relegated the nuptial cortege and public festivities to a secondary position? Can we say that a decisive division occurred between the necessary and sufficient condition represented by the *verba de praesenti* and the popular rite—respectable but not indis-pensable—imposed by the "custom of the place"? If this were the case, would not such an evolution indicate the growing influence of the Church by its emphasis on the act that was the basis of the sacrament of marriage, the free exchange of consent?

In fact, it is possible that statistics take away with one hand what they seem to have given with the other. The shift in meaning of the term *menare* makes it extremely ambiguous and suggests that the limited number of

40. Ibid., 73, 81.
41. G. Salvioli, "La benedizione nuziale fino al Concilio di Trento," *Archivio giuridico* 53 (1894): 169–97.

counts that led me to this interpretation need to be looked at carefully. Indeed, it often happens that a domestic chronicler notes that he *menò* his bride and "consummated" the marriage (or "slept with her") "in the house of [his father-in-law]"; and then will write, three lines farther down, that several days later, he "led her *(menò)* to his house." In the second case, *menare* keeps its meaning of the physical transfer of the wife to her new dwelling, but in the first it is evidently contaminated by the idea of the consummation, with which it had long been associated, and it came to signify the consummation itself. Thus it becomes difficult indeed to distinguish what the expression *menare* refers to when it is used in isolation in the texts of the later period. The many mentions of wives "led" for whom we do not know the moment of the consummation of the union might refer to the practice of the Trecento, when consummation followed transfer. In these conditions, the change suggested by the spread of the dates of consummation may refer only to exceptional cases in which the writer thought further explanations were needed.

The fact remains that contemporaries, both preachers and simple observers, seem to support our first impression of a coincidence of the "ring day" and the consummation.[42] Antoninus complains[43] that in his day engaged girls found it difficult to avoid "shameful acts" during the visits of their *sponsi* to their father's house.[44] Bernardine of Siena (San Bernardino) sharply criticized the newlyweds' habit, "encouraged by senseless relatives," of "rushing into the union of the flesh" as soon as the ceremony of the *desponsatio* had ended, and occasionally even before.[45] For him, those acting like "wild animals or dogs" were victims of a base credulity inspired by the devil and by "the fear of spells and enchantments" threatening the couple with impotence. Altieri also indicates that the Romans of his day dreaded the casting of evil spells, particularly on the day of the nuptial cortege, when the publicity given the young couple exposed them to all manner of possible expressions of ill will.[46] Thus, advancing the moment

42. It does not seem to me that the lowering of the average age at marriage for women, toward the end of the fifteenth century, can explain the earlier consummation of marriage, until that time put off until the fiancée had reached the canonical age. The latter was taken into account, in fact, at the recital of the *verba de praesenti.*

43. Antoninus, *Summa,* 4:15:7, fol. 300.

44. Well before the Council of Trent the Florentine synodal statutes of 1517 forbade the future husband to make more than two visits to his promised bride between the engagement and the *verba de praesenti (Sacrorum Conciliorum,* ed. Mansi, 35, col. 248.

45. S. Bernardini, *Opera omnia* (Florence: PP. Collegii S. Bonaventurae, 1950–1978), 4:469–70.

46. "Alguno incantatorio et malefico legame, da prestarce impedimento al succeso quale dal coniugio se spera" (some enchanting and evil-doing spell, to urge on us an impediment to the success we hope from the union), Altieri, *Li nuptiali,* 68. The author describes many rites designed to avoid this threat (particulary, eating fish) or to assure the couple's fertility (pp. 76, 79, 81, 83, 88). On these rites, see also E. Westermarck, *History of Human Marriage,* 5th ed. (New York, 1922), 2:543–72; and E. Le Roy Ladurie, "L'aiguillette," in *Le territoire de l'historien* (Paris, 1978), 2:136–49.

of consummation (legitimized, what is more, by the preliminary exchange of consent) represented a way to prevent an enemy's occult interference.

There is one further reason, institutional and financial this time, that explains the haste with which Florentines of the well-to-do classes hurried to consummate the union to which they had just expressed consent. In the fourteenth century it was common for the marriage, at least the *nozze* and the wife's arrival at her husband's house, not to be celebrated until the dowry had been paid.[47] This norm suffered innumerable exceptions and loopholes, but at least it subordinated the "perfecting" of the marriage, and its culmination in the union of the flesh, to the execution—at least in part—of the dotal agreement. After 1434, Florentines of sufficient wealth could invest in a new financial institution, the Monte delle Doti, in order to provide dowries for their daughters.[48] At the end of a term of five to fifteen years, the husband received all or a part of this sum after the marriage had been consummated and the *gabella* had been paid on the dowry. Here we see a reversal of the previous scenario. Where the payment of the dowry had been a necessary condition put for the consummation of the union, consummation now became a necessary condition for payment of the dowry. How did Florentines, imbued as they were with the old principle according to which the dowry must be paid before the wedding could be solemnized, arrive at this state of affairs? No doubt the parents of a marriageable daughter saw it as a useful guarantee against second thoughts concerning a union that had already been celebrated or against the husband's refusal to take in his wife on the pretext that the dowry had not been paid.[49] Moreover, the shift in the moment at which the marriage was consummated became acceptable, without threatening the honor of the families that had concluded the alliance, when the payment of the dowry (now firmly linked to the consummation of the union) was assured by a state agency, permitting the son-in-law and his family to consider the engagement irreversible.

This shift in the nuptial scenario thus tipped the balance in favor of the "ring day"—the day when the *verba de praesenti* were spoken—and legalized sexual union at that time. The following morning, bright and early, the happy bridegroom could rush to pay the *gabella* so that he could then withdraw what the Florentine government owed him, or at least could make sure that his rights were recognized. The wedding proper could be

47. See Herlihy and Klapisch-Zuber, *Les Toscans*, 592, n. 34.

48. J. Kirshner, "Pursuing Honor while Avoiding Sin: The Monte delle Doti of Florence," *Studi senesi* 89 (1977): 177–258; J. Kirshner and A. Molho, "The Dowry Fund and the Marriage Market in Early Quattrocento Florence," *Journal of Modern History* 50 (1978): 403–38.

49. This is a piteous theme found in the declarations to the *catasto* of 1427: taxpayers complain of having to keep their married daughter at home and of not being able to pay the dowry so that her husband will "lead" her away. See chapter 10 below, "The Griselda Complex."

put off until later, or could even be omitted completely: the essential had taken place and the marriage was *perfetto* (completed). One example among many others: when messire Niccolò Altoviti married Antonia, the daughter of Bernardo Rinieri, he "swears and gives her the ring" Thursday, 24 November 1485, and "that evening, he *leads* her in the house [of Bernardo Rinieri] with no other manifestations of *nozze*." Monday, 28 November, he pocketed the dowry, and it was not until 1 February 1486 that he gave his wife the traditional presents and sent for her to come to his house.[50] We see here a real clustering of several moments of the scenario around the capital moment of the ring. Although the reasons for this clustering may have been varied, they all worked to the benefit of the central ceremony and the detriment of the other rituals, annexed or eclipsed by the "ring day." Thus around 1500, out of a nuptial ritual that had been extended and dispersed among several poles, there emerged a new, more centralized ceremonial complex, grouped around the *verba de praesenti*—the first indication of the modern marriage that would be instituted definitively by the Tridentine reform.

The agreement of the financial institutions of the republic to guarantee the payment of dowries was indicative of a new attitude on the part of the well-to-do classes toward state intervention in family affairs. The connection becomes clearer if we look at the families that supported Lorenzo de' Medici after 1470. The skillful role the Medici played as marriage brokers is well known, and its political significance is evident, since they used the matrimonial alliances to keep a tight rein on their supporters and allies.[51] A few specific examples will clarify in what ways and on what occasions they did so. Several books of *ricordanze* show how the Medici, making use of the traditional roles of arbiters and *mezzani* (the friendly go-betweens for families interested in becoming allied by marriage), became securely entrenched as guarantors of marriage *par excellence,* first among their adherents, then in the whole of the urban aristocracy. In the third quarter of the fifteenth century they often substituted for family members in the preliminary negotiations, and more and more often their presence alone came to lend validity to engagements concluded in such negotiations. At this point there was no need for solemnity, no need for the public setting of a church; neither was there any need for the presence of all the "relatives and friends" to solemnize a *giuramento*. Most of the

---

50. ASF, *Conventi soppressi*, 95, 212, *Ricordanze di Bernardo di Stoldo Rinieri,* fol. 169v and also fols. 169r (1483) and 171 (1487). After 1472, Lorenzo de' Medici expresses his desire for simplicity in nuptial feasts. See also *Ricordi storici di F. di C. Rinuccini dal 1282 al 1460,* ed. C. Aiazzi (Florence ,1840), cxlviii.

51. See F. Guicciardini, *Storie fiorentine,* chap. 9, in *Opere inedite,* ed. G. Canestrini (Florence, 1859), 3:90–91. The register of the notary ser Niccolaio Michelozzi contains a great number of these marriage contracts concluded *in domo Laurentii de Medicis;* see ASF, *Not. Antecos.,* M. 530, fol. 15r–15v, 18r, 20v, 21v, 30r–30v, 40r, 42v, 43r, 44r (1472–75). See also D. Kent, *The Rise of the Medici: Faction in Florence, 1426–1434* (Oxford, 1978).

*ricordanze* that note that the *impalmamento* took place under the aegis of Lorenzo, in his chambers in the Palazzo della Signoria, at his bank, or at his own family palace, either mention no other ceremony of the *giure* or explicitly note that there was no other.[52] The ritual process was thus telescoped, in comparison to the basic sequence by which lineages had made their alliances public a hundred years earlier. Here again, the rituals clustered around the "ring day."

Does this rearrangement of the internal balance among the various secular marriage rituals show that the Church in Florence had gained stronger direct control over them? Following what has just been said, it had not, and I would see in this the second archaic element of ritual in Italy, as compared to France. Unlike French rituals—which in the eleventh and twelfth centuries began to bring rites that had previously taken place in a domestic setting or on the public streets closer to the sanctuary or even within it and concentrated functions that laymen had formerly had taken on in the hands of priests[53]—Florentine rituals persistently kept ecclesiastical presence and the religious consecration of marriages to a marginal role. For evidence of this, we need to look briefly at various aspects of the Florentines' indifference to the recommendations of the Church, an attitude in which they persisted up to the Council of Trent.

Paradoxically, Sunday seemed to Florentines a particularly propitious day and the sanctuary a propitious place for a nuptial ceremony precisely because the ceremony was less subjected to the Church's meddling. As we have seen, Sunday was not chosen for the celebration of the *giure,* the "ring," or the *nozze* out of an interest in making these activities part of a religious rite. The "peace" of the lineages who were to be allied or the ritual procession of the bride acquired their solemnity from the feast days on which they took place. Similarly, the choice of the church or its immediate surroundings for the celebration of the *giure* seems above all aimed at creating a climate of neutrality and conferring a degree of public sanction on the peace sealed by the *osculum* and by the engagement between the two families. When the Florentine commune emitted a decree in 1356 (renewed in 1384) that *sponsalia* take place in a church, its efforts were aimed particularly at reinforcing this promise of public peace.[54]

52. A few examples: G. Buongirolami, *Ricordanze* (ASF *Strozziane,* 2d ser., 23, fol. 129), an agreement concluded 11 December 1499 without being followed by *giure;* the same for T. Guidetti, *Ricordanze* (ASF, *Strozz.,* 4th ser., 418, fol. 3v, 2 October 1481); Luigi Martelli (ASF, *Strozz.,* 5th ser., 1463, fol. 119, 24 April 1487); Bartolomeo Valori (Biblioteca Nazionale Centrale, Florence, henceforth abbreviated BNC, *Panciatichi,* 134, fol. 7, 1 March 1474; fol. 8, 2 January 1476; fol. 9, 7 July 1476; fol. 10, 22 November 1481); Recco Capponi (ASF, *Conventi soppressi,* S. Piero a Monticelli, 153, fol. 24v, 20 February 1469).

53. Ritzer, *Le mariage dans les Eglises chrétiennes,* 388–95. Molin and Mutembé, in *Le rituel du mariage en France,* appendixes, 283–300, include a dozen of the *ordines* of marriage.

54. *Statuti,* ed. R. Caggese, 1:222. The substance of this was repeated in the *Statuta* of 1415, 3:366.

Neither through its representatives nor through its legislation did the Church enter directly into the ceremony of the *giure*. Its absence is just as noticeable on the "ring day." In medieval France, it was the Church's penetration into the rites of the *verba de praesenti*—through use of the sanctuary as well as the presence of clergy—that had permitted clerical control and subsequently the "liturgization" of this capital moment. For the Tuscan families we are examining here, however, the ceremony by which the spouses expressed consent remained a largely domestic rite until the eve of the Council of Trent. The "ring day" was almost always celebrated at the home of the engaged girl's father, guardian, or employer. I can cite only one exception to the rule of the priest's absence, and it is an exception that clearly confirms the rule. When Filippo Strozzi took Vaggia Gianfigliazzi as his second wife 19 September 1477, in the country, the notary invited to put the questions and record the couple's consent was nowhere to be found; so Filippo fell back on a priest who was among them, asking him to do so.[55] There could hardly be a better illustration of the priest as a substitute solution. Well into the sixteenth century, statutory texts and synodal legislation continued to charge the notary with these important functions.[56]

The most surprising aspect of Florentine nuptial rituals and their archaic autonomy remains the virtual omission of religious benediction. Antoninus, both in this *Summa*[57] and in his constitutions of 1455,[58] repeatedly stresses the obligation to hear mass at the ceremonies for a first marriage, particularly in the *contado,* where the faithful probably demonstrated an even crasser ignorance than the city dwellers. But although they were better surrounded by the Church and its preaching, city folk seem to have been no more assiduous than peasants when it came to the wedding mass, which was not part of the day's festivities as it was in Rome. Rarely do the domestic journals note that a *messa del congiunto* was celebrated at one point or another in the nuptial scenario. Only a dozen of these journals (two before 1430 and ten after that date) report that the couple—or the wife alone—heard mass and received the blessing of the Church. To judge

55. ASF, *Strozz.*, 5th ser., 22, fol. 105.

56. See the synodal statutes of 1517: "Nessuno ardisca contrahere sponsalitii ne de futuro ne de presenti se prima non chiama el prete suo o vero un notaio, el quale faccia le parole tra loro in questa forma" (Let no one be so bold as to contract a *sponsalitio* either with the *verbis de futuro* or *de praesenti* if he does not first call his priest or a notary, who will pronounce the words between them in this manner) (*Sacrorum Conciliorum*, ed. Mansi, 35, col. 247).

57. *Summa*, 3:1, *De statu conjugatorum*, fols. 6 and 32v.

58. Published by R. C. Trexler in *Quellen und Forschungen aus den italienischen Archiven und Bibliotheken* 59 (1979): 111–39. "Item perche abiamo inteso in alchuno luogo in contado . . . da alchuno ignorante farsi le nozze prima senza la benedictione overo messa dil Congiunto secondo à ordinato la sancta Chiesa" (Item: Since we have heard that in some place in the *contado* . . . some ignorant person has gotten married before [receiving] benediction or [hearing] the nuptial mass as ordained by the holy Church), pp. 138–39.

by this sparse evidence, Florentine spouses who sanctified their union did so preferably on the "ring day," before the exchange of consent, or occasionally during the preceding days. Not one of the twelve masses was celebrated on a Sunday.[59] Are we to believe that the religious ceremony was so automatically part of the proceedings that a narrator would not even feel the need to note it, and that the expenses involved were so small that they were never recorded (or hardly ever) among the other minuscule amounts spent by the head of family? It seems to me more probable that Florentines' attitude toward the Church's blessing was just as casual as that of the rustics or of Machiavelli's Nicomaco and that they simply accepted people's behaving like "wild animals" as far as marriage was concerned, permitting the *sponsa* to skip this bothersome formality.[60] In the last analysis, the individual's piety left him the judge of the utility of the Church's blessing. The heart of the nuptial ritual lay elsewhere.

Among the lower echelons of society, the succession of juridical acts that surrounded marriage was more concentrated and shorter by several episodes; but the clergy did have the possibility of playing a greater role than among the families who kept *ricordanze*.[61] Notarial acts present a great number of brief scenarios of these marriages of artisans and even of *contadini*.[62] We know little about popular gestures and symbols of betrothal in Tuscany. Antoninus admits that an engagement could be established in different ways: by simple promise; by the giving of a down payment "such as money, jewels, etc."; by the gift of a ring; by an oath or by a pledge resembling an oath; or by words spoken to dedicate the future marriage to an "honest and useful condition."[63] Several of these forms, then, were open to all sorts of popular rites that were relegated to the background in the solemn *giure* of the patriciate. In his study of notarial acts of alliance, Samuel Cohn notes that among the unions that occasioned a notarial act only about 10 percent had been preceded by an *instrumentum sponsalitii* drawn up during the *giure*. All of these, or nearly all, pertained to rich families.[64] On the contrary, artisans and workers in Florence went

59. Altieri, *Li nuptiali*, 73, reports however that in Rome, couples often had mass celebrated *in the house of the bride* three days before the wedding, so that they could consummate the union the evening of the wedding and still respect the three "Nights of Tobias" that the Church imposed on them.

60. Machiavelli, *Clizia*, act 3, scene 7. On the religious celebration of marriage in Italy, see F. Brandileone, *Saggi*, 88–96.

61. One example of rural marriage in 1302 is given in G. Pampaloni, "Le nozze," 35–36. Many peasant unions must have done without formalities, however, like the one mentioned in 1409 by one Florentine: "Ed è vero posto che la detta donna fosse stata con detto G. più anni, non era però fatto sponsalizio né dato annello o confessato dota" (And it is given as true that the said woman has been with the said G. for many years, but no marriage was performed, no ring given, nor dowry agreed on) (BNC, *Manoscritti*, 77, fol. 34).

62. S. Cohn, *The Laboring Classes*, 21, 24.

63. *Summa*, 3:1:18, "De sponsalibus."

64. S. Cohn, *The Laboring Classes*, 19–21.

regularly to the notary to register the dowry—even a minuscule dowry—given to their daughters. The notary also registered the exchange of mutual consent and the giving of the nuptial ring, usually soon after these ceremonies took place. But among the poor the ring seems to have been given more often in church or before a priest or monks who served as witnesses.[65] It was more natural for the clergy to play the required role of mediator and privileged witness in relation to people for whom the economic stakes of marriage were smaller. In these more modest circles, the young wife followed her husband as soon as the ceremony of the ring had taken place, if the dowry had been paid.[66]

All this information, whether it concerns the rich or the poor, demonstrates that the nuptial blessing was less than imperative, but it also shows that it was associated with the ceremony of the ring. The exchange of mutual consent, on which marriage was founded, undoubtedly took place in a domestic setting and did without the presence of a representative of the Church. Although marriage was still seldom celebrated with a religious ceremony, people nevertheless felt that such a ceremony was a desirable preliminary to the sacrament of marriage. Hence a religious solemnization tended to be drawn closer to the exchange of consents, and the ring, the symbolic object given at the time of that exchange, tended to become connected with the religious rite.

### The Nuptial Ring in Tuscany and the *Sposalizio* of the Virgin

The ring, that symbolic object, has a long history in the nuptial rites of the West, and we shall not repeat it here.[67] The Roman engagement ring, the *anulus sponsalitius,* which was the token of a promise, was later enriched with the Oriental notion of an advance on the promised dowry. During the early Middle Ages, the ring became a part of the ceremony of the Germanic *desponsatio,* which was considered a binding engagement. When the Church had better imposed its conception of the consensual character of the union and after the preliminary ceremony in which the families expressed their pledges to one another became distinct from the ceremony of the *verba de praesenti,* the *anulus sponsalitius* shifted from the first occasion to the second.[68] It retained its character of a promise that definitively

65. One example can be found in the *ricordanze* of Piero Strozzi (ASF, *Strozz.,* 4th ser., 354, fol. 168v). At the marriage of a poor young girl dowered by charity 31 January 1508, her husband "gave the ring . . . in [the church of] Santa Trinità in the presence of the monks of the church."

66. As the *ricordanze* show when they report on the marriages of servant women, slaves, poor women, and girls married by charity.

67 .Chénon, "Recherches historiques," 3–13, 33–35; F. Brandileone, *Saggi,* 318ff; *Dictionnaire d'archéologie chrétienne et de liturgie* (1932), s.v. "mariage," 10, col. 1890–93.

68. Antoninus distinguishes clearly between the two moments possible for the giving of the ring: the *sponsalia* are accomplished by the gift of the ring; "alicubi tamen datur anulus

engaged the couple in marriage and authorized the consummation of the union. The Roman idea of a token or a promise and that of an advance on the promised dowry were eclipsed by a more intimate interpretation but were never totally eliminated. In Florence in the fifteenth century, the ring was no longer a token or a pledge, *stricto sensu,* for material promises; and terms like *subarrata* or *waidiata* had almost ceased to be applied to the spouse who was *anellata.* When an educated Florentine says that he sees the nuptial ring that he places *maritali affectu* onto the ring finger of his wife as a sign of the faith pledged, he is referring first and foremost to his spouse's fidelity. Furthermore, although there was an exchange of mutual consent, there was no exchange of rings. The husband alone gave the ring, on which the aristocratic Romans described by Altieri[69] engraved the arms of their lineage rather than one of the symbols of fidelity that the ancients were so fond of.[70] The affective and personal bond of the union affirmed by the ring is thus not without implicit restrictions.

These connections with very diverse legal and symbolic acts, as well as the ring's origin in popular ritual of alliance, are probably what made the ring a central symbolic object,always open to new interpretation and new classifications, but always seen as necessary. This polysemy and symbolic richness very early attracted the attention of the Church[71] and opened the way to the ring's annexation into the liturgy of marriage as the one object to remain universally licit in the context of the religious ceremony. Marked by the various changes incurred in its long history, the ring also offered the Church a way to guide an evolution, of which I have found fresh traces, amid all the fluctuation of Florentine popular rituals, as late as the fifteenth century. The ring fitted well into the new conjugal policy founded on a comprehension of the consensual nature of marriage. And it is of course the ring that we find at the center of visual representations of the *Sposalizio* in the fourteenth and fifteenth centuries.

The story of the marriage of the Virgin and the miracle by which Saint Joseph was designated the terrestrial father of Christ have seen many different versions. The proto-gospel of James, an apocryphal writer of the third century, offers the oldest known eastern version.[72] Mary, still a young girl (twelve years old) reaches the age at which she might sully the temple

---

quando contrahitur per v. de pr. et tunc non sunt sponsalia sed perfectum matrimonium" (in some places, however, the ring is given when [marriage] is contracted by the *verba de praesenti;* then it is a completed matrimony and not a *sponsalia) (Summa,* 3:1:18, fol. 19).

69. Altieri, *Li nuptiali,* 51.

70. *Dictionnnaire d'archéologie chrétienne,* s.v. "mariage," 10 cols. 1891–93 and 1931– 42.

71. As early as the seventh century, bishops wore a ring to signify their marriage to the Church (ibid., s.v. "anneaux," 1: cols. 2181–86). Similarly, on nuns' rings, see R. Metz, *La consécration,* appendixes.

72. E. Hennecke and W. Schneemelcher, *Neutestamentliche Apokryphen,* 3d ed. (Tübingen, 1959–64), 277ff.

in which she has been brought up. The High Priest learns from an oracle that he is to entrust her to one of the widowers of Judah: a sign will designate the chosen one. Then, it is from the rod carried by Joseph, a good old man with grown sons, that the divine dove emerges. Bewildered, Joseph demurs, arguing his sons and his age. But in vain: the priest entrusts little Mary to his care, without any question of marrying the old man to the future mother of the Redeemer, however.

Four or five centuries later, in the apocryphal text of proto-Matthew—the most direct source of the representations of the *Sposalizio* in the West—the theme of the election of Joseph appears in a new guise.[73] Although the Church soon refuted the widowhood of Joseph, the motif, repeated here, once more justifies the modesty and the hesitation of the old man. A dove alights on the rod that he, like all the men of Judah who were "free from conjugal ties," has brought to the temple, and all congratulate him at this sign of divine election. Here again, his protests do not stop the High Priest from entrusting the Virgin to him until the day he is to marry her. The decisive step is taken with an abridged version of this legend, written in the ninth century and long attributed to Saint Jerome under the name of the "Book of the Nativity of the Virgin."[74] Influenced by the staff of Aaron, the rod here flowers at the same time as it receives the dove in a doubly miraculous sign that obliges Joseph—now just an old man, with no mention of widowhood or preceding paternities[75]—to receive Mary. Their *sponsalia* are celebrated immediately. In his reelaboration of the *Golden Legend*, Jacobus de Voragine adopted the theme of the *desponsatio* that makes Joseph return home "to prepare everything for the wedding."[76] As the evolution of the written legend ends and its iconographic developments begin, an aged Joseph is thus chosen, from among all the bachelors of Judah,[77] as the husband of the Virgin by virtue of miraculous signs distinguishing the "little rod" that he carries. Under pressure from the Church, the apocryphal theme of his widowhood—which western theologians judged incompatible with their doctrine of the purity of Christ's parents—disappears, but its silhouette can still be seen, we might say, in the advanced age that the West continues to attribute to the saint. The other distinctively western trait is the disappearance of the "placing under guardianship" of the young Mary and the appearance of the theme of her engagement,[78] then of her marriage. This transformation

73. J. Lafontaine-Dosogne, *Iconographie de l'enfance de la Vierge dans l'Empire byzantin et en Occident* (Brussels, 1964–65), 2:135–53. L. Kretzenbacher, "Stabbrechen in Hochzeitsritus? Zur apokryphen Erzählungsgrundlage eines Bildmotivs im Sposalilizio-Thema," *Fabula* 6 (1963): 195–212.

74. Lafontaine-Dosogne, *Iconographie de l'enfance*, 135–36.

75. *Dictionnaire d'archéologie chrétienne*, s.v. "Saint Joseph," 5, cols. 2656–66.

76. *Legenda aurea*, ed. T. Graesse (Breslau, 1890), 589.

77. "Nuptiis habiles non conjugati" (capable of marriage but unwed) (ibid.).

78. This is still the interpretation of Antoninus (*Summa*, 4:15:7), referring to Jewish custom.

took place between the ninth and the end of the thirteenth centuries, at the same time that the *sponsalia* were splitting into two ceremonies.[79] The *Legenda aurea* does not describe the formal aspects of the sacred couple's marriage, but art was soon to give definition to these forms when it adopted the theme and brought it to life on the walls of Italian churches.

The iconography of this pious legend between the eleventh century and 1300 is based on traditions that are both ancient and varied.[80] To the south and to the north of the Alps alike, some previous representations still seem not to have been influenced by the apocryphal texts: they present a simple marriage, pictured according to the forms inherited from ancient art, in which a central figure unites the hand of a young Joseph with that of the Virgin in the traditional Roman *dextrarum junctio*. In certain sculptures the eastern story of the election of Joseph transmitted by the Gospel of James or by proto-Matthew can be read in certain details that were later abandoned in western versions but that return up to the mid-thirteenth century north of the Alps, such as the small size of the Virgin, not fully grown, and the High Priest's gesture, better adapted to entrusting Mary to the guardianship of the old man than to their union. The representations of the marriage of the Virgin that multiplied in the twelfth and thirteenth centuries in French and German lands refer more clearly to the Book of the Nativity: an older Joseph often carries a leafy or flowering branch, sometimes crowned with the dove, the useless rods abandoned by the men of Judah litter the ground or the altar, and the High priest unites the hands of Joseph and Mary.

Around 1300, these depictions of the Marriage of the Virgin, numerous north of the Alps, were almost unknown in Italy. Byzantine models had indeed inspired a mosaic in San Marco, in Venice (beginning of the thirteenth century) and a fresco in the upper church in Assisi, but it was with Giotto in the Arena Chapel in Padua that this antiquated iconography was brought up to date and the pattern set for some time to come.

The cycle that Giotto devoted to the life of the Virgin repeats preexistent models of the election of Joseph and the *Sposalizio,* reworking them into a novel synthesis and following the *Golden Legend* faithfully (see plate 9.1). First, the setting: the scene takes place at the doors of the temple. The Byzantine altar on which the rods had been placed in expectation of the miracle is enclosed within the building, and the matrimonial destiny of Mary and Joseph is played out at its threshhold. Some critics have seen a reference to Jewish custom in this choice of setting: since marriage was not a sacrament, the scene could not take place in a consecrated place and would necessarily occur outside, outdoors, but near the temple in which

79. Chénon, "Recherches historiques," 13. See above.

80. Lafontaine-Dosogne, *Iconographie de l'enfance*; L. Réau, *Iconographie de l'art chrétien* (Paris, 1955–59), 2:2:170–73 and 3:2:752–60. E. Sépulcre, "Saint Joseph et l'intimté dans l'art médiéval: Étude iconographique" unpublished thesis, Brussels, 1952.

Plate 9.1 Giotto, *Marriage of the Virgin*. Padua, Scrovegni Chapel, about 1306.
(Photo Anderson-Giraudon 27017)

Mary had lived.[81] But how likely is it that Giotto or the monks who
commissioned the frescoes would have worried about respecting Jewish
customs? Does this not attribute to them an interest in historical reconstruction rather far from the aims of medieval iconography? The square
in front of the temple, where Giotto sets the holy marriage, could have
an explanation closer to hand than such antiquarian scruples.

Next, the actors: Joseph, on the left, is an aged graybeard. The lily he
holds in his left hand is weighed down by the dove that has alighted on
it. Mary, her hair floating free, is crowned with flowers. The ages and the
attributes of both Joseph and Mary are clearly borrowed from the *Golden
Legend*. Their respective positions are also different from any Byzantine
models that Giotto could have studied in the vicinity of Padua. Joseph on
the left and Mary on the right frame the High Priest, who, facing the
spectator, brings their two right hands together. The frontal position of
the priest reflects the schema inherited from the Romans in which *Juno*

81. L. Réau, *Iconographie*, 171.

*pronuba*, and later her heir, Christ *pronubus*, presided over the *dextrarum junctio*, the symbolic gesture repeated north of the Alps in both ritual and iconography.[82]

Giotto, however, departs from this tradition by representing his compatriots' gift of a nuptial ring. His innovation lies in this ritual object, placed in the center of the composition. The Virgin seems to be presenting the fourth finger of her right hand, which is supported by Zacharias, while Joseph's right hand, guided by the priest, offers the ring. The gesture, the finger, and the object were to figure from about 1300 on in a wealth of representations of marriages: the mystical marriages of Saint Francis of Assisi with Poverty and the two Saints Catherine with Christ, or lay marriages depicted on the sides of *cassoni* or in Italian miniatures.[83]

As for the other participants in the miracle of the staffs, the *Golden Legend* suggested their presence at the *Sposalizio* and their assent. In Giotto's fresco, the crowd of the men of Judah standing behind Joseph are shown commenting on the proceedings with some excitement. One of them breaks his unflowering rod over his knee, while seven others still hold theirs, now useless, in their hands. Although the faces of the unlucky rivals—nearly all of whom are younger than Joseph—express some astonishment and disappointment, we cannot read real hostility in them. (The lack of acrimony also faithfully reflects the apocryphal texts.) One young man, to be sure, raises his hand behind Joseph's back, but the gesture is in no way threatening. Rafaello Corso has seen it—and rightly so—as depicting a popular custom (which was condemned by Italian synods of the eighteenth century, however): a rather heavy clap on the husband's back, given by his *compater anuli* at the moment of the exchange of consent.[84]

When our Tuscan painter introduces this gesture from popular ritual into his illustration of the apocryphal tale, he calls attention to the freedom of his pictorial interpretation, and we can sense that for him the ceremony evoked a living reality. The *Golden Legend* and its models, which said

---

82. A. Rossbach, *Römische Hochzeits- und Ehedenkmäler* (Leipzig, 1871). S. Ringbom, "Nuptial Symbolism in some XVth Century Reflections of Roman Sepulchral Portraiture," *Temenos* 2 (1966). *Dictionnaire d'archéologie chrétienne*, 10, cols. 1895ff.

83. Meiss, *Painting in Florence*, 108–113, illus. 100–107. G. Kaftal, *Saints in Italian Art: Iconography of the Saints in Tuscan Painting* (Florence, 1952), 235–47, illus. 244, 247, 248. On the diffusion of the legend of Saint Catherine of Alexandria, see B. Beatie, "St. Katherine of Alexandria: Traditional Themes and the Development of the Medieval German Hagiographic Narrative," *Speculum* 52 (1977): 785–800. On the *cassoni*, see P. Schubring, *Cassoni* (Leipzig, 1915), 2 vols., with annotated index; E. Callmann, *Apollonio di Giovanni* (Oxford, 1974).

84. R. Corso, "Tre vecchie costumanze aretine: il baccio alla sposa, la rottura della scodella, il pugno allo sposo durante la celebrazione nuziale," *Reviviscenze*, 1st ser., 6 (1927): 71–83; A. Basile, "Usi popolari nuziali nello Sposalizio della Vergine della grande pittura italiana: Il pugno e la rottura della bacchetta," *Folklore* 10 (1956): 3–11. Synodal texts can be found in C. Corrain and P. L. Zampini, *Documenti etnografici e folkloristici nei sinodi diocesani italiani* (Bologna, 1970), 49. Statutes against hitting people who are getting married appear in many communal statute books.

nothing of the rites followed in the marriage of the Virgin, were thus completed by the painter. By borrowing this gesture from his contemporaries, Giotto performed a radical revision of the Nordic interpretations of the ceremony; he anchored them in Italian reality. We have a right to ask how all these images related to the conceptions that the Church was attempting to establish in the ritual order of weddings. Could not the *Sposalizio* be considered an instrument of propaganda by means of which the Church was attempting to dominate popular ritual? Or, conversely, what welcome did the Church give to the symbolic gestures of popular ritual? In point of fact, Italian painters—particularly the Tuscans—continued and developed Giotto's setting of the legendary miracle and took his various discoveries very far indeed, prompting the Church to refine the edifying and militant functions it assigned to the *Sposalizio*.

The setting, the actors, and the objects that Giotto set in place were to enjoy enormous success in Italy. The Tuscans were the first to imitate certain details of his frescoes again and again.[85] In the fourteenth and fifteenth centuries nearly all of them—Florentines and Sienese alike—followed Giotto in setting the scene close to the temple: under the portico or in the atrium, at the foot of the stairs, in the garden, or on the street beside it. This near unanimity is all the more striking because painters of other regional schools who took up the theme in the fifteenth century were often to give it a different setting: the entrance to the church or inside the church. The Umbrian school alone[86] remained faithful to the tradition of Giotto, and Raphael, striving to better Perugino, painted the definitive version of this interpretation. In his painting in the Brera Museum, the temple, freestanding and placed dead center, dominates with its triumphant mass the marriage taking place at the edge of the vast paved square.

It was *in facie ecclesiae*, then, or, more precisely, *ante foras ecclesiae* that Tuscans, Umbrians, and many Lombards placed the *Sposalizio*. If the church were not outlined in the background, many of the porticos in Tuscan paintings might suggest the *loggia* of the ancient Florentine dwellings, where festivities—*giure*, the swearing of peace, weddings[87]—took place when the great lineages wanted to give them particular luster and publicity. These loggias do not appear, however, to have been the usual site of the exchange of consent on the ring day. Hence the portico of Tuscan pictures depicts the atrium of the santuary. We might ask why painters did not place their *Sposalizio* at the heart of the consecrated space, in front of the

85. In all, about a hundred Italian paintings of the fourteenth to the sixteenth centuries have been analyzed.

86. In this region, the vogue of the *Sposalizio* was based on the cult of the relic of Mary's ring, a cult in Perugia that developed in the fifteenth century. See A. Rossi, *L'annello sposalizio di Maria Vergine che si venera nella cattedrale di Perugia: Leggenda* (Perugia, 1857).

87. F. W. Kent, "The Rucellai Family and its Loggia," *Journal of the Warburg and Courtauld Institutes* 35 (1972): 379–401.

altar or at the entrance to the nave, as the Venetians and many Romans, Neapolitans, and even Lombards were to choose to do. The Church, in fact, aimed at bringing control of the legality of the union and the freedom of the couple's consent closer to the sanctuary; and in medieval France and in parts of Italy, perhaps influenced by Norman ritual,[88] these procedures took place at the door to the church. The portico in Tuscan painting thus indicates a desire to ensure the transfer of legal control over marriage to the Church's representative, rather than highlighting the religious blessing of the union. A study of Zacharias's gesture confirms this.

The *Sposalizio* of Giotto confers an undeniably religious tone on the giving of the ring to Mary, but at the same time it reflects the gestures of ritual practice among Tuscans, merely putting an ecclesiastical actor where Tuscans placed laymen. In Tuscan and Umbrian paintings the priest always occupies the central place, but he does no more than draw the hands of the future spouses toward one another, or sometimes only Mary's hand toward that of Joseph.[89] It is quite exceptional before the sixteenth century for painters from these two regions to portray the priest blessing the couple. Thus, Zacharias was put in the place of the notary, but also in the place of the father or the guardian of the bride, whose role was to give her to the husband on the ring day.[90] The ecclesiastical goal of regulating and administering domestic rites united the roles of the Tuscan notary and the father in the person of Zacharias but, curiously enough, refused him the role of the priest sanctifying the marriage by his blessing. Through the *Sposalizio* the Church affirmed the necessity of its intervention *before* the transfer of the woman to her husband, *before* the consummation of the marriage, and *at the moment* at which the ring best symbolizes the consent and the faith sworn by the spouses. In Tuscany, however, it did not use this iconographical theme to preach the need for the nuptial blessing, necessary in its eyes but not indispensable to the validity of the union.

Painters who treated the *Sposalizio* occasionally let themselves be carried rather far in this distortion of popular rites. Giotto's followers added figures or details unknown in the legendary tale but reminiscent of the gestures the spectator could observe around him. Musicians and trumpeters playing at a nuptial feast, a *maggio* (may tree) being carried by a young man, the

---

88. On rites "at the doors of the church" in Gaeta, see F. Brandileone, *Saggi*, 77–79, 90–91.

89. In one-half and one-third of the cases respectively.

90. The representation of the marriage of a poor young girl dowered by the charity of the *Buonomini di san Martino* is particularly interesting: The girl's father stretches out his right hand toward the ring held out by the husband, while the *Buonomo* places the dowry in his left hand. Father and dowerer occupy the central space—the space in which other painters placed Zacharias. At the left, seated, the notary draws up the *instrumentum matrimonii* (Fresco of Francesco d'Antonio del Chierico, ca. 1478, in the church of San Martino al Vescovo, Florence).

children carried by one or several women as a propitiatory rite—all these secondary motifs, which nevertheless reveal exchanges between popular culture and ecclesiastical culture, were to be either eliminated in later representations of the scene or reinterpreted in an allegorical manner, as in the *putto,* the little dog as an emblem of conjugal fidelity, and the dove of the Holy Ghost soaring above the saint's rod. But it is the ritual clap on the back, as it was taken up by Giotto's successors, that provides the best example of the way iconography's permeability to popular practices weakened the *Sposalizio's* glorification of religious marriage.

Tuscan painters of the fourteenth century, in fact, distorted Giotto's invention by making it stand for an exasperated confrontation between age classes. It took the Church a long time to combat the incongruity of this interpretation and reject the story of the rods as apocryphal. During the whole of the fourteenth and fifteenth centuries, painters and sculptors in Tuscany charged the group of suitors with more and more hostile— even hateful—sentiments toward the saint, who turns his back on them to place the nuptial ring. Soon after 1330 Taddeo Gaddi had already introduced a certain amount of contained violence in the attitudes of the rejected suitors. The sticks, more numerous, are broken energetically by the men who were carrying them, and the clap on the back is given more rudely, with a closed fist, by a young man to an old Joseph.[91] Around 1360, in a chapel in Santa Croce in Florence, Giovanni da Milano (or one of his students) took the suitors' gestures one step farther: there are now two of them threatening the saint, raising their hand or their fist at him. Agnolo Gaddi in turn repeated his predecessors' motifs in the cathedral of Prato, with even more insistence on the hostility if not the fury of the men of Judah. Two Sienese painters, Bartolo di Fredi and Niccolò di Buonaccorso, also stress the frank hostility and the excitement of the men massed behind Joseph's back.[92]

In all these Tuscan paintings, Joseph has an old man's gray beard and white hair. The artists emphasize the contrast between this late arrival to marriage, who seems so humble and reserved, and the group of bachelors— young, for the most part beardless, curly-haired, and dashing—whose frustration grows the farther we get from Giotto. In the fifteenth century the conflict between generations that the *Sposalizio* had become is described with an increasing wealth of detail: frustration, resentment, and blind violence set these "young men" against the old man who has defeated them. Two[93] or even three[94] of them raise their fist at him around 1480– 1510, their faces distorted by anger (see plate 9.2). Children carrying

---

91. See also the medallion by Orcagna (ca. 1350) in the church of Orsanmichele.
92. Bartolo di Fredi worked before 1367; Niccolò di Buonaccorso died in 1388.
93. See Andrea di Giusto (Prato, Duomo, ca. 1450), Fra Angelico (San Marco), Giovanni di Paolo (Rome, Galleria Doria), and Benozzo Gozzoli (Vatican Museum, predella).
94. See Fra Angelico (Prado) and Bartolomeo di Giovanni (Florence, Innocenti, predella).

Plate 9.2 Fra Angelico, *Marriage of the Virgin* (detail). Prado, Madrid. (Photo Anderson-Giraudon 16013)

sticks add to the agitation.[95] Luca Signorelli, pushing to paroxism the emotions of the young against an old man who wins a lovely girl from them, eliminates all reference to the miracle of the rods, leaving nothing but the conflict between age groups; here it is no longer necessary to invoke legend in order to justify the violent emotions attributed to the actors.[96]

When Tuscan painters[97] interpreted the ritual gesture that Giotto, straying from the legendary version, had painted at Padua, they accentuated and focused on the supposed hostility of the suitors; they came to make the gesture the sign of intergenerational conflict, of matrimonial censure on the part of young bachelors toward an old man entering into legitimate matrimony—a censure close, indeed, to that expressed in the charivari. A gesture from popular ritual, misinterpreted, opened the way to other symbolic gestures taken from the ritual of weddings. A whole group of doubly apocryphal gestures that were lent to the witnesses to the marriage of an

95. For example, with Ghirlandaio (Florence, S. Maria Novella, 1488–90), Franciabigio (Florence, SS, Annunziata, 1513), Tribolo (Loretto, S. Casa).

96. The painting is now listed as in a private collection. In the copy in the National Gallery, Washington, the animation of the stick breakers sets off a sort of general riot.

97. With some exceptions: Lorenzo Monaco (Florence, S. Trinita); D. Beccafumi, another early-sixteenth-century Sienese; V. Tamagni of San Gimignano (1492–1530).

old man with a virgin—the classical motif of the charivari—thus came to be grafted onto the central theme of the *Sposalizio*.[98]

It seems to me important that the Church tolerated the Tuscan painters' fondness for the theme of the "charivari of Saint Joseph" until the beginning of the sixteenth century. Church acceptance of the further development of the miracle of the rods probably comes from the fact that it preferred to ignore such excesses as long as the proclamation of holy matrimony *in facie ecclesiae*—the mission assigned to the *Sposalizio*—remained the work's central theme. Furthermore, charivaresque references were more attenuated outside Tuscany. In Umbria and in the Marche, the many painters who illustrated the Marriage of the Virgin and the miracle of the rods around 1500 removed all rancor from the suitors' gestures.[99] At the beginning of the sixteenth century, Lombard painters as well softened the young men's expressions to vague discontent or anxiety, sometimes even edification. The backslap and the clenched fist disappear, and one of the figures points to Joseph as an exemplary husband.[100] Joseph has grown younger or else his rivals have grown older; in any event, the opposition between age groups is tempered.[101] When reference to the miracle of the rods finally disappears, Venetians, Lombards, and Romans—unlike Signorelli—see in the *Sposalizio* only a pretext for a grave meditation on marriage (see plate 9.3)[102] In one-quarter of the hundred or so paintings studied, both suitors and rods are gone, and a calm, thoughtful atmosphere reigns among the witnesses to the scene, who are often older. Allegorical figures and simple worshipers abound in these compositions, which rarely come from Tuscany.[103] This interpretation becomes increasingly frequent toward the mid-sixteenth century, and carries the day with the Counterreformation.

98. See chapter 12 below, "The Medieval Italian Mattinata."

99. Antonio da Viterbo, called Pastura (Tarquinia, ca. 1478), Marco Palmezzano (Milan, Museo Poldi Pezzoli), Pinturicchio (Spello, 1501, Rome, S. Maria del Popolo, 1490); Ragazzini (Macerata, ca. 1520–1547); Andrea da Iesi il Giovane (Cingoli, S. Sperandio). On the other hand, Monaldo da Corneto (Detroit, Institute of Fine Arts) and Lorenzo da Viterbo (Viterbo, S. Maria della Verità) show the anger of the young people. Perugino and Raphael are still the best examples of this school and of its interpretation of the Sposalizio (the former at Fano, S. Maria Nuova, and Caen, Musée; and the latter at Milan, Brera).

100. B. Luini (Saronno and Milan, Brera) and the painters of the first two-thirds of the sixteenth century, G. Marchesi, G. Romanino, O. Samacchini.

101. Masolino da Panicale (Castiglione d'Olona, 1435); Bartolomeo dei Rossi (Parma, Duomo); B. Loschi (Carpi).

102. The best example is possibly that of Lorenzo Costa (Bologna, Pinacoteca). Here Joseph is a beardless young man. For the fourteenth century, see also P. Cavallini (Naples, Museo Civico). For the fifteenth century, see B. Fungai (Florence, Berenson Collection; Gotha, Landesmuseum). For the sixteenth century, see Rosso Fiorentino (Florence, S. Lorenzo) and Sodoma (Subiaco). The latter, like Palmezzano (see note 99), totally eliminates the priest: the spouses really administer the sacrament of marriage to each other by their own will alone.

103. As in the works of Rosso Fiorentino, F. Zaganelli, Brescianino, G. Marchesi, V. Salimbeni, E. Salmeggia (the last three still refer to the miracle of the rods).

Plate 9.3 Lorenzo Costa, *Marriage of the Virgin*. Pinacoteca, Bologna. (Photo Alinari-Giraudon 10744)

Why did the other schools of Italian painting not choose to stress the conflict between age groups as explicitly as the Tuscans? The principal reason is that the development of the theme in Tuscany predates its success in the various provinces in which it later became popular, in particular toward the end of the fifteenth century. At that later time a veritable campaign undertook to spread the cult of Joseph by glorifying his virtues. The best-known partisan of this rehabilitation at the beginning of the fifteenth century was the Frenchman Jean Gerson, but the movement did not bear fruit throughout Europe until the end of the century.[104] By then, the figure of the saint was purified of his comic or possibly ridiculous aspects,[105] and Joseph's merits as the foster father of Christ and the chaste husband of the Virgin were stressed. It became indecent to continue to show young people insulting such a noble figure on the walls of the churches or in the theatrical mystery plays of northern Europe. The violence of the suitors abates, the grimaces melt into smiles, and if the painters still dared to show the fury of the unlucky rivals, it was to show the absurdity of their excessive gestures against the saint—that is to say, at the sacrament of marriage. Thus Franciabigio in the church of the Annunziata in Florence, or the sculptor Tribolo at Loreto, show urchins breaking sticks and crying with rage (plate 9.4). Derision of the saint here becomes derision of his detractors. Even before the Council of Trent, which was to attack the remaining vestiges of the apocryphal story—the miracle of the rods, the advanced age of Joseph—the rehabilitated saint had become, with some banality, a model of the good husband taking part in marriage ceremonies that only the Church could sanctify. The couple, serious and imbued with the solemnity of the moment, the priest, active and indispensable in the proceedings, blessing the spouses and guiding their hands, the transformation of the accompanying figures into allegorical figures, the scene set inside the sanctuary—all of these worked together to the eventual rejection of the fabrications that Giotto's successors were so fond of.

Thus the propositions central to the iconography Giotto had inspired ended up converging with the evolution and the extension of the liturgy of marriage, perhaps hastening this evolution, but in any event losing their own inner necessity. By the time the blessing of the ring before the altar and the ecclesiastical *magisterum* had been imposed everywhere by the Roman ritual, the *Sposalizio* had quite outlived its usefulness. The apocryphal legend and the elements of popular wedding ritual that painters had introduced into it had lost their reason d'être in the face of an apologetics and a liturgy that were now sure of themselves. And the ambiguous marriage scenes of the thirteenth century, in which a child Virgin is put

104. J. Seitz, *Das Josephfest in der lateinischen Kirche in seiner Entwicklung bis zum Konzil von Trient* (Fribourg, 1908). E. Sépulcre, "Saint Joseph," 20. In Florence the feast of Saint Joseph did not become a holiday and a day of rest until 1508, by decree of the Constitutions of Cosimo de' Pazzi (I. da San Luigi, ed., *Etruria sacra* [Florence, 1782], 1:56). To cite one example of the effects of preaching on the image of Saint Joseph traditional among the faithful: the Bolognese mason Gaspare Nadi tells of hearing a sermon given by "uno frate de Santo Zoane in Monte" in the church of San Petronio. He reports, "Disse chome santo Usse yera zovene quando spossò Madona Santa Maria, non lo credo" (He said that Saint Joseph was young when he married [the] holy Lady Mary [but] I don't believe him). (Gaspare Nadi, *Diario bolognese* ed. C. Ricci and A. Bacchi della Lega, [Bologna, 1886], 164).

105. Sépulcre, "Saint Joseph," 51. Caricatures of the saint were found particularly in Flemish and German artists and writers. In Italy, Joseph was rarely mocked to the extent of showing him occupied with women's domestic chores: respect for the paterfamilias was still much too widespread and strong.

Plate 9.4 Franciabigio, *Marriage of the Virgin*. Santissima Annunziata, Florence. (Photo Alinari-Giraudon 3816)

into the hands of an old man, were replaced by the Catholic marriage of an adult and harmonious couple in which the *subarratio per anulum* was accepted as the central symbolic gesture. The ring—and the Church—had won the day.

## The Outlook for Further Research

In emphasizing some of the places, gestures, and objects involved in wedding ceremonies, the Marriage of the Virgin served the Church in its attempt to consolidate its presence. The Church had done so by the seventeenth century, when it finally retired its old iconographic tool, the neutralized *Sposalizio* stripped of its explosive charge. By absorbing or integrating elements of popular ritual that could be reduced to Church doctrine, by transmuting into allegory elements that it did not condemn as pagan but could not integrate into its liturgy, by rejecting as anecdotal or apocryphal certain rites it denounced as inappropriate or violent, the clerics prevailed over the artists and their sensitivity to contemporary practices.

Religious ritual was enriched as the Church purged itself of irreducible elements, which became folklore. But this complementary and dual process—illustrated in the limited area of iconographic propaganda by the representation of the *Sposalizio*—does not exhaust the problem of the constitution and survival of the rituals. For one thing, social variables beyond the scope of the materials analyzed here enter the picture. Such variables lead us directly to the problem of the strategies invented by the Church (and other institutions)—strategies that differed according to the various practices of both the upper and the lower classes and that were directed at controlling rituals of alliance.

Among the lower orders of society, the function sometimes attributed to the priest and the setting chosen for the gift of the ring, the telescoping in time of the various episodes of the nuptial scenario, the disappearance of the *giure,* and the central importance of the ring giving seem to make marriage somewhat more in conformity with the wishes of the Church than among the great and the rich. But if this is true, we still have to define by what channels and with what motivation marriage among the humbler people, at least in the cities, came to conform somewhat better to the model submitted by the Church, avoiding the temptation to imitate patrician customs and reflecting instead the image of the good Christian marriage. We need to study the proselytizing of marriage, preaching on the subject, and—to return to the *Sposalizio*—the nature of the orders, religious confraternities, or individuals who commissioned painters to illustrate this theme. This means also that we need to evaluate the autonomy an artist enjoyed in relation to his patron, lay or ecclesiastical, and even the autonomy of a lay patron in relation to the church in which he commissioned the decoration of a chapel.[106]

Signs of a possible direct influence of the religious model of marriage on the rites of the Florentine bourgeoisie are tenuous indeed. It was not the Church that presided over the reorientation of ritual expressed, after 1470, in an increasingly frequent omission of certain phases or in the more intimate character of the marriage celebration. In Florence, the *ricordanze* suggest that the problem of the dowry had detached the consummation of a marriage from the celebration of the *nozze* to link it more closely with the ring day, contracting into a single, more compact ceremonial the creation (by the *verba de praesenti*) and the accomplishment (by consummation) of the marriage and thus making the *nozze,* the wedding itself, superfluous. The fact that unions were more often celebrated *alla dimestica*—almost as if on the sly—seems more a direct response to economic pressures and to the matrimonial market than a response to the teachings of the Church. As the fifteenth century progressed, the oblique solution to the problem of the dowry brought on by the Monte delle Doti did

---

106. See F. Haskell, *Patrons and Painters: A Study in the Relations between Italian Art and Society in the Age of the Baroque* (London, 1963); P. Burke, *Culture and Society in Renaissance Italy 1420–1540* (London, 1972).

more to change nuptial ritual in upper-class Florentine society than the policies of the Church. Similarly, thanks to the efforts of the Medici, marriages among the urban aristocracy paradoxically came to approach humbler unions in their simplicity, eliminating the festivities of the *giure* and the *nozze*. These examples reveal that in elite Florentine circles the motivation to simplify the nuptial scenario did not for the most part come from the Church.

These internal changes had the effect of making marriage a more private affair rather than interiorizing the consensual character of marriage. The Church, first of all, insisted less on the essence of consent than on the need to control it according to models—as the Tuscan *Sposalizio* has shown— that were closer to the Norman than to the French model of reciprocal donation. Even marriage legislation did not really further the practice of expression of consent or freedom of consent between the two spouses. According to the most authoritative theologians of the time, the assent of the son of the family or of the wife could be reduced to a sign, even to their simple presence, or to an absence of overt contradiction.[107] The search for "signs" of consent obviously opened the way to interpretations most pleasing to parents and friends. The practical limitations of doctrine concerning consent are just as evident in the synodal statutes of Florence of 1517. At that date the Florentine clergy proposed to combat the common practices of "ignorant [people who] do not understand the force of the words they pronounce, often believing that they are becoming engaged when they are pronouncing the very words of marriage." The remedy that the synod proposed in order to put these common people's *sponsalia* in their proper place was to require the parties involved to call for the parish priest or the notary, who would ask the husband-to-be if he would agree to marry the girl when her family requested it of him. There is no question here of the bride's pronouncing *verba de futuro* instead of the humbler formulas or rites by which she might give her personal promise.[108] In combating the ambiguity of the nuptial agreement among common folk, the Florentine Church of 1517 condemned—perhaps not in all innocence—the reciprocal character of that agreement. And when it reinserted the celebration of the engagement into the domestic setting, under the supervision of the notary or the parish priest, the Florentine Church was really imposing upon the lower orders habits of the ruling class, who were

107. "In filiis familias sufficit tacitus cum expressione eorum in quorum sunt potestate" (Among children in families it is sufficient [for them] to be silent, with a statement on the part of those in whose power they are); "Si . . . illa nihil respondeat, dico quod si mulier consentiat animo sed ex verecundia taceat, permittitur tamen se subarrhari per anuli immissione voluntarie vel dotari ipsa taciturnitate et patientia consensus eius exprimitur etiam si lingua taceat . . .sufficit quod non contradiceat" (If she does not respond at all, I say that if the woman consents in spirit but remains silent from modesty, it is permitted to marry her, as a consenting party, giving her a ring or a dowry; [for] by that very silence and passivity her consent is expressed even if her tongue is silent. . . . It suffices that she not speak against it) (Antoninus, *Summa*, 3:1:19, fol. 20.

108. R. C. Trexler, *Synodal Law,* 125. See above, note 56.

less than enthusiastic about submitting their matrimonial strategies for the approval of a giddy girl.

In Florence, then, we can see changes in nuptial ritual—changes that occurred late and were incomplete and psychologically and socially limited, but that were to become clarified and widespread from the end of the sixteenth century onward.

These changes were indeed late, in comparison to those in France and, perhaps, other parts of Italy such as Venice or Rome. There the Church's hold was established earlier; in Florence, nuptial practice did not really give a privileged place to the ring day until the fifteenth century, and even the choice of that day did not place the priest at the heart of the ceremony, except in the imaginary world of iconography.

The changes were incomplete because most Florentines demonstrated a nonchalance toward the religious blessing that lowered them to the level of those "animals" condemned by the preachers and the more observant of their flock. Also because, as a domestic ceremony, the transfer of the woman to her husband in exchange for the gift of a ring still conformed to very ancient forms of the matrimonial contract. To be sure, these forms were subject to control by the presence of the public agent, the notary, who made sure that consents were given according to the rules. Still they perpetuated gestures and behaviors in which the woman remained basically a pawn to be placed as favorably as possible on the social chessboard.

The changes were limited because they seldom reflected a deep awareness of the sacrament of marriage; they reflected the families' financial or political needs just as much as they did the doctrines of the Church. They were also limited socially because the lower strata of society found them more congenial than did the "good and ancient families," for whom the stakes involved in alliance, and therefore the rites designed to bring families closer together, remained all-important to their survival and advancement.

To what factors and to what structures did Florence and Tuscany owe the existence, around 1500, of this somewhat exceptional situation? I believe the establishment of patrilineality in urban clans from the twelfth century onward, what amounted to a decline in the legal and social status of women, and the triumph of the dotal system served to maintain and fix contractual and legal forms of the ritual of marriage, retarding the emergence of an image of the married couple and the household based on reciprocal donations and mutual and freely given consent. The *Sposalizio*, in an ambiguous and rather timid fashion, prepared the terrain for the Church's penetration into these rituals. But the only way it could influence ideas and attitudes was by proposing, on its own initiative, the figure of a High Priest who, both in his gestures and his role, resembled the traditional giver of the bride and guarantor of the contract.

# 10

## The Griselda Complex: Dowry and Marriage Gifts in the Quattrocento

 *Chi to' donna, vuol danari:* He who takes a wife wants money. In a recent study, Diana Owen Hughes has traced the fundamental change in the West from a system of marriage assigns based on a "brideprice," or an "indirect dowry," to the dowry system.[1] This transformation, which differed from one region to the other, affected most of western Europe between the eleventh and the fourteenth centuries. It came particuliarly early and was most sweeping among the aristocracy, followed by the business-oriented middle class in centers of commerce. It accelerated and broadened with the increased circulation of money and with the increasing complexity of economic exchanges. Finally, it went hand in hand with the more clearly defined affirmation of the rights of male heirs to their fathers' real property, to the exclusion of their sisters. "Perhaps men now preferred to endow the female members of their own descent group [than] to [invest] in their wives, who were necessarily alien members [of their lineage] since both custom and ecclesiastical law required exogamy."[2] When daughters were thus excluded, they became wives inevitably more subjected to their hus-

Originally published as "Le complexe de Griselda," *Mélanges de l'Ecole Française de Rome* 94, no. 1 (1982): 7–43.

1. D. O. Hughes, "From Brideprice to Dowry in Mediterranean Europe," *Journal of Family History* 3 (1978): 262–96. A listing of the essential literature on the origins and the spread of the dowry system in the Middle Ages can be found here. We might add D. Herlihy, "The Medieval Marriage Market," *Medieval and Renaissance Studies* 6 (1976): 1–27.

2. Hughes, "From Brideprice," 287–88.

bands, who in turn managed to "assert their power over the whole of the conjugal estate."[3]

During the age that interests me here—the two last centuries of the Middle Ages—this evolution was fully accomplished in metropolitan centers like Florence as well as more generally in central and northern Italy. Here a woman was virtually excluded from a share in the paternal estate. Her father or her brothers dowered her "appropriately," but they made every effort to keep her from removing any of the lands that constituted the nucleus of their patrimony or any of the houses in which their ancestors had lived. The need for this dotal practice was fully taken for granted: what Florentine would have questioned it around 1400? From the top of Tuscan society to the bottom,[4] families ran to the notary to establish a dowry, and a marriage without dowry seemed more blameworthy than a union unblessed by the Church. The dowry penetrated to the very heart of the social ideology of the time. It was what guaranteed honor and the share of respect due each individual: it ensured the nubile girl and the widow a marriage that respected the taboos concerning feminine purity; it conferred and proclaimed before all the social rank of the marrying couple and of their families.[5] It was therefore a regulating force in society. Since funding a dowry was a charitable work when the dowry was set up for a poor and deserving girl, charity also furnished a device to keep the social machinery from grinding too fine, assuring the salvation of the donor as well.[6] After 1430 an important financial innovation placed the dowry at the center of the apparatus of the State. When the Florentine commune instituted a sort of dowry insurance to stimulate an increase in marriages, it guaranteed a "decent" dowry at the account's maturity to any girl whose father had thought to make a deposit in the Monte delle Doti when she was a child.[7]

In this way the dowry system penetrated the entire structure of Florentine society, politics, and people's thinking at the end of the Middle

---

3. G. Duby, *Le chevalier, la femme et le prêtre: Le mariage dans la France féodale* (Paris, 1981), 103–15, esp. p. 107.

4. On the spread of the dowry in the popular classes in Florence see S. Cohn, *The Laboring Classes in Renaissance Florence* (New York, 1980), 16–25. For the urban upper classes, see D. Herlihy and C. Klapisch-Zuber, *Les Toscans et leur familles: Une étude du catasto florentin de 1427* (Paris, 1978), 414–18.

5. J. Kirshner, *Pursuing Honor while Avoiding Sin: The Monte delle doti of Florence,* Quaderni di *Studi Senesi* 41 (Milan, 1978).

6. L. Passerini, *Storia degli Stabilimenti di Beneficenza e d'Istruzione della Città di Firenze* (Florence, 1853), 501–15; R. C. Trexler, "Charity and the Defense of Urban Elites in the Italian Communes," in F. Jaher, ed., *The Rich, the Well Born, and the Powerful: Elites and Upper Classes in History* (Urbana, 1973), 64–109.

7. J. Kirshner and A. Molho, "The Dowry Fund and the Marriage Market in Early Quattrocento Florence," *Journal of Modern History* 50 (1978): 403–38; D. Herlihy, "Life Expectancies for Women in Medieval Society," in R. Thee Morewedge, ed., *The Role of Women in the Middle Ages* (Albany, 1975), 1–22. On the Monte delle Doti and its role in Florentine society of the fifteenth century, see also M. Becker, *Florence in Transition,* vol. 2: *Studies in the Rise of the Territorial State* (Baltimore, 1968), 236–37.

Ages. Its triumphant success seems to have erased all memory of the practices that preceded it. The dowry, however, did not achieve its empire smoothly and without tensions. Toward the middle of the fourteenth century, complaints arose regarding the excessive and ever-increasing amounts of dowries. Literary figures as prominent as Dante and Giovanni Villani protested the effects of the system and its hypertrophy.[8] The principle, however, was never seriously questioned. Had Florentines of the fourteenth and fifteenth centuries really forgotten that 150 years earlier the husband brought at least as much to a marriage as the wife? Were they unaware that women at that earlier time were not excluded from the paternal estate, which could fall to their lot as well as to their brothers'? The new system must have been responding to very strong exigencies, or else it contained mechanisms for self-correction for people to have adapted to the tensions engendered by the pursuit of dowries.

One of the chief conditions often cited for the establishment and development of this system has been a numerical imbalance between men and women as possible partners. It is extremely difficult, however, to weigh this imbalance at a time when the system was on the brink of change and when the dowry, brought by the woman, prevailed over other forms of payment.[9] Furthermore, even if one can admit the existence of a "matrimonial market" in which supply and demand for spouses of both sexes varied in relation to some demographic factors and influenced others, it is nevertheless difficult to apply this argument to a comparison of variations in the amount of the dowry with variations in the price of merchandise. Dowries and wives changed hands in only one direction, and it would be absurd, in market terms, to pay in order to sell one's merchandise. In a society like that of Florence at the end of the Middle Ages, where filiation was strongly patrilineal and marriage strictly virilocal—not the case in all contemporary European societies—the absurdity of the analogy is even more evident. Why indeed would the family into which a woman was about to enter demand supplementary payments—a dowry, a trousseau— when by the marriage of one of its sons it had already acquired rights over the bride, her labor, and her descendants? As recent anthropological studies have emphasized, this conundrum exists for all economically oriented interpretations of marriage portions that see them as deriving from a cost/profit relationship.[10]

---

8. Dante, *Paradiso*, XV: 103–5; G. Villani, *Istorie fiorentine* (Florence, 1823), 2:96.

9. See Herlihy, "The Medieval Marriage Market," 13–20, and the remarks of Hughes, "From Brideprice," 285–87. See also Herlihy and Klapisch-Zuber, *Les Toscans*, 414–18.

10. J. Comaroff, "Introduction," in J. L. Comaroff, ed., *The Meaning of Marriage Payments* (New York and London, 1980), 1–47; D. B. Rheubottom, "Dowry and Wedding Celebrations in Yugoslav Macedonia," in ibid., 221–50. Historians are all the more willing to admit this working hypothesis because it takes into account social mechanisms posited as measurable and permits a quantitative approach.

The function that the jurists of the time assigned to the dowry—taking care of household expenses, then of the widow's needs, before returning to her descendants—did little to resolve the intrinsic contradiction in the dowry system or the problem posed by the imbalance in the respective contributions of the allied families.[11] Indeed, how could one justify the fact that the Florentine husband, after enjoying the benefits of administering the dowry for the duration of his marriage, contributed so little to the maintenance of his widow? Or that he provided no widow's dower, and in the fourteenth and fifteenth centuries his marriage gift to her was reduced to a ridiculously low *donatio propter nuptias* required by law?[12] In practice, it proved extremely difficult for a widow even to recuperate the dowry on which she was to live and which her legitimate heirs or their guardians tried desperately to keep until her death. Was it true that the dowry primarily assured a flow of goods from the families that gave the wives to the heirs of the families that took them in? This is the role that Jack Goody assigns to it when he sees the dowry as characteristic of the complex societies of Europe, societies of agricultural working families of bilateral filiation.[13] For Goody, the dowry was equivalent to the daughter's share of the inheritance. When she brought it to her husband, she effected a transmission of goods from the male lineage. One of the results of the system was that it worked in favor of a greater social diversification, since each negotiation of an alliance redistributed the cards economically and redefined the rank and status of the partners. It is difficult, unfortunately, to apply this attractive theory to late medieval Europe, where bilateral filiation had been obliterated both in law and in practice, and where the principle of male transmission of goods—land in particular—had been adopted. Here the dowry was not considered a female share in inheritance; to the contrary, it worked to exclude its beneficiary from inheritance. In Florence, daughters, dowered or not, could inherit from their fathers, in the absence of brothers or nephews, only up to one-quarter of the fathers estate, the remainder going to agnatic kin. Needless to say, heiresses were rare.[14]

11. See M. Bellomo, *Ricerche sui rapporti patrimoniali tra coniugi* (Milan, 1961), 65ff; G. S. Pene Vidari, *Ricerche sul diritto agli alimenti*, vol. 1: *L'obbligo ex lege dei familiari nei giuristi dei secc. XII–XIV,* Memorie dell'Istituto giuridico dell'Università di Torino (Turin, 1972); vol. 2: *Mem.* 144.

12. Bellomo, *Ricerche*, 15–23, 46ff.; R. Caggese, ed., *Statuti della repubblica fiorentina,* vol. 2: *Statuto del podesta dell'anno 1325,* (Florence, 1921), 98; *Statuta populi et communis Florentiae (1415)* (Fribourg, 1778–81), 1:156–59. In Florence, a widow seemed to keep this sum only if her husband died without male heirs: see the *ricordanze* of Luca di Matteo da Panzano, Archivio di Stato, Florence, henceforth abbreviated ASF, *Strozziane*, 2d ser., 9, fol. 21v, 2 December 1422.

13. J. Goody, "Inheritance, Property and Women: Some Comparative Considerations," in J. Goody, J. Thirsk, E. P. Thompson, eds., *Family and Inheritance: Rural Society in Western Europe, 1200–1800* (London, 1976), 10–36; "Bridewealth and Dowry in Africa and Eurasia," in J. Goody and S. J. Tambiah, eds., *Bridewealth and Dowry* (Cambridge, 1973), 1–58.

14. There is no study that calculates whether female dowries were equivalent to the male portions of the inheritance; at first sight, however, they seem to be situated generally

In Florence, then, the dowry system functioned counter to modern anthropological theory. What is more, it functioned badly, created unbearable tensions, and aroused innumerable complaints on the part of those involved with it on a daily basis. It did function, however, and it became the subsoil in which psychological reflexes and social customs took root. Should we, then, not question the traditional approach to the phenomenon? Have we adequately described the whole of the system when we have analyzed the legal aspects and the demographic or economic implications of the circulation of dowries? Perhaps we should look elsewhere, beyond dowries, for other kinds of matrimonial assignments and for the elements that would legitimize the working of this circulation by placing it back into a whole, certain terms of which are generally underestimated. It seems to me that an exploration of the fringes of the Florentine dowry system reveals a series of assignments of which the dowry can be considered a priori only one part. Yet historians, once they had concluded that the dowry played a predominant part in marriage law, lost interest in the assignments based on custom, which are mentioned in a great many documents, although in less than clear terms. When these exchanges, which had been judged marginal, became the prey of folklorists, they left the area of "historical facts," those privileged objects studied by analysts of medieval law or the medieval economy. At best, historians have judged them a residue of a defunct system and of little economic or social importance, abandoning them to the curiosity of antiquarians who collect practices and rituals of the good old days.[15] What I want to do here is to reexamine certain of these marginal assignments to see whether they might have constituted a counterweight to the dowry by remaining of functional importance in the economics of the exchanges connected with formation of a married couple.

What leads should we follow to explore these fringes? The usual materials of the legal historian lend themselves poorly to such an inquiry. There are few notarial acts during the fourteenth and fifteenth centuries that mention anything but the dowry and the legal actions that governed its determination and delivery. Normative texts of communal or religious

---

at a lower level, which implies a general male hypergamy. On female rights of succession, see *Statuta* (1415), 1:222–25.

15. For Tuscany, see the studies of O. Bacci, *Usanze nuziali del contado della Valdelsa* (Castelfiorentino, 1893); J. Del Badia, "Fidanzamento e matrimonio nel sec. XV," in *Miscellanea fiorentina di erudizione* 1 (1886): 189–92; A. Funaioli, "Usanze del comune di Pomarance," *Rivista delle tradizioni popolari* 1 (1894): 619ff.; O. Targioni-Tozzetti, *Le strenne nuziali del sec. XIV* (Livorno, 1873); and particularly L. Zdekauer, "Il dono del mattino e lo statuto più antico di Firenze," *Miscellanea fiorentina di erudizione* 1 (1886): 33–36; Zdekauer, "Le doti in Firenze nel Dugento," ibid., 97–103; Zdekauer, "Usi popolani della Valdelsa," *Miscellanea storica della Valdelsa* 4 (1896): 64–66, 205–12. The position of P. Toubert, in *Les structures du Latium médiéval* (Rome, 1973), 1:742, who rejects one after the other the "alembical exegeses of the romanists, canonists, historians of law, and folklorists" concerning the ritual and customary practices in weddings, seems to me to do away rather hastily with social indices that are also interesting to the simple historian.

origin say somewhat more, but they only tell us what was considered excessive or deviant from current practice without describing those practices in detail. On the other hand, the Florentine family sources, the *ricordanze*, exceptionally plentiful in that epoch, are equally exceptional for their abundant and precise descriptions of the minute details associated with private and public marriage ritual.[16] The author of a book of *ricordanze*, in order to establish his own eventual rights or to acknowledge engagements he has agreed to, carefully notes the chronology of the entire process of the alliance. He notes all the credits and debits that have marked its course, the contributions controlled by law, and the more or less clandestine exchanges that the law prohibited or tried to contain. Through these assignments the donor increased the number of persons obliged to him; if he was the recipient, he contracted an obligation that he considered important to remember or to recall to his heirs. The dowry itself and all that made it up—trousseau, financial obligations or credits in the public debt, coin, etc.—can be found detailed in these books with much greater care than in notarial registers. Occasionally we have access to papers that have generally disappeared from the other types of documentation—private *scritte* resembling a marriage contract, revealing the agreement arrived at by the families' appointed negotiators. The husband or the bride's father often copied down a detailed description of the items in the trousseau—the *donora*—which was brought to the husband's house the day after the wedding ceremonies and appraised independently by two clothes dealers. But above all what appears in the *ricordanze* in all its diversity is the collection of gifts that the couple and their families exchanged. With a little effort we can discern in the calculations and the narrative entries in these journals a network of exchanges infinitely more complex but also more intelligible than the unilateral and simplistic gesture of the dowry alone.

## Marriage Gifts: A Clandestine Counterdowry?

Any operation that concerned the dowry and the trousseau in the Quattrocento required publicity and legal procedures that took it out of the familial sphere. Thus the payment of the monetary portion of the dowry (the total amount of which had been proclaimed before the two family groups at the time of the solemn *giuramento*) began at the moment of the exchange of consent, and each installment required an official act duly

---

16. On the *ricordanze*, see C. de la Roncière, *Un changeur florentin du Trecento: Lippo di Fede del Sega (1285 env.–1363 env.)* (Paris, 1973), 11–21; F. Pezzarossa, "La memorialistica fiorentina tra Medioevo e Rinascimento: Rassegna di studi e testi," *Letter italiane* (1979): 96–138; Pezzarossa, "La tradizione fiorentina della memorialistica," in G. M. Anselmi, F. P. Pezzarossa, and L. Avellini, eds., *La "memoria" dei mercatores* (Bologna, 1980), 39–149.

notarized and drawn up before witnesses.[17] The payments could continue for years, the acknowledgment of the final payment sometimes occurring many years after the wedding. It was extremely rare, however, for a bride to establish herself in her husband's house before at least part of the dowry had been paid, usually in hard cash and full-weight coins. As for the trousseau, it was obligatorily delivered on the day of the wedding or the following day,[18] and its conveyance, in baskets or coffers sometimes provided by the husband,[19] signified that the marriage had been consummated and cohabitation established. The principal ceremonies in the nuptial scenario—the families' agreement and oath taking, the *verba de praesenti* (the couple's marriage vows), and the wedding ceremonies—were thus highlighted by a public act that expressed in broad daylight and in a form made official by a document or by material conveyance, the transfer of goods that accompanied the wife.[20]

There were other exchanges that were carried out with less publicity, however. During the days or months preceding the marriage and within the year following, the husband provided what was in effect a wardrobe for his wife, a kind of countertrousseau, about which the notarial acts of the time say not a word. These marital gifts had an influence, however, on the supposed imbalance between the respective contributions of the two parties, an asymmetry, let me recall, that has been reputed typical of

17. On the nuptial scenario and its evolution in Florence, see also chap. 9 above, "Zacharias, or the Ousted Father."

18. The trousseau generally arrived on the Monday following the Sunday of the wedding, or with the bride herself on her wedding day. Two examples among many others: the wife of Giovanni Buongirolami, who, 7 August 1499, "venne a stare qui in casa et rechò in tre zane le infrascripte cose e donora" (came to live here in [this] house and brought in three wicker baskets the things and trousseau listed below) (ASF, *Strozz.*, 2d ser., 23, fol. 131, Ricordanze di Giov. di messer Barnardo Buongirolami); Marco di Parente Parenti, who married off his daughter Marietta Sunday 9 April 1475: "Andò a marito a casa di detto Tomaso e consumarono la sera il matrimonio" (She went to [her] husband to the house of the aforementioned Tomaso, and they consummated the marriage that evening); April 10: "Mandai le donora della detta M. a chasa del sopradetto T. Stimate insino a dì 7 da . . . rigattiere overo sensale . . . con due zane nuove in che si portarono le sopradette donora" (I sent the trousseau of the said M. to the house of the aforementioned T. They were appraised on 7 [April] by . . . clothes dealer and marriage broker . . . along with two new baskets in which the abovementioned trousseau was transported) (ASF, *Strozz.*, 2d ser., 17 bis., fol. 72, modern numeration. Dates are given in modern style, as the Florentine year began March 25).

19. Aside from the baskets cited in n. 18, see G. Niccolini da Camugliano, *The Chronicles of a Florentine Family, 1200–1400* (London, 1933), 140: The husband sends for his wife, the daughter of Paolo Niccolini, and Paolo sends him the trousseau "in two baskets, because he [Giovanni, the husband] had not sent me coffers, nor had I had them made." Two *zane* and two painted coffers, on the other hand, figure in the trousseau of Gostanza, Marco Parenti's daughter, in 1472, but for his own marriage, Marco had had two coffers painted that were not completely ready on the day of the wedding (ASF, *Strozz.*, 2d ser., 17 bis, fols. 69 and 4).

20. On the conveyance of the trousseau, see A. van Gennep, *Manuel de folklore français contemporain* (Paris, 1976), 1:1, 352–63; N. Belmont, "La fonction symbolique du cortège dans les rituels populaires de mariage," *Annales, E.S.C.* 33, no. 3 (1978): 650–55.

the dowry system. They form a sort of counterweight provided by custom to the dowry brought by the bride, a counterweight that must be studied not only for its economic value but also in the context of the symbolic process by which new relationships were established between lineages or within families.

Marco Parenti, a rather exceptional husband, to be sure, as his own mother-in-law, Alessandra Strozzi, emphasizes in her correspondence, is a case in point.[21] Between 1447 and 1449—from the moment of the *giuramento* to a year after the wedding—Marco spent on his wife a sum that represented more than two-thirds of the dowry.[22] The outfits—clothes and jewelry—that he offered her cost him nearly 700 *fiorini,* while the dowry, including the trousseau, amounted to less than a thousand *fiorini.* His mother-in-law considered him infatuated beyond all reason with his young spouse and eager to satisfy her least desire. But the reason for these eccentric expenditures lies above all in the hypergamy of the husband: Parenti was a newcomer by comparison with the Strozzi with whom he allied himself, and Alessandra needed to justify her choice of son-in-law to her son, who was in exile in Naples. She could have found a more honorable party, she explains, but the dowry would have cost 500 *fiorini* more and the suitor would not have accepted the delayed payment that she had proposed.[23] The fact remains that the husband's contribution— here exaggeratedly high—reveals the prevalent trend in Florentine practice. The young husband spent considerable sums to adorn his wife and to "make the chamber" in which the couple was to live. Although the law prescribed nothing of the sort and attempted to limit excess,[24] responsibility for clothing the wife during the nuptial period was felt as an ineluctable necessity by the Tuscan husband. And this customary obligation more often than not exceeded the value of the trousseau that the wife brought. In the case of Marco Parenti, the expenditures he made for his marriage and for his wife more or less devoured all the cash dowry that she brought him. All husbands did not show equal generosity, but the information that can be gleaned from the *ricordanze* demonstrate that for the most part they spent for this purpose between one- and two-thirds of the promised dowry (in holdings or in cash), trousseau included. In this manner Valorino Ciurianni marries his son Lapozzo to a Cavalcanti in 1410: he is promised 700 *fiorini* of dowry, but he spends 430 *fiorini* on clothing for his daughter-in-law, a sum to which the expenses of furnishing

---

21. Marco Parenti is known not only through his *ricordanze* (see notes 18 and 19) but also through the correspondence of his mother-in-law, Alessandra Macinghi negli Strozzi, *Lettere di una gentildonna fiorentina del secolo XV ai figliuoli esuli,* ed. G. Guasti (Florence, 1877, reprinted 1972).

22. The expenses for the wedding are listed on fols. 3–12 and 28; they are partially reproduced in A. Macinghi, *Lettere,* ed. Guasti, 15–22.

23. Ibid., 3–6.

24. See below, notes 91–100.

the bridal chamber (74 *fiorini*) and of the wedding festivities (20 *fiorini*) must be added.[25] Giovanni Venturi shows equal generosity when he takes a Boninsegni as his second wife in 1439, spending 750 *fiorini* for the adornment of his bride when the dowry was only 1,300 *fiorini*.[26] The sums that most husbands devoted to this purpose remained within more reasonable limits. In 1457 Jacopo di Giovanni Attavanti married Oretta Malifici, whose dowry was 350 *fiorini*, of which only 78 was in coin. The husband in this case spent as much as 93 *fiorini*, or 27 percent of the total dowry, to "clothe" his wife.[27] Tribaldo dei Rossi recapitulates, in 1482, the expenses involved in his marriage: his wife had a dowry of 1,250 *fiorini di suggello*, in which the trousseau counted for 250 *fiorini*. He himself spent 270 *fiorini larghi* to clothe her, provide her jewels, and decorate the conjugal chamber.[28] At one pole of these marital expenditures, one Lorenzo Morelli spent only the equivalent of 12 percent of the 2,000 *fiorini* of dowry received from his wife, Vaggia Nerli, on gifts, the wedding festivities, and furnishings.[29]

This obligation was not exclusive to the upper level of urban society: dowries among humbler folk were counterbalanced by the husband in exactly the same manner. Like the dowries of the daughters of merchants and bankers, those of the daughters of the *popolo minuto* of Florence or of peasants in the Tuscan countryside were made up of a trousseau and of a certain cash sum, rarely of real estate. Custom thus dictated the dual nature of the dowry, although the trousseau occupied a relatively more important place in it since it counted for a third to a half of the total.[30] In like manner,

25. ASF, *Manoscritti*, 77, fols. 35v. An extreme case: in 1351 messer Luca di Totto da Panzano receives at his marriage 450 *fiorini* of dowry, but he spends 550 *fiorini* for the "forzierino, e le robe sue e le nozze e la gabella, e che lasciai per donora a messer Bindo" (jewel case, her clothing, the wedding, and the tax, and that which I left as a gift to messer Bindo [his father-in-law] ) ("Frammenti della cronaca di messer L. di T. da P. da una copia di V. Borghini," ed., P. Berti, *Giornale storico degli archivi toscani* 5 [1861]: 68). Similarly, one Carlo di Ugolino Martelli, in marrying Oretta, daughter of Giovanni d'Antonio Medici with 2,000 *fiorini* of dowry, spends 330 *fiorini* in clothing for his wife and 820 *ducati* in jewels (ASF, *Strozz.*, 5th ser., 1464, fols. 117r–117v, 1478).

26. ASF, *Manoscritti*, 86, fols. 4–5.

27. Archivio degli Innocenti, *Estranei*, 53, fols. 6–7; 54, fols. 8v–9v.

28. Biblioteca nazionale, Florence (henceforth abbreviated BNF) 2, 2, 357, fols. 2–6v.

29. ASF, *Carte Gherardi*, Morelli 137, fols. 63v.–79, 164.

30. The trousseau in Florentine dowries before 1433 known by means of the *ricordanze* accounted for nearly 13 percent, on the average, of the total value of what the female dowry brought in; and that proportion remained the same after that date, that is, after the institution of the Monte delle Doti, and until about 1520. J. Kirshner, *Pursuing honor*, 3, n. 3, citing two examples, remarks that occasionally that equilibrium was not respected in Florentine dowries and that the trousseau might constitute (as for the illegitimate daughter of Francesco Datini) 84 percent of the dowry, or it could drop to 8 percent (in the case of Paliano Falcucci marrying a Scolari in 1390). Our sampling of more than forty cases contains only one other case this extreme, in which the trousseau represented less than 3 percent of the total dowry. Peasant dowries are known through allusions to them in the fiscal declarations of the *catasto* of 1427 and of 1470.

the rustic husband felt obliged to "put on the back" of his wife a sum equivalent to the other half of the dowry. And as he rarely had ready cash at his disposal for the "clothing" of his spouse, he too, just like the more fortunate Florentines, had to wait for the cash payments of the dowry to enable him to receive his wife, who already wore his ring, before too much time had passed.

The interdependence of the two parties was thus extremely finely tuned. Some frankly admit it. A notary, ser Agnolo Bandini, who married a noble girl, Nanna Tornaquinci, in 1453, was promised a modest dowry of 350 *fiorini,* not including the trousseau. His father-in-law, *grand seigneur,* promised to pay 200 *fiorini* of this before the bride joined her husband, "so that," as the latter says, "I can dress her and can make my chamber."[31] Much good it did him, for the needy noble was never to pay what he owed and continued to live—even luxuriously—at his son-in-law's expense. It is clear that the husband did not always consider the payment of the dowry a godsend: even when a father sent his daughter off with a trousseau and hard cash, the husband would often whine that he would just as soon not take a wife, since the liquid portion of the dowry would go to clothing his bride. "When my son gets the dowry," one future father-in-law complains, "he will have to spend this amount *or even more* to clothe his wife."[32] The discomfiture that this obligation to clothe the bride engendered can be measured by the complaints that we can hear from both sides, echoed in the tax records. Since the bride's father does not have the money that he must pay his son-in-law, he is unable to send his daughter to him— even when she in duly betrothed and *anellata*—and the husband is equally unable to produce his countergift of the bride's clothing. An alliance without both parties' contributions or lacking gifts to the bride would be considered incomplete, hastily and carelessly fashioned.

All this evidence permitting us to pinpoint the importance of the husband's customary gift of clothing to his wife suggests that a portion of the dowry was diverted from the satisfaction of the needs of the household to the personal needs of the married woman. This use of the dowry seems to contradict juridical theory (in which the dowry meets the needs of the marriage) and also to contradict many of the conclusions historians have reached on the role of dowries in economic life. Certainly the dowry could not launch a young husband in business when the greater part of it was blocked in shares of the Monte delle Doti and when the portion that was paid in cash—a much smaller portion in the fifteenth century than was customary in the fourteenth—was immediately spent by the husband on clothing for his wife.[33] How then are we to explain why Florentine hus-

31. ASF, *Conventi soppressi,* 102, 84, fol. 17v: "per vestirla e farmi la camera mia" (to clothe her and make my bedchamber); fol 104, on his quarrels with F. Tornaquinci.

32. ASF, *Catasto,* 266, fol. 334, declaration of Giuliano di Michele Fusacchi of San Gimignano: the dowry is 60 *fiorini.*

33. On the utilization of dowries as an indicator of social advancement, see L. Martines, *The Social World of the Florentine Humanists, 1390–1460* (Princeton, 1963), 18ff; D. Herlihy,

bands showed so little resistance to these customary demands, which, with the institution of the Monte, denied them the access to professional autonomy and the flexibility of investment that the dowries of the fourteenth century had offered them? Were not gifts of clothing and even the furniture of the bridal chamber mere survivals and feeble echoes of a legal system that had been abolished and that had disintegrated into customary obligations as ruinous as they were constraining, as senseless as they were mechanical?

To be sure, marital gifts should not be confused with the *donatio propter nuptias,* the marital counterpart of the dowry. Since the twelfth century and the rebirth of Roman law, the *donatio propter nuptias* had coexisted with the *Morgengabe* of Germanic origin, first as a deformation of it and then as a substitute almost everywhere in southern Europe. It is common knowledge that, beginning with the thirteenth century, this donation was kept within strict limits that took all real pecuniary importance from it, just at the time when the sums involved in dowries among the urban classes were rising.[34] In the fifteenth century, the required 50 *lire*—approximately 12 *fiorini*—accounted for little in comparison with the thousand or two thousand *fiorini* that the daughters of merchant families brought with them. Thus the marital donation declined, in law as well as in practice. Nevertheless, it expressed the need, respected by law from late antiquity; to establish a reciprocal and almost equal exchange between the two parties. We can find this same need in the *Morgengabe* (the *morgincap* of Tuscan documents) or the gift that the husband made to his wife the morning after the wedding night.[35] Originally composed of movable goods, the *Morgengabe* introduced by the Lombards into Italy soon aroused hostile reactions, expressed in limits placed on the wife's free enjoyment of this gift. Little by little it became established that the *morgincap* returned to the husband's heirs, as did the portion of his wealth (*quarta, tertia*) that he had ceded to his wife.[36] In spite of these limits, it was the husband's gift that long served to proclaim to all the consummation of the marriage and, in the last analysis, its validity. The legal revolution that took place

---

"The Medieval Marriage Market," 10–11; Herlihy and Klapisch-Zuber, *Les Toscans,* 414ff.

34. Zdekauer, "Le doti in Firenze," and Bellomo, *Ricerche,* 15, 27–60, 223–44.

35. Zdekauer, "Il dono del mattino"; Hughes, "From Brideprice," 273–76. The *mancia,* or gift of money that the Florentine of the fifteenth century made to his wife the morning after the wedding night, recalls the older *Morgengabe:* 22 *fiorini* in 1410 "per donare alla detta sposa la mattina seguente che la menò" (to give to the said bride the morning after I had 'led' her) (ric. Ciurianni, ASF, *Manoscritti,* 77, fol. 35v); 25 *fiorini* in 1416 (ricordanze di Antonio Rustichi, ASF, *Strozz.,* 2d ser., 11, fol. 8v); 20 *fiorini larghi* and 100 *grossoni,* or 26 fiorini, in 1477 ( ric. d: Bartolomeo Sassetti, ASF, Strozz., 5th ser., 1751, fol. 135); 30 fiorini larghi and 200 *grossoni* in 1482 (ric. di Tommaso Guidetti, ASF, *Strozz.,* 4th ser., 418, fol. 5); 20 gold *fiorini larghi* and 35 *lire* in 1499 (ric. di Giovanni Buongirolami, ASF, *Strozz.,* 2d ser., 23, fol. 130); 35 *ducati* in 1542 (ric. d'Andrea Minerbetti, Biblioteca Laurenziana, Florence, *Acquisti,* 229, 2, fol. 158).

36. Bellomo, *Ricerche,* 5–13; Hughes, "From Brideprice," 276–80.

at the end of the eleventh and the beginning of the twelfth centuries certainly was not able to eliminate with one pen stroke a deep-rooted structure of exchanges in effect for half a millennium. It seems to me that the husband's customary obligation to dress the bride perpetuates the *function* that the *Morgengabe* had fulfilled. It would be wrong to see it as the deformation of a legal form, however. This would too quickly reduce the debate to the single point at which historians and folklorists have confined it. Furthermore, it would neglect the deeply felt significance of these assignments, for without the reciprocal exchange of goods between families and between spouses, the establishment of a new alliance would remain incomplete. Even more important than the material worth of these gifts, in fact, was the need that people engaged in the process of alliance felt—on all levels of society—to make such offerings. They took great pains to reestablish an equilibrium perturbed by the official modalities of the dowry system when an alliance was made and a new couple set up housekeeping. The obligation honored by the husband to "dress" his wife thus *acted* as a countergift. It reestablished equality between the partners, an equality that had been destroyed by the initial gift and by the superiority that it momentarily conferred to the giver over the receiver.[37]

If there is a husband's counterbalance—and a sizable one, financially— to the one-way contribution of the wife's dowry, then an analysis of the dowry cannot be confined to its economic terms alone. These assignments have all of the traits characteristic not of a market economy (or even of a "matrimonial market"), in which the respective contributions theoretically adjust to the solicitations of supply and demand, but of a structure of exchanges founded on gift and countergift—odd as that might seem in the context of a great merchant city.

## The "Clothing" of Griselda

The husband's gifts not only responded to a demand for reciprocity: they were also indispensable symbolic agents in the integration of the wife into another household and another lineage. They were signs that relations had been initiated between the husband's group, redefined to include his wife, and the wife's family of birth.[38]

When the linens and the personal belongings that make up her trousseau were sent to the bride's new dwelling, her family of birth signified that it was breaking with her in some way, that it was renouncing its rights over

37. See M. Mauss, "Essai sur le don: Forme et raison de l'échange dans les sociétés archaïques," in *Sociologie et anthropologie* (Paris, 1968), 143–279.
38. A. van Gennep, *Les rites de passage* (Paris, 1909; trans. M. B. Vizedon and G. L. Caffee as *The Rites of Passage* [Chicago, 1960] ); A. van Gennep, *Manuel de folklore*, 1:1:111–13; Max Gluckman, "Les rites de passage," in *Essays on the Ritual of Social Relations* (Manchester, 1962); C. Lévi-Strauss, *L'homme nu* (Paris, 1971), 597ff.

her.[39] Moreover, ethnological literature has often shown that the dressing of the bride is a rite of passage, more precisely, a rite of integration.[40] Florentine practice confirms this: when he "marks" her with dresses and jewels, often bearing his crest,[41] the husband introduces his wife into his group, signals the rights he has acquired over her, and initiates her into her new role as a married woman. A little-noticed fact, but an important one, clearly demonstrates the function assigned to this finery: in Florence the husband's gifts were temporary. Once they had played their role, the husband could repossess them. They were thus only momentarily "invested" on her back—just long enough for her to pass from one group to another.

The Florentine husband remained, indeed, the virtual proprietor of the objects (dresses, jewelry, furniture) offered to his wife during the wedding period. What happened to these gifts at the dissolution of the marriage depended on his last wishes. If his wife managed to keep possession of them until her husband's death, he would have to have mentioned them in his will to ensure her continued enjoyment of them, and it is on this condition alone that his heirs would allow the widow to leave their house with her festive clothes and her rings either to live independently, or, worse, to remarry.[42] Thus the notary ser Antonio Bartolomei left his wife, by a codicil to his will dated 12 October, 1492, her "clothes, her linen, and her rings," to which he added 12 *fiorini* "to dress herself" and an annual income provided she remained unmarried and chaste.[43] An Orvieto notary, ser Matteo di Cataluccio, indignantly accuses his daughter-in-law, widowed in 1457 by the death of his son, of coming surreptitiously to take back from the coffer in his bedroom the "cioppa de pavonazzo" (blue-black cloak) the departed had had made for her for their wedding.[44] Fur-

39. On the trousseau, see van Gennep, *Manuel de folklore,* 1:1:353–66; N. Tamassia, "Scherpa, scerpha, scirpa," *Atti del R. Istituto veneto di sc., lett. ed arti,* 66, no. 2 (1906–7): 725–35; R. Corso, "Pittacium," in *Patti d'amore e pegni di promessa* (S. Maria Capua Vetere, 1942), 81–94.

40. Van Gennep, *Manuel de Folklore,* 1:2:389ff; for Italy, R. Corso, *Patti d'amore*; Corso, "I doni nuziali," *Revue d'ethnographie et de sociologie* 2 (1911): 228–54.

41. See below, note 83.

42. See the *ricordi* of Doffo di Nepo Spini, 1415–39, ASF, *Strozz.,* 2, 13, fol. 87v (1436).

43. ASF, *Acquisti e doni,* 11, 1, fol. 38 (ric. di ser Antonio di ser Battista Bartolomei, 1488–94). I could give many other examples: *casa* Ciurianni (ASF, *Manoscritti,* 77, fols. 19 and 22), where the widow of Barna di Valorino leaves her children in 1380 *in spite of* her husband's will, which ordered his heirs to keep her "in tutte cose onorata come si conviene" (in all things honored as is appropriate) and had left her as guardian of the youngest child. This widow nevertheless took back possession of her dowry (a farm) immediately, and the heirs also granted her "certi pannetti che di nostro volere rimandamo, di pichola valuta" (certain garments of little value that we gave back of our own accord). On the situation of widows, see chapter 6 above, "The Cruel Mother."

44. "Ricordi di ser Matteo di Cataluccio da Orvieto (a. 1422–1458)," in L. Fumi, ed., *Ephemerides Urbevetanae e cod. Vat. Urb. 1745,* 1 (Città di Castello, 1920), 529 (*Rerum italicarum scriptores,* ed. altera, 15/5).

ther, he demands that his daughter-in-law give back "the rose-colored sleeves that our [son] Francesco had made for her" and the three rings she had received from him the day of their exchange of consents.[45] Another notary, Florentine this time, ser Agnolo Bandini, cuts short his accounting of all the expenses he had incurred for his young wife, "because [these gifts] need not be given back" if he should predecease her and the dissolution of their union oblige his heirs to give back the dowry and the trousseau.[46]

More than one widow left the conjugal roof under such conditions, leaving behind to the heirs (who might be her own children) not only the dowry and the trousseau, which they were slow indeed to return to her, but also the ritual wardrobe of her wedding. In Venice the rights of the widow to her husband's estate drew their very name—the *vestis vidualis*—from the outfits that had been cut to her measure when she came under his roof.[47] I might touch, here, on the hypothesis that will be discussed later in this volume: that the musical or charivaresque manifestations of the Italian *mattinata* were connected, when they were sweet and harmonious, with the gifts the husband made to his young bride, just as they were connected, in a discordant and critical form, with the possibility that the widow who remarried might remove those gifts from the inheritance.[48] "Give me a way to be dressed," one widow implores as she is about to leave her children and her children-in-law at the insistence of her family, who want her to remarry. We can translate: "Leave me not only the trousseau that I have the right to take back but these clothes, these jeweled rings that my husband (your father) had me wear when he was alive and that are part of your estate."[49] Some widows found themselves in a pitiful

45. Ibid., 528. And he adds: "Vestimenta debent fieri expensis mariti olim viri sui. . . . Ego non sum heres filii mei, non teneor ad vestimenta. . . . Vide quod mulier non potest petere alimentari ab heredibus mariti" (The clothes must be made at the expense of the bridegroom, her former husband. . . . I am not the heir of my sons, and I am not liable for the clothing. . . . Note that the woman cannot ask for support from the husband's heirs), which is a restrictive interpretation of the widow's right to *alimenta*, to say the least. (See above, note 11.)

46. ASF, *Conventi soppressi*, 102, 84, f. 7v: "Non seguirò qui perche mi sarebbe tedio sanza utile perche nonn'anno a essere renduti e olle affare tante cose che questo libro s'inpierebbe e questo basti" (I will not continue here because it would be useless toil since they need not be given back and I have so much to do for her that this book would fill up, so let this suffice) (1458). See the *consilia* on this question edited by T. M. Izbicki, " 'Ista questio est antiqua': Two Consilia on Widows' Rights," *Bulletin of Medieval Canon Law*, n.s. 8 (1978): 47–50.

47. Corso, "I doni nuziali," 238 n. 4; P. Molmenti, *La storia di Venezia nella vita privata*, 1 (Bergamo, 1927); *Statuti di Venezia* (Venice, 1477), 1, chap. 60; 3, chap. 43.

48. See chapter 12 below, "The Medieval *Mattinata*."

49. See the *ricordanze* of Cambio and his son Manno Petrucci, ASF, Strozz., 2d ser., 15, fols. 61v–65: a lengthy tale of the squabbles of a widow with her stepchildren when her own family takes her back to marry her off again. See chapter 6 above, "The Cruel Mother," note 44. The dowry is at stake, but also the household linen and her clothes. The phrase cited (*Datte modo ch'io sia vestita*) can be found on fol. 64. On the *alimenta* see *Statuta* (1415) 1, 223–25.

state when heirs turned nasty: the new wife of ser Andrea Nacchianti, for example, had to borrow "a few clothes" to cross the street in order to make a decent entrance into the house of her new husband—who had a dress and an overdress cut for her that very day.[50]

Long before a couple was separated by death and the nuptial costumes became a definitive part of the heirs' estate, one can see, by following the destiny of these objects in the account books, that gifts of clothing and jewelry made to a bride were frequently taken back by her husband soon after the marriage. Often he had borrowed them, just for the nuptial period, from relatives, friends, jewelers, or professional lenders, and returned them after a certain time, generally within the year.[51] Occasionally he even sold these offerings once the rite was performed, and they graced the bride only during her very first years as a married woman.[52] Once again we can cite the case of Marco Parenti: the enormous sums he spent led him to equally great regrets. This loving husband was soon to pick apart pitilessly, pearl by pearl, gem by gem, sleeve by sleeve, the various festive garments that in his ardor he had had made during the two year period that spanned his wedding.[53] Three years after the ceremonies, practically nothing remained of the treasures he had poured out on his young wife. The ritual jewels, the jeweled necklace, the precious diadem, all had vanished. When a husband had not borrowed such items but had bought them or had had them made, he could often turn a profit, once the first

50. Archiv. Innocenti, *Estranei*, 633, fol. 97 (18 May 1491): "La detta Madalena ne venne a casa con panni achatati perche aveva piatito co' cognati, et detto dì le tagliai et feci tagliare una gamurra rosata et una cioppa di saia nera" (The said Madalena came to this house with borrowed clothing because she had quarreled with her family-in-law, and that same day I cut and had made for her a rose-colored dress and a black twill overdress).

51. Thus, when Bartolomeo di Tommaso Sassetti marries Antonia della Tosa in September 1447, he borrows pearls and various jewels from several persons during the eight months preceding and the six months following the wedding (ASF, *Strozz.*, 5th ser., 1749, fols. 164v–166). Similarly, Antonio Rustichi borrows two necklaces from jewelers for weddings (*Strozz.*, 2d ser., 11, fol. 9, 1416). Giovanni Buongirolami borrows two jewels in February and March 1499, gives the ring to his wife in April with a ruby which he returns in July 1500, and gives back the other jewels as early as summer 1499 (ASF, *Strozz.*, 2d ser., 23, fols. 129v–134v). An ashamed borrower transforms the pearl necklace received on loan from Francesco di Matteo Castellani in 1450 "perchè non gli fussi ricognosciuto" (so that it not be recognized) and gives it back to him without having it returned to its original state (ASF, *Conv. sopp.*, 90, 84, n. 2, fol. 38, 1450).

52. Niccolò Ferrucci sells the pearls of his *pendente* in 1482 (*Carte Galletti*, 39, fol. 5v) (his wedding had been celebrated in 1472).

53. See the *ricordanze* of Marco Parenti, ASF, *Strozz.*, 2d ser., 17 bis, fols. 3v–23, where the author recapitulates what happened to the various items offered to his wife (1447–59). The dismantling of the wedding finery was planned from the moment the clothes were made. Marco's mother-in-law advises her own son, Filippo Strozzi, not to skimp on pearls, since "s' e' panni non s'adornano con perle, bisogna adonarlle con dell'altre frasche; che si spende assai, ed è gittato la spesa. Sì che a spendere utile ti conforterò" (if clothing is not decorated with pearls, it must be decorated with other trinkets; much is spent and the money is thrown away. So that I will encourage you to spend usefully) (*Lettere*, ed. Guasti, 466, 31 August 1465).

year of marriage was past, by allowing professional lenders to lend them to other husbands in search of ritual nuptial baggage.[54] The fact that these nuptial "gifts" could be borrowed and that later they had to be given back as soon as possible shows that this mandatory offering from husband to wife had a primarily ritual role.

The Griselda immortalized by Boccaccio in the last story of the *Decameron* stands as emblematic of just such a cruelly restricted husbandly generosity.[55] Behind the edifying story, some have deciphered the plot lines of a popular tale.[56] Both characteristics—the tale and the moralization—explain the immense popularity the novella enjoyed even as late as in the salons of the seventeenth century and in the Bibliothèque bleue.[57] But something else may have added to the success of the story, at least with Florentines. In Griselda—taken virgin, poor, and naked (in Pesellino's iconography, reproduced here as plate 10.1, she does not even have a shift to throw on to receive the ring),[58] richly adorned for the wedding cere-

---

54. Tommaso Guidetti lends "his" pendant, through jewelers, for several different limited periods and on many occasions from 1489 to 1496 (he was married in 1483) (ASF, *Strozz.*, 4th ser., 418, fols. 9v, 18v, 22v). Similarly, Niccolò Ferrucci, married in 1472, lends his pendent from 1483 on, by the month, through Piero Rucellai (*Carte Galletti*, 39, fol. 6). Bernardo di Stoldo Rinieri also lends a jewel "che disse per isposare la donna (that [the borrower] said [was] to marry his wife) (ASF, *Conv. soppr.*, 95, 212, fol. 157v, 1458).

55. On the *Decameron* and its diffusion, see especially (from a vast literature): V. Branca, *Boccaccio medievale* (Florence, 1956); Branca, *Tradizione delle opere di Giovanni Boccaccio* (Rome, 1958); Branca, "Per il testo del Decamerone: La prima diffusione del Decamerone," *Studi di filologia italiana* 8 (1950): 66ff.; Branca, "Per il testo del Decamerone. Testimonianza della tradizione volgata," ibid. 11 (1953): 163–234.

56. R. Köhler, *Kleinere Schriften zur erhzälenden Dichtung des Mittelalters* (Berlin, 1900), 2 vols.; E. Castle, "Über die Quelle von Boccaccios Griselda Novelle," *Archivum romanicum* 8 (1924): 281ff; W. Küchler, "Über Herkunft und Sinn von Boccaccios Griselda-Novelle," *Die neueren Sprachen* 33 (1925): 241–65; A. Arne and S. Thomson, *The Types of the Folktale: A Classification and Bibliography* (Helsinki, 1928), 425, 887; D. D. Griffith, *The Origin of the Griselda Story*, The University of Washington Publications in Language and Literature, 8, no. 1 (1931), 7–120; W. A. Cate, "The Problem of the Origins of the Griselda Story," *Studies in Philology* 29 (1932): 389–405.

57. On the posterity of Boccaccio's Griselda, as revised by Petrarch, see V. Pernicone, "La novella del marchese di Saluzzo," *La cultura* (1930): 961–84; V. Branca, "Sulla diffusione della Griselda petrarchesca," *Studi petrarcheschi* 6 (1956): 221–24; E. Golenistcheff-Koutouzoff, *L'histoire de Griseldis en France au XIV^e et au XV^e s.* (Paris, 1933); Golenistcheff-Koutouzoff, *Etude sur 'Le livre de la vertu du sacrement de mariage et réconfort des dames mariées' de Philippe de Mézières* . . . (Belgrade, 1937); G. Martellotti, "Momenti narrativi del Petrarca," *Studi petrarcheschi* 4 (1951): 5–33; R. Hirsch, "F. Petrarca's Griseldis in Early Printed Editions, ca. 1469–1520," in *The Printed Word, its Impact and Diffusion* (London, 1978); *Il marchese di Saluzzo e la Griselda, novella in ottave del secolo XV,* ed. G. Romagnoli (Bologna, 1862). To restrict citation concerning the diffusion of the novella in particular countries to classical France, see especially: P. Toldo, "Come il La Fontaine s'inspirasse al Boccaccio," in *Miscellanea Torraca* (Naples, 1912), 1–15; N. Cacudi, "La Fontaine imitateur de Boccace," *Rassegna di studi francesi* 1 (1923) and 2 (1924); M. Soriano, *Les contes de Perrault: Culture savante et traditions populaires* (Paris, 1968), 99–112.

58. Pesellino develops Boccaccio's text here, which was to pass into only some of the later versions and into literature of the type of the Bibliothèque bleue and which puts the disrobing of Griselda before the assembled vassals before the exchange of vows. Griselda's reduction to nudity was attenuated by Petrarch and the many who followed him. On the

Plate 10.1 Pesellino, *Story of Griselda* (detail). Accademia Carrara, Bergamo. (Photo Anderson-Alinari 12865)

monies in the presence of her baron husband's vassals, then sent back by him *en chemise* to the hut in which she was born—Boccaccio's contemporaries would have recognized acts and behaviors rooted in the nuptial practices of their times. Toward the middle of the fourteenth century, the husband's dressing of his bride still possessed the quality of compelling ritual action, and the compulsion would have been immediately perceptible to the readers or hearers of the tale. The archaic aspect of the details of Griselda's wedding have been argued to conclude that the novella embodies

---

reactions of contemporaries and of Petrarch to Boccaccio's tale, see G. Martellotti, "Momenti narrativi," 22. On the first illustrations of Boccaccio, see Branca, *Boccaccio medievale*, 219–23; on the iconography of Griselda, see L. Negri, "Per la iconografia della novella di Griselda nel Rinascimento," *La bibliofilia* 27 (1925): 13–18; and C. L. Ragghianti, "Studi sulla pittura lombarda del Quattrocento," *La critica d'arte* 1949: 48–49.

historical fact interpreted as legend.[59] Conversely, the ahistorical character of these same details have been argued in the interests of a structural study of the tale.[60] Although the second approach has proved much more productive than the first, I must admit that the argument invoked by the best champion of this cause misses its mark:[61] the references to contemporary weddings are undeniable. Boccaccio rationalized the supernatural elements of the old tale when he gave the Marchese di Saluzzo—a more plausible transformation of the monster or the being come from another world to marry a mortal—the actions (I am tempted to say the automatic ritual gestures) of a husband of his own time. Boccaccio recast the tale in the taste of his day when he brought the supernatural gifts of the monstrous husband down to the level of human experience, but he respected the structure of the story.

In order to cross the frontier that separates the human world from the supernatural, Griselda has to take on, then rid herself of, the clothing appropriate to that passage. Rites of clothing have a profound unity, whether they signal a passage from this world to the supernatural or, as here, are taken by Florentines almost as law. This unity emerges clearly in the formula *Tibi res tuas habeto* that Apuleius puts in the mouth of Cupid as he rejects Psyche (another version of the same tale), since this was the very formula that signified divorce in classical antiquity.[62] Similarly, a Florentine widow would carry away her dowry goods, and Griselda only her chemise,[63] leaving the rich garments and jewels offered by the husband under his heirs' roof. Both wore their finery and their jewels only as long as their marriage lasted, be that for a long period of conjugal union, sometimes further prolonged by a chaste widowhood, or for the short span of the nuptial period.

The *vestizione*[64] of Griselda, and the "vesting" of the bride, keeps the husband's "gifts"—an indispensable ritual counterpart to the goods brought by the wife and the agents of her transfer under his roof—within the symbolic sphere. This ritual role obviously does away with any interpretation that sees only economic or affective motivations in the husband's gifts. Admittedly, it is difficult for the historian, who cannot interrogate

59. C. E. Patrucco, "La storia nella leggenda di Griselda," *Piccolo archivio storico dell'antico marchesato di Saluzzo* 1 (1902); Patrucco, "Le famiglie signorili di Saluzzo fino al sec. XIII," *Studi saluzzesi* 1901: 57–114; Castle, "Über die Quelle."

60. See Küchler, *Über Herkunft*; Golenistcheff-Koutouzoff, *L'histoire de Griseldis*, 25–26, on the tradition of historicization from the fifteenth century on.

61. Griffith, "The Origin of the Griselda Story," 94.

62. Ibid., 23–42. On popular versions of the tale of Cupid and Psyche, see E. Tegethoff, *Studien zum Märchentypus von Amor und Psyche* (Bonn and Leipzig, 1922).

63. Griselda gives back the ring and the dresses given her "in premio della mia verginità" (as a reward for my virginity)—that is, as a *Morgengabe;* she goes off "con la dote che tu mi recasti" (with the dowry that you brought me), says the marchese in Boccaccio's novella—that is, with her one shift.

64. This term is used both for the robing of a new bride and for a nun taking the veil.

his subjects directly, to grasp what function they themselves assigned to the husband's offerings when new relations were established between individuals and between family groups. A meticulous analysis of all the exchanges included in the matrimonial ritual might enable us to see how the husband's contributions related to all the other "gifts" of foodstuffs or objects and then to consider this whole in terms of other exchanges connected to the individual life cycle or the cycle of family development. This is certainly too vast an ambition for the limits of the present study. Nevertheless, the nature and special characteristics of certain other gifts offered by the two kinship groups to the bride clarify the context within which the husband adorned his wife and welcomed her under his roof.

## The Ring Game

In Florence, either on the day of the wedding or the next morning, the father of the husband and members of his family presented the young bride with rings, some set with stones. Women closely related to the husband figure prominently among the donors, and are often in the majority. Several typical documents identify them for us. The account written following his marriage in 1433 by one of the Medici, Francesco di Giuliano d'Averardo, first cousin twice removed to Cosimo, is particularly rich in details on the festivities for his wedding.[65] Francesco lists some fifteen rings given to his wife by members of his family—seven men and seven women, besides himself. Three of the women are his paternal aunts, one his paternal grandmother, two the wives of cousins of his paternal grandfather, and a sixth a maternal aunt. Among the men are the husband's paternal grandfather and paternal uncle, two more distant cousins, a first cousin, and a business associate and the manager of one of his lands (figure 10.1). When she marries Bernardo Rucellai in 1466, Nannina Medici receives twenty rings from eighteen people, among them ten of her husband's kinswomen, her mother-in-law at the head of the list.[66] Not one unmarried girl takes part in this game: only wives, born into the lineage or who have entered it, offer a ring to the young wife. This fact keeps us from interpreting the gift of rings simply as an echo of the ceremonial exchange of mutual consent at the house of the bride's father, when the husband offered two or three rings.[67] Why should these married women

65. ASF, *Mediceo avanti il Principato* (henceforth abbreviated MAP), 148, 31, fols. 32–39.

66. A. Perosa, ed., *Giovanni Rucellai ed il suo Zibaldone: 1 Il Zibaldone quaresimale,* Studies in the Warburg Institute, 24 (London, 1960), 29. The passage concerning the wedding had been published by G. Marcotti, *Un mercante fiorentino e la sua famiglia nel sec. XV.* (Florence, 1881), Nozze Nardi-Arnaldi.

67. As recalled by Francesco di Giuliano Medici himself, who (as was normal) gave two "little rings," one with a diamond, the other with an emerald (MAP, 148, 31, fol. 34).

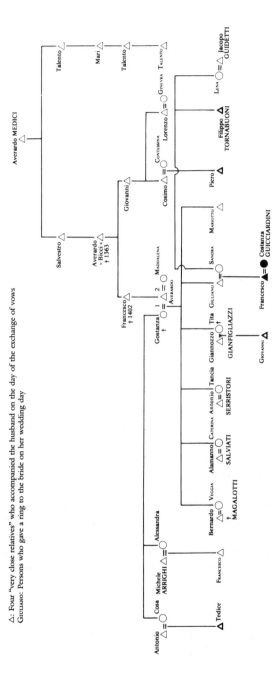

△: Four "very close relatives" who accompanied the husband on the day of the exchange of vows
GIULIANO: Persons who gave a ring to the bride on her wedding day

Figure 10.1 Gifts of Rings at the Wedding of Francesco di Giuliano d'Averardo dei Medici (13 June 1433). Source: Archivio di Stato, Florence, *Mediceo avanti il Principato*, 148 n. 31.

be charged with making this gesture of alliance, when the Florentine woman was never considered a full member of the lineage into which she entered by marriage? But is it just to the husband's lineage that the young bride is integrated by this act? And are these women acting autonomously, or are they expressing other interests involved in the nuptial ritual?

The rings seem to assign the new wife to her place in a kinship group but, more precisely, within a group of women. They situate her within the conjugal family—the family she forms with her husband—and it is that central situation that is consecrated by the many rings her husband offers her. Nannina Medici received two rings from her husband-to-be upon the agreement to marry, two others at the *sponsalitium,* the cere- monies of the "ring day," and two others at the *nozze,* "the morning of the giving of rings."[68] The three stages that mark the realization of the union are signaled by these gifts, which are considered more important than those of other relatives. The married woman is then introduced into the domestic group of her husband, often directed by his father. The "elders" of the family then signify their authority and her place in their home by means of another gift of rings. Sisters and sisters-in-law, wives of uncles and of cousins then surround the new arrival in a larger circle of kinship.[69] All these many gifts somehow reinforce the alliance: they define its limits and install the bride within its concentric circles.

But the rings have still another meaning. In the presence here of so many women of the husband's kin and in their prominent role in ritual activity we can read an insistence on impressing the new bride with her status of wife within a new lineage. The bride finds herself transplanted by her marriage, not only into a new universe of kinship, but also out of her former group (daughters subjected to a father) into the more uncertain world of married women. It is a world dominated by a hierarchy of authorities: that of her husband, her father-in-law, her brother-in-law, and the men of the husband's lineage who take part in important decisions.

When the husband's female relatives give a ring to the new bride, moreover, they are relinquishing a gift that was made to them in the same circumstances. The *ricordanze* tell us clearly and precisely that these gifts have meaning only in the ritual process, and that they no more enter into the definitive possession of the bride than do the clothes and jewels offered by the husband. When Pandolfo Pandolfini leads home a wife in 1481, his brother Jacopo notes that "we (my wife and I) gave her a diamond

---

68. Perosa, ed., *Zibaldone,* 92. Similarly, Bartolomeo di Tommaso Sassetti gives his young wife six jeweled rings (worth a total of 48 *fiorini*), and she receives others from various relatives worth 53 *fiorini* (*Strozz.,* 5th ser., 1749, fol. 169, 1447).

69. Tommaso Guidetti's father gives a pearl to his daughter-in-law, after which the husband's married sister, his brother's wife, a cousin (rather, his wife), and the latter's son follow suit: a total of five jeweled rings, to which the husband adds a diamond on the same day (*Strozz.,* 4th ser., 418, fol. 3v, 1482).

worth . . . , a diamond that we received from him when I 'led' Marietta my wife [in 1473]"[70] At the marriage of his brother-in-law the same year Jacopo notes: "We will give him a ruby set in gold that I bought twelve years ago for 15 or 16 *fiorini* . . . and that I ought to have returned to me when one of my sons takes a wife."[71] By the same token, Pandolfo, Jacopo's son, gives a diamond in 1493 to the wife of a first cousin, and his father notes gravely in his book that "the said ring should be returned when Pandolfo takes a wife or, if not he, at least the first of my other sons [to marry], because myself [his father] and Pier-Filippo [father of the bridegroom], we are even, since I made a gift to his wife when he married her and he made me one when I 'led' my wife. I note this so that my descendants will know the whole picture"[72] (see figure 10.2).

Although rings were given to new brides by wives who were already established, it was the men standing behind them who remained masters of the game, deciding on the occasions and the destination of the rings that had been "given" to their own wives at their marriage. Rectifications frequently appear in the *ricordanze* attesting that the wife was the bearer and the ritual agent of gestures the strategic direction of which remained in male hands. Our memorialists often write: "My brother (or my cousin, etc.) X, that is, *(cioè)* his wife, Madonna Y, gave my wife . . . etc."[73]

70. Innocenti, *Estranei*, 648, fol. 170, see also fol. 153v (1473). The rings were sometimes replaced by precious fabrics: Giuliano, Francesco Medici's father gives his daughter-in-law *una* "peza di vellutato in chermisi" (a bolt of scarlet velvet), her mother "ciento martore" (one hundred sable skins) (MAP, 148, 31, fol. 33v). M. A. Altieri, *Li Nuptiali*, ed. E. Narducci (Rome, 1873), 51, notes these gifts of precious fabrics, but on the part of the mother-in-law to the friends of the husband (see below, note 83, and chapter 11, "An Ethnology of Marriage"). Shirts were also given instead of rings: Bernardo di Stoldo Rinieri notes that "mia sorella . . . mi donò una perla leghata in anello d'oro la quale ebbe da me e per ischambio mi donò sei overo otto chamice" (my sister . . . gave me a pearl set in a gold ring that she had had from me, and in exchange gave me six or eight shirts) (ASF *Conv. soppressi*, 95, 212, fol. 150v, 1459).

71. Innocenti, *Estranei*, 648, fol. 173v, 10 December 1481. On the contrary, Luigi di Ugolino Martelli states in November 1487 that he was obliged to give back a diamond to the son of the man who had given a diamond to his wife (ASF *Strozz.*, 5th ser., 1463, fol. 120), and two years later Martelli returns the gifts to the donor (*Strozz.*, 5th ser., 1468, fol. 113v, 30 January 1490).

72. Innocenti, *Estranei*, 652, fol. 118 (3 October 1493). Similarly, Manno di Cambio Petrucci notes the three rings received at his marriage in 1444 and adds "e la moglie di Cieseri mi donò uno anello, che inprima n'avevo dato a lui simile a quello, si ché di casa Domenico non ebi altro (nè da altri ch'io abi a rendere)" (and Cieseri's wife [the wife of Cieseri di Domenico di Tano, a first cousin] gave me a ring similar to the one I had first given him, so that I had nothing else from Domenico's house [nor from others that I must return]) ASF, *Strozz.*, 2d ser., 17, fol. 33v.

73. "E Filippo mio fratello, coè la Piera sua donna gli donò . . ., E Lucha mio chugino coè la Giovanna sua donna gli donò . . ., E la Piera mia sorella e donna di Bernardo Altoviti mi donò" (And Filippo, my brother, that is, Piera, his wife, gave her . . . and Lucha, my cousin, that is, Giovanna, his wife, gave her . . . and Piera, my sister, wife of Bernardo Altoviti, gave me) (Ric. di Bernardo di Stoldo Rinieri, ASF, *Conv. soppr.*, 95, 212, fol. 150v, 21 January 1459). Manno di Cambio Petrucci comes right out and says that it was to him that the diamonds and rings were given: "Donomi la dona di. . ., mi donò, etc." (The wife of . . . gave me, X gave me) (*Strozz.*, 2d ser., 17, fol. 33v, 29 June 1444).

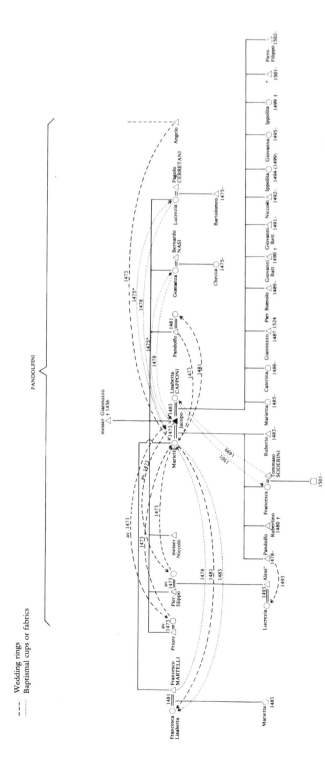

Figure 10.2 The Circulation of Ritual Objects in the Family of Jacopo Pandolfini (1473–89, 1493–1502). Source: Archivio degli Innocenti, Florence, *Estranei*, vols. 648, 651, 652.

followed by a meticulous accounting of rings given and received. Filippo Strozzi heads a new page in his book *Anelli Donati* and notes on it "the persons who logically and to all reason *(ragionevolmente)* ought to restore them to the wife of Alfonso [my son].[74] After 1500 Andrea Minerbetti keeps records of the sort in his *ricordanze* under the heading *Dono*. The best example of this is that of Giovenco di Giuliano Medici, who notes thirty of these transfers of rings between the date of his own marriage (1448) and that of his third son (1492).[75] These passages in the domestic books testify to the importance attached to the rite and to the need to keep the rings circulating.

The rings thus had several combined functions. They marked the limits of the kinship circle into which the wife entered, and they welcomed her into that circle. They established her in the female roles that she, like their donors, was to play there. Finally, they reinforced a solidarity among the kin themselves and sent it echoing from one generation to another, and they permitted the women who had been initiated in this way at their own marriage to replay the terms of the alliance and to have their turn at exercising a mediating role toward women younger than themselves. Periodically, the marriage rings skipped a generation. When they did, their transmission or their restitution reinforced the solidarity and the ties established with the allied families that had formerly received daughters of the lineage as wives. As the examples of Pandolfini or of Francesco Medici demonstrate, the nephew would renew ties, through his wife, with his aunts, with wives of his father's or his mother's brothers, with the cousins of those marriages, or with his father's sisters' sons. The multiform symbol of the ring, the circular form of which recurs in many of the objects and ritual presents of alliance and marriage—necklace, diadem, belt, etc.—was widely used by the Florentines of the fourteenth and fifteenth centuries not only to link the wife to her husband and the daughter-in-law to her family-in-law, but also to take each marriage as an opportunity to renew all of the already established alliances that still played an important role and were worth preserving.

The circulation of rings, however, sometimes became blocked for a time, and ties of alliance, poorly maintained, could slacken. Indeed, a cycle

74. ASF, *Strozz.*, 5th ser., 41, fol. 161v (1486): "Apresso sarà richordo d'agneli dati e che darò per l'avenire a persone che ragonevolment 'gli aranno a rrendere alla donna d'Alfonso" (Follows a list of [seven] rings given, and that I will give in the future to persons who logically will have to give them back to Alfonso's wife).

75. Biblioteca Laurenziana, *Acquisti*, 229, 2, fols. 36, 57; Baker Library (Harvard Business School), Selfridge Collection of Medici Papers, Ms. 500, fol. 4r, 6v. Bartolomeo Sassetti notes what happened to four of the eight jeweled rings offered to his wife: a saphire is "given" to the wife of the preceding donor, "il suo medesimo, per non errare" (his own, so there can be no mistake) (ASF, *Strozz.*, 5th ser., 1749, fol. 169). The care with which the worth of each "gift" is registered in the *ricordanze* shows that they aimed at giving back, if not the object itself, at least its exact equivalent: one must not appear "unequal." (See Mauss, "Essai sur le don," 211.)

of gifts between affines could be initiated only by a married man, since in Florence the wife's kin did not participate in the offering of gifts, which took place under the husband's roof on the wedding day. It was thus a husband who made the initial gift and who renewed the alliance between the families by offering the first ring to the wife of his brother-in-law—a ring that could not be returned to him until the marriage of his own son. Such was the case with Jacopo Pandolfini, who decided to offer his wife's brother's bride, on her marriage, a ring that could not "in all good reason" be returned until the following generation, when one of his sons married.[76] Although the ritual relations that maintained and constantly redefined the alliance depended on the initial act of the family that had received a wife, these relations were neither clearly drawn nor obligatory. If payment of the dowry was delayed too long and relations between the families turned sour, for example, the husband would hardly seek to inaugurate a cycle of regular exchanges. Thus the alliance did not automatically open up continuing and cyclical ritual relations between lineages. Once inaugurated, however, these relations had every chance of being carefully cultivated. But how could this aim be met if marriages were separated by two long an interval, given that it was reciprocity that gave substance and meaning to the rite?

In Florence, another series of interconnected exchanges took place after those of the rings and the marriage gifts. These exchanges occurred at the birth of children born of a union, and they carried the same obligation to return the object "given." Florentines saw in this act an explicit renewal of the ring-exchanging game. At the birth of a child in a middle-class Florentine family, it was the custom to offer the mother a silver cup decorated with the arms of the two families allied by the marriage.[77] This goblet renewed the cycle of exchanges if the ring had already made its round trip or had long remained blocked with one couple because all the possible partners were already married. Cup and ring had parallel functions without being really interchangeable. As Andrea Minerbetti says in his book in 1504 under *Dono:* "Note well—reason being changeable [read: since errors can be made in accounts]—that since my brother-in-law Zanobi Corbinelli has 'led' a wife, I ought to give a ring in compensation

76. See notes 72 and 74 above.
77. Andrea Minerbetti sends his daughter Gostanza "per havere facto fino adì 24 detto una fanciullo maschio . . . uno nappo d'ariento coll'arme nostra e de' Saxetti pieno di pinochiati" (for having had on the 24th a male child . . . a silver goblet with our arms and those of the Sassetti full of pinenut cookies) and worth nearly 20 *fiorini* (Bibl. Laurenz., *Acquisti,* 229, 2, fol. 91, 30 August 1512). Similarly, Filippo Strozzi sends his daughter Marietta, *sposa* Ridolfi, at her first childbirth (a son): "uno nappo d'ariento a fette e dorato tutto il fondo e horllo chol'arme de' Ridolfi e Strozi . . . e pieno di pinochiati" (a striated silver goblet gilded inside and with a gilded border, bearing the arms of the Ridolfi and the Strozzi . . . and full of pinenut cookies) (ASF, *Strozz.,* 5th ser., 41, fol. 163v, January 1488). His son-in-law had sent Filippo's wife this same *nappo,* also full of *pinochiati,* in February 1487, at the birth of a daughter.

[*ricompensa*] for the goblet that he sent Ermellina [my wife] when she gave birth to Maria . . . but we agreed on this day, 25 November, Zanobi and I, that the goblet I lent him at the end of August for him to give to Bernardo Lanfredini, his own brother-in-law, constitutes the compensation of the said ring, and that I am not obliged to give him anything else."[78]

Since the offering of foodstuffs of all sorts that accompanied and punctuated the nuptial proceedings should be taken into account if we want to establish a more complete model of nuptial exchanges, we should remark that they shared this quality of reciprocity and circularity with the gifts to the married couple. It was a Roman, Marco Antonio Altieri, who best and most explicitly expressed this when he said them as "loans full of love, designed to provide more easily for the expenses of the wedding, loans which in similar circumstances will have to be returned with all good will and love [by those who are now beneficiaries] acting as persons filled with gratitude and appreciation."[79] Altieri refers here to the gifts *(segno)* and the contributions of foodstuffs that the friends and relatives of the husband's family brought on the eve of the wedding.[80] He speaks in similar terms of gifts to the bride from the women relatives on both sides invited to the wedding, gifts that were delivered the day following the wedding and that were to be "considered only as a free and well-intentioned loan, which the father [of the husband] will have to return on analogous occasions to all the persons from whom he notes in writing that he has received them."[81] Florentine practice, as it surfaces in the notations of the

---

78. Bibl. Laurenz., *Acquisti*, 229, n. 2, fol. 57. Also, forks and spoons bearing the arms of the two families were often offered on the occasion of a childbirth (see ASF, *Carte Gherardi*, Morelli 137, fols. 137, 165v, 1477), as were lengths of cloth to make outfits for the newborn (ASF, *Conv. soppr.*, 95, 212, fol. 159, 1482, where fabrics, capes, and forks offered to the wife of Bernardo Rinieri are listed). These "gifts" involved the same implicit obligation to return the compliment: see Jacopo Pandolfini giving 5 *braccia* of cloth: "Ce ne l'aranno a rendere quando noi aremo uno figliuolo, che llei a partorito uno figliuolo maschio" (They will have to return [the gift] to us when we have a son, she having had a male baby) (Arch. Innocenti, *Estranei*, 652, fol. 118, 1494). The same was true for silver forks (ASF, *Strozz.*, 4th ser., 418, fol 11v, 21 December 1494). It is clear that these childbirth presents involved accountings as complicated as marriage gifts: Tommaso Guidetti (ibid., fol. 8) registers the gifts made by his wife in his absence for a period of six years.

79. Altieri, *Li nuptiali*, 58.

80. In Rome in the fourteenth and fifteenth centuries these gifts of foodstuffs, known as the *parte*, consisted in a fish or part of a sturgeon. On fish as it enters into matrimonial fertility rites, see E. Westermarck, *The History of Human Marriage* (5th ed., New York, 1927), 2:484–85.

81. Altieri, *Li nuptiali*, 88. On sharing in wedding expenses, van Gennep, *Manuel de folklore*, 1:2:507–8. Martine Boiteux notes that in Alatri the family of the husband registers in a *Libro dei presenti* all the gifts brought, noting their worth, and that "anyone whose name is not inscribed in the book not only is not invited but, further, is stricken from the list of family members. The feast confirms the family" ("Recherches sur les fêtes de printemps à Rome," Mémoire de l'Ecole française de Rome, unpublished MS [1978], 143). On the

*ricordanze,* testifies to the care with which these loans and their movement back and forth were recorded. They were men's business, as were the written memoranda kept of them.

In this manner, ritual defined and relaunched the cycles of exchanges within the lineage and between allied lineages. The quotation from Altieri invites us to examine this system as it operated among the Florentine middle-class families and compare it to that of the Roman aristocracy he described. In Rome, if Altieri is to be believed, the gifts occasioned by a marriage demanded that the *two* family groups be united in one place. At the exchange of mutual consent, which took place, as in Florence, under the roof of the father of the bride, "the husband's closest relatives," who had accompanied him, repeated his gesture immediately after him and offered "rings or other little presents" to his wife.[82] This was immediately answered by the mother of the bride, who offered her son-in-law a bowl decorated with the arms of the two families[83] and presents lengths of cloth "to those who had made a present to the bride." In Florence, on the other hand, the contribution of friends and relatives of the husband was limited on that day to small gifts (*merce*) of sweetmeats or foodstuffs for the collation that ended the day. After placing the ring on his wife's finger, the Florentine husband distributed veils, rich fabrics, coifs, and shoes or

customary contribution (*porter à la noce*) in the village of Minot before 1914, see Y. Verdier, *Façons de dire, façons de faire: La laveuse, la couturière, la cuisinière* (Paris, 1979), 285–86: "The present in foodstuffs here puts into operation a generalized principle of reciprocity, and the sphere of exchange goes far beyond the sphere of the two families who have become allied: it includes the entire village." See also ibid., 327–28, on the role of the young, who carried the foodstuffs.

82. Altieri, *Li nuptiali*, 51.

83. Ibid. See also M. Mauss, "La notion de personne," *Sociologie et anthropologie*, 344, on the relationship between crests, names, and ancestors. As we have seen, the "joined arms" of the allied families were added, in enamel, to the goblets that circulated at births: thus they could be transformed if needed. See Filippo di Matteo Strozzi: "Alla Brigida di Donato Bonsi . . . pel primo suo parto, uno nappo d'argento adorato di oncie 13, chostòmi chollo smalto . . . fior. 14 s. 15" (To Donato Bonsi's Brigida . . . for her first childbirth, a gilded silver goblet weighing 13 ounces that cost me, with the enameling, . . . 14 *fiorini* and 15 *soldi*) (ASF *Strozz.*, 5th ser., 41, fol. 161v). Jacopo Pandolfini sends his sister a "nappo coll'arme sua e nostra . . . pieno di monzellatti" (a goblet with her arms and ours . . . full of sweetmeats), and when his wife gives birth, he receives one "coll'arme sua e nostra e de' Martelli di peso d'incircha oncie 18, e da nnoi n'ebbe quando ebbe la Checha uno choll'arme nostra e sua di tal peso" (with her arms and ours and those of the Martelli, weighing about 18 ounces; when she had Checha, she had one from us of the same weight with our arms) (Innocenti, *Estranei*, 648, fols. 161v, 168v, 1475, 1478). See also ibid., fol. 173v (1481) on the addition of enameled crests. The arms of the two families also decorated the marriage coffers. See C. Aiazzi, ed., *Ricordi storici di Filippo di Cino Rinuccini dal 1282 al 1460 colla continuazione di Alamanno e Neri suoi figli fino al 1506* (Florence, 1840), 251: the sum of 33 *fiorini* was owed to "Apollonio dipintore per un paio di forzieri dipinti e messi con oro coll'arme nostra e de' Martelli" (Apollonio, painter, for two coffers painted and with our arms and the Martelli arms in gold) (1461). Crests also decorate the copper *bacino* in the bride's trousseau: see for example the *ricordi* of Marco Parenti, ASF *Strozz.*, 2d ser., 17 bis, fol. 3 (1448).

clogs to the women of the *famiglia*—domestics included—of his wife.[84] In Florence, then, all gifts were made in one direction on the "ring day."[85] The same is true of the wedding day, when the wife was "led" by her husband and when she received the rings and gifts mentioned above. The response and the countergifts did not follow until the next day, when the trousseau arrived and the wife in her turn distributed veils, shirts, slippers, or small gifts to the members of her husband's household.[86] It seems to me remarkable that Florentines preferred to associate the husband's relatives with the installation of the bride under his roof rather than with the rite of the formation of the couple, "according to the precepts of the Holy Church," at the house of the bride's father. The sequences of the nuptial scenario must have been clearly separated in their minds and their actors seen in isolation. The two families' participation and giving was more restricted than in Rome, more limited in the number of recipients, in the place chosen to make the gifts (which in Florence coincided strictly with the dwelling of the spouse of their own blood), and in the moment at which they offered them (for the husband's kin this was confined to the moment of the wife's "initiation" into her new family). Florentines, it appears, wanted to accentuate the rites of separation and admittance of the wife, whereas in Rome the two families seemed to emphasize ritually the relations of alliance that involved them jointly. In Rome the participants interacted, individually and collectively, at all moments of the nuptial ritual and at all stages of the exchanges that it governed.[87] The Florentine ritual, using the same elements but arranging them differently, aimed particularly at defining where the wife belonged and in effecting her in-

84. Lapozzo di Valorino Ciurianni thus offers a ring to his mother-in-law (ASF, *Man-oscr.*, 77, fol. 35v, 1410). Tommaso Guidetti gives "chalze due alla divisa e uno paio nera . . . a tre servitori de' Richasoli . . . quattro sciugatoi fini donate alle serve de' Richasoli" (two pair of hose in the livery and one black pair . . . to three servants of the Ricasoli [his family-in-law] . . . , four fine towels given to the Ricasoli's women servants) (ASF, *Strozz.*, 4th ser., 418, fols. 3v–7v, 1482). Lorenzo di Matteo Morelli distributes *chalze a divisa* to the servants of the Nerli (*Carte Gherardi*, Morelli 137, fol. 76, 1472).

85. However, Tommasa di Giovanni Niccolini, following the Roman model, offers a purse to her brother-in-law, who had come to accompany her husband to the ring ceremony. (Niccolini da Camugliano, *Chronicles*, 64, 1353.)

86. Altieri, *Li nuptiali*, 86. There are frequent examples in Florentine trousseaux of these presents that the bride distributed in the following days: see, for example, the *donora* of Gostanza Benci when she married Bernardo Gondi in 1518 (L. Pagliai, *Una scritta nuziale del secolo XVI, Nozze Schiaparelli Vitelli* (Florence, 1904), or the trousseau of Nannina Medici when she married Bernardo Rucellai in 1466 (Marcotti, *Un mercante*, 92, n. 66). Bonaccorso di Vettorio Ghiberti gives 6 "fiorini larghi tra grossi e oro" (6 florins in mixed coins) the morning of 22 June 1500 to his wife Lionarda, "disse per dare mancia . . . ; non s'usi" (she said, to give gratuities. . .; she did not use them) (Innocenti, *Estranei*, 547, fols. 60v–61; see also ibid., 546, fol. 43v). The *mancia* is thus perhaps used by the wife to be redistributed to the husband's family.

87. I may be too much influenced on this point by the presentation Altieri makes of Roman wedding celebrations: his analysis of nuptial rites starts from a political choice—restoring peace between family groups—and thus, in conformity with that end, he gives an idealized vision of the practices of the past. See chapter 11 below, "An Ethnology of Marriage."

tegration into the lineage of the husband. Such an interpretation strongly accentuates the limits to Florentine interlineage solidarity, when lineages are considered as collective actors in the nuptial ritual and as partners in the political life of the city.[88]

## Sumptuary Display

The exchanges of presents between families enables us to understand better the nature of the husband's "gifts," how they were specific to this role, and why they were provisional, remaining as part of the husband's estate if the woman was widowed. The husband's ritual "clothing" of his spouse was carried on with all the more solemnity since at that epoch the transfer of a dowry to form an alliance could engender a severe shift in the economic and social imbalance between lineages. The wedding gifts went some way toward filling the gap left in the domain of the law by the disappearance of the husband's assignments. They did so, in Florence, by lending greater value to the ties that bound each of the two spouses to their respective families by alliance rather than by emphasizing the new and permanent relations between these families. The part custom played in the nuptial assignments draws its importance, then, from the need to define the status of the dowered women, to mark them with the husband's seal when they "entered" his *casa,* and to blend them in with the group of *care donne* who had entered before them—in short, the need to keep the dowry from escaping as soon as the personal tie between husband and wife broke. The presents, which might seem fictitious because they were provisional and of short duration, were nevertheless *doni* (gifts) in the full root sense of the word: in order to function, they had to be returned. That is why Florentines made every effort to see that certain gifts circulated not only during the period of the establishment of the alliance, but also for the whole time during which the marriage remained alive and useful—that is, as long as there were children being born.[89]

Public authorities tried to impose guidelines to the playing of this game, which escaped its control. It is fair to ask why. What good did it do to set limits on the ritual expression of alliance and on its local peculiarities?

88. The contrasts between the principles of political life in Florence and in Venice are outlined by F. Gilbert, "The Venetian Constitution in Florentine Political Thought," in N. Rubinstein, ed., *Florentine Studies: Politics and Society in Renaissance Florence* (London, 1968), 463. The mechanisms of the rivalry between lineages and the formation of clienteles have been shown by Dale Kent in *The Rise of the Medici: Faction in Florence, 1426–1434* (Oxford, 1978). For the general political background in Florence, see G. Brucker, *Florentine Politics and Society, 1343–1378* (Princeton, 1962), and his *The Civic World of Early Renaissance Florence* (Princeton, 1977); N. Rubinstein, *Il governo di Firenze sotto i Medici (1434–1494)* (Oxford, 1966).

89. Mauss, "Essai sur le don," 250–55; E. Benvéniste, *Le vocabulaire des institutions indoeuropéennes, vol. 1: Economie, parenté, société* (Paris, 1969), 65–86.

On this point sumptuary laws can teach us much indeed, and they are abundant enough to deserve a study of their own. Here, I make only a few observations.[90]

Laws in the fourteenth century were aimed more toward limitations on ceremonial banqueting than toward limitations on the worth of the gifts or the number of givers.[91] Beginning at that time, however, certain statutes reflect the apprehension of religious or communal authorities when the giving of gifts and countergifts forced the expenses involved in a union to reverberate far beyond the circle of close relatives. One instance among many is the statute of Arezzo, dated 1327, which forbids anyone, but in particular the six women relatives of the husband who participate in the ceremony, to offer the least *donum* to the wife on "the ring day" or to send the couple *donamenta* during the entire year following the wedding.[92] In Lucca a sumptuary statute of 1362 not only limits the number of invitations to the wedding and the dishes that can be served and forbids "presents" of foodstuffs on the ring day or the day that the wife returns to her father's house for a banquet; it also prohibits the gifts that the bride might make "to her father-in-law, her mother-in-law, the brothers and sisters of her husband, or to any other person of the house or family of the husband."[93] The ritual *donamenta,* brought or sent by the members of both kinship groups and consisting of foodstuffs, sweetmeats, or objects are thus thrust into a quasi clandestinity. The Church frowned on these alimentary liberalities, misuse of which could soon take on "the force of custom," for encouraging the sin of gluttony. The lay authorities saw them mainly as an opportunity to gather too many members of restless family groups. In Florence itself, a limit was first set to the number of people at public gatherings on the occasion of *sponsalia,* before daring to aim directly at the family groups at the nuptial banquets. Thus in 1415 two hundred male guests could still participate in the festivities of the *sponsalia* of rich Florentines, but only thirty guests of both sexes could be summoned to join in the wedding feast.[94]

90. For Florence, the statutes of ecclesiastical origin have been published with comment by R. C. Trexler, *Synodal Law in Florence and Fiesole, 1306–1518* (Vatican City, 1971). Trexler remarks (p. 113) that after 1310 and with the exception of 1354, it was the commune that took the initiative and enacted laws in this domain. The sumptuary statutes of civil origin are included in the communal statutes of various periods, particularly in book 3 of those of 1415, *Statuta populi et comunis Florentiae* (Fribourg, 1781), 2:366ff: "Ordinamenta circa sponsalie et nuptias."

91. Trexler, *Synodal Law,* 114, 116–17, 271.

92. *Statuto di Arezzo (1327),* ed. G. Marri-Camerani (Florence, 1946), 4:85:238–40.

93. G. Tommassi, "Sommario della storia di Lucca dall'anno MIV all'anno MDCC, compilato su documenti contemporanei," *Archivio storico italiano,* 10 (1847): 1–632 (the "Statuto suntuario" is on pages 95–102).

94. On the laws of 1322, see R. Davidsohn, *Storia di Firenze* (Florence, 1965), 7:680, where he cites the statutes of the captain and the ordinances of 1356. See *I capitoli del comune di Firenze: Inventario e regesti,* ed. C. Guasti and A. Gherardi (Florence, 1893), 2:101, 167. In 1388 the "radunata degli uomini" (gathering of men) at the *sponsalizi*—that is, at the

More interesting for my purposes are the dispositions concerning the *vestizione* of the wife by the husband and the customary gifts which, after the *donatio propter nuptias* was eliminated, perpetuated the functions of the former "morning gift" in nuptial practice. Certain statutory texts speak clearly of the interdependence of the dowry and the husband's gifts, a phenomenon also evoked, as we have seen, by the complaints of husbands waiting for the dowry in order to receive their spouse properly adorned according to rite. The sumptuary laws sometimes reveal the mechanism by which dowries and the husband's gifts were swept up in an inflationary spiral, in what contemporaries, as early as the fourteenth century, experienced as a mad race. The Arezzo statute of 1327 limits the value of the *cofanellum vel aliqua areda* sent by the husband to his wife. It does so by linking its value to that of the dowry, saying that these presents must not exceed one-third of the value of the dowry.[95] There are articles in statutes of communes farther to the south that are even more explicit: certain of them describe, occasionally in luxuriant detail, the gifts that were permitted or forbidden.[96] One such article deserves citation at greater length for its analysis of the inflation of dowries.

In May of 1308, articles were added to the statutes of Tivoli to regulate wedding procedures.[97] The legislators note that nobles and commoners were crushed by "the enormous and unusual dowries that they must pay for their daughters, nieces, or sisters." What is more, "by evil custom and abuse" they must also deliver *"dona et exenia* and other things as well as the dowry . . . which are worth more than the dowry itself." To hear them tell it, this situation was peculiar to Tivoli: "Neither in Rome nor in the other nearby lands, nor even much farther away in Italy, does one see such custom and abuse." The remedy: limit the number of guests at the various nuptial ceremonies, forbid "on the Monday or the Tuesday [following the Sunday wedding] the relatives of the bride from sending a gift or *exenium* to the house of the husband . . . in addition to the dowry, with which the husband should be satisfied." The husband, "reciprocally," is forbidden to send to the parents or relatives of his wife *guarnimenta* (silk, shoes, slippers, etc.) aside from those destined for his spouse. Up

---

public conclusion of the alliance—is limited, as in 1356, to one hundred "invited" persons. See the *Ordinamenta,* ed. D. Salvi, in the appendix to G. Dominici, *Regola del governo di cura familiare* (Florence, 1860), 221–37. For 1415, see *Statuta populi,* 366, 369.

95. *Statuto di Arezzo,* 4:85:238.

96. For example, the statutes of Montalboddo in the Ancona Marche, which enumerate the "mannatum, insenium seu donum . . . de panibus, carnibus, planellis, centuris, marsupeis, denariis" (offerings or gifts . . . of bread, meats, clogs, belts, purses, money) that can be given by the husband or his close kin to the bride or her family; the husband can send his wife only simple items for the wedding (*Storia d'un comune rurale della Marca Anconetana,* ed. A. Menchetti [Iesi, 1913], 261, in appendix to bk. 2: "Gli statuti di Montalboddo dell'anno 1366 con le modificazioni e le aggiunte degli anni 1369, 1371, e 1375").

97. V. Federici, ed., *Statuti della Provincia Romana,* Fonti per la storia d'italia, 48 (Rome, 1910), 253–55.

to this point the analysis is classic. It is the excessive expense of the wedding, festivities, or trousseau that raises the price of the dowry. It is the avidity of those who take a wife that, in the last analysis, is the cause of inflation.

In September of the same year (1308), the people of Tivoli took up the problem again. The new text that is inserted in the city statutes shows that in refining their first analysis they reversed its terms.[98] They have "heard it said that in many cities and places which, outside the city of Rome, are nobler and richer than the city of Tivoli, women, both nobles and commoners, are dowered by their parents or by their brothers with no more than a light and moderate dowry, approved by good and praiseworthy uses and customs, because of the modesty of the clothing and belts that they [the husbands] have had made for their wives [the description of these outfits follows]; in this way, this very restricted dowry profits those who receive it more than their large dowries profit the people of Tivoli. For, in Tivoli, excessive, useless, and superstitious[99] garments are made for women, for which he who receives the dowry does not hesitate to spend it entirely or partially; since he puts aside practically nothing of this dowry to take care of the necessities of life, he shortly finds himself constrained to strip his own wife and to pawn out to the Jews, under most pressing need, those very garments with which he had adorned her, thus drowning them in usury at the lenders', against a small sum." Considering the debts and the charges that these "garments and excentricities"[100] led to, the wise men of Tivoli firmly prohibited the adorning of a spouse for more than 40 *lire*.

Tivoli offers an example that highlights the reciprocal relationship that sent both the wife's dowry and the husband's "gifts" spiraling upward at the beginning of the fourteenth century. The statutes of that city were innovative in their insistence on the husband's excesses in starting a movement that was slipping dangerously out of the family's control. The husband's role was difficult to perceive. The dowry was visible, proclaimed, legally registered, and guaranteed. It provided the measure of the couple's social standing. That is probably where the shoe pinched. The hypergamy of husbands, which characterized many marriages in urban settings at the end of the Middle Ages, brought to the husbands dowries requiring the countergifts that the Tivoli authorities had condemned as useless and "out of measure" with the resources of the overambitious husbands. Interestingly women are not denounced here as responsible for these vestimentary excesses and for the absurd prodigalities of their husbands. We may well imagine, however, that they did little to discourage the sumptuary display

98. Ibid., 256–57.
99. "Immoderata, inutilia et superstitiosa indumenta" (ibid., 256).
100. *"Ex talibus indumentis et curiositatibus"* (ibid., 257). The limit was placed at 60 *lire* for nobles, *milites* and the like.

by means of which the social rank of the new couple was proclaimed and even exaggerated during the wedding period. Displaying themselves under the pearls, jewels, and precious fabrics that for a short time they were allowed to wear, they must have found consolation for the frustration of having consented to an unequal marriage or an inferior alliance.[101] In this way, even a minimal dowry—as the case of Marco Parenti shows us—a dowry that barely reflected the social status of the couple, particularly of the wife, required customary gifts in return that were disproportionately sumptuous. When these gifts became the rule,[102] husbands were prompted to demand, and fathers to grant, dowries in cash capable of paying for this display.

Among the reasons given by the Tivoli statutes for the inflation of dowries and their wrongful use (diverted from their true function and frozen in clothes and jewels soon lost to the moneylenders), one last reason is suggested by the term *superstitiosa* applied to the feminine adornments that led families to ruin. The epithet may express the deep-rootedness of these customary gifts, the obstinate attachment to assignments that had recently been eliminated by the dowry, and the almost magical value that those entering into the married state accorded to them. The tendencies to display on the woman the signs of the rank and power of a husband or of a lineage—even to the detriment of their real fortune—may have been judged severely, but it was constantly reborn and is in evident accord with the ambiguous situation of the dowry, an instrument for social promotion as well as the only remaining visible term of a formerly bipolar system.

Thus rite and custom filled in for law. When the gifts that formerly had been given to show proof of the carnal consummation of the marriage and to give it popular legitimacy were eliminated from the purview of the law, they survived, but hidden and often forbidden. The dowry system was able to function because an equilibrium was maintained between the parties when what had formerly been the husband's contributions were transferred into the symbolic realm. This equilibrium was expressed, if not on the level of the law, at least in the reality of acts of interchange, of reciprocal and even renewed gestures of giving. Hence, the more the rules

101. The 1473 sumptuary statutes of Lucca stipulate that girls, from the age of ten, could wear pearls for no more than one year after the wedding ceremonies; brides could wear what they wanted to when they "went to husband" (Tommassi, *Sommario*, 118, n. 94). In Florence, the limit was fixed in 1388 at the moment at which the wife "wears the cloak" (*Ordinamenta*, ed. Salvi, 223, 224, 226). From 1373 on, wearing a silver belt and jeweled rings was reserved to engaged or married women (*I capitoli del comune*, II, 173–74). According to the doctrine of the jurists, female clothing should show the social rank of the husband; see Izbicki, " 'Ista questio,' " 49.

102. Hughes, "From Brideprice," 288. The statutes of Aspra Sabina denounce the fascination of the bad example of the *superchie spese* (superfluous expenditures) undertaken at nuptial feasts, which, "nel tratto del tempo, pigliano forza di consuetudine et passano al'altri en esempio" (with the passage of time take on the force of custom and pass to others as a model) (*Statuto d'Aspra Sabina, 1397*, Fonti per la storia d'italia, 69 [Rome, 1930]), 493 [additions of 1417].

of filiation and inheritance became patrilineal within a social group, the more deeply that group accepted the dowry with all its faults, and the more it broadened the interplay of gifts that gave alliance its cohesion. The traditional gifts that replaced the "indirect dowry" made up a symbolic investment, the material worth of which was far from negligible, even if it was not appraised officially. Stripped of strictly legal value, this symbolic investment figured in social bookkeeping and tempered the unilateral excesses of the system founded on the dowering of women. In her own way Griselda stands as a witness—naked, wearing only her chemise, or "clothed"—to an unsuspected complexity in the matrimonal regime toward the end of the Middle Ages, and it would be unjust to forget that it was her evil husband who clothed her in order to make her his wife. At the heart of the nuptial practices of the Quattrocento lived a hidden "Griselda complex" which assured that women and dowry goods pass, without too much friction, into the houses of the husbands.

# 11

## An Ethnology of Marriage in the Age of Humanism

In the dialogue of Marco Antonio Altieri entitled *Li nuptiali,* which appeared not long after 1500, one of the protagonists declares: "Many are the mysteries [in the nuptial rites], and I am persuaded that a great many of them have been commanded by our holy mother the Church in order to exalt the sacrament of marriage, . . . but I find myself led to doubt that the same is true of certain of these rites which, I believe, come from the hidden corners of dark antiquity."[1]

This doubt, however, does not lead Altieri to contrast a Christian model with a pagan model of the ritual order of the wedding. If he had done so, he might indeed have been led to reject as superstition common practices unrelated to the sacramental nature of marriage, and to see progress or decline in the evolution from ancient festivities to modern rites—in short, to lay down a norm by excluding certain practices.[2] Altieri's work is interesting for different reasons: because it treats relationships and the exchanges between learned culture and "popular" practices without postulating the supremacy of learned culture's models—those of the clerics or the humanists—over the popular ones, at least, not in the rites and festivities, particularly the

Originally published as "Une ethnologie du mariage au temps de l'humanisme," *Annales, E.S.C.* 36, no. 6 (1981): 1016–27.

1. M. A. Altieri, *Li nuptiali,* ed. E. Narducci (Rome, 1873), 70.
2. See J.-C. Schmitt, " 'Religion populaire' et culture folklorique," *Annales, E.S.C.* 31, no. 5 (1976): 941–53; C. Ginzburg, "Folklore, magia, religione," in *Storia d'Italia,* vol. 1: *I caratteri originali* (Turin, 1972), 601–76.

nuptial rites, that he has taken as his domain. As a legitimate heir to fifteenth-century humanism, Altieri seeks to reconcile civic order and religious order. To decipher the ritual heritage of these two orders, traditions that at first sight seem incompatible, he gauges them by the standard of classical antiquity. In doing so, he lays the foundations for an ethnology of marriage (we could even say an anthropology of alliance) that reveals surprisingly innovative sources for humanist thought before the Counterreformation.

The intellectual itinerary of the author of the *Nuptiali* cannot be understood without reference to his political itinerary. Marco Antonio Altieri[3] was born in 1450 and died in 1532. He belonged to the urban nobility of Rome, the wealth of which was grounded, in the fifteenth century, on urban properties but also on rural domains progressively converted to pasturage at the end of the Middle Ages. By tradition, this minor nobility also exercised public functions in the city and held Capitoline offices.[4] Altieri held many public offices: in 1511, before he had finished his *Nuptiali,* he was *conservatore* of the commune of Rome, a high municipal office.[5] He took a wife in 1472 from an old family of his part of the city, the Albertoni, and one of his sons, Giulio, was to marry a Casali, another family of the urban aristocracy.

Toward the end of the fifteenth century this communal lesser nobility saw its traditional political privileges eroded by the competition of newcomers. Relatives or favorites of the popes, these intruders relied on the extension of pontifical bureaucracy to round out their stipends, often at the expense of the Roman commune.[6] In those of his writings that have

---

3. Biographical information on M. A. Altieri can be found in the introduction to the E. Narducci edition of the *Nuptiali*; A. Reumont, review of this edition in *Archivio storico italiano* 20 (1874): 449–63; *Enciclopedia italiana* (Milan, 1929), s.v. "Altieri" (E. Re); *Dizionario biografico degli Italiani* (Rome, 1960), s.v. "M. A. Altieri" (A. Asor-Rosa); D. Gnoli, "Marco Antonio Altieri," in *La Roma di Leone X* (Milan, 1938), 32ff; M. E. Cosenza, *Biographical and Bibliographical Dictionary of the Italian Humanists and of the World of Classical Scholarship in Italy, 1300–1800* (Boston, 1962), 5 vols, 1:146. On Altieri's family, see also A. Schiavo, *Palazzo Altieri* (Rome, 1963).

4. See J. Delumeau, *Vie économique et sociale de Rome dans la seconde moitié du XVI<sup>e</sup> siècle* (Paris, 1959), 526–29, 566–68, 578–80 on the progress of raising grazing animals and on the behavior of the "barons" hostile to grain culture. On Capitoline administration up to the end of the fourteenth century, see E. Dupré-Theseider, *Roma dal Comune di popolo alla signoria pontificia,* vol. 11 of *Storia di Roma* (Bologna, 1952); "Nuptiali," 23.

5. He was *castellano* of the fortress of Viterbo after 1482, *maestro delle strade* in 1493; see Narducci, Introduction, *Li nuptiali,* v–vi.

6. On the administration of the curia during the second half of the fifteenth century, see R. Aubenas and R. Ricard, *L'Eglise et la Renaissance, 1499–1517,* vol. 15 of *Histoire de l'Eglise depuis les origines jusqu'à nos jours* (Paris, 1951), 74–75, 87–88, 112–13, 138–43, 146–49. On increasing venality and nepotism, see L. von Pastor, *Histoire des papes depuis la fin du Moyen Age* (Paris 1892–98), 4:213–26 (on the entourage of Sixtus IV, 1471–84); 391–95 (on the diversion of municipal funds). See also Pio Paschini, *Roma nel Rinascimento,* vol. 12 of *Storia di Roma,* (Rome, 1940), 241–46, 253–54.

come down to us[7] Altieri reflects clearly the rancor of the older Roman families more interested in local administration and municipal prosperity than in the affairs of the universal Church. With the new course of papal policy, this group felt stripped of its prerogatives, denied in its identity, and rejected by its "father" the pope, who prefered the services of "foreigners" to theirs.[8] The troubles that periodically shook the city became even more intense toward the end of the reign of Julius II, at the time when Altieri was putting the finishing touches on the *Nuptiali*. In August of 1511 the Roman nobles, who had gathered at the Capitol under the leadership of several great "barons," speculated openly on the death of the pope (whom they thought to be on his deathbed) and demanded the reestablishment of "republican liberty." When the pontiff miraculously recovered, Altieri acted as an intermediary, with other citizens, to help the barons and their followers save face and to avoid an armed confrontation by swearing peace and fidelity to the pope.[9] In contributing to a peaceful resolution of the crisis, Altieri played a role more of peacemaker than of political partisan, and in a discourse given in 1511 he lucidly analyzes the causes of the malaise that reigned among the Roman nobility.[10] He does not mince his words when he denounces the errors of his caste. For him, the misfortunes that struck his compatriots were not to be imputed to consistent bad luck that seemed to single out the Romans, nor to divine punishment, for their woes had lasted too long for that explanation to be credible. The Romans had no one to blame but themselves, and would have to mend their ways if they wanted to see the course of events change and to reestablish their political and economic position. Their moral disorder, the spirit of lucre that had begun to pervert them, and political mistakes coupled with political irresponsibility were leading them to perdition more surely than any external intervention. The same lucidity dictated Altieri's analyses of Roman decadence—understood as

7. On Altieri's works, see E. Narducci, Introduction, *Li nuptiali*, xiv–xix, where he presents the discourse given in 1511. V. Zabughin has published a novella written by Altieri: "Una novella umanistica, 'L'Amorosa' di M. A. Altieri," *Archivio della R. Società Romana di storia patria* 32 (1909): 335–94. F. Cruciani, in *Il teatro del Campidoglio e le feste romane del 1513* (Milan, 1968), gives an "Avviso" in which Altieri, describing the commune's celebration in honor of the granting of citizenship to Giuliano and Lorenzo Medici, takes this as a pretext for a veritable political manifesto (4ff). Both "L'Amorosa" and the "Avviso" were part of Altieri's *Baccanali*, an anthology of political and literary works, never published and half of which seem to be lost (see Cruciani, *Il teatro*, xxxvi–xxxviii and 127–30).

8. See in particular the diatribes against the papacy and the venality of the pontifical entourage or the pope's ingratitude toward Roman families, in *Li nuptiali*, 21–33, 186–88. The theme reappears in "L'Amorosa," ed. Zabughin, 374–75.

9. On the riots of 1511 and the sequels of the "Pax Romana," see Pastor, *Histoire des papes*, 6:345–46; Paschini, *Roma nel Rinascimento*, 393–96.

10. The discourse Altieri gave in 1511 is published in *Li nuptiali*, ed. Narducci, xiv–xix, and the 1513 discourse, given after the death of Julius II, in Zabughin, ed., "Una novella," 342.

the decadence of the urban aristocracy—that serve as preface to the *Nuptiali*
and reveal its political dimension.

The introduction to *Li nuptiali*[11] declares it an occasional work—a
eulogy of friendship, of alliance, and of their expression in the wedding
celebration, composed on the occasion of the wedding of a Roman friend.[12]
Written in the vernacular and in the form of a dialogue, the work puts
before us ten gentlemen, relatives or friends of Altieri, all imbued with
the greatness of the Roman past and with the antiquity of their own titles
of nobility. Under the pretext of contributing to the proper conduct of
the wedding festivities of his friend, Altieri declares that he will answer
their questions and submit for their deliberations what he knows of marriages of the past. Our author, then, who was nearly sixty, presents himself
as a sort of expert whose learning, humanist education, literary talent, and
political consciousness allow him to satisfy the curiosity of his friends on
ancient festivities. Under cover of enlightening them on nuptial rites,
however, Altieri is obviously pursuing political ends.

In Altieri's eyes, his contemporaries show themselves extremely ignorant
of wedding etiquette because—and this is a much worse vice—they are
on the verge of forgetting the very principles of social solidarity. Speaking
of the abuses of ancient rites—of the way the Romans of his times "are
going astray from those curious and sacrosanct ceremonies that until the
beginnings of our epoch one saw celebrated daily with such fine order
and so much propriety in the company of friends, relatives, and other
associated persons"[13]—he declares that these modern vices arise from the
scorn his fellow citizens display toward marriage and procreation. To
restore ancestral rites in all their fullness would thus be to treat the disease
through its symptoms. Unity could be restored to a "debased" social class
by the practice of traditional ceremonies; it could be helped, by this means,
to regain its hope and its taste for life, to procreate, and to busy itself for
the good of the city. Altieri argues that this sort of reassessment would
attenuate the decline—numerical, political, economic, and moral—of the
Roman nobility that he denounces in the first section of *Li nuptiali*. The
title of his work cannot mask its civic ambition. For Altieri it was indeed
a question of resuscitating a moral order and a political power—the order
and power that had formerly assured the permanence and strength of his
caste.

Altieri's analysis of the material and psychological roots of the decadence
that had struck the Roman aristocracy thus leads him to praise their former
mores and to search for the customs followed by the city's nobility at the
time of its most brilliant prosperity. The second part of the *Nuptiali* extracts

11. The original manuscript of *Li nuptiali* (composed between 1506 and 1509, with
additions after 1513) is owned by the Altieri family heirs. Several copies circulated as early
as the sixteenth century; see Narducci, Introduction, *Nuptiali*, xxv–xxix.

12. *Li nuptiali*, Proemio, 1–2.

13. Ibid., 30–31.

all possible meanings from the rites that previously had accompanied the conclusion of a marraige alliance. The model that he outlines permits him, in the third section, to broaden his analysis of the social functions of celebrations and to examine the role that those who best personify "nobility" and "civility"—his own friends of the lesser urban nobility—should play in them. It is in the central section of the work, the part devoted to nuptial rites as they had been practiced not long before and as Altieri would like to see them reinstated in all their splendor, that our humanist comes to pose questions on the relations between practice and tradition.

Spurred on by his friends' questions, Altieri comments on former matrimonial customs and on their roots in antiquity. He knows these customs firsthand since in his youth, before the deplorable reign of Sixtus IV and the Borgia, he had attended traditional weddings, when they were less perverted by a mercantile spirit and by the demoralization of the nobility than around 1500. Altieri also declares he has asked people older than himself to describe the celebration of marriages a century earlier. He may well also have done some documentary research, for example, comparing these accounts with the stipulations of sumptuary legislation at the time of Paul II.[14] These are his sources for his description of the celebration of weddings in "modern" times. Altieri's knowledge of the ancient rites to which he constantly compares them springs from his humanist education. In his youth, Altieri had participated in the meetings of the Roman Academy under the leadership of Pomponio Leto and Platina.[15] He assures his interlocutors of the *Nuptiali* that in those distant days he had discussed with his "perceptors and friends" the ancient equivalents of the customs they could observe around them,[16] and his knowledge of ancient Rome and of the best classical authors does in fact seem solid.

He proceeds differently, however, from his teachers and from their own forerunners—Lorenzo Valla, for example.[17] The Roman humanists had been forced to search for the perfect forms of classical antiquity in the degraded state to which those forms had fallen in later periods. Traditions and archaisms, ruins and vestiges thus constituted the backdrop of their melancholy journey, the outcome, always rejected, that enabled them to exalt the ancient model all the better. Altieri, on the other hand, starts

14. In 1471, Pope Paul II approved the Roman statutes that included a good deal of sumptuary legislation, particularly concerning marriage (given by Narducci in preface to *Li nuptiali*, xliii–l).

15. On Altieri's formation, see Narducci, Introduction, *Li nuptiali*, xxii–xxiii; Zabughin, ed., "Una novella," 351; Reumont, review cited (note 3 above), 450. On Pomponio Leto (1428–98) see V. Zabughin, *Giulio Pomponio Leto* (Rome and Grottaferrata, 1909–12), 2 vols.; Cosenza, *Dictionary*, 4:2906–14. On Bartolomeo Sacchi, known as Platina (1421–81), see Cosenza, *Dictionary*, 4:2839–46; Zabughin, *Pomponio Leto*, 1:58.

16. *Li nuptiali*, 30–31, 42, and *passim*.

17. On Lorenzo Valla, see Cosenza, *Dictionary*, 4:3550–69; S. I. Camporeale, *Lorenzo Valla: umanesimo e teologia* (Florence, 1972); G. di Napoli, *Lorenzo Valla: filosofia e religione nell'umanesimo italiano* (Rome, 1971); P. Giannantonio, *Lorenzo Valla: filologo e storiografo dell'umanesimo* (Naples, 1972).

from a set of fairly recent practices, taken as a whole, and goes back in time to understand their meaning and their function. This method is based more on a grasp of analogies than on a systematic search for the origins of contemporary reality. The network of correspondences that Altieri patiently constructs around each gesture, each symbol of the nuptial ritual, leads him in the long run to question the central significance of ritual forms, a significance that legitimizes ancient rites as well as more modern ones. Indirectly, the key to the cipher that he elaborates in the *Nuptiali* furnishes him not only with a valuable ideological weapon in the political combat that had inspired his investigation, but also with a more general theory of alliance.

An investigation of this sort was less likely to provoke the ire of the Church than were the Roman academicians' flirtations with antiquity in their day.[18] Altieri did not claim a priori that the customs of the ancients should be restored. This would inevitably have led him to deny or ignore the contribution of Christian doctrine to marriage. Quite to the contrary, the rituals of the golden age of the Roman commune that he hoped to bring back to life were those that, according to his own words, "our fathers," "our ancestors" observed with pomp and exactitude. This was not a remote past time but the end of the fourteenth and the beginning of the fifteenth centuries, three or four generations back—the threshhold at which memory falters. Those times, which indeed saw an autonomous Roman commune at its zenith, were nevertheless Christian times: the model they offered was irreproachable from the point of view of the theology of marriage that the Church had launched near the beginning of the thirteenth century. Constant references to that historical period keep Altieri within an impregnable Christian framework. He is equally free to discuss nuptial rites: they were still common ground, not the preserve of the Church they were later to become. Around 1500 the freedom with respect to the form of marriage ritual left the way wide open to anyone who might want to reflect on the actions and symbols associated with it. There was no rigid, universal codification of dogma, no prescribed liturgy to restrict or paralyze the thoughts of anyone curious as to the meaning of ritual. For the pre-Tridentine Church, especially the Italian churches, rituals of marriage were admitted in all their variety, as long as they observed the "custom of the land."[19] Religious liturgy of marriage, more strictly speaking, varied enough from one place to another to merit the same critical examination as popular rites of alliance. Without counter-

18. On the Roman Academy's plot and Paul II's persecution of those responsible, see Pastor, *Histoire des papes*, 4:34–59; Aubenas and Ricard, *L'Eglise et la Renaissance*, 68–70; Paschini, *Roma nel Rinascimento*, 224–27.

19. K. Ritzer, *Le mariage dans les églises chrétiennes du Ier au XIe siècle* (Paris, 1970). A. Esmein and R. Génestal, *Le mariage en droit canonique* (Paris, 1929–35). F. Brandileone, *Saggi sulla storia della celebrazione del matrimonio in Italia* (Bologna, 1906). See also chapter 9 above, "Zacharias, or the Ousted Father."

vening the articles of faith, Altieri had every right to consider and analyze every part of the celebrations. In the absence of a doctrine setting up norms for these rites, he could study them in their variety, ask how they fitted together, and consider their history and their most recent variations. In short, Altieri ran little risk of being accused of impiety when he proposed to bring to light *lo antiquo costumato . . . l'ordine et modo* (the ancient custom . . . order, and fashion) of weddings.[20]

Nevertheless, when he tells his friends that his historical frame of reference is the time of the "ancients" and the "ancestors," our amateur ethnologist is playing on a certain ambiguity in his terminology right from the start in order to establish a continuum in ritual. Altieri repeatedly legitimizes the rituals of his own time by citing texts from classical antiquity. His method consists in making his audience conscious of the gap between the debased ritual of 1500 and that of "our fathers"; then, in order to strengthen the model and the image he has isolated, he leaps boldly beyond the obscure centuries of the early Middle Ages to the ritual order of antiquity, to the rites of "our most ancient ones." As he reaches the end of each of his analyses, the gap of a good millennium and a half separating classical antiquity from the communal era seems less to him than the hundred years separating him from the latter era. Yet the comparison—often implicit—between "our ancient ones" and "our most ancient ones" results not so much in an affirmation of the classical origins of medieval rites as in a comprehensive explanation of the rituals to contemporaries no longer mindful of tradition.

His description is coherent. *Li nuptiali* is not a simple collection of curiosities and anecdotes, of scattered observations gathered with a philologist's, a jurist's, or a moralist's care.[21] Altieri reconstitutes a ritual *ordo* by means of which he reads a social system. Like the ordering of festivities or dances, the ritual order has the aim of *making*—that is, of constructing and maintaining friendships and the networks of solidarity that war and aggression unmake.[22] Marriage and alliance are an antidote for aggressiveness, for conflict, and for misunderstood interest. If *all* members of the Roman aristocracy ought to participate in the marriage of one of its sons, it is because they needed to be resoldered, to be "linked together" *(incatenati),* according to Altieri's rather strong expression.[23]

Admittedly, Altieri presents an amalgam of disparate explanations for each of the rites he examines in *Li nuptiali*. There are philological inter-

20. *Li nuptiali*, 185. These are the last words and the key to the work.
21. F. Brandileone has used *Li nuptiali* more thoroughly and more systematically than anyone else; see especially his study "La celebrazione del matrimonio in Roma nel sec. XV ed il concilio di Trento," *Rivista di diritto ecclesiastico* 6 (1898): 216–49, republished in his *Saggi*, 291–340.
22. *Li nuptiali*, 3–4. On the dance, see note 33 below.
23. Ibid., 7: "*Parentato incatenatose per modo, che pochi qualificati citadini hora ne sonno, chella parentela nolli astringa intervenirce*" (an alliance forged in such a way that there are few citizens of quality whose bonds of kinship do not oblige them to participate in it).

pretations, first of all, consisting of lists of etymologies that are lifeless and poorly organized, also steeped in the writings of classical or Christian authorities. Thus, when he attempts to understand why, in his youth, weddings were celebrated on Sunday, Altieri arrives at a far-fetched enumeration of reasons that might have pertained in antiquity for placing marriages on that day. After the Lord *(dominus)* and the house *(domus)*, where the festivities and dancing took place, the sun, "universal dominator and genitor" is called to the rescue to explain the Sunday *(domenicale)* celebration of weddings because, as he says in scholarly fashion, it is logical that, "legitimate marriage being the instrument of human generation, in order to make that divinity [the sun] propitious and favorable to us by games, feasts, and public gaiety, we celebrate them [marriage and the sun] on the same day."[24]

Historical, moral, juridical, and allegorical interpretations flow from Altieri's pen one after the other and spin a web of meanings around each element of ritual. This network is not very well structured, however, and the author often admits his perplexity as he tries to get at "the real meaning."[25] This is the case with the sword that in the fourteenth century was held over the heads of the couple at the exchange of vows. This rite, most probably of barbarian origin, suggests three or four hypotheses to Altieri. "Some think that the sword is brandished in imitation of those most ancient ones who parted the bride's hair with the blade of a lance, seeking to show in this way that iron alone could break a union. Others think that [the husband] seeks to show the wife his valor and his warlike character, and that he would be able to defend her courageously by means of arms. Many believe that this gesture shows what authority the husband holds over the wife, freely being able to go as far as killing her if need be." The interpretations do not stop there: the last and most delectable brings him a key to elucidate many other rites "utterly obscured by a corrupt and lazy negligence." "Some," he declares, "are of the opinion that the sword is produced in this manner in eternal memory of the very first marriages performed by Romulus, sword in hand, on the occasion of the rape of the Sabine women."[26] It makes little difference, in fact, whether a sword figured in ancient ritual or not. Altieri had grasped here an element decisive to his understanding of ritual events. Rite is the putting into action of the symbolic resolution of a real situation, a conflictual relationship of forces. When he reads the story of the Romans' first wives into each of the nuptial rites of his own times, Altieri means to recall to the Roman aristocracy that the shortest road from disorder to order, from

24. Ibid., 57.
25. Ibid., 52.
26. Ibid. The *ferro hastato* is an allusion to the Roman rite of the *hasta caelibaris*, a curved lance blade placed in the hair of the bride, a rite for which even ancient commentators of the classical age had no explanation. See J. Bayet, *Histoire politique et psychologique de la religion romaine* (Paris, 1957), 69.

war to peace, from political blindness to social harmony, is the rite of alliance.

For our humanist, in fact, aggression and violence underlie alliance, and many nuptial ceremonies have no other meaning than that of perpetuating the memory of the legendary Roman origins: the violence of the founding of Rome, built on a murder and on marriage by force, but also on the peace that ensued.[27] References to that ancient legend return constantly to his pen: "Every nuptial act recalls the rape of the Sabines";[28] "the least gesture in the espousal ceremonies puts us in memory of the rape of the Sabines; when someone takes his wife by the hand, he is showing that he is using violence on her."[29] And elsewhere: if the father of the bride does not accompany her to the church on the wedding day, it is because "in all logic, it would seem inconceivable and totally indecent that the father show himself consenting to the violent act that our founder's memory recalls to us."[30] Finally, if at the entrance to his house, the father-in-law welcomes his daughter-in-law by roughly taking her to a group of women, "if he thus shows her violence in leading her into his house, it is to call constantly to mind the kidnapping of the women."[31]

The violence is primarily that of one sex toward the other, of the sex that has physical, economic, moral, and juridical power over the other. But when Altieri's interlocutor, Mezzocavallo, remarks that marriage "has from the earliest times broken the law of hospitality to satisfy unbridled desires," Altieri replies that the force employed then was afterward transformed into love by the bonds of the "honored, holy, venerable marriage that came out of it."[32] Marriage and its rites *consecrate* force and violent forms of the appropriation of women and goods. They sanction the return to a social equilibrium that must follow the first phases of the alliance—phases that are necessarily aggressive and destructive—if the fabric of human relations is not to be torn asunder.

Altieri is never clearer about the underlying meaning that he attributes to the nuptial rites than when he describes and interprets the dance of the *giaranzana,* a sort of complicated farandole performed by all the wedding guests on two different occasions. Each guest was placed according to his degree of kinship with the husband and according to his "condition." The movements of the dance led each of the participants to "recognize" each of the others in turn—that is, to greet each one and touch his or her hand.

---

27. On the literary constitution and transmission of the legend of the Sabine women, see J. Poucet, *Recherches sur la légende sabine des origines de Rome* (Louvain, 1967); H. J. Erasmus, *The Origins of Rome in Historiography from Antiquity to Perizonius* (Assen, 1962); J. Seznec, *La survivance des dieux antiques: Essai sur le rôle de la mythologie dans l'humanisme et dans l'art de la Renaissance* (London: Warburg Institute, 1939), 13–34.
28. *Li nuptiali,* 73.
29. Ibid., 93.
30. Ibid., 68.
31. Ibid., 79.
32. Ibid., 48.

This could go on for hours if the wedding party was large. The responsibility of placing the dancers and leading the dance was a formidable task,
entrusted to a dependable relative of the husband: any error on his part
might well be taken as an insult and could cause the retreat of an entire
branch of the family, thus breaking the fragile fabric of the alliance that
the *giaranzana* was intended to express and consolidate. "Everyone greatly
feared making an error in disposing such a large number of persons, all
closely related and all of quality, and dreaded sowing serious discord,
inadvertantly or for any reason, so that each person performed this dance
in fear and circumspection."[33] The only classical origins Altieri can find
for this dance—the dance instituted by Theseus in memory of his victory
in the Labyrinth over the Minotaur—are uncertain indeed.[34] It seems to
him more appropriate, "when one considers the way in which this dance
begins, is performed, and ends, to see in it . . . a demonstration of love
and gratitude toward one's friends, and then toward all of one's relatives,
in joy for the marriage celebrated on that day."

Here, then, we have no ancient model, no analogical recall of other
ages and other cultures. Behind the *giaranzana,* however, Altieri does
decipher the same fundamental theme of alliance for which the kidnaping
of the Sabine women and the resulting marriages provide a legendary
outline. The exchange of ritual salutations and the "recognition" of the
family to the remotest degree that took place in the turns and twists of
the dance followed after an initial stage of hostile exchange—whether
expressed in physical blows (the alliance between enemy families was, after
all, the normal conclusion of many a private war during the Middle Ages)
or, symbolically, in the slowness and the caution of the initial negotiations
for the marriage, conducted by third parties. The violence underlying the
acquisition of a wife[35] and "the genital act must, if we wish to be distin-
guished from the wild animals, be celebrated in such a way that not only
the name of marriage renders them honest, but, thanks to the numerous
ceremonies that take place then, they are offered in sacrifice to the supreme
Creator and proposed, amid public rejoicing, as a mystery regarding God
alone."[36]

In the third book of the *Nuptiali* Altieri echoes this discussion of the
*giaranzana* when he elaborates on the theme of social peace founded in
respect of hierarchies and enhanced by collective festivities. Here the pretext of his reflections is the cavalcade that traditionally went to fetch the
bride and escort her to her spouse. Altieri takes the opportunity to list the
persons who should take part in this ceremony to examine the rank they

33. Ibid., 85. The dance took place the Saturday night before the wedding and the
Monday evening that followed (ibid., 58).
34. Ibid., 58.
35. Ibid., 46.
36. Ibid., 45.

occupy in society, as represented by their place in the procession.[37] Thus the nuptial procession figures as a symbol for a society reconciled in festivity. The *ordine et modo* (order and ponderation) that must be observed here express, as in the feast and the dance,[38] the fragile equilibrium between kin, affines, and friends or, beyond that, between social and professional groups, whose respective values are discussed at length by Altieri and his interlocutors. Ritual recapitulates social order.

We can now understand why Altieri proposes that Roman nobles of 1500 restore the nuptial rites and the feasts of their "fathers." To neglect these rites is to omit the reparative part of the alliance; it is to "depreciate kindred and the relations of friendship among family members." To found the alliance only on the lure of gain is to deny "the union, the cohesion, the solidarity of the entire city, welded [to the contrary] in sure and perpetual fashion by love when all concerned maintain relations like those of father and sons, or as if they were born of one progenitor or had been nourished by the same milk."[39] Aristocratic misalliances with "avid and sordid merchants" and weddings that failed to respect tradition "provoke discord among us; the consciousness of having concluded a bad affair debases us; these unions strip us of all humanity. Once an alliance is agreed upon and brought to pass, it is no longer recognized, except in disputes, it is only rarely honored at weddings, and never at funerals; one cares no more when a relative by marriage is sick than if this had occurred at Tenos, Salamis, or Mitylene centuries ago."[40] Incomprehension and a criminal—or suicidal—neglect of the rites of marriage thus reach into all corners of the life of society and destroy its very mainsprings.

Since Altieri sets himself the task of elucidating all ritual, not religious liturgy alone, antiquity proves highly useful to him and he calls on "our most ancient fathers" whenever a problem arises. Thus he presents the bride—the coin and the object of disputes and amicable transactions alike—in an essentially passive role. She remains passive, even when Altieri admits, with little enthusiasm, that Christian marriage rests on mutual consent (the foundation of the sacrament) and expresses his hope that reciprocal desire will arise between the spouses. At most this leads him to justify the occasionally long delays that separated the marriage proper (that is, the

37. ibid., 185. Altieri attempted to put his ideas on the revival of festivities into practice by contributing to the celebration of the anniversary of the foundation of Rome, the *Palilie*; see Gnoli, *La Roma di Leone X,* 102; and Cruciani, *Il teatro*, xxi–xxxv (on Altieri's will, dated 1513, instructing his son to contribute to its expenses).

38. On festivities as occasions of peace and alliance, see *Li nuptiali*, 4. Curiously, Altieri gives little description of the practical arrangements for wedding feasts.

39. *Li nuptiali*, 26.

40. Ibid., 27–28. The "sordid merchants" he had in mind seem to have been above all Florentines, who were extremely active in Rome under Julius II. On the simplification of marriage rites among the Florentine merchant class at the end of the fifteenth century, see chapter 9 above, "Zacharias, or the Ousted Father."

exchange of vows) and the wedding festivities and the consummation of
the union—a delay during which espoused Roman couples finally had the
right to an "honest frequentation" and could get to know one another
under the matrons' vigilant eyes.[41] In preaching reserve and submissiveness
to the bride, Altieri of course takes as his model the well-known virtues
of the chaste wives of antiquity, the Sabines first and foremost, who accepted the union imposed on them and proved their fidelity to their Roman
husbands as much as to their families of birth. Here the classical Roman
model permits Altieri to leave modestly veiled the Christian idea of the
sacrament established on the *initial* free will of the two parties. It is once
again the seal of antiquity that legitimizes, in his eyes, the magic rites that
are to insure the fertility of the wife and of the couple. The references to
classical authors give meaning to certain bewildering nuptial customs that
our aristocratic humanist judges at first sight "ridiculous," "vile," or
"obscene."[42]

What seems to me important is that Altieri, with classical examples to
back him up, can examine not only the contributions of Christian liturgy
but all that the post-Tridentine Church was to judge to be meaningless
claptrap or ritual tainted with "superstition" and to eliminate from marriage ceremonies. Altieri rejects nothing: he considers all ritual gestures
substitutes for the violence of human relations. He creates an anthropology
of alliance in which the stakes are not so much salvation and the happiness
of one particular couple as equilibrium between lineages, social peace, and
social renewal. Antiquity offers him not an insuperable model, reconsti-
tuted by erudite research and considered the inimitable paragon for modern rites, but a historical and mythical frame of reference that permits him
to formulate theories on the relationship of ritual to society. Altieri credits
the Christian centuries, as well as antiquity, with creating ritual forms that
were admirable, provided these forms were "civil" and worked for the
good of the country and the family. What he takes exception to is recent
"bad custom," which, by its omissions, adulterates the legacy of the past.
Ancient customs are bastardized only when they are neglected, forgotten,
impoverished. Today, Altieri says, the pressure of the spirit of lucre makes
us neglect the symbolic exchanges of the weddings of yesteryear—exchanges of salutations, of foodstuffs, of presents—and people are content
with "two, three, or four jigs in company,"[43] with a meal—and with a
dowry. For him, on the other hand, a ritual must be enriched and its
meaning must be multiform or it will desiccate and perish.

Altieri, a well-educated aristocrat and a good Christian, thus totally
excludes superstition and popular customs, which were, on the other hand,

41. *Li nuptiali*, 53–54. On male supremacy and its consequences in remarriage, adultery,
and repudiation, see ibid., 97–99, 101.

42. Ibid., 79, 81, 83, 86, 87.

43. Ibid., 85: "Non già con doi, tre, over quattro salta in zeppi, come hogie assai
diversamente se costuma" (as today, quite unlike [then], is the custom).

to provide a framework for the Catholic clergy's thinking after the Tridentine reform, when "remnants of paganism" were catalogued for the purpose of extirpating them.[44] The oppositions implicit in Altieri's interpretation are the civil and the base, festive order and disorder, charity and friendship, and avidity and egotism. Superstition has no place in his thought,[45] since the modern equivalents of ancient rites retain the social importance of their classical counterparts rites "even when their name, place, and moment are changed."[46] Furthermore, at no time does Altieri really pose the question of the social diversification of his rituals. What seems to him at first sight "vulgar" or "obscene" will shortly be rehabilitated in the name of its "civil" function. For him the "popular" simply does not exist. Not out of class ostracism, but because the nuptial rituals and festivities celebrated by his peers display most explicitly and completely the multiple elements inherited from previous centuries. Rites form an open symbolic whole, which had become frozen only in his degenerate times, but it is not an unlettered or unbelieving "people" that Altieri accuses of such perversion. The danger that lay in wait for Roman ritual comes from the parvenu, from the bourgeois or the merchant, much more than from the rustic or the illiterate.

Altieri, motivated by the political resentment and the reactionary nostalgia typical of his social class, opens his eyes to all ritual behavior of his day, including customs he does not understand. This fresh view helped him to invent a sort of retro-ethnology that postulates universality in the practice of his social class. A look at oneself, made possible by comparison with a recent past, becomes a look at another reality made of historical stratifications, Christian and ancient. Thus it is not the ethnology of the savage, the barbarian, or the benighted peasant that Altieri invents, but that of the "world we have lost." A consciousness of the passage of time rather than a spatial or social uprooting invites him to take inventory of the mores of his group, proudly ignoring all differences other than the historical. But his vision of alliance was free of the blinders later imposed in the categories for the observation of ritual established by Catholic authorities: it was limited by caste spirit, but it remained lucid. Altieri uses the ancient story of the Sabine women to look into the heart of alliance and decipher a dialectic of violence and "friendship" underlying human relations, which the nuptial rites resolve in their own manner.

44. On superstition as a category, see the thoughts of R. Chartier and J. Revel, "Le paysan, l'ours et saint Augustin," in *La découverte de la France au XVIIᵉ siècle*, Colloques internationaux du C.N.R.S., no. 590 (Paris, 1981): 259–64; J. C. Schmitt, "La 'religion populaire,' " 944–46.

45. The word appears, as far as I know, only once in *Li nuptiali* (73), where Altieri speaks of "Tobias's nights" and "the superstitious observance that [our ancestors] made of them"—"a three-day abstinence," concerning which Altieri notes, however (72), "that it seems to me little observed today," but to which he again finds ancient correspondences that permit him to evoke the violence associated with marriage.

46. Ibid., 38.

This position is not very different from the doctrine of the Church, for which charity and love of one's neighbor are renewed by marriage, the true social cement when bonds of kinship have become too lax. By emphasizing, but in a rather different way, the fundamentally violent nature of social exchange, and by trying to show that rites regulate this violence or conjure it away, Altieri was moving in the same direction as the Church, which had long opposed marriage based on kidnaping or force.[47] His proposals, however, were intended to please the families of his peers rather than the Church, for their social position was at stake with each new alliance. He entreats husbands and wives to stifle their feelings until their marriage has restored peace to their families, and reminds his audience that women owe obedience to the law of men at all times. In this sense, Altieri's *Nuptiali* are an example of the resistance that the Catholic reform of marriage would soon provoke from post-Tridentine families.

There is, however, a counterpart to the revelations that Altieri makes to his Roman friends on the deeper meaning of their festivities. When he tries to give them a weapon to help restore their old "republican" values, he is really proposing a role tailor-made for a domesticated aristocracy in modern times: that of curators of the accumulated ritual that his patient archeologist's labor had sorted out for them, and of docile heirs of a past whose meaning had become shrouded in obscurity.

47. See the analysis of the positions of Hincmar, archbishop of Reims in the ninth century, recently offered by G. Duby in *Le chevalier, la femme et le prêtre* (Paris: Hachette, 1981), 37–40, and of the Church tradition in this matter, ibid., 186–87, 221. On Peter Damien, see D. Herlihy and C. Klapisch-Zuber, *Les Toscans et leurs familles* (Paris, 1978), 526–30.

# 12

# The "Mattinata" in Medieval Italy

For some time now, a large body of material has been available on the charivari in Italy. Several decades ago G. C. Pola Falletti, in a work that is both poorly organized and over systematic, attempted to clarify the place of traditional youth associations in the *ciabre* celebrations of Piedmont.[1] But is the *capramaritum* of medieval Piedmont, which closely resembles the French charivari, to be taken as the model or even the origin of the other Italian forms of this rite? We need to define what was specific to charivaris over a rather extensive area (Emilia, Romagna, the Veneto, Tuscany, etc.), where this rite is—or was—known by one name: the *mattinata*.[2] In more than one area, however, other terms came into use,[3] which referred instead to the various instruments used.[4] There were other occasions for noisemaking that go, or went, by the name of *mattinata*. These homonymic uses provided a starting point for research on the origins

Originally published as "La 'mattinata' médiévale d'Italie," in *Le Charivari*, ed. J. Le Goff and J.-Cl. Shmitt (Paris: La Haye, 1981): 149–63.

1. G. C. Pola Falletti-Villafalletto, *Associazioni giovanili e feste antiche: Loro origini* (Milan, 1939); *La juventus attraverso i secoli* (Monza, 1953).

2. See map 816, entitled "Scampanata," in K. Jabert and J. Jud, *Sprach- und Sachatlas Italiens und der Südschweiz* (Zofingen, 1932), vol. 4.

3. See, for example, the remarks of P. B., "Usi nuziali nel Ferrarese," *Rivista delle tradizioni popolari italiane* (henceforth abbreviated *RTPI*) 2 (1894): 305, on the shift from *maytinata* to *tempellata* between the beginning and the end of the nineteenth century.

4. Such as *scampanata, tamburata,* etc. See G. Cocchiara, "Processo alle mattinate," *Lares* 15 (1949): 31–41; 16 (1950): 150–57.

and the functions of this rite. Two types of sources have been used in the present study: communal statutes and the synodal constitutions published roughly from 1300 to 1550. These texts came rather belatedly to consider the charivari punishable by law, for it is only toward the end of the fifteenth century that they began to restrict and regulate it. The allusions they made well before that time, however, to other occasions for music and hubbub throw light on the ritual context in which the medieval *mattinata* should be placed.

We need first to review the earliest references to the charivari on the occasion of remarriages and within the geographical area in which the term *mattinata* was used. Next, a comparison with the other meanings the word took on will underline the ambivalence of the rite—an ambivalence not always understood during the period that interests us but that offered the jurists (with the halfhearted encouragement of the Italian Church, to be sure) a means of attacking this "custom." The very vacillation of this repression suggests that we should return the *mattinata* to its context within popular wedding ritual. It is by investigating the connections between the *mattinata* and nuptial gifts that we can best attempt to grasp its earliest history.

## Italian *mattinate*: Charivaris Aimed at the Widowed

Statutory texts in Italy referring to discordant and noisy performances like the charivari were rare before the mid-fifteenth century. Various bodies of materials recently made available can be systematically exploited, however—numerous rural statutes, for example, published since 1930,[5] or the synodal statutes of the early modern period, which have now been listed[6] and surveyed.[7] Certain of these sources mention noisy disturbances. The earliest mention of a charivari that I have noted dates only from 1362, however. It can be found in the sumptuary statutes of Lucca,[8] which prohibited various excesses characteristic of wedding celebrations, particularly the custom of saluting the bride, "be she maid or widow," with a great uproar *(rumore)*. They also forbade "making noise with basins, bells, plaques or any other sort of metal, or blowing on horns." These boisterous displays in Lucca did not take place on the wedding day alone: they were

---

5. Especially in the collection *Corpus statutorum italicorum* (henceforth abbreviated *CSI*) directed by P. Sella, 22 vols. (Milan, 1912–45), and in *Fonti sui comuni rurali toscani*, 6 vols. (Florence, 1961–69).

6. Silvino da Nadro, *Sinodi diocesani italiani: Catalogo bibliografico degli atti a stampa* (Vatican City, 1960); *Studi e Testi*, vol. 1, 16th–19th cent., 207.

7. C. Corrain and P. L. Zampini, *Documenti etnografici e folkoristici nei sinodi diocesani italiani* (Bologna, 1970).

8. G. Tommasi, "Sommario della storia di Lucca dall'anno MIV all'anno MDCC . . . ," *Archivio storico italiano* (henceforth abbreviated *ASI*) 10 (1847): 1–632; *Documenti*, 95–109.

prohibited during the three-day period preceding and following the marriage—that is, during the customary duration of the wedding festivities. This first mention shows that the custom we call charivari existed in Tuscany independently of the French *charivari* or the *zabramari* of Piedmont, which were never mentioned by name in the Lucchese statutes. In Lucca, however, the noisemaking was addressed not only to remarrying widows but to every bride, "even a virgin."

During the fifteenth century, rites resembling a charivari on the occasion of a remarriage were mentioned with increasing frequency in both urban and rural statutes. Between 1445 and 1473, an addition to the statutes of Cadore, in the Veneto,[9] made punishable with a high fine (50 *lire*) and three days in prison "those who would stop and demand payment of a ransom of the nuptial procession of a widow, or who would address brazen *matinatas* to these couples." The statutes of Montemerano, a village in the Maremma (1489),[10] also defined the limits of these cacophonic displays, prohibiting *campanate* (the ringing of bells, big or small) at weddings and "barriers or any other obstacle or lack [of respect] shown a widower or widow." The statutes of Parma of 1494 forbade going about at night *"maytinando . . .* with various instruments, or making, particularly for remarried men or 'bigamists,' a *maytinatam* in any manner whatsoever."[11] They also opposed the practice of stopping or delaying the bridegroom, once again, particularly a man about to marry a widow. In Reggio Emilia the statutes revised in 1501[12] prohibited the uproars, both vocal and instrumental, known as *matutinate,* aimed at older people and the widowed who remarried. One chronicler from Modena, Tommasino de' Bianchi, describes more than fifteen of these charivaris between 1527 and 1547,[13] and in every one the *mattinata* was directed toward a double remarriage involving a widow and a widower. The disturbances that resulted from some of these demonstrations—in 1528, for example—incited the municipal authorities to prohibit, in the revised statutes of 1547, all such ceremonies "carried out by day or by night, accompanied by horns, basins, drums, and other bestial instruments, to loud shouts and disreputable words."[14] As late as the eighteenth century, the *mattinate* of Modena, like those of Mantua,[15] occurred only with dual remarriages.

9. *Statuta communitatis Cadubrii* . . . (Venice, 1545), fol. 80v, chap. 127.
10. Cited by L. Zdekauer in *Miscellanea storica della Valdelsa* 4 (1896): 128.
11. *Statuta Magn. communitatis Parme* (Parma, 1494), fol. 131v.
12. *Statuta Magn. communitatis Regii* (Reggio, 1582), fol. 197v.
13. T. de'Bianchi detto de' Lancelloti, *Cronaca modenese,* C. Borghi, ed. (Parma, 1862–70), *Monumenti di storia patria delle provincie modenesi,* 10 vols., Serie delle cronache, II–XI. Subsequent reference will be made to the volume of the *Cronaca* and not of the series.
14. Bianchi, *Cronaca,* 2:333 (28 January 1528); 9:187 (24 October 1547).
15. L. A. Muratori, *Antiquitates Italicae Medii Aevi* (Milan, 1836), Dissert. 23, 1:490. There is record in Mantova toward the middle of the sixteenth century of an *asouade* inflicted on a widowed couple: see A. D'Ancona, "Delle mattinate; memoria dell'Abb. G. Gennari," *Archivio per lo studio delle tradizioni popolari* (henceforth abbreviated *ASTP*) 4 (1885): 379.

The morning serenades of "countermusic" addressed to couples, particularly to remarrying widows and widowers, are thus attested in central and northern Italy outside of the confines of Piedmont. The rite relied on improvised instruments, which shared the characteristic of producing disagreeable sounds. It was not restricted to the larger cities: we can see its rural roots in the statutes of small towns such as Montemerano, Pomarance (near Volterra),[16] and Castelnuovo,[17] or in the rural communities of Cadore (in the Veneto). A 1534 addition to the statutes of the Lombard town of Mirandola[18] referred briefly to these "*mattinate* that it was the custom to make for widowed persons" and that the victims could buy their way out of.

One element typical of the French or Piedmontese charivari of the fourteenth and fifteenth centuries does not appear in the contemporary documents of the Po valley, or in the center of the Italian peninsula. Masked revelers, often costumed as animals, harlequins, demons, or *larvae* (souls of the dead), led the French charivaris of the Middle Ages;[19] yet neither Tommasino de' Bianchi (who nevertheless describes with a wealth of detail the maskers' growing monopoly of Modenese festivities) nor the statutes, which forbade certain masked plays or regulated the wearing of masks, ever specify that masked persons or even disguised persons took part in the *mattinate*. Masks, to be sure, were opposed above all by the Church, which saw in them survivals of paganism and beliefs concerning the world of the dead that were incompatible with Christian doctrine, whereas the documentation that we have considered up to now is principally of lay origin. In Piedmont, however, innovation came from the civil authorities, not from episcopal decisions, and it was they who began to discourage the wearing of masks. Nothing of the sort seems to have occurred in the regions under consideration here. We can conclude, at least provisionally, that masks were indeed absent in the clamorous serenades offered the widowed and repeat newlyweds, and that outside of Piedmont, during the fourteenth and fifteenth centuries, the rites surrounding marriage were dissociated from popular beliefs concerning the other world.[20]

16. A. Funaioli, "Usanze del comune di Pomarance (1526)," *RTPI* 1 (1894): 619.

17. Cited by G. Targioni-Tozzetti in *Relazioni di alcuni viaggi . . . nella Toscana*, 8th ed. (Florence, 1751–52), 3:424; statutes dated 1525, article 98.

18. F. Molinari, ed., *Statuti della terra del comune della Mirandola e della corte di Quarantola, riformati nell'anno 1386* (Modena, 1885), 86.

19. See P. Fortier-Beaulieu, "Le charivari dans *Le Roman de Fauvel*," *Revue de folklore français et de folklore colonial* 11 (1940): 1–16. P. Toschi, *Le origini del teatro italiano* (Turin, 1955), chap. 6, 166–227. K. Meuli, "Maske, Maskereien," in *Handwörterbuch des deutschen Aberglaubens* 5 (1932), cols. 1820–23,1774–88.

20. See the texts cited by Pola Falletti, *Associazioni*, 1:32; F. Neri, "Le abbazie degli stolti in Piemonte," *Giornale storico della letteratura italiana* 40 (1902): 3–4: ordinances of 1343, 1401, 1420. G. B. Borelli, ed., *Editti antichi e nuovi dei sovrani prencipi della R. casa di Savoia* (Turin, 1681), 199–200, Decree of Amedeo VII, 17 June 1430, "Ne fiant larvaria in desponsationibus."

Another feature of the *mattinate* and the *rumori* directed at the widowed in central and northern Italy (always with the exception of Piedmont) is the identity of their participants. In Piedmont the "young," grouped in their "abbeys," assumed responsibility for these ceremonies from the fifteenth century onward. But in Emilia, Lombardy, and Tuscany, the statutes prohibiting the *mattinate* show no indication that the young or the unmarried as a class played a predominant role in them. The "joyous companies," the activities of which are known in Florence[21] and in Venice[22] from the fourteenth to the sixteenth centuries, and which included not only youths but adult males who were active in organizing festive occasions, do not seem to have included charivaris among their responsibilities. The immediate family, friends, kin, and neighbors, on the other hand, took part in them more or less spontaneously, though they took on the role of assiduous censors when they met with resistance. Here the Modenese Tommasino Lancelotti de' Bianchi offers us a valuable firsthand report.

Tommasino, as he approached the age of sixty, was a member of a group of *buoni compagni*, established men, local notables, notaries, master craftsmen, and some of the nobles living in the same *quartiere*—men of an age and fortune that might easily offer an opportunity for remarriage. As soon as they heard that a local widow and a widower were preparing to marry, these solid citizens would offer to *diffendere la mattinata*.[23] They then dispatched a prominent member of their group to the widower, their "friend" and "neighbor," to persuade him to come to terms with them, threatening him with a "great *mattinata*" if he failed to do so.[24] The price for this varied from two to six *ducati* under ordinary circumstances, but it could climb a good deal higher if the victim rebelled or if he wanted to display his wealth and his liberality.[25] The "defenders" of the *mattinata*

---

21. On the Florentine companies, see Toschi's remarks in *Origini*, 92, 100; P. Gori, *Le feste fiorentine attraverso i secoli: Le feste per San Giovanni* (Florence, 1926); R. Hatfield, "The Compagnia dei Magi," *Journal of the Warburg and Courtauld Institutes* 33 (1970): 107–61; R. C. Trexler, "Ritual in Florence: Adolescence and Salvation in the Renaissance," in C. Trinkaus and H. Oberman, eds., *The Pursuit of Holiness in Late Medieval and Renaissance Religion* (Leiden, 1974), 201–71. The only mention of a charivari that I have found in Florentine *ricordanze* comes from ser Andrea Nacchianti, who remarries and leads his new wife home to his house 28 May 1501. "La notte vi venne certi per fare giuochi come s'usa. Bisognomi dare loro trebbiano et altre, che mi costò più che fior. 2 larghi" (That night some people came to play tricks as is customary. I had to give them Trebbio wine and other things and it cost me two *fiorini larghi*). See Innocenti, *Estranei* 633, fol. 126.

22. On Venice, see L. Venturi, "Le compagnie della Calza, sec. XV–XVI," *Nuovo archivio veneto* n.s. 16 (1909): 161–221; 17 (1910): 140–233.

23. Bianchi, *Cronaca*, 2:311, 333; 3:322, 349; 4:101, 119–20, 240, 288, 328, 366; 6:315, 408; 8:41, 53.

24. Ibid., 2:333 (28 January 1528); 3:126 (11 October 1530); 3:305, 315 (3 September 1531); 6:307.

25. Messire Andrea Molza pays 25 *scudi* after the ramsacking of his house (ibid., 2:333); Ser Zirolamo Manzoli pays 10 *scudi* unwillingly after three days of "great" charivari (3:305, 315); Ser Antonio Carandin settles the 50 *scudi* for a festive meal with good grace (4:288, 26 June 1533); and count Uguzon Rangon (a ringleader in *mattinate*) pays 60 *scudi* when he in turn remarries in 1534 (4:366).

spent the money on celebrations, which were to be conducted *honorevol-mente* and *galantamente:*[26] they went off to feast, democratically grouped around one table, at the best inn in the city, and they honored the bridal couple with a serenade, hiring fifers to play in front of their house for one, two, or three evenings, to the light of bonfires.[27] In this way "neighbors and friends," often under the leadership of a relative of one of the couple—men of mature age and a certain social standing—were "given," as in Modena, or else "took," or "relieved" the widower of his *mattinata* to celebrate it themselves—joyously if they succeed in obtaining "ransom" from him, but with "horns and other bestial instruments" if the widower was intractable and refused to pay up immediately.[28]

One of Tommasino's accounts, however, reveals a more brutal train of events and involves the young.[29] In 1533 a master lime-slaker "gave" the defense of his *mattinata* into the hands of some of his neighbors, our chronicler among them, for a rather modest sum (2 *ducati*), barely enough to cover a simple meal in his honor and send him four fifers. Nevertheless, the *mattinata*'s defenders acquitted themselves of their mission with vigilance, particularly since a band of "young show-offs of the city" arrived during the afternoon to celebrate in their own way, "with an enormous racket," the *mattinata* that had already been bought off by the others. Our kindly neighbors thus spent the night keeping the intruders away from the house of the newlyweds, using "the force of reason" but also threatening to call the captain of the guard, already alerted of the presence of the troublemakers. The young hooligans finally put away their noisemakers—"horns and disagreeable instruments"—and went off to bed.

This anecdote reveals an obvious rivalry between two age groups, and perhaps between two different conceptions of the *mattinata*. By both their age and their conjugal aspirations, the neighbors feel a solidarity with one of their own who is threatened with having to confront a minor neighborhood tempest that would outrage his "honor" if they failed to intervene to "defend" it—intervene, that is, both by protecting him and by defending their own right to the *mattinata* that he rightly deserved. They constitute, as a group, a kind of mutual protection society for widowers and potential repeat bridegrooms. Tommasino draws the moral of the affair: "Thus it goes in Modena when a widower takes a wife: the neighbors, and no one else, defend the *maitinada* for his honor, and so that the young be enabled

---

26. These terms reappear in several of his accounts: 2:311, 3:315, 350; 4:101, 119, 240, 288; 6:408.

27. Dinners at an inn: 3:316, 350; 4:101, 288, 327, 366; collation: 4:240; fifers and musicians: 3:322 and 349 (three nights running); 4:101 (also three nights); 4:240 (four fifers and bonfires), 288 (fifers and singers), 328 (bonfires, which set off a fire); 6:408.

28. "Rough" *mattinate* are noted in 2:333; 3:305, 313; 6:307 (here the widower throws stones out of the window at the participants).

29. Ibid., 4:240 (20 March 1533).

to respect it, a collation is offered." In the last analysis, the latent conflict between age groups was simply shifted. Instead of setting the young against the newlyweds in a charivari, it set the pot-whacking youths against both the couple and its defenders—who gratified the newlyweds with music of a sweeter sort.

These texts raise the question of whether charivaris in Modena were a recent development: if they were, the function of collective censure would have been weakened if not totally distorted as older people acted in their own defense to take over "to their honor" the rite of raising a rumpus. Should we not also ask how both actors and victims of these neighborhood psychodramas spontaneously judged the proceedings? Whether their intentions were benevolent or not, their actions were focused on the "honor" of the couple. The question becomes even more significant when we recall that the *rumori* that enlivened weddings in Italy seem originally to have been addressed to the virgin bride as well as to the widow. The uncertain nature of the rite—as it is seen in these earliest texts—suggests that we examine other occasions for noise or music designated by the word *mattinata*.

## Amorous and Satirical *Mattinate*

The statutes of Parma forbade, in general, going *maytinando* "with lutes, horns *(cum alpibus et tronis)*, organs, and other instruments," later specifying that *mattinate* directed at the widowed were forbidden.[30] Similarly, in Reggio in 1501 the particular case of *matutinate* directed at the widowed and at older people is mentioned only after the repression of nocturnal *matutinate* in general—cases of "insults" not necessarily aimed at newlyweds—has been treated. From the end of the thirteenth century on, in fact, many of the communal statutes mention *mattinate* among the causes of disturbance and noise, without specifying their exact nature. The Florentine statutes of 1415 set heavy penalties for nocturnal musicians who, armed with "bagpipes, trumpets or any other instrument, accompanied by other musicians or singers,"go through the streets "playing music, singing, or making *mattinatas*."[31] This prohibition was repeated from the older statutes of the Podestà (1324) and from the even earlier statute of 1284, in which the only difference is in the list of instruments ("lutes, viols, or other") used at night *causa mattinandi*.[32] Nocturnal vagabondage

---

30. See above, note 11.
31. *Statuta populi et communis Florentiae* (Fribourg, 1778–81), 3 vols.; bk. 3, heading cxciii, vol. 1, p. 403, "De poena citarizantis vel facientis mattinatam."
32. R. Caggese, ed., *Statuti della Repubblica fiorentina* (Florence, 1910–23), vol. 2. G. Rondoni, ed., *I più antichi frammenti del constituto fiorentino* (Florence, 1882), 52.

to musical accompaniment was condemned in nearly identical terms in the statutes of Ferrara in 1287, of Bologna in 1288, of Verona in 1296, and so forth.[33]

In the larger cities of central and northern Italy, then, the term *mattinata* designated not only the charivari of the widowed but all the serenades that city dwellers seemed so fond of at the end of the Middle Ages. Lovers, first of all: singing was obligatory to courtship, and the tone-deaf lover hired a professional.[34] A proper burgher like the Florentine Giovanni Morelli complied with the rite of amorous courtship, although within certain limits imposed by propriety—and by thrift.[35] If he felt the need to restrict his outpourings of music, it was because communal authorities from the thirteenth century onward penalized nocturnal *mattinate:* they indeed did disturb public order and represented an obvious infraction of curfew. Most of the communal statutes proscribed such behavior, and many prohibited vocalizations that, at night, risked a poor reception from sleeping townsmen.[36] Musical deambulation brought not only the confiscation of the instruments—as people were relieved of their arms if they were arrested at night—but also a fine usually higher than the one levied for simple nocturnal vagrancy.

Nighttime noise, however, is insufficient to explain the heavy sentences that occasionally were meted out to moonlight songsters. The communal authorities had every reason to fear that such concerts might degenerate into brawls and general commotion, since they were not always a simple matter of lovers' serenading their beloved. According to the statute of 1339,[37] the Podestà of Padua was charged with prosecuting nocturnal musicians and meting out the stipulated sentence, unless the musicians "had had just cause to play music or to have music played." The wording of the text is deliberately vague and fails to state the criteria according to which those responsible for public order could judge how "just" the cause was. The fact remains that a sense of justice might inspire someone out of revenge and provided with a sharp tongue or with bells, pots, and horns just as much as a lover. The nocturnal music of the *mattinate* was played in many keys and with lyrics that were often "not honest." In Trieste, the

---

33. W. Montorsi, ed., *Statuta Ferrariae a. MCCLXXXVII* (Ferrara, 1955), 375; G. Fasoli et P. Sella, eds., *Statuti di Bologna dell'a. 1288* (Vatican City, 1937), 229 (Studi e Testi, 73); G. Sandri, ed., *Gli statuti di Verona del 1276 colle correzioni e le aggiunte fino al 1323* (Venice, 1950), 2:89.

34. Du Cange, s.v. "Maitinata," cites a text that recognizes arranging for *maitinatas* as one of the three obligations of the lover.

35. G. Morelli, *Ricordi,* ed. V. Branca (Florence, 1949), 262: if the lover did not want to seem inexperienced, he ought not to throw away more than two *fiorini* for his serenade.

36. We could cite the statutes of Pisa (1286, 1313); Padua (1339); Gambassi, near Florence (1322); Lecco, in Lombardy (fourteenth century); Ascoli Piceno (1377); Brescia (1473, 1557); Crema (1484); Bergamo (1491); and so forth. Although the prohibited instruments are designated here, the infraction is not qualified as a *mattinata.*

37. *Statutorum magn. civitatis Paduae libri sex* (Venice, 1747), 2:322.

statutes of 1421 absolve in advance any family head who might in his anger wound an offender planted before his door at night singing "aliquam inhonestatem."[38] What amounted to an "antiyouth decree" dating from 1451, furthermore, threatened pursuit to all those "over 14 years old" about at night, and heavy fines or prison awaited anyone caught "singing shameful, reprehensible, or insulting things in any place whatever in the city."[39] In 1491, the statutes of Bergamo prohibited night owls from stopping to play an instrument or sing "*cantilenas* [or] outrageous or defamatory words" before the door of an honest citizen.[40] Judges and municipal police often had dealings with such disorderly persons when they attacked peaceable burghers by speech, song, and noisemaking, or made use of the time-honored methods of popular justice.[41] In 1501, the statutes of Reggio clearly allow that a plaintiff might feel himself "injured" by a *mattinata*. These texts clearly indicate that where the word *mattinata* was the prevalent term, it referred to nocturnal song and music of both a joyous and an insulting variety. Where in one place the *mattinata* sprang up to honor a young girl or an attractive couple, in others it became satirical or injurious, and brought ignominy to the family.

Thus, at the end of the Middle Ages the same word designated occasions for noise that were very differently received. Several scholars have already commented on this fact, but may not have drawn its full consequences. Another group of researchers, exemplified by Father Giuseppe Gennari and his editors Francesco Trevisan (1820) and Alessandro D'Ancona (1885), have concluded that the word *mattinata* underwent a deliberate inversion; that at an ascertainable moment in history the term that had designated a love song was applied, in mocking antinomy, to the satirical song or to the brouhaha aimed at punishing certain disapproved forms of love.[42] As late as 1949, G. Cocchiara reiterated essentially the same interpretation.[43]

Despite such high authorities, I tend to believe that the medieval texts display a unity of content in the lovers' *mattinata* and the *mattinata* aimed

38. M. de Szombathely, ed., *Statuti di Trieste del 1421* (Trieste, 1935), 3:9:199.

39. *Ibid.*, 228. According to the statutes of Chiusa Pesio (Piedmont) in 1472, *zabramari* was regarded as a "verbum iniuriosum" that one should avoid shouting.

40. *Statuta communitatis Bergomi (1491)* (Brescia, 1491), collatio 9: 52–53. Many towns under the control of the Church included in their statutes the punishment of *libelli diffamatorii* condemned by the *Costituzioni Egidiani* of Cardinal Albornoz in 1357 (P. Sella, ed., *CSI* [Rome, 1913], 1:181): their paragraph 33 forbade going out at night for the purpose of leaving in front of a neighbor's door "cornum sive cornia bestiarum, feces fetidas vel aliquod valde turpe aut scripturam sive cedulam continentem aliquod diffamatorium vel obbrobriosum domino vel habitatori domus."

41. Texts cited by G. Perusini, "Antiche usanze friulane," *Lares* 15 (1949), 58–65. Participation in *mattinate* was forbidden to the Venetian clergy by a fifteenth-century synod (J. D. Mansi, *Sacrorum conciliorum nova et amplissima collectio* [Florence and Venice, 1758–98], 31A: 289–328), and to the Sienese clergy in 1336.

42. D'Ancona, "Delle mattinate," 377.

43. Cocchiara, "Processo alle mattinate," 37–38.

at the widowed, and a coherence in the various rites of music, satire, and "countermusic." The *mattinata* was a public display centered on love; it also proclaimed the formation of a new couple, the guarantee of social reproduction; finally, it expressed reprobation of certain members of the community, particularly those who contracted an atypical marriage. The characteristic common to these episodes was the celebration—approving or critical—of a union. According to Tommasino's expression, which is also ambiguous, the "defenders" of the *mattinata* in Modena "guarded" (kept, respected) it, but also stood guard for their remarried friend. After they had struck their pact with him, all their actions were directed toward his honor: the fifers, the bonfires, the more or less burlesque spectacles— donkey races in particular,[44] in which the most awkward racer was declared the winner—drew the entire city into the rejoicings; and all the diversions and the drinking bouts organized with the "ransom" money were con- ducted "galantly" and "honorably." They used laughter to increase the "honor" of the new couple. These honors, however, always verged on the satirical: there was in the donkey races a whiff of the old *asouades,* the popular punishment of an ass-back parade with which widowed people who remarried were threatened in many towns in this area during the early modern period.[45]

The playful activities that the *mattinata* brought to Modena in the beginning of the sixteenth century seem somewhat contaminated by car- nival celebrations or festivities of the church calendar, even though they could occur at any time of the year. Yet, this very contamination allows us a better understanding of the behavior of the *mattinatori* and their "victims." During carnival, any joke thrown out to swell the great collective laughter—whether offered in simple derision or in accusation—had to be accepted good-heartedly. There was no such thing as an insult at carnival time.[46] To lodge a complaint against a jokester who had raised laughter at your expense was almost inconceivable. The same was true of the public displays aimed at the widowed who remarried. The couple was expected to take it all without flinching, no matter how stinging the *lazzi,* how cacophonic the serenade, how burlesque the spectacle. Where indeed was the borderline between a good hullabaloo and disturbing the peace? Be- tween grotesque music and racket? Between earthy humor and obscenity or insults? Between the horn of plenty and the horns of the cuckold? In short, between honor and offense? In some strange way, the propitiatory function of jokes, rough play, shouting, and noisemaking forced their acceptance. And this continued to be true as long as such ritual nighttime

44. Horse races: Bianchi, 8:53 (5 August 1545); 9:121, 129 (July, August 1547). Donkey races: 8:41–42 (19 July 1545), 9:150 (11 September 1547).

45. As in Mantua, according to Gennari; D'Ancona, "Delle mattinate," 379.

46. Toschi, *Origini del teatro,* 106–21, 220.

dins were felt as essentially "gratifying." In more than one place in the world this is still true of the boisterous noise of the charivari.[47]

These ritual rackets could become a dangerous weapon in the hands of someone moved by anger, envy, and resentment, however. In France, letters of remission granted around 1400 to participants in a charivari whose rejoicings had taken an ugly turn show that disorder could arise when the implicit rules of the "game" were no longer observed.[48] It is understandable that in Italy the widowed who remarried might have dreaded the moment of the *mattinata*, when all could be said or sung, even when the participants were brimming with goodwill. The attitude of Lucrezia Borgia, a widow with a particularly rich past, gives evidence of such fears when she arrived, in February 1502, at the court of Ferrara to marry Alfonso d'Este.[49] At his first wedding Alfonso had accepted with good grace the ritual jokes at the bedding of the couple. This time, the pair called off the *mattinata* that their closest kin were preparing for their delectation, probably on their arising from the nuptial bed. One of the disappointed *mattinatori*—the marchesa of Mantova, Isabella d'Este, Lucrezia's acid-tongued sister-in-law—later confessed that her brother's nuptials were "rather cold."[50] It is true that a *mattinata* such as this one permitted high hopes: this was Lucrezia's third wedding and her husband's second. "Under the guise of congratulations," to repeat one jurist's expression, the *mattinata* came close to being offensive, even at the bedside of a princely couple.

"Shocking and injurious congratulations . . . presented by impudent mimes who held second marriages up to ridicule,"[51] the *mattinata* does indeed seem in this anecdote to be a parodic extrapolation of the nuptial ritual rather than its negation. The ambiguity of the Italian word used in this region is thus a sign of the dual nature of the rite. In the period that interests us here, it was because one particular aspect of this ritual behavior—its "injurious" significance—was increasingly misunderstood that

47. In the Tyrol, *Katzenmusik* accompanies the happy couple on their return from the church; and, in the Oberland, the spouses consider themselves honored by a propitiatory racket. The *Schareware* offered newlyweds of Baden an hour after they go to bed is also welcome, since it expresses the community's recognition of the couple. See A. Perkmann's article "Katzenmusik," in *Handwörterbuch des deutschen Aberglaubens* 4 (1931), cols. 1125–32. The American shivaree seems to have retained this aspect.

48. R. Vaultier, *Le folklore pendant la guerre de Cent Ans d'après les lettres de rémission du Trésor des Chartes* (Paris, 1965).

49. See M. Catalano, *Lucrezia Borgia duchessa di Ferrara* (Ferrara, n.d.), 16.

50. The newlyweds took to their bed "without any preceding ceremony." Isabella adds later: "Non gli havemo facto la mattinata, come s'era sì [?] ordinato, perchè, a dire il vero, sono pur queste nozze fredde" (We did not make them a *mattinata* as we were ordered, because to tell the truth this wedding is really cold) (ibid., 54–55).

51. *Joannis Fabri Burdegalensis In Iustiniani imp. institutiones iuris civilis commentarii* (Lyon, 1593), 380: "Charevarisans, is dicitur, qui sub specie gratulationis conviciis premit, aut quadam molestia eos afficit, quibus gratulari fingit, ut petulantes illi mimi in contemptum secundarum nuptiarum."

this aspect finally came to be isolated and emphasized to the detriment of the other, honorific aspects. This may well be, in the last analysis, the entire "story" of the *mattinata* or of the charivari, a rite whose forms and accents remained so remarkably impervious to the passage of time.

## The Right to the *Mattinata*

The *mattinata*—a parody of honors, a reversal of *congratulazione*—remained an honor and a collective gesture of congratulations only as long as those to whom it was destined accepted it as such. Farce and derision could take over ritual gestures, and rite could become a cruel game. The breaking point depended less on the contents of the satire, however, than on the state of mind of the protagonists.

With this in mind, we should look at the interpretation—condoning or repressive—that civil and religious authorities placed on the ritual uproar and the ritual insults, and consider this interpretation in light of the synodal and communal statutes—normative or repressive texts that reveal what meaning the actors in it attributed to the rite and how attitudes toward it evolved.

City statutes at the end of the thirteenth century had forbidden nocturnal noise and music in the most general sense as infractions of the curfew and a source of trouble. The representatives of the middle class who were in power had every intention of controlling nocturnal agitations and delinquency,[52] but these level-headed men also sought to curtail amorous courtships and liaisons that imperiled lineages and family fortunes. If they wanted to discourage the serenading of widows and widowers in particular, the authorities could consider it simply as a particular instance of disorders provided for in the communal statutes and pursue it ex officio. It is true that the statutes added specific prohibitions bearing heavier penalties to the more general ones. Thus offensive words were punishable with a fine, just as noisemaking and the exchange of blows were, and the fine was heavier if the words spoken against someone were uttered in front of his house, in church, or in the municipal council. It was considered a further aggravating circumstance if a funeral, a wedding, or a baptism were taking place in the house, if the uproar took place at night, or if it took place on the occasion of a widower's or a widow's remarriage. The field of application of the law thus seems to have become progressively more specific.

---

52. See J. Rossiaud, "Prostitution, jeunesse et société dans les villes du Sud-Est au XVᵉ siècle," *Annales, E.S.C.* 31 no. 2 (1976): 289–325. See also the *Statuti di Trieste*, 199, 228, 303.

Does this mean that certain *mattinate* were consciously perceived as more illicit than others? Was it not the case, rather, that a custom formerly not judged reprehensible, which consequently escaped repression, came to constitute a crime? Custom, it seems, originally permitted the noisy rituals accompanying ordinary marriages (and particularly remarriages) to escape the stipulated penalties, or at least allowed an appeal to clearly mitigating circumstances. Dissonant music, insults, and din raised at the door of newlyweds, tolerated up to the fourteenth century, slowly came to be considered objectionable conduct. Between 1330 and 1550 these activities joined a category of behavior that the authorities took it on themselves to supervise or for which they sometimes expressly delegated supervisory power to neighbors or the young.

This was accomplished by arguing the "injurious" nature of such disturbances. If the victim of a *mattinata* declared himself "injured" and considered that the insult had been abusive and launched in anger *(irato animo et iniuriose commissa)*, or, on another level, if the stone thrown at his house was evidence of malicious *(malitiose)* or injurious *(injuriose)* intent,[53] he theoretically had a right to lodge a complaint, whatever custom dictated. Anyone could be plaintiff—and even pocket part of the fine. There may have been some jurists in the fourteenth century who still refused to admit complaints lodged against those who took part in a charivari on the grounds that, good or bad *(etiam prava)*, custom excused the act.[54]

In the fifteenth century, however, most jurists concurred in the contrary opinion, which became the rule in the sixteenth century. "One cannot excuse the *charivariseurs* by appealing to custom, since custom goes counter to good morals," Jean Favre affirms; these manifestations result from a spirit of vengeance, jealousy, and contempt, they engender scandals and brawls, and they fetter the liberty of marriage, Jean des Garrons added.[55] Thus it was possible to bring suit against those who indulged in the disorderly activities of the *capramaritum*, or *carivaritum*, "as is done against those who make *matinatas*," one Italian jurist, Nevizzano, concluded.[56] Seen in this light, even though *mattinate* fell under the special domain of

53. For example, the statutes of Tivoli (1305) in Tommasetti, ed., *Fonti per la storia d'Italia*, 38:215; those of Bologna (1288), 207; those of Gambassi in Tuscany in *Statuti della Valdelsa dei sec. XIII e XIV*, ed. A. Latini, *CSI*, 7 (Rome, 1914), 1:42. According to the Florentine statutes of 1415 *(Statuta . . .* , 1:371), a stone thrown at a house during wedding festivities or during carnival incurred only a 10 *lire* fine, as against 50 *lire* and 25 *lire* respectively if it occurred at night.

54. The jurists' opinions are given in E. Bouchin, *Plaidoyez . . .* , 2d ed. (Paris, 1728). Bartolus and Benedictus thus sustain that "quae consuetudo etiam prava excusat, quamvis actum non validat" and that "Ubi mos est crimen non est."

55. J. Fabri . . . *commentarii*, 381; *Joan. Garonis Tractatus IV . . .* (Hanover, 1598), tr. 4: "De poenis et remediis secundo nubentium," 245, paragraph 35.

56. G. Nevizzano, *Sylvae nuptialis libri sex* (Lyon, 1545), 144.

custom, their injurious nature would justify a much more severe treatment than that accorded to ordinary curfew infractions. This was what prompted fines two, five, or ten times heavier.[57] Furthermore, by a parallel process, Carnival itself no longer escaped this new notion of injury. In their concern for public order, authorities in Orvieto around 1500 reached the point of totally ignoring the ritual meaning of carnival insults, for which they stipulated fines similar to those for insulting speech in a house where a wedding was taking place.[58]

Those charged with keeping public order had a choice between two lines of action: they could prosecute nighttime trouble-makers ex officio, or they could wait to act on charges of conducting charivari and on complaints from those who declared themselves "injured" by a *mattinata*. In practice, however, both the victims' complaints and ex officio arrests continued to meet with the resistance of custom. In Modena in 1528, when one "defender" of the *mattinata* felt that he and his companions had been humiliated by his brother (a widower who refused to pay up as promised), he first sought out the captain of the local constabulary to assure his neutrality, then launched a general attack on the house in which the wedding was being held, which his men devastated from top to bottom.[59] When the hapless bridegroom complained to the governor of the damages he had sustained, he was told that he had gotten no more than his due: "One must not go against the constitution of the city, and that this is how people act toward widowers who take a widow to wife."[60] In Reggio, after 1501, the Podestà had the power to prosecute, "ex officio and as it sees fit," *mattinate* aimed at the widowed and the elderly; but the penalties and suits for delinquency of duty that threatened the men of the watch if they failed to pursue the malefactors suggest that they carried out their task halfheartedly. Custom permitted them to fall back on a more or less implicit "constitution" of the city, like the governor of Modena, or to excuse the participants before the fact on grounds of the inoffensive and playful nature of the ceremony or their good "intentions." The written law, by leaving it up to the authorities to decide whether

57. In Ravenna (1590) the sentences for infractions of the curfew were quadrupled for the *mattinatores*; in Ascoli Piceno (1377), doubled; in Pisa (1286, 1313) they ranged from 40 *soldi* for nocturnal vagrancy to 100 *soldi* for singers; and in Florence fines ran from 12 to 20 *soldi* in 1284 but from 3 to 100 *lire* in 1415.

58. *Statutorum civitatis Urbis veteris volumen et reformationes* . . . (Rome, 1581), 165: the fine was 10 *lire* instead of one.

59. Bianchi, *Cronaca*, 2:333 (28 January 1528). The participants tore down the roof and the doors, "ruined" the well by throwing horse saddles into it, broke up the stairs and the bedroom fireplace, threw grain and nuts into the courtyard: in short, used the time-honored methods of popular justice (see on the subject K. Meuli, "Charivari," in *Festschrift Franz Dornseiff* [Leipzig, 1953], 231–45) after having treated the bridegroom to a *martinada* "with drums, horns, and other bestial instruments."

60. Ibid., 333–34. The governor adds that he had married a woman "who brought him many goods," a theme that often "excused" a charivari in Modena (see 3:305, 4:327; 6:315).

injury had occurred, long provided a convenient way to avoid direct confrontation with custom.[61]

The inertia of the authorities shows that moral condemnation of the charivari penetrated only slowly into the thought and the practices of the laity in Italy. The men who drew up statutes and the municipal powers charged with putting them into effect followed the lead of the people under their administration, rather than preceding them. Only belatedly did they draw arguments from the jurists' reflections on the notion of injury from the thirteenth century onward and apply them to the charivaris or *mattinate*. Nor did they deliberately ignore the positions of the Church: their reluctance to suppress this custom came rather from the weakness of those positions in a society in which the marriage ritual eluded Church control much more than it did in France.

In France, the condemnations of the charivari that appear in synodal texts from in the first third of the fourteenth century onward are consistent with the Church's increasingly vigorous effort to moralize marriage and gain control of this sacrament, starting with the Lateran council (1215) and the council of Lyon (1247). The Church's struggle against "clandestine" marriages moved it to provide the nuptial ritual with a religious framework; the more "inappropriate" aspects of marriage were consequently eliminated as all the more shocking in a sacred setting.

As the French churches increased the majesty of the sacrament by the presence and the more active participation of the priest, they also reaffirmed the licit and equally sacramental nature of second or subsequent marriages. To be sure, the Church traditionally refused to renew its benediction of "bigamists."[62] Its attitude, however, was not totally consistent in the fourteenth century. After 1300, if the widowed party was the husband, or if one of the spouses, although widowed, had remained virgin, the Church occasionally permitted that "in certain places" custom authorized the repetition of the blessing.[63] For doctrinal reasons, then, the Church seems here to have preceded the evolution of practice. The same was true in Italy. Here synods experienced the same hesitations or the same compromises when faced with the problem of blessing second marriages. Thus it was that the provincial councils of Florence in 1346, of Venice between

61. *Statutorum Urbis veteris*, 166: "quod autem turpe sit et iniuriose factum iudicantis arbitrio reliquatur." In Viterbo (1251) a paragraph is consacrated "de eo quod factum est causa ludi non auferatur pena"; R. Morghen et al., eds., *Statuti della provincia romana* (Rome, 1930); *Fonti per la storia d'Italia*, 69, p. 221. On the musicians' intentions, see the statutes of Padua cited above in note 37.

62. See A. Del Vecchio, *Le seconde nozze del coniuge superstite, studio storico* (Florence, 1885); A. Esmein and R. Genestal, *Le mariage en droit canonique*, 2 vols. (Paris, 1929–31), 2:99–108.

63. Del Vecchio, *Le seconde nozze*, 248–49, citing Guillaume Durand, before 1296. The author seems to interpret the synodal statutes of Avignon of 1337 prohibiting charivaris as the consequence of a decision of John XXII abolishing the interdiction on the blessing of second marriages.

1418 and 1426, and of Benevento in 1470[64] all prohibited the benediction of remarriages, but for different reasons. In Florence the prohibition was without exceptions; in Venice the presence of priests and their blessing of the ring were discouraged only when second weddings were celebrated *ex parte mulieris* (on the wife's part); in Benevento the council admitted that a "legitimate and approved custom" authorized local exceptions to the rule that refused blessing to widowed persons of either sex. Three churches, three different situations.

Condemnations of noisy disturbances, dances, or "obscenities" taking place in or near a church abound in Italian synodal constitutions of the thirteenth and the fourteenth centuries just as they do in France. However, like the communal statutes, which they often prompted, and unlike the French texts, these Italian constitutions before the Council of Trent include no particular prohibition of noisemaking or "iniquitous games" accompanying remarriages, in church or not.[65] Was the Church in Italy more sensitive to popular disparagement of second marriages than in France? Probably it was more tolerant of expressions of this reprobation because they took more ambiguous forms than in the French charivaris—less violent, and less contaminated by carnival rites and calendar feast rites. In short, they took less "pagan" forms. Another factor, however, certainly contributed much to the silence of the Church in Italy. Nuptial ceremonies remained within the domestic sphere in Italy longer than in France.[66] Nearly everywhere, in the fourteenth and the fifteenth centuries, the exchange of the *verba de praesenti* and the gift of the ring to the bride were likely to take place in her home and not *in facie ecclesiae,* as had become customary in France from the twelfth century on. In Italy, well into the sixteenth century a notary could dispatch the business of this ceremony just as well as a priest, if not better. After the gift of the ring, which ushered the young girl into the married state, her solemn departure for her husband's house and the nuptial festivities could easily be put off for a few days or even a few years, while the consummation of the marriage was not tied to its solemnization in church.

64. J. D. Mansi, *Sacrorum conciliorum nova et amplissima collectio* (Florence and Venice, 1758–98), 26, col. 57 (Concilium Florentinum, 1346, art. "De secundis nuptiis"); 31–A, col. 358 (Synodicon Venetum, Ex synodo Marci ep., art. "De sponsalibus et matrimoniis"); 32, col. 369 (Concilium Beneventanum, cap. V, "Contra presbyterum bigama benedicentem excommunicatio proponitur").

65. Even in Turin and from the middle of the fourteenth century, civil ordinances forbade or regulated charivaris; see Pola Falletti, *Associazioni,* 1:5, 32. A so-called council of Verona dating from 1445 or 1448, cited by several Italian authors, was supposed to have condemned the "charivarium" (see A. Balladoro, *Folklore veronese: Il matrimonio dei vedovi* [Turin, 1899], 5). In reality this seems to refer to the council of Tours of 1448, can. 12 and 13; J. Hardouin, *Conciliorum collectio* . . . (Paris, 1710–15), 9, cols. 1346–47.

66. See A. Brandileone, *Saggi sulla storia della celebrazione del matrimonio in Italia* (Bologna, 1906); J.-B. Molin and P. Mutembé, *Le rituel du mariage en France du XII*e *au XVI*e *siècle* (Paris, 1974).

Under these conditions, the Italian churches could judge it less urgent to emphasize respect of the sacrament in second marriages than to increase their direct control of the celebration of all marriages. Italian churches, from the fourteenth to the sixteenth centuries, had to carry out the task that the French clergy had completed as early as the twelfth and thirteenth centuries. Protecting the "liberty" of second weddings probably appeared as a mission of secondary importance, compared to the enormous enterprise of supervising first unions. The proclamation of banns, for example, seems to have been quite generally absent in Italy at the end of the Middle Ages. Thus the noisy displays that accompanied remarriages remained widely ignored by Italian synods before the Council of Trent, whereas their constitutions reiterate an insistence that weddings be public and licit. When the Tridentine reforms hastened change in Italy by placing the essential part of the nuptial ceremonies firmly within the church setting and by reserving to the priest functions that until then had been more generally exercised by laymen, the time had at last come to bring order to the popular rituals surrounding second marriages.

Before the sixteenth century, then, the Italian Church exerted only halfhearted pressure on civil authorities to punish the rowdy tumult of the *mattinata* aimed at widowers. Those responsible for public order, only feebly encouraged or supported by their pastors to track down jokesters who noisily saluted "abnormal" and "ridiculous" marriages, could defend themselves in all good conscience by appealing to custom, should a victim of a charivari's practical jokes decide to lodge a complaint.

## Nuptial Gifts and the Charivari

The ambiguity of the *mattinata* derives from the propitiatory nature of a rite that was not simply an act of censure, and the relations of the *mattinata* with the law, before 1550, show that the problem lay in how the rite was received. Thus we need to return to a consideration of the *mattinata* within the context of popular wedding ritual as a whole. The Italian term in itself invites us to question at what time of day the rite took place. Several authors have seen the *mattinata* as the matutinal equivalent of the evening *serenata*. Only one has mentioned, and in passing, the hypothesis that the *mattinata* might be linked to the *Morgengabe* as something like its musical accompaniment.[67] Let us return to that hypothesis, bringing some new elements to bear.

The popular ritual surrounding the wedded couple's arising from the marriage bed had the principal function of proclaiming the consummation of the union and recognizing the formation of a new couple. During the

---

67. D'Ancona, "Delle mattinate," 377.

early Middle Ages it was at this moment, solemnized by the presence of friends and relatives, that the bridegroom under Germanic law—in Italy, Lombard law—turned over the *Morgengabe,* the "morning gifts," to his wife "as soon as she rose from his side," amid the joyous confusion that greeted the new couple.[68] In more than one place in Italy, the father of the bride and family friends sent their presents to the bride on the Monday following the wedding night. At the end of the Middle Ages, the gifts were no longer presented obligatorily on the day following the wedding, and the Florentine *morgincap,* for example, Romanized as a *donatio propter nuptias* and mixed in with the other gifts and marital contributions, came to be fixed by the marriage contract along with the dowry.[69] The congratulations of friends and relatives, their arrival to musical accompaniment, their indiscreet or inquisitorial pleasantries—all the rites of the *mattinata*—were no longer strictly linked to the solemn presentation of the *donum matutinum:* from this point on, it was on the evening preceding the wedding ceremonies that the Florentine husband sent a coffer containing his gifts and the bride's raiment. At this point the timing of the musical *mattinana* could be shifted, and it could become attached to some other important moment of the nuptial ritual also dedicated to the giving of gifts. Nevertheless, perhaps because of its ancient contribution to the newlyweds' arising, this part of Italy maintained the term alluding to the moment of the original ceremony, maintaining it, moreover, for its more violent and more satirical forms.

The connection between the charivarilike *mattinata* of northern Italy and the nuptial morning after ritual or the husband's gifts to his wife finds a convincing linguistic parallel in France. In the fifteenth century, at least, the term *charivari* still bore a meaning that has been neglected because it seems too distant from the noisy rites. A poem of Coquillart, written around 1440, gives the word a meaning of coquetry, taking on airs, simpering affectation.[70] Another text of the fifteenth century, however, throws light on the connection between these feminine "airs" and the noisy disparagement of a disapproved marriage. One Latin-Roman glossary[71] twice

68. E. Besta, "Gli antichi usi nuziali del Veneto e gli statuti di Chioggia," *Rivista italiana per le scienze giuridiche* 26 (1898): 204–19: "cum primum surrexit a latere," "quando primo cognovit eam in conjugio," "in die lune nuptiarum."

69. L. Zdekauer, "Il dono del mattino e lo statuto più antico di Firenze," *Miscellanea fiorentina di erudizione* 1 (1886): 33–36; "Le doti in Firenze nel Dugento," ibid., pp. 97–103: at the beginning of the fourteenth century, rural notaries still speak of the gift "propter nuptias mephi et morgincap." Well into the fifteenth century, Florentine husbands noted in their account books the *mancia* given to their wife after the wedding night. *See* chapter 10 above, note 35.

70. G. Coquillart, *Oeuvres,* ed. P. Tarbé, 2 vols. (Reims, 1847), 2:191 ("Monologue de la botte de foin") and 204 ("Monologue du puits"). Jault, when he edited the *Dictionnaire étymologique* of Ménage in 1750, deduced from this that the origin of the word lay in the Old French *chiere* (face, expression); see G. Peignot (known as Dr. Calybariat), *Histoire morale, civile, politique et littéraire du charivari* (Paris, 1833), 37–38.

71. R. Gachet, *Glossaire roman latin du XVᵉ siècle extrait de la Bibliothèque de Lille* (Brussels, 1846), 10. This passage of the glossary is extracted, without comment, by G. Phillips, "Über

gives the word *chalivali* as the French equivalent of the Latin terms *larnatium* (urn, box, coffer) and *morganicum* (matutinal). *Chalivali* is found in both definitions included under the glossary heading *de paramentis mulierum* (on women's clothing), where it figures among various attributes related specifically to female clothing, housekeeping, or sewing. *Larnatium* might refer to the coffer, box, or wedding basket that the husband offered his wife—ritual gifts that were at one time or another confused with the *donum matutinum*. This morning gift seems, finally, to be connected with the *morganicum*, which this glossary also translates as *chalivali*. Thus the text appears to establish an identity between nuptial gifts and phenomena called *charivari* in France and *mattinata* in northern Italy. By a process of degeneration parallel to the juridical decline of the *Morgengabe* itself, the name of the rite (and perhaps that of the objects given in the course of the ceremony) may thus have remained connected with feminine frivolities or, in an abstract sense, to the "airs" and affectations of the weaker sex. At the same time, however, the ceremonial noisemaking that signaled the moment at which the husband "recognized" his wife may have undergone a contrary process of expansion of sense.

We can take this one step further. Historians and ethnologists have noted the frequent mention in Italy of furs in the trousseaux traditionally sent or paid for by the husband—from the Middle Ages down to our own times. In the fourteenth and fifteenth centuries, furs appear in trousseaux in Tuscany as well as in Venice, in southern Italy, and in Sicily.[72] The domestic utensils, furniture, and clothing that the young woman received over and above her dowry almost mandatorily included furs or sheepskins, and originally these were given by the husband.[73] In one example among many, a Venetian husband of the twelfth century offers his bride a goatskin *(pro dono pellem unam caprarum)* on her arising from the nuptial bed.[74] In Venice, the terms for widows' weeds, *pellicia vidualis* or *vestis vidualis,* eventually designated the widow's rights to her husband's estate.[75] Furthermore, some Italian jurists of the fifteenth and sixteenth centuries established an equivalence, at first sight incomprehensible, between the "skins" and the charivari. Rocco Corti, the first of them in date, reports that in

---

den Ursprung der Katzenmusiken," in the second edition of his *Vermischte Schriften,* 3 vols. [Vienna, 1856–60], 3:26–93, and by A. Tobler and E. Lommatzsch, *Altfranzösisches Wörterbuch,* s.v. "charivari" (Frankfort, 1925–73), vol. 2.

72. See the *Petri Excerptiones* cited by A. De Gubernatis, *Storia comparata degli usi nuziali in Italia e presso gli altri popoli indo-europei* (Milan, 1869), 93; N. Tamassia, "Scherpa, scerpha, scirpa," *Atti del Reale Istituto veneto di scienze, lettere ed arti* 66 (1906–7): 725–35, and 728 for the document from Lucca of the year 1009 cited; L. Zdekauer, "Usi popolani della Valdelsa," *Miscellanea storica della Valdelsa* 4 (1896): 64–66 and 205–12. R. Corso, "I doni nuziali," *Revue d'ethnographie et de sociologie* 2 (1911): 228–54, esp. p. 252; *Patti d'amore e pegni di promessa* (Santa Maria Capua Vetere, 1924), "Pittacium," pp. 81–94.

73. Corso, "Doni nuziali," 247–52; *Patti d'amore,* 92–93.

74. Cited by Besta, "Antichi usi nuziali," 215 for the year 1193.

75. Corso, "Doni nuziali," 238, n. 4.

his city of Pavia toward the end of the fifteenth century a deplorable custom reigned: "shameless" young people forced those who married for the second or third time to pay them a sum of money that they claim as their due *pro pelle sponsae*.[76] Nevizzano, a Piedmontese from Asti, notes somewhat later that "in certain regions custom dictates that the remarrying spouses pay for the pelt or the *zabramari (pro pelle seu sabramari)*.[77]

Although interpretation of the connection is a delicate task, the offering extorted by the youths from the "bigamous" bridegroom in exchange for the "bride's skin" or in place of the *zabramari* (charivari)—the buying off of the ritual gifts or the musical ceremony that ought to accompany them—establishes an irrefutable link between the nuptial gifts, the participation of the young, and the noisy rites of the charivari or the *mattinata*. Why must the furs of the remarrying bride be ransomed, in this instance from the "shameless young people" and their *abbas juvenum* and elsewhere from the staid "defenders" of the middle-class *mattinata*? Can we say that when they "cry *charivari* at someone" the young were demanding that the bride's ritual gifts, or compensation for them, be delivered into their hands? And by what right did they do so?

First, we might consider the participants in a charivari as representatives of the material or moral interests harmed by a remarriage. Movable goods given by the husband—in Italy, the *sirpa*[78]—generally remained the property of the widowed wife even when she remarried. Toward the end of the Middle Ages the unanimous reproach to a widow who remarried was that she was wronging her children of the first marriage. If she brought them into their stepfather's house, he might neglect their patrimonial interests in favor of his own; if she abandoned them to the care of her first husband's lineage, this would deprive them of both her dowry and her share in the marital donation—the *sirpa* in particular—to which she had a right. The actions of the young could be justified, under these conditions, by an age-class solidarity encouraging them to take the part of the children of the first marriage and to demand (in their name?) at least payment of a transfer fee on the goods the widow carried away. This explanation contains its share of truth, but it is far from adequate: the ransoming of the charivari (that is, according to my hypothesis, the compensation for the marital gifts) sets the role of the young at another level.

The gifts involved, which sanction the passage from maid to married woman, are incompatible with the wedding of a widow. This is what the

76. Rocco Corti, *De consuetudine* (Lyon, 1550), fol. 18.

77. Nevizzano, *Sylvae nuptialis*, 144. In the Bergamo region in the nineteenth century, the new bride returning to her father's house was said to be going there "a prendere la pelle" (to take the pelt).

78. Tamassia, "Scherpa." In many places in Italy the term *sirpa* still refers to the trousseau or the movable goods of a household; see Corso, *Patti d'amore*, 87–93. Does the word perhaps come from the Latin *sirpea*, a reed basket? Or from the German *scherbe*, part, mosaic tile, coin? See the examples cited by Du Cange, s.vv. "schelfa," "schelpus," "scirpha," "scirpus," which contain a good many contradictions.

young are saying when they use their charivaris in harsh condemnation of what the theologians called "honest fornication." But they also keenly sense that the absence of the gifts and their attendant rites was a dangerous reduction of their own role as mediators. In many places, in fact, the young "friends" or peers of the husband accompanied him when he came to carry his *donora* to his future wife, and they often delivered the gifts in his name.[79] This mission no longer took place at a woman's second marriage, when the nuptial gifts were kept discreet and publicity, instead of being sought, was carefully avoided. The introduction of the wife into another lineage no longer involved clearly defined rites of admission, as in the case of a fresh young bride, and the wedding celebrations showed none of the pomp and display in which the young had such a leading role in ordinary marriages.[80]

A woman to whom widowhood had brought ownership of property was free to bring it to a new husband without compelling him to reciprocate with ritual gifts. On both counts, she had no need of the mediation of the "young" in order to take a second husband. Thus widowhood curtailed the rites of passage in a remarriage, frustrating the young of their role as paranymphs, because it simplified both the transfer of material goods and, on another level, that of the woman herself. Not only did the young thus demand a sort of reparation of the "loss of gain" involved in festivities denied them,[81] but in their charivaris in Piedmont or in Lombardy they also seem to have been demanding compensation for this transfer of goods that escaped their control (a compensation that in the early modern period was often to take the form of a percentage of the dowry). When they broke into the "countermusic" of the charivari, the demonstrators remedied the loss of "honorable" rites, but their integrative social function remained fundamentally the same.[82]

79. See the description of roman wedding festivities in M. A. Altieri, *Li nuptiali*, ed. E. Narducci (Rome, 1873), 56, for the solemn presentation of the nuptial gifts and the basket by the groom and his friends.

80. Altieri, *Li nuptiali*, 57 and 94, on the marriage of widows: the bride goes to her new husband's house on a weekday, hidden among a group of women who accompany her discreetly. Bernardo Rinieri leads his second wife home to his house: "e la sera la menai a chasa mia sanz'altra dimostrazione" (and that evening I led her to my house without any further ado) (*ASF, Conventi soppressi* 95, 212, fol. 171, 18 January 1487). Antonio Rustichi remarries his sister Niccolosa and "la sera cho' nome di Dio n'andò a marito a chonpagnia di donne" (that evening, with the name of God, she went to [her] husband accompanied by women) (*ASF, Strozziane* 2, 11, fol. 13v, 26 January 1418). Jean des Garrons also clearly indicates that a widow receives no gifts, either monetary or material, but in their place "solet fieri canonizatum" (for "charivaritum"). This is the 48th degree of her punishment, the charivari being the 35th (*Tractatus*, 4:255). The connection established by des Garrons between the "donaria et iocalia in favorem et gaudium matrimonii novi" refused to the second-time bride, and the charivari that takes their place, would seem to corroborate the indications of other jurists and my own hypothesis.

81. A. van Gennep, *Manuel de folklore français contemporain* (Paris, new ed. 1976).

82. See the conclusions of C. Gauvard and A. Gokalp, "Les conduites de bruit et leur signification à la fin du Moyen Age: Le charivari," *Annales, E.S.C.* 29, no. 3 (1974): 693–704.

These remarks should make it clear that I have no intention of reducing the medieval charivari to the role of a demographic—or even a matrimonial—control mechanism exercised by young people.[83] Furthermore, could the young have guaranteed the fecundity of the population when charivaris were aimed exclusively at dual remarriages, which deprived their own peers of no marriage partner desirable for her youth or fecundity? In reality, the role of the participants in the charivari exceeded the simply regulatory functions to which some scholars have attempted to restrict them. The medieval texts invite us to reflect anew on the ritual mission of the *mattinatori* and on the origins of this practice, which, as I have attempted to show, was linked to an important aspect of popular wedding ritual. This analysis of the Italian *mattinata* has aimed at demonstrating that such a mission long maintained its underlying coherence under the contrasting forms of honor and insult.

83. To reach a clear conclusion regarding this function of the young men's or the bachelors' actions, we would need first to ascertain that an increase in charivaris (and how could this be measured?) coincided with a disequilibrium in the matrimonial market that worked to the disfavor of the young. This may have been the case before 1350, when demographic pressure delayed marriages and discouraged second unions. Remarriages then would seem a provocation to young men lacking access to women. That the Church in this period was more flexible in carrying out its policy of refusal to bless subsequent marriages may have increased the number or the violence of charivaris, the response to which was the synodal condemnations around 1330. In later years, however, pestilence and population decline relaxed the constraints that weighed on the marriage of the young. Widowhood and opportunities for remarriage multiplied between 1350 and 1450, but the young also gained easier access to marriage. As it happens, there was much more frequent mention of charivaris. Is this an illusion caused by documentation? Conclusions drawn from the presence or absence of normative texts, as compared with a demographic evolution that is as yet imperfectly known, seem to me premature.

# 13

## The Name "Remade": The Transmission of Given Names in Florence in the Fourteenth and Fifteenth Centuries

When Florentines of the Renaissance spoke of their "name," they referred, if they belonged to the ruling class, to the name of their lineage. These great theoreticians of the family seem to have given little thought to the social significance of the given name. Conversely, if they showed an interest in the collective family name that one generation transmits to another, it was because this hereditary name, which appeared even before 1200, had long remained an indication of social rank and political responsibilities. Although use of a family name had spread downward in society during the previous three centuries, it was for the most part reserved to the ruling class.[1] The given name that all Christians receive at baptism seemed to them less obviously connected to their social status and to the survival of their lineages, sorely threatened by repeated attacks of the plague. In fact, the explicit ideology of the lineage and the reflection on the role of

Originally published as "Le nom 'refait': La transmission des prenoms à Florence (XIVᶜ-XVIᶜ siecles)," *L'Homme* 20, no. 4 (1980):77–104. A much abbreviated version of this study was presented at the CUERMA colloquy, "L'Enfant au Moyen Age," held at Aix-en-Provence in March 1979. That version was published in the proceedings of the colloquy, *Cahiers du C.U.E.R.M.A.* 1980. My thanks go to R. C. Trexler for a reading of an early version of this study that led to many revisions.

1. See D. Herlihy and C. Klapisch-Zuber, *Les Toscans et leurs familles: Une étude du catasto de 1427* (Paris: Presses de la Fondation nationale des Sciences politiques, 1978), 537–50. In 1427 a good third of Florentines had a family name, as opposed to only one out of ten persons living in the countryside.

alliance in maintaining the lineage—the object of tested strategies and close analysis—did not include the area of the more obscure processes by which the choice of given names functioned within the family. This is because individual impulses might come into play here, as well as other phenomena—fashion, pious practices, etc.—that the lineage group did not feel it controlled. There is enough onomastic diversity among the great Florentine families, however, to persuade us that the processes of name giving and those of the continuance of the lineage were interconnected. And, although Florentines do not theorize on the matter, these processes are mentioned often enough in the Florentine *ricordanze* to tempt the historian to investigate this shadowy area of family consciousness.

The arrival to power of the merchant class in the thirteenth to the fourteenth centuries coincided with a profound change in the structures of the family and of kinship—which perhaps explains why the men of the early Renaissance were so sensitive to familial themes. As early as the thirteenth century, in imitation of the noble lineages of the twelfth century, the great merchants and bankers of Tuscany asserted their lineage solidarity by giving themselves a family name, transmissible in the male line.[2] By reinforcing the dotal system, which excluded women from the transmission of patrimonial goods, they further accentuated the patrilineal orientation of the system of filiation and inheritance.[3] This can be seen not only in the evolution of matrimonial law but also in the taste for genealogy that became the hobby of a great many Florentines. The genealogies that they draw up, however, were often uniquely masculine: daughters and wives were eliminated, or mentioned only when the alliances they helped to acquire had been particularly useful to the lineage. Excluded from the system of filiation and inheritance, a woman, when widowed, had to leave her children to the husband's lineage if she wanted to regain her freedom and get back her dowry. At the end of the Middle Ages (1360–1530), the period under consideration here, inheritances everywhere were divided, at the father's death, into equal parts among the sons, their sisters having been "appropriately" dowered. A father might leave more to one son, in general the eldest, but the practice was not current before the sixteenth century, and equality among the male heirs remained the rule. If a father died without sons, his estate went to his agnates, according to an order of precedence duly established by the statutes of the commune.

2. See O. Brattö, *Studi di antroponimia fiorentina; il Libro di Montaperti (An. MXXLX),* "Acta Universitatis" (Göteborg, 1955); A. Gaudenzi, "Sulla Storia del cognome a Bologna nel secolo 13: Saggio di uno studio comparativo sul nome di famiglia in Italia nel medio evo e nella età romana," *Bullettino dell'Istituto storico italiano* 19–20 (1898): 1–163.

3. M. Bellomo, *Ricerche sui rapporti patrimoniali tra coniugi: Contributo alla storia della famiglia medievale (120–130 sec.)* (Milan: Giuffrè, 1961); Bellomo, *Problemi di diritto familiare dell'età dei comuni: Beni paterni e pars filii* (Milan: Giuffrè, 1968); Bellomo, *La Condizione giuridica della donna in Italia: Vicende antiche e moderne* (Turin, 1970).

The exclusion of women from inheritance, which can be dated histor-
ically, was relatively recent at the time. Shunted between two lineages—
her father's and her husband's—a woman was not a full member of either.
She had an excellent chance of spending her life under several roofs, as
her successive marriages dictated, and of never seeing her identity fixed in
a definitive name. On the other hand, equality among the male heirs
produced fraternal communities that persisted after the father's death and
lasted at least until all the brothers had reached majority and could take
possession of their share of the inheritance.[4] These familial communities
sometimes survived a great deal longer, until cousins could no longer
tolerate living under the same roof. By their residence, which at the beginning of the fifteenth century remained close to that of their cousins
and their "consorts," by the collective expression of their particularity,
sanctioned by the hereditary name they bore and their common coat of
arms, by the overlapping of their patrimonial interests, Florentines of the
same lineage demonstrated an active familial solidarity and acquired at
birth a firm identity founded on filiation through the male line.[5]

What, then, went to make up the "name" that designated a Tuscan?
The great majority of people, in the fourteenth to the fifteenth centuries,
were addressed by the given name—or the first of the given names—they
had received at baptism, or sometimes by its diminutive or a nickname.
As further reference this was followed by the given name of their father
and quite often by that of their grandfather, on the model of "Giovanni
di Bartolomeo di Bernardo." Thus each man was identified by a series of
two or three male given names in a series that was elongated if genealogical
memory had to help consolidate social status, but into which a female
given name never entered. When these linked given names were not enough
to distinguish between individuals, other individual characteristics served
to complement the name.[6] As a reminder of the professional group or the
family group to which he belonged, a Tuscan would be designated by his
work, his title, his origin, or the hereditary name of the paternal lineage.
Thus, in the small city of San Gimignano, among a sample of one hundred
men registered in 1427 by the tax officials, there is not one who is designated by his given name alone: 80 persons are noted with their given
name and their father's name, while 18 add to it that of their grandfather
and two others that of their great-grandfather. Among the first group of
80 men, 23 also give a collective "family" name, as opposed to only 3 of

---

4. C. Fumagalli, *Il Diritto di fraterna nella giurisprudenza da Accursio alla codificazione*
(Turin, 1912). Herlihy and Klapisch-Zuber, *Les Toscans,* 469–522.

5. See F. W. Kent's lucid analysis, *Household and Lineage in Renaissance Florence: The
Family Life of the Capponi, Ginori and Rucellai* (Princeton, 1977), in fundamental disagreement
with R. W. Goldthwaite's thesis in *Private Wealth in Renaissance Florence* (Princeton, 1968).

6. This is the way the name was treated by the jurists and writers of the *Artes notariae*
of the thirteenth and fourteenth centuries. See the texts cited by A. Gaudenzi in "Sulla storia."

the 18 who give their grandfather's name. Eight others who belong to the first group have a personal nickname, 6 give the name of their profession, and 27 an indication of their residence or their origin. There are only 15 persons left who seem to be sufficiently individualized by two names.

In the constellation of the "name," then, the profession, title, nickname, or family name had equal value from the point of view of a demanding bureaucracy, since they served equally well to individualize possible homonyms and to identify the taxpayers. In the survey of 1427 in Florence, even if only the given name of a taxpayer and his father's name were registered, mention of his profession sufficed to distinguish most of the homonyms. For example, if we look at the group of "Giovanni di Bartolomeo," which appears 19 times, those who have no family name bear, in 9 cases out of 11, the name of their profession or a title, while of the 8 who bear a lineage name, only one also mentions his profession.

It should be stressed that a simple chain of three given names—a reduced filiation that could be kept in mind without excessive ancestor worship—was enough to avoid most of the confusions within a lineage, even an extended lineage. Even if a very small number of given names are repeated indefinitely, confusion is well-nigh impossible when reference to the given names of the father, the grandfather, and the great-grandfather are coupled with a skip of a generation in direct line before a given name is used again. With a chain of only four given names, for example, perfect homonyms cannot appear within the same generation, and the risk of homonymy strikes only the members of the elder branch in relation to their grandfathers and their great-uncles, and to the latter's first cousins (see figure 13.1)

Thus the various members of a sibling group, girls or boys, were recognizable by the series of the given names of their male ancestors in direct

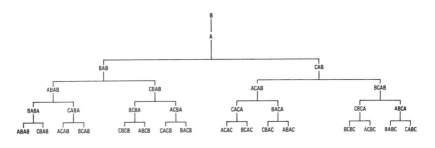

A = Andrea     B = Bartolomeo     C = Cristofano
ABCB = Andrea di Bartolomeo di Cristofano di Bartolomeo

Figure 13.1 Possibilities for Homonymy in the Anthroponymic System in Florence

line. Did the personal name that individualized them and that was given to them at birth modify this agnatic specification by attaching the newcomer more particularly to one of his two lineages or by privileging one ancestor or another within one lineage? Did it serve to recall the bilateral nature of filiation, even while the kinship group accented its patrilineality? And if so, why? Since after 1350 the child often received not one given name but two, and even three at the end of the fifteenth century,[7] parents had enough choices open to them to respond to different solicitations (as one name alone could not) and to multiply the child's material and spiritual chances. By investigating this question we can perhaps comprehend the parental strategies behind the choice of given names.

In many parts of Europe studied by ethnologists and historians of the modern period, name giving was strictly connected with the godparents, and they in turn were restricted to close blood relatives.[8] The godfather and godmother were selected from among the spouses' immediate kin in both lineages, and his or her given name or, conversely, that of the symmetrical relative not chosen as godparent, was given to the godchild. The couple struck a balance between the paternal and maternal lineages for their children's names, either by choosing the godparent's name for the child or by alternating between one line and the other for each of their children.

In Florence during the fourteenth and fifteenth centuries, natural kinship and spiritual kinship were juxtaposed but almost never overlapped. An infinitely small number (1.5 percent) of godfathers and godmothers were among the blood relatives or the close affines of the parents of the baptized child, at least in the social levels of those whose "family books" have been conserved.[9] The overwhelming majority of godparents of children born to these families of the urban middle class, upper or lower, were recruited among neighbors, colleagues, political acquaintances, or business associates of the child's father. If there was a set of rules that tied the choice of the given name to kinship in Florence, it did not operate through the godparents.

7. Second given names appear much earlier here than in France, where they are not noted until the end of the sixteenth century in the Midi and in the seventeenth century in the North. Approximately 60 percent of the nine hundred children of Florentine bourgeois families studied by means of familial documentation bear a second given name in the period 1360–1530.

8. See F. Zonabend, "La Parenté baptismale à Minot (Côte-d'Or)," *Annales, ESC* 33, no. 3 (1978): 656–76; Zonabend, "Pourquoi nommer?" in *L'Identité: Séminaire interdisciplinaire dirigé par Claude Lévi-Strauss, professeur au Collège de France, 1974–1975* (Paris, 1977), 257–86 and 348 (bibliography).

9. For a first approach to the question of the godparent relationship in Florence, see chapter 4 above, "Kin, Friends, and Neighbors," and C. Klapisch-Zuber, "Le *comparatico* à Florence: Parenté spirituelle et relations familiales avant la Contre-Réforme (14ᵉ–16ᵉ s.)" (to be published). On the family books or family journals (*ricordanze*, also *ricordi*), see D. Pezzarossa, "La Memorialistica fiorentina tra Medioevo e Rinascimento: Rassegna di studi e testi," *Lettere italiane* 1979: 96–138.

Plate 13.1 Giotto, *Naming of John the Baptist by His Father*. With restoration by
Gaetano Bianchi, late nineteenth century (detail). Santa Croce, Florence. (Photo
Alinari 3929)

The name was given primarily by the father. In general, the writer of
the family book stressed his own responsibility—without mention of his
wife—in the choice of a child's given name.[10] Direct maternal intervention,
clearly indicated, remained rare. As far as naming their godchild was concerned, the godparents had no role beyond that of transmitting to the
priest and presenting before God, at a baptismal ceremony that the child's
parents did not attend, the name or names that the child's parents had
chosen. According to family journals in Lucca and Bologna, the second
given name was given at the door to the church and the principal name
at the baptismal font.[11] The father often indicates in his book which given
name had priority: if the godparents deviate from this injunction, it is
purely by accident, perhaps due to distraction when, standing before the

10. As can be seen by the expressions currently used, such as "puosigli nome . . . " (I
put the name . . . to him).

11. Archivio di Stato, Lucca, Archivio Guinigi, Manoscritti 29, Ricordanze di Girolimo
Guinigi, 1433–59, passim. V. Montanari, ed., "Cronaca e storia bolognese del primo Cinquecento nel Memoriale di ser Eliseo Mamelini," *Quaderni culturali Bolognesi* 3, no. 9 (1979):
18 (4 October 1507), 22 (6 June 1509), 45 (23 August 1522).

priest, they invert the various names given the baby.[12] It was up to the father, then, or exceptionally to both the child's parents, to specify the given names that the godparents were to repeat.

From what stock of names did the father draw and how can we understand how he chose them? The selection of given names, the mechanisms by which they were transmitted, and the fashions that could influence the choice and distribution of names are phenomena difficult to perceive before the appearance of sources of systematic data such as parish registers. When such data do exist, they make it possible to reconstruct complete genealogies for entire sibling groups. To be sure, the medievalist has recourse to lists of given names, and he finds them useful for the study of fashions, religious practices, and social and regional differences.[13] As for genealogies, they abound toward the end of the Middle Ages among the urban families of Florence. As we have seen, however, their patrilineal emphasis gives us few cases in which we can study maternal lineages and thus discern the place that names coming from the maternal side really came to occupy in the stock of given names. The influence, direct or indirect, that the mother or the father's allies were able to exert on the process of name giving remains, in these conditions, harder to perceive than that of the father or his kin.

We can analyze the various reasons for the choice of first names only when we have full data on both the sibling group and its cognatic ascent group. We can find both categories of these precious data—biographical information and genealogical material—in the vast corpus of Florentine diaries and journals. In Florence, the *ricordanze* served in effect as civil registers of births, marriages, and deaths. It was to these books that the families who belonged to the ruling class consigned the birth dates of their sons (in order to be able to prove them eligible for political and professional tasks when they came of age) and of their daughters (with a view to their dowry and their marriage). These notations often proved useful for taxation purposes as well. Thus the head of family wrote down day by day all the events that marked the life of members of his household, including births, marriages, and deaths. When he had his children or his grandchildren baptized, he not only wrote down the name the child had been given but those of its godfathers and godmothers. Finally, he often took the trouble to give his reasons for the names he had chosen for the child.

12. This is what happened when the godparents of one of Luca di Matteo da Panzano's sons did him the disservice of inverting the given names Bartolomeo and Salvadore planned by the father: "He was given as a name by those who baptized him Salvadore and Bartolomeo, because my wife was remaking the name of her father . . . although I had said before Bartolomeo, a name which I strike out below" (Archivio di Stato, Florence, henceforth abbreviated ASF, *Strozziane* 2d ser., 9, fol. 90v, 24 August 1435).

13. This was the method followed by Brattö in his studies on the variations in the stock of given names in the thirteenth century (see above, note 2).

Here is one notation, typical in its simplicity, taken from the *ricordanze* of Carlo di Niccolò Strozzi when a first daughter, Francesca, was born to him 14 December 1497: "A baby of female sex—may all go well with her! —[named] Francesca, because of monna Francesca my mother. . . . Held at the baptismal fonts by [the names of three godparents follow]."[14] Or this one, longer and more explicit, which figures in the first book of the *ricordanze* of Francesco di Tommaso Giovanni under the date "on which my son Piero was born . . . Tuesday 26 March 1443, about twenty-two o'clock [i.e. about 4 P.M.] of Mea [my wife]. . . . He was baptized the 28th, giving him the name of Piero in honor of Saint Peter the Martyr, to whom [the mother] had made a vow to give this name at the birth of Giantommaso [an elder brother]. The second name that I have had given to him, Giovanni, is in honor of Saint John the Evangelist: the devotion I bear him had made me intend to baptize [one of my children] with his name; but it is also to remake (*rifare*) Giovanni, our brother. He was held at the baptismal fonts by [the names of five godfathers and one godmother follow], all doing so for the love of God. May God grant him life and health." The baby's death is noted three days later. "May God be praised for all," the father concludes, with resignation.[15]

This second document raises a series of problems. Somewhat exceptionally, it notes the direct intervention of the mother in the choice of a given name. But, above all, it shows the complexity of the reasons for giving the child the second name of Giovanni. This was, in fact, the name of the paternal lineage; thus several of Francesco's sons received it in second position or combined with another name. It is also the name of an important saint, homonym to the patron saint of Florence. Finally, it was the name of a paternal uncle of the baby who had died in 1431 and whom the father now wanted to "remake." This strange term seems at first sight to refer to the idea that an ancestor or a close relative would find himself reincarnated in a newborn child through the reattribution of his given name. As the term *rifare* indicates, the child was connected in a special way with this one member of his family, both by the symbolic attribute of his given name and by something more corporal. It is precisely the nature of this bond that I shall attempt to clarify.

Texts of this type, which are fairly frequent, give the reasons that underlay parental choices. There are explanations of 27 percent of the attributions of first given names and 18 percent of the second and third names in a sampling of about nine hundred children. The genealogical and biographical information that abounds in many of the *ricordanze* permits us, furthermore, to enrich this preliminary catalogue of explanations. A systematic comparison of the name given at baptism with that of the saint celebrated on that day or on the day of the child's birth adds an entire set

14. ASF, *Strozz.*, 4th ser., 74, fol. 50v.
15. ASF, *Strozz.*, 2d ser., 16, fol. 25.

of notations useful to the study of religious practices. For several hundred children born into the Florentine middle class, it is thus possible to untangle the complex interplay of rules and practices that led their fathers to fix on the name they were giving.

It will simplify the problem to consider first a small group of 33 unions, nearly all taken from the fifteenth century, with a total issue of 266 children, or an average of 8 children per couple.[16] This group is unusual in that the father, the author of the *ricordanze*, is particularly prolix concerning his reasons for the choice of given names. Furthermore, the genealogy of the families involved is fairly well known. Despite this detailed information, it is difficult to ascertain the origin of the first given name of 26.3 percent of these children. The uncertainty is particularly strong for the girls.[17] Among the children with a given name of known origin, we can see that one-half—girls as well as boys—bear a name taken from the stock of names in the paternal lineage. One boy out of six and one girl out of ten take their first given name from the maternal line, as far as we can tell. It is true that the greater uncertainty regarding female names might make these figures undependable. Were girls' names more often chosen from this lesser-known maternal pool? Such a preference, masked by the size of the group of all first names of uncertain origin, might escape us. It would be difficult to understand, however, following this hypothesis, why the maternal name stock is better represented among boys than among girls when the father gives the name. If we overlook the idea that this uncertainty can lead to appreciable distortions, and if we keep to given names of clear provenance, we can suppose, as a first approximation, that the paternal line furnished three to four times more names than the maternal line, and that this preference affected girls at least as much as boys.

The rest of the given names for which Florentine *ricordanze* give a direct or indirect explanation show a further characteristic of the system of name giving. A great many girls (nearly one-third of all female names for which origin is known) bear the name of a sister who had died; boys less often receive the name of a dead older brother (13 percent). Might these names carried over within a sibling group also hide a preference for names taken from one family name pool or the other? In point of fact, out of 20 girls whose names repeat that of a dead sister, 14 are indirectly attached by this means to the paternal line, and only 2 to their maternal grandmother,[18] whereas for boys paternal and maternal name origin are somewhat better

16. These unions represent approximately one-quarter of the total corpus of the families studied, and the children (144 boys and 122 girls) represent one-third of those whose precise birth date is known, sometimes along with other biographical information. A certain number of extracts from *ricordanze* cited here are taken from families who are not included in this smaller sampling of thirty-three families.

17. Or 41 girls (33.6 percent) and 29 boys (20.1 percent).

18. The origin of the given name is unknown for three others. A youngest girl repeats a name previously given to her sister on the occasion of an important political event. Finally, four girls bear the name of their father's first wife (see below, notes 34 and 35).

balanced. This preliminary examination leads to the necessary conclusion that paternal given names, as corrected by the addition of names attributed a second time after the death of the first bearer of the name, far outweighed others among girls, where they make up two-thirds of the total explained names, as opposed to 53 percent among boys. Given names from the maternal line, similarly corrected, occur somewhat more frequently among boys (19 percent) than among girls (13 percent).

Compared to these names from the family stock, principal first names taken from godparents or inspired by them were the exception: in this sampling, there are no more than five of these for all boys and two for girls.[19] In the urban circles from which the *ricordanze* come, the rare occasions on which a godparent's name is passed on to a child can usually be explained by the choice of an illustrious godparent.[20] The infrequency of such cases confirms, *a contrario*, that the choice of given name was normally restricted to within the confines of natural kinship: a less prestigious godparent did not transmit his or her name to the godchild.

The system of name giving does not depend on the kinship structure alone, however. One group of principal given names—a small but significant minority—indicates the modest beginnings of another orientation: 17 percent of male first names and 9 percent of similar female names were selected, according to the writer of the family journal, for reasons of piety. The father might name a child out of personal attachment to a particular saint, sometimes to fulfill a vow; he might, somewhat more automatically, choose the name of the saint whose feast day it was; or he might choose the name of a saint associated with a particular type of birth. For example, children baptized privately, usually under conditions of urgency, were named Giovanni or Giovanna and placed then and there under the protection of the Baptist; children born with a caul were named Santo or Santa, and so forth.[21] The exiguity of this group of first given names shows

19. It does not seem pure coincidence that the tenth and eleventh sons of Matteo di Niccolò di Duccio Corsini, born in 1376 and 1378, bear the five given names of their five godfathers, but the case is nevertheless exceptional. A. Petrucci, ed., *Libro di ricordanze dei Corsini (1362–1457)* (Rome, 1965),100.

20. Thus, in 1467, Filippo di Matteo Strozzi named his eldest boy by his first wife Alfonso, the godfather being Don Alfonso of Aragon, the duke of Calabria, "who happened to be in these parts" and who was represented by Lorenzo de' Medici at the baptism (ASF, *Strozz.*, 5th ser., 17, fol. 189v). His daughter Lionora was so named, in 1473, because Eleonora, the daughter of the king of Naples, married the duke of Ferrara when Filippo himself was in Naples (ASF, *Strozz.*, 5th ser., 22, fol. 90).

21. See ASF, *Strozz.*, 3d ser., 346, fol. 90v, Ricordanze di Bernardo di Tommaso Strozzi, 1 November 1419: "Antonia e Santa, naque vestita." Because of the religious character of children born with part of the amnion covering their heads at birth, they were also named for the Virgin. See also Archivio degli'Innocenti, *Estranei* 648, fol. 174, Ricordanze di Jacopo Pandolfini 24 March 1490, birth of Giovanbattista Mariano: "mi naque . . . vestito." Even today children born in this manner are named Santino or Santina. On children born *vestiti* in Italy, see C. Ginzburg, *I Benandanti: Stregoneria e culti agrari tra Cinquecento e Seicento* (Turin, 1966), 23–25 (*The Night Battles: Witchcraft and Agrarian Cults in the Sixteenth and Seventeenth Centuries*, trans. J. and A. Tedeschi [Baltimore, 1983]). For a more general approach see N. Belmont, *Les Signes de la naissance* (Paris, 1971).

once again how heavily the naming process depended on family tradition, as found in its stock of names, and how little influence individual piety had on it.

The stamp of the paternal line is particularly evident among eldest children: 63 percent of male and 60 percent of female firstborns bear a name from the paternal line.[22] Beginning with the second child, these percentages sink to 48 and 44, respectively, and borrowings from the maternal stock increase slightly. These contrary trends continue up to the fourth child, after which borrowings from the paternal and maternal line come into balance. The share of names attributable to religious motives, on the other hand, remains much more stable at all points in order of birth. These collective data therefore eliminate the idea that any systematic alternation from one lineage to the other was observed in the choice of given names. In Florence the massive preference for paternal names was to some extent tempered by the introduction of names from the maternal line's stock, a tendancy that increases with later position in birth order.

Second names[23]—those given at the entrance to the church in Lucca and Bologna and subsequently little used—are less difficult to situate, since religious references account for three-fourths of the names we can explain. Pious practices have the upper hand here. The protection of a patron saint is invoked for the newborn in 73 percent of male names and 80 percent of female names—a saint personally revered by the parents or, more frequently, the saint whose feast day fell on the child's day of birth or baptism. Furthermore, more than half of these "devotional names" were given to the child automatically: whole sibling groups, after 1470, are given Romolo or Romola as a second or third name, after the patron saint of the cathedral church of Fiesole, near Florence. A great number of girls are just as automatically named Maria in second position (although the name is rare in first position) or Margherita. Saint John the Baptist, patron saint of the city, is invoked for many boys. Children born or baptized on Sunday are very often given Domenico or Domenica as a second name, which had the advantage of placing them under both divine protection and that of Saint Dominic.[24] Babies were not baptized with the name of all calendar

22. If names of unknown origin are excluded, these percentages rise to 76 and 86.

23. Out of 266 children, 179, or 67.3 percent, bear at least a second given name; 41 have a third name (15.4 percent of the total). These percentages are close to those based on 900 children (see above, note 7).

24. The feast of Saint Romolo bishop was added to the list of *dierum feriatorum seu inutilium* (nonwork days) in Florence only in 1508 (I. da San Luigi, ed., *Etruria sacra* [Florence, 1782], 1:56). It is difficult to verify whether all the children born on Sunday were given Domenico or Domenica as their second name, but it is certain that out of 30 children who are so named, 26 were born or baptized on Sunday and only 4 received their second name because their birth coincided with the feast of Saint Dominic (5 August). Two children baptized with this name as principal given name perhaps show the father's personal devotion to Saint Dominic. On the diffusion of these new pious practices in the fourteenth century, see C. M. de La Roncière, "L'Influence des Franciscains dans la campagne de Florence au XIVᵉ siècle (1280–1360)," *Mélanges de l'Ecole française de Rome, Moyen Age–Temps modernes* 87 (1975): 27–103.

saints, however: often a child born on the feast of an obscure saint would be named for a more powerful celestial patron whose feast day was near.[25] The mechanisms for the introduction of religious references, one may infer, are not simple. One thing that is clear, however, is that preachers, who from the end of the thirteenth century urged the faithful to place each new Christian under the direct protection of an incontestable saint, contributed to the appearance of second given names at the end of the fourteenth century in Tuscany.[26]

As a result, fewer second given names than first names linked the child to an ascendant line. Only 14 boys and 4 girls (20 percent and 14 percent, respectively, of those for whom second given names are explained) bear names that reflect ties to the paternal line; 9 percent and 4 percent, respectively, were similarly linked to their maternal line. On the other hand, godparents occupy a more important place among second given names, and godparent collectivities such as religious communities, political bodies, and communes subject to Florence sometimes transmitted their names to a godchild.[27]

The choice of the second given name seems to respond to a need to reconcile a desire for religious protection with the necessity to link the child to one of its kinship groups. Furthermore, the father could often play on the ambiguity of a given name to show his piety while he recalled an ancestral name or made a gesture toward the opposite lineage. Bartolomeo Valori, in 1456, notes that his eldest son's second name came from the feast of Saint Peter, celebrated that day, but his genealogy reveals that Piero was his father-in-law's name as well.[28] He could thus tip his hat to both the saint and, discreetly, to his wife's father.

Although name-giving after maternal relatives was relegated to a minor place, the field was not left totally free to the child's paternal kin. The father sought to keep on good terms with his allies and submitted to the teachings of the Church by making room for their representatives. Second names express better than principal names the contradictory tendencies of a system of name-giving founded essentially on the paternal kin but which opened up enough to accept both the great patron saints of the Church

25. In particular, the feast days consecrated to the Virgin overflow to the surrounding days. The same is true for Saint John the Baptist, patron of Florence. Saint Reparata, on the other hand, the other patron saint of the city, has only a few followers.

26. See de La Roncière, "L'Influence des Franciscains."

27. The commune of San Gimignano gave the name of its saintly eponym in this manner to one godson, Buonaccorso Pitti's son, in 1417 (A. Bacchi della Lega, ed., *Cronica* [Bologna, 1905], 29). The commune of San Miniato did the same for a son of Lapo Niccolini in 1398 (C. Bec., ed., *Libro degli affari proprii di casa* . . ., [Paris, 1969], 89). The second name of one of Andrea Minerbetti's daughters was Marta (1497); the sisters of Santa Marta di Montughi, represented by their chaplain, figured among her godparents (Biblioteca Laurenziana, *Acquisti e Doni*, 229, 2, fol. 14).

28. Biblioteca Nazionale Centrale, Florence (henceforth abbreviated BNF), *Panciatichi* 134, fol. 5v.

and some obscure saints tucked away in a corner of the calendar, representatives of new cults as well as extremely ancient religious traditions, some godparents, and a small number of affinal relatives. But were second names enough to resolve the latent conflict between the two families? Global evaluations like those that precede cannot guarantee that we grasp strategies of choice, so we must turn for a model to several families whose particularly full genealogy and full explanations provide an opportunity for closer examination.

The first example, that of Piero di Marco di Parente Parenti, illustrates preferences current in Florence at the time (see figure 13.2).[29] Piero's children show how their father, after having fulfilled his duties toward their grand-parents, first paternal and then maternal, felt freer to give homage to other dead members of his kinship group and to show his reverence for important saints of the Catholic calendar: Saint Francis, Saint Vincent, and Saint Sylvester. As for second names, he places his daughters under the protection of the Virgin, Saint Margaret, and Saint Francis and his boys under that of the saint whose feast day it was. Francesco, his second son, born on the feast of the Stigmata was named Antonio as a second name to honor his maternal grandfather of that name. This was premature, as the next boy was called Antonio as well, as a principal given name this time. The maternal grandfather appears once more, in second position, for his sixth son, Benedetto.

Multiple examples of families that showed a similarly low sensitivity to given names from the maternal side, grandfathers excluded, could be found from one end of the social scale to the other. The coppersmith Bernardo Masi shows a clear preference for the paternal line in his choices of names for his two sets of children. He also demonstrates how the father handled the stock of family given names to adjust to deaths in the family (see figure 13.3).[30] His oldest son, Piero, receives the name of his paternal grandfather, who had died twenty years earlier, and his second son, Bartolomeo, that of his father's maternal grandfather, which had passed on to one of Bernardo's brothers who had died in infancy. The first girl, whose two grandmothers were still living, is named Maria, since she was baptized on the vigil of the feast of the Assumption, 14 August 1482. In August of 1484 the child's maternal grandmother died, and her name, Agnola, was immediately given to a daughter born in November. Bernardo was to have ten children by his second wife. The first daughter, born 18 September 1496, is named for his dead wife, Caterina, but the second is named for her paternal grandmother, Piera, who had died 31 December 1496. A third daughter born of this second marriage also bears this name, precious

29. ASF, *Strozz.*, 2d ser., 17bis, fols. 76v, 77v, 83v.
30. ASF, *Manoscritti* 88, *passim,* Ricordanze di Piero di Bernardo Masi, fols. 140–140v (1478–1513). G. O. Corazzini, ed., *Ricordanze di Bartolomeo Masi calderaio fiorentino dal 1478 al 1526* (Florence, 1906).

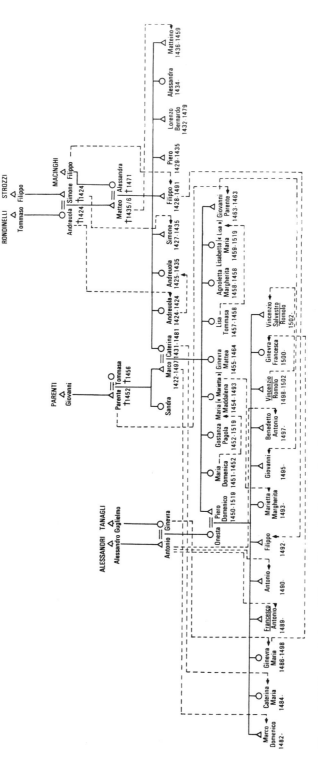

Figure 13.2 Transmission of Given Names in the Family of Piero Parenti. Names underlined repeat the name of the saint whose feast falls on the day of the child's birth or baptism. The observation of children stops in 1520.

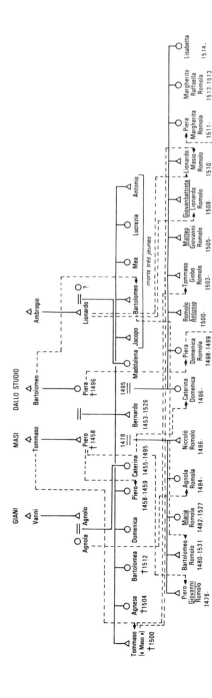

Figure 13.3 Transmission of Given Names in the Masi Family. Names underlined are explained by the father's piety. Observation stops in 1526.

to her father, since the death of her sister in 1499 had left it vacant. As for the boys born of this second union, their names alternate between devotional names, for the first, third, and fourth child, and the names of a paternal uncle who had died three years earlier or the maternal grandfather (the name of the paternal grandfather common to both sets of children, Piero, was still in use by their half brother). Almost all of Bernardo's children are also given Romolo as a second name, and for some of them a third and less stereotyped name is added. The father signals a more individualized religious affiliation in this way, or attaches the child to his own affines and to the maternal line. For example, the sixth son by the second wife, which devotion prompted him to name Giambattista, made the maternal grandfather, Lionardo, skip his turn. No matter: this negligence was corrected with the next boy.

While the attribution to the elder children of the given names of paternal grandparents was generally respected, alternation between paternal and maternal lines was not the rule. The father is more apt to have recourse to relatively distant paternal kin or to his own maternal kin than to his affines. The paternal given names easily supplant the maternal ones. Thus Bernardo's second son by his second wife is named in 1503 for his paternal uncle, Tommaso, who had died recently, and the reuse of the maternal grandfather's name, Lionardo, has to wait for the fifth child. What is more, calendar saints often take over the place that should belong to maternal grandparents.[31] By their vulnerability, given names from the maternal line point to a conception of kinship that the Church asserted to be dependent upon bilaterality, but that in lay practice and the law was most often treated as unilateral.

How do our Florentines justify giving other relatives priority over the child's grandparents? The following example should permit us to see this more clearly. Bartolomeo di Giovanni Morelli gives his first son, born in 1376, the name of one of his own brothers who died in the plague of 1374, while his second son receives the name of his paternal grandfather, Giovanni, who died in the previous plague of 1363.[32] Bartolomeo thus gives priority to his brother, whose grave was still fresh, over his father, thirteen years dead. It is evident that he sets aside the child's grandfather here because his uncle's death is more recent. Death gives a priority that could break the usual hierarchical order of the attribution of given names. The precedence accorded to those most recently dead apparently resulted

31. This order was also upset by surprises like the one Benventuto Cellini reports in his autobiography. His given name means "welcome," and his parents, persuaded that they would have a second girl, had thought to call her Reparata after her maternal grandmother, the elder having been named after the paternal grandmother (B. Cellini, *Vita*, Biblioteca universale nos. 771–72 (Milan, 1954), 1:3:18–19.

32. Giovanni di Pagolo Morelli, *Ricordi*, ed. V. Branca (Florence, new ed. 1969), 166–68.

in an obligation stricter than that of any hierarchical order between lineages or within a lineage.

The writers of the *ricordanze* confirm this analysis. They often note that they have chosen one name or another because they felt themselves obliged to *rifare* a relative who had recently died. A living person was not "remade," but the "remaking" of a dead member of the lineage was on the contrary felt as a duty, and the preceding example shows that the operation had to be carried out as soon as possible after the person's death. This obligation generally resulted in the appearance of names given for paternal relatives strangely distant from the child. Thus Francesco di Tommaso Giovanni notes 23 October 1449 that his son-in-law, Giovanni Arrigucci, named his third son Bernardo "because of his cousin Bernardo di Pagolo Baroncelli, who died in September 1449."[33] It is also by this necessity to "remake" the recent dead that we can explain the appearance of the few maternal given names lost among names that were in the majority paternal. Recourse to maternal names that were not those of the child's direct grandparents must be explained by the recent death and also the prestige of their former bearer, a prestige that it was tempting to capture and carry over to a newborn. Virgilio Adriani comments on the names Tommaso Vitale Antonio, given to his fourth son 27 April 1470 in the following terms: "Tommaso for his uncle, his mother's brother, dead 31 March 1470, to give pleasure to the mother. He was a good man . . . dead very young at the age of 26 or 27. His death was a great loss, for he was the last of his house, the branch of Ubertino di Tommaso d'Ubertino Strozzi, who descended from the branch of Rosello Strozzi, the first builder of the chapel of Santa Maria Novella, who initiated the consecration of chapels in the name of the house of the Strozzi in the church of Santa Maria Novella." With the death of little Tommaso at the age of six died the memory of those affinal relatives whom the father had agreed to perpetuate in his own lineage, under pressure from the mother but also through a sensitivity to the added prestige that this alliance brought him.[34]

The urgency to reattribute the given name of a dead relative is felt particularly keenly, however, within the narrower sphere of the conjugal family. This is expressed first by the virtually automatic carrying over of the name of the father's first wife to the first daughter born of a second marriage, taking precedence over any ancestral name for the child. Biagio Buonaccorsi offers one example of this with his eldest daughter by his second wife, whom he names Alessandra "to remake Alessandra, who was my wife and who well deserves that I have her name eternally remembered."[35] Similarly, Bartolomeo di Francesco Salvetti, a maker of gloves

---

33. ASF, *Strozz.*, 2d ser., 16 bis, fol. 4.
34. ASF, *Strozz.*, 2d ser., 21, fol. 70.
35. BNF, *Panciatichi* 101, fol. 19, 3 April 1512.

and purses, names his second daughter (the first had been given emergency baptism) after his first wife, giving her his own mother's name only as a second name.[36] An asymmetry between lineages appears once more in these reuses of a name, since it would have been inconceivable for a widow who remarried to give a son of a second marriage the name of her first husband. The attribution of the father's name to a posthumous son was also common,[37] and the premature death of the father explains the aberrant cases in which the son bears the same given name as his father.[38]

Within a sibling group the shifts of names from a dead brother or sister to a younger sibling reveal even more clearly this community of the living and the dead of a lineage. Piero di Marco Parenti, in the example analyzed above, names his last child Vincenzio Salvestro Romolo "because," as he says, "I remade his brother Vincenzio, who died not long ago, and because he was baptized on Saint Sylvester's Day." His fourth daughter had been named Ginevra Francesca in 1500 "in exchange for the first, who died [in 1498]."[39] Such an attitude—and we should note that almost without exception the former and the new bearers of the name are of the same sex—was not unique to the ruling class in Florence. It can be found from one end of society to the other, as seen in the *ricordanze* of minor notaries and artisans and of inhabitants of secondary cities of the territory. It can be found, by allusion, even in the tax declaration of a humble sharecropper, explaining to the tax officials, who may have been surprised to encounter a three-year-old Antonio whom they could see listed as older in a previous survey: "He died and I remade him."[40]

This carrying over of given names, which, as we have seen, particularly affects girls, leads to astonishing repetitions among siblings. The Valori family, in which girls were particularly numerous, gives examples that extend over three generations. Bartolomeo di Filippo names three of his ten daughters Pichina—his mother's name—between 1453 and 1470. His son Niccolò has three Lucrezias between 1497 and 1509, and his grandson Filippo no fewer than four Ginevras—the name of their paternal grandmother—between 1523 and 1534![41] "Remaking" the dead applied not

36. ASF, *Manoscritti* 96, fol. 12.

37. Bartolomeo di Bartolomeo di Jacopo di Doffo Spini, posthumous son, "received his name because his father died leaving his mother pregnant" (ASF, *Strozz.*, 2d ser., 13, fol. 18.). Piero di Bernardo di Piero Masi had an uncle, Piero di Piero, who died at six months, who was so named by his mother because he was born three months after the death of his father (ASF, *Manoscritti* 88, fol. 140, 1459). See also Biblioteca Laurenziana, *Acquisti e Doni* 229, 2, fol. 69, 1508, Ricordanze d'Andrea Minerbetti; ASF, *Strozz.*, 3d ser., 270 (18 October 1340), Ricordi di Rosso d'Ubertino Strozzi.

38. For the given name most frequently found in Florence, Giovanni, which returns 854 times in the *catasto* of 1427, only eighteen taxpayers (2.1 percent) can be found at that date whose father was also named Giovanni.

39. See above, note 29.

40. ASF, *Catasto*, 934, fol. 175, declaration of Bernardo Lanciani (1469–70). See chapter 5 above, "Childhood in Tuscany."

41. BNF, *Panciatichi*, 134, 1, fols. V, Vv.

only to dead children whose given name was used again. The names of ancestors, which it was urgent and logical to give to new bearers, were "remade" through their namesakes. But the process also involves the "devotional names": first introduced into the familial stock for religious reasons, once given to a child they were integrated into this pool of names. The case of a notary from Prato, ser Jacopo Landi, is one example of this. Because of repeated deaths from plague, he keeps trying to "remake" his mother, his maternal aunt, and his paternal grandmother in the children he had by two wives (see figure 13.4).[42] But he also remembers two saints, Saint Paul and Saint Nicholas, who watched over him in his first series of misfortunes, by giving their names a second time to children of his second marriage. The story of this provincial notary shows clearly how new familial cults could be consolidated and could leave a lasting mark on the stocks of given names of certain families. All that was needed was for one member to proclaim his devotion by naming one of his children, or several in succession, after a patron saint, and this new given name and the obligation to "remake" it were bequeathed to his descendants.

When pressed by sudden death, parents even went so far as to change the name of a child who had already been baptized to that of the dead near relative—father, mother, or elder sibling. When they did so, they always took the sex of the dead person into account. Conjugal devotion prompted a mother to rename her youngest son for her husband when he died: Filippo di Filippo Strozzi had been baptized Giovanbattista in

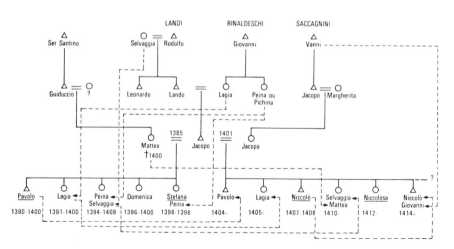

Figure 13.4 Transmission of Given Names in the Landi Family. Names underlined are explained by the father's piety. Observation stops in 1415.

42. BNF, *Manoscritti Palatini* 1129, Ricordanze di ser Jacopo di Lando da Prato (1383–1414).

1489, but when his father died three years later, his widow renamed the child Filippo "to renew the memory of his father."⁴³ These practices seem to have been ancient. Uguccione di Mico Capponi simply changes the name of his daughter, Cilia, born in 1436. As he says, "since, afterward, this name no longer pleased us, we have named her Vaggia, because my eldest daughter who died bore that name."⁴⁴ We can find this same attitude in *ricordanze* of the first half of the fourteenth century. Thus Pepo Albizzi took away the given name of his illegitimate daughter Piera, born in 1350: "When she went off to nurse, we named her Margherita, and so she is called today." In 1361 he gave the name Piera to another daughter— legitimate this time—by his third wife.⁴⁵

Another example illuminates the priorities that parents established among the dead of the lineage and of the immediate family. At the birth of a daughter 6 August 1476, Filippo di Matteo Strozzi "remakes our mother," Alessandra, who died in 1471. The mother died soon after the child's birth. When the child was confirmed 1 January 1478, her father "orders that in the future she be called Fiametta so that she will bear the name of her mother," and from that time on the little girl was known by the diminutive "la Fiamettina." We should note that Filippo's brother Lorenzo had already "remade" their mother in the person of his eldest daughter in 1471, the year of the grandmother Alessandra's death, and subsequently he "remade" his sister-in-law Fiametta before his brother did, only a few months after her death in 1477. Filippo, however, insisted on "remaking" his mother on his own, since her given name had been vacated among his own children in 1478. He gave it immediately to the eldest daughter of his second marriage in 1479, "in memory of our mother and of the one [the Alessandra] that she had had."⁴⁶ Here conjugal devotion temporarily sets aside the venerated name of the paternal grandmother for the youngest child of the first marriage, but the father reembodies the name Alessandra as soon as he can. Filippo's second wife was to return the compliment in debaptizing their youngest son after his father's death to give him his father's name.⁴⁷ The history of Filippo and his brother Lorenzo also reveals that there was no competition between the two brothers to reattribute the name of a "dear departed," but that each one felt and respected an obligation to honor her memory, to show the place that she had occupied

43. Lorenzo di Filippo Strozzi, *Vite degli uomini illustri di Casa Strozzi* (Florence, 1872), 85–86. Other examples are cited in Kent, *Household and Lineage in Renaissance Florence,* 47. One child in Bologna was renamed with the name of the saint whose intercession had cured him (see the *ricordanze* of ser E. Mamelini, "Cronaca e storia," ed. V. Montanari).

44. ASF, *Conventi Soppressi,* San Piero a Monticelli 153, fols. 4–4v. The precise date of the death of the first Vaggia is not known but must have been between 1438 and 1444.

45. Newberry Library, Chicago, Ricordanze di Pepo Albizzi, 1339–1358, fol. 35v.

46. ASF, *Strozz.,* 1st ser., 22, fols. 72, 97. Filippo was thinking of one of his sisters, born in 1434 and married in 1451, who had herself received her name, Alessandra, not from their mother but from an aunt of their father's (ASF, *Strozz.,* 5th ser., 11, fol. 155v).

47. See above, note 43.

in the life of the family, to honor her closest survivor, and to emphasize their ties of affection to her (see figure 13.5).

The children of Giovanni Buongirolami, a jurist from a lineage of men of law who came from Gubbio to Florence at the beginning of the fifteenth century, have names that reappear in equally complex cycles.[48] Giovanni's eldest son, Bernardo, received the name of his paternal grandfather in 1500, but died at five years of age. His fourth son, Girolamo, born in 1504, named for a paternal great-uncle, was then debaptized, and his father says that he "gives him for name Bernardo, by which he must be called from now on." The name Girolamo, now freed, was to be attributed to a sixth son born in 1507. In the meantime, twin girls had been born in 1505, one named Milia after her paternal grandmother and the other Alessandra, after her maternal grandmother. Milia died at 22 days old, and her father decided that "the above-named Alessandra will in the future be called Milia in exchange for the dead girl." The second Milia died at 17 months. The next daughter, born in 1511, took her place, while a fourth daughter, in 1514, was to "remake" both her maternal grandmother and her dead and rebaptized sister, Alessandra. Here the maternal grandmother was ousted twice, while the father's paternal uncle was obliged to cede his place to his brother, the child's paternal grandfather. In all of these cases, the names of grandparents that were set aside were reused for a succeeding child (see figure 13.6).

The corollary of the practice that consisted in "remaking" the dead was that two *living* members of the same group of siblings or the same conjugal family could not bear the same given name.[49] The inextricable puzzle well known to modern demographic historians of certain regions, who find homonyms within one family at one time, therefore does not exist for Tuscany. But if this is the case, when a Florentine had to "remake" the dead of his family by giving their names to the living as soon as possible, could he give the living only the names of the dead? Was it impossible for him to "remake" an honored member of his family prematurely? Until about 1460 it does seem that fathers, who so often carried over to a newcomer the name of an ancestor or a relative who had died recently, spontaneously refrain from "remaking" the living. In the last third of the century and the beginning of the sixteenth century, on the other hand, not only are attributions of names that still belonged to living persons more frequent,[50] but the explanations given by the father show that he

48. ASF, *Strozz.*, 2d ser., 23, fols. 129–36, 171v–80.

49. Children baptized under conditions of urgency, who were often named Giovanni or Giovanna even if they had a living sibling of that name, do not fall under this rule. They occasionally take the name of a living person because they are themselves felt to be condemned. Two examples of this can be found among the children of Matteo di Niccolò Corsini (see above, note 19).

50. Among the Rinieri, the paternal grandfathers were "remade" in the two following generations while they were still living (ASF, *Conventi Soppressi*, 220, fol. 5v, 1508, and fol. 102v, 1544).

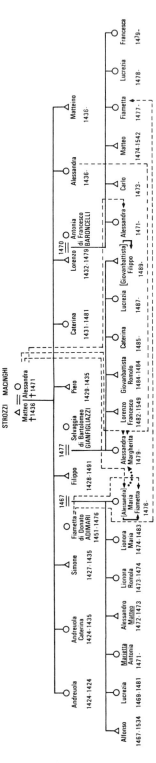

Figure 13.5 Renaming of Children—Family of Filippo Strozzi. Repetitions of the names Fiametta and Alessandra alone are given here. The solid arrow indicates a renaming; the brackets indicate the abandoned given name. The broken arrow indicates any other transmission of a given name.

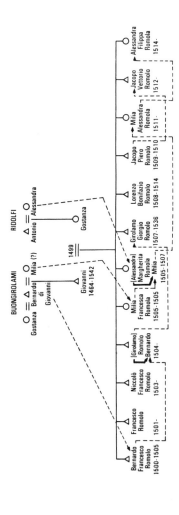

Figure 13.6 Renaming of children—family of Giovanni Buongirolami. The solid arrow indicates a renaming; brackets indicate the abandoned given name.

was conscious of violating a sort of taboo, implicit until then. Piero Strozzi "remakes" his father Carlo in 1459 in the person of his eldest son, "although our father is still living."[51] The second name given to the child, Viva (literally, "may he live!"), is perhaps there to dispel the threat that such a precipitous reattribution of the name might offer one or the other of its bearers. Similarly, Biagio Buonaccorsi "remakes" his own step-mother, Agnola, in his first daughter, "even though she is alive." After both died, he gave the name to his second daughter by his second wife, "to commemorate Monna Agnola, my stepmother, whose behavior [toward me] did more for me than a mother." The taboo applied, therefore, not to a father's transmission of his own name to his son, but to the passing on of the name of a living person to another living person, and Florentines did not choose to violate it lightheartedly. Tribaldo dei Rossi is a good illustration of this. He bows, seemingly against his will, to the pleadings of his father, "asking as a grace of [him]self and [his] wife to remake him while he was living."[52] Good or bad, handsome or ugly,[53] rich or poor, the members of the lineage had to be "remade." But before their name could be reincarnated in a new body, they had to pass to the rank of ancestors. Giving the name of a living relative would be equivalent to making him enter prematurely into the group of ancestors and would threaten the child. For the dead were dangerous as well as protective, whatever they might have been during their lifetimes. The double sense of the word *rifare*—"revive" and "indemnify"—indicates that in honoring and reincarnating the dead, the living avoid alienating them; they neutralize them, "buy them off," and prevent them from floating free in the indefinite and threatening space reserved for shades.

When Florentines carried on this sort of "reincarnation" of the dead person they appear to have aimed less—before the end of the fifteenth century—at transmitting the personal qualities or the merits of an ancestor to a new member of the family than at investing the name itself with a provisory flesh-and-blood body. In 1497 one rich Florentine, Tommaso Guidetti, discovers in the family archives that the given name of one of his distant ancestors was Mannello: the name had not been used in his branch of the family for five generations, and all memory of the personality of the original bearer had certainly faded into the obscurity of the past. Tommaso nevertheless decides to "re-make this ancient name of our house," and he gives it, in spite of its antiquated tone, to one of his sons.[54] Here

51. ASF, *Strozz.*, 5th ser., 16, fol. 1 (14 September 1459).

52. BNF, *Panciatichi* 101, fol. 3v (14 April 1503) and fol. 31 (12 February 1517), Ricordanze di Biagio Buonaccorsi; BNF 2, 2, 357, fol. 59, Ricordi di Tribaldo d'Amerigo dei Rossi, fol. 59.

53. See the anecdote reported by Poliziano, cited in Kent, *Household and Lineage*, 47: A small child of the Rucellai family protested when he learned that his parents proposed to *rifare* a ridiculous-looking uncle. " This time don't make him so ugly! " he demanded.

54. ASF, *Strozz.*, 4th ser., 418, fol. 33.

again, the individual is without attributes and it is instead the name itself that is brought back to life.

Given names formed a sort of family patrimony, no part of which should be neglected or lost. One definition of the ideal "house," which included all members of the lineage, living or dead, can be found in the collection of given names that were reactivated among the living in each generation. Ultimately, all members of the lineage of the same sex were interchangeable. The individual, the child particularly, would be named or renamed *in cambio*—in exchange for—the elder family member cut down by death. In the parents' memory, homonymic children ended up being merged into one person whose permanence was guaranteed by the use of the same given name. Cambio di Tano Petrucci gives two of his sons successively to the same nurse, the second "remaking" the first, and when he draws up his accounts with the nurse's husband, around 1409, he condenses his two sons into one: "Manno, whom he raised for me twice!"[55] The spiritual birth of a child, who received his name with the waters of baptism, thus annuls the death of the preceding bearer of the name. We see a conscientious father, Niccolò di Carlo Strozzi, carefully striking out in his journal the notation he had made of the death of a first son, Carlo, in 1473, for the child had been "remade" two months later in a new Carlo.[56] Each child offered his body as a perishable habitat for a name, the perennity of which was assured only through the corporeal reality of its successive bearers. To "remake" someone was to prevent the disappearance of a name and to assure the continous circulation, within a family, of a capital of given names that the dead passed on to the living. A name that was dropped impoverished the whole community of the lineage, and its attribution—its "remaking"—gave bodily reality to the community.

Thanks to his given name, the new bearer of the name participated in the collective person that was the lineage and that Florentines called the *casa*. Some Florentines used the identifying mark that a given name gave its user—which tied him to several links in a long chain of ancestors—by applying it, short-circuiting these connections, to their bastards. Luigi di Valorino di Barna Ciurianni names "Ciurianni" a son that he had had by a slave woman "because of the name of the house."[57] Luca di Matteo da Panzano, who had a son by a servant woman, names him "Ridolfo and Mariotto, that is, Ridolfo because of the ancient name of the Firidolfi da Panzano, and Mariotto because 2 March [error for February?], the day on which I was born, I, Luca, was Santa Maria Candelora [Candlemas Day]; thus have I given him for second given name Mariotto, in honor of holy Mary to whom I, poor sinner, am devoted."[58] This insistence

55. ASF, *Strozz.*, 2d ser., 10, fol. 17v.
56. ASF, *Strozz.*, 4th ser., 71, fols. 40v and 42 (1473).
57. ASF, *Manoscritti* 77, fols. 36 and 39 (1415).
58. The child himself was born 5 February 1423 (ASF, *Strozz.*, 3d ser., 9, fol. 22).

brings the illegitimate son into the lineage by attaching him immediately to his eponymic ancestor, jumping over the ancestors who transmitted less strongly marked names to one another. But the aim was the same, even if the means differed. For these bastards as for legitimate children, what was important was to proclaim the community of interests among the living and the group of their dead.

The "houses" of Florence used their symbolic or genealogical patrimony, just as they did their patrimony of houses or of lands, as trump cards in the social game: given names, and not just the family name, figure as the high cards here. All male children were potential beneficiaries of this capital, which was both material and symbolic. They were the ones who stood to inherit, in equal shares, lands and houses, shares in commercial associations, the right to participate in professional and political life, the right to the family crest and to lifetime enjoyment of the hereditary name. As order of birth had no influence on inheritance rights,[59] names could be carried over from a forebearer to an elder child and then to a younger child, as deaths dictated and without immutable preferential order. Equality among male heirs assured the free circulation and the repetition, on the level of the sibling group, of time-honored given names, since the obligation to "remake" the dead, this Italian *anastassi*,[60] could not be utilized with the hidden thought of transmitting to one particular heir the whole or a privileged part of the patrimony.[61] And as the maternal line had nothing to transmit but a dowry, the prestige of alliance, and the fecundity of the wife's womb, names borrowed on that side were easily reduced to hommage to the child's immediate forebears.

On the female side, women received dowries, generally composed of movable goods, which could vary according to the urgency of the family's desire for the matrimonial match. Women of course had no professional or political capacities, and they would find themselves brought into the lineages of their husbands, the name of which they would add to their own given name. The negotiation of their marriage would be based on the "social capital" their fathers and brothers enjoyed, but they could not hope to benefit directly from it. Thus it was less important that women be recognized, through transmittal of their given names, as members of a male kinship group in which names were perpetually passed from one temporary owner to another. This is what is reflected in the greater uncertainty that characterizes the origin of women's given names; fashion, friendship, the godparental relationship, and also affective ties with certain

59. At least not before the sixteenth century, which was to see the institution of majority and primogeniture in the transmission of goods in the great families.

60. A Greek term that seems equivalent to the Italian *rifare*. See B. Vernier, "La circulation des biens, de la main d'œuvre et des prénoms à Karpathos: Du bon usage des parents et de la parenté," *Actes de la Recherche en Sciences sociales* 31 (1980): 63–87.

61. Which is contrary to the Greek strategies analyzed in Vernier, ibid.

close relatives probably played a freer role in the choice of female names. Male names depended more closely on community of interest and inter-generational obligations.

Finally, while the names of apostles and important saints were feminized at will in this pre-Tridentine period, female and male given names in the family stock were not interchanged. When a father sought to "remake" a dead member of the family, he went out of his way to respect the gender of his or her name: girls almost never borrow and feminize the name of a male ancestor, and boys are not named for a female relative. According to this sex distinction, which assigns different places to men and women within the lineage, women cannot "remake" men. In the Florentine system of filiation, women did not furnish memorable ancestors as men did; therefore they could not perpetuate a female lineage identity that would benefit one group alone.[62]

In Florence, the reincarnation of the dead had little to do with short-term strategies by which a father might seek to assure one particular child the good will or the inheritance of a wealthy relative. The mechanisms governing the choice of given names were nevertheless deeply influenced by the structure and lasting cohesion of the lineage. The concepts under-lying these customs did, it is true, weaken somewhat after 1500. "Re-making" someone was then more often phrased as a "commemoration" of the dead person, whose qualities and example were supposed to have a favorable influence on the destiny of the new bearer of his or her name. It became more common for a father to choose from among his ancestors, even from among his affines, a person whose given name would invoke the particular virtues he displayed during his lifetime or the prestige he had enjoyed. Parents eliminated given names that displeased them and gave privileged status to given names that pleased them in the familial stock, thus conforming with the teachings of the Church, for which the name of a patron saint was supposed to induce in the individual who bore it the virtues of the eponym. It was less a question of giving temporary embodiment to a name than of influencing the child's attributes and moral identity. The name, which previously had established an identity for the child, now recalled the road to virtue laid out by the Church or the child's ancestors. The name was now intended to set an example; it explicitly forged personality. At this point, nothing stopped families from appealing to different systems by giving the child several given names. The choice of the name narrowed to closer degrees of kinship, while at the same time it opened to extrafamilial values.[63] As the solidarity of the agnatic descent

62. In a city like Bologna, in which daughters seemed less strictly excluded than in Florence, we can indeed find mention—absolutely unknown in Florence—of a maternal grandfather "commemorated" in his granddaughter after his death (Montanari, ed., "Cronaca e storia" 42 [1520]).

63. Alessandra Strozzi seems upset when her sons, after a long period in exile, show little respect for Florentine customs. She complains in a letter to Filippo, dated 8 May 1469,

group gradually crumbled, so did the coherence of the medieval system of name giving, governed by ancestors, in which "strictly speaking, there was no birth, because the ancestor had not disappeared; he had only disappeared from view."[64]

that after naming his first son Alfonso (a foreign name; see above, note 20) he now wants to call his second child Alessandro. (Fortunately, the child was a girl). The younger son, Lorenzo, comes to the support of Filippo, saying: "E' no' steremo freschi, se a' nostri figliuoli noi non potessimo por nome a nostro modo!" (we'd be in a fine fix if we couldn't name our children as we please!). The good lady responds: "Ed i' ho auto tanti degli altri dispiaceri, ed hogli passati, e così passo questo; e sare' passato avendo fatto Allessandro, come passò Alfonso; benchè allora v'era ragione rispetto di chi lo battezzò. Insino allora m'avvidi, che'l nome di tuo padre non ti piaceva. Ora Iddio provvide che fece la Lucrezia" (I have had so many other tribulations and gotten through them, thus I will get through this one; and I would have supported [Filippo's] making an Alessandro as I supported Alfonso; although then there was a reason, given who baptized him [see above, note 20]. Since that time I have come to understand that your father's name did not please you. Today God willed that Lucrezia be born). (Alessandra Macinghi negli Strozzi, *Lettere di una gentildonna fiorentina del secolo XV ai figliuoli esuli,* ed. C. Guasti [Florence, new ed. 1972], 590–91).

64. E. Benvéniste, *Le Vocabulaire des institutions indo-européennes* (Paris, 1969), 1:235.

# 14

# Holy Dolls: Play and Piety in Florence in the Quattrocento

The borderline between devotional practices and play activities is a narrow one. Historians of toys have noted the similarity between medieval marionnettes or dolls and devotional figurines of that epoch, and it is not always easy for archeologists or ethnologists to classify the objects they find into one category or the other.[1] Small modeled or molded statuettes in terra-cotta, sometimes mass-produced and found in abundance in the four corners of Europe;[2] pewter, tin, or earthenware objects that the manufacturers of household utensils and bric-a-brac added to their displays;[3] marionnettes to enliven preachers' sermons or to present sacred dramas[4]—all these ambiguous objects, both those repre-

Originally published as "Les saintes poupées: Jeu et dévotion dans la Florence du Quattrocento," in *Les Jeux à la Renaissance,* ed. J.-C. Margolin and Ph. Ariès (Paris:Vrin, 1983): 65–79.

My thanks to Richard C. Trexler for his generous guidance on the paths of Florentine religious history onto which the dolls led me. By permitting me to read several chapters of his book in proof, he enabled me to put certain of my overingenuous hypotheses into perspective. My thanks also to Daniela Lamberini and Amanda Lillie for their invaluable help — photographic, bibliographic, and iconographic.

1. Henri R. d'Allemagne, *Histoire des jouets* (Paris, 1902), 98–99. Michel Manson, "Introduction," Catalogue of the exposition Histoire de la poupée, Musée Roybet-Fould, Courbevoie, 1973–74; Manson, "La poupée française," in *Histoire de la poupée* (1980), 5–6.

2. D'Allemagne, *Histoire*, 149–50; C. van Hulst, "La storia della divozione a Gesù Bambino nelle immagini plastiche isolate," *Antonianum*, 19 (1944): 33–54; R. Berliner, *Die Weihnachtskrippe* (Munich, 1955), 157, n. 25.

3. D'Allemagne, *Histoire*, 149.

4. P. Jeanne, *Bibliographie des marionnettes* (Paris, 1926); C. Magnin, *Histoire des marionnettes en Europe* (Paris, 1862), 57; C. Sezan, *Les poupées anciennes* (Paris, 1930), 133, 136–39.

senting the divine and those used for play activities, reveal a confusion of attitudes toward the sacred and toward play on the part of those who were to manipulate them.[5] Florence in the Quattrocento offers one example of a type of sacred image with a dual purpose. These objects were considered a practical means to open up the way to God to women and children by exciting their imaginations (ingenuously or deliberately). By the contemplation of these objects, by their manipulation in play, ritual or dramatic fantasizing, these souls of "weaker" and more "malleable" constitution were led to a spiritual vision of the sacred verities. Play, dream, and rite were three facets of a drama that was played out between the believer and his God, in which the former gave life to the image of the latter, set it up as a sentient actor, and conversed directly with it.[6]

What devotional toys are we speaking about? A scholar of the last century, Giuseppe Marcotti, noted that "a *bambino* [a child doll] with a damask dress embroidered with pearls" figured in the wedding trousseau of the young Nannina Medici, sister of Lorenzo the Magnificent, in 1466.[7] In a recent article on the new domestic architecture of the fifteenth century, Richard Goldthwaite also expresses surprise to see a similar doll that was given in 1452, not to a young bride, but to a sixteen-year old nun who had entered a convent five years earlier, the daughter of a wealthy Florentine, Francesco Giovanni.[8] Nor are these two examples totally isolated. The trousseau inventories listed in Florentine *ricordanze* between 1450 and 1520 occasionally include mention of these dolls given to young brides by their parents and even, as in the case cited by Goldthwaite, to girls entering a convent.[9]

5. See Max von Boehn, *Puppen und Puppenspiele* (Munich, 1929).

6. R. C. Trexler, "Florentine Religious Experience: The Sacred Image," *Studies in the Renaissance* 19 (1972): 7–41; Trexler, "Ritual Behavior in Renaissance Florence: The Setting," in *Medievalia et humanistica: Studies in Medieval and Renaissance Culture*, n.s., 4 (1973): 125–44; Trexler, *Public Life in Renaissance Florence* (New York: Academic Press, 1980), esp. chap. 3, "Exchange."

7. G. Marcotti, *Un mercante fiorentino e la sua famiglia nel secolo XV* (Florence, 1881), 90. The citation is repeated in Aby Warburg in "Bildniskunst und florentinisches Bürgentum, 1: Domenico Ghirlandaio in S. Trinità," in his *Gesammelte Schriften* (Leipzig, 1932), 1:342.

8. R. A. Goldthwaite, "The Florentine Palace as Domestic Architecture," *American Historical Review* 77, no. 4 (October 1972): 1011. The *ricordanze* of Francesco di Tommaso Giovanni, 1422–58, are found in the Archivio di Stato, Florence (henceforth abbreviated ASF), *Strozziane*, 2d ser., 16 and 16 bis; the mention figures in 16 bis, fol. 16v. Sister Angelica, baptized Gostanza, was born 5 July 1436; she entered the order of Saint Clare of Monticelli in 1446 and made her final vows 8 February 1450 (ibid., fol. 5). Dates are given in modern style.

9. The *ricordanze*, which were both account books and personal journals, were written among the entire Florentine bourgeoisie and even into artisan circles. The dozen or so that I cite here are the work of merchants and jurists who belonged to the wealthier strata of society: their daughters' dowries averaged around 1,500 *fiorini* and ranged between 1,000 and 2,000 *fiorini*. Their daughters who entered the religious life brought an "alms" of 100 *fiorini* and a trousseau evaluated at about 30 *fiorini*, or one-tenth the amount of that of their sisters who marrried.

In most instances these *bambini* were effigies of children; male babies that were not nude but generally richly dressed. Some of them seem completely nonreligious in character, such as the one owned by Nannina Medici, or another "child with pearls" that figured in the trousseau of Jacopo Pandolfini's second wife in 1483,[10] or the "child dressed in brocade and pearls" that Tommaso Guidetti received from his father-in-law in his wife's wedding basket in 1482.[11] In 1505, Tommaso's daughter Maddalena entered a convent, taking with her the "child dressed in crimson velvet, in a little coat of green brocade, with the sleeves of its dress embroided with pearls, that her mother had brought at her wedding; the value of this was at the time . . . *fiorini.*"[12]

Most of the time, however, the dolls that belonged to Florentine girls had a more evidently Christian personality. In 1486, Antonia, the daughter of Bernardo Rinieri, received with other items in her two wedding baskets "a child dressed in fine linen in the image of Our Lord."[13] Marietta, daughter of Filippo Strozzi (who built the family palace), had in her trousseau in 1487 "one Messire Lord God with brocade robe and crown of gold and pearls."[14] Similarly, in 1515, Francesca, daughter of Carlo Strozzi, brought a "Messire Lord God, fully dressed, with pearls."[15]

A few of the female saints of the Christian Pantheon made a timid appearance among these richly dressed figures of the infant Jesus. In 1493 "one saint Margaret, with a dress of gold brocade, with gold lace and pearls and gold buttons on top," followed Andrea Minerbetti's first wife into his house,[16] and a "saint Mary Magdalen dressed in red satin with pearls" arrived in 1499 in one of the three baskets containing the trousseau of Giovanni Buongirolami's wife.[17]

When the identity of the dolls is not specified, we can still infer from the preceding examples and from the nature of the objects that accompanied them that these *bambini* had a religious function. The doll sent in 1452 by Francesco Giovanni to his daughter, sister Angelica, was "made of wood, with two robes, one of crimson satin with a pearl clasp and the other of Alexandria velvet with gold trimming, a crimson velvet bonnet,

10. Archivio degli Innocenti, *Estranei*, 648, fol. 173 (1 November, 1483).

11. ASF, *Strozz.*, 4th ser., 418, fol. 4v (31 January 1482).

12. Ibid., fol. 51v (19 August 1505).

13. ASF, *Conventi soppressi* 95, no. 212, fol. 169v (1 February 1486).

14. ASF, *Strozz.*, 5th ser., 41, fol. 169 (3 February 1487). The *donora* (trousseau) of her sister Fiammetta when she marries Tommaso Soderini included "una Santa Maria Maddalena" (ASF, *Strozz.*, 5th ser., 59, fol. 13v, 5 July 1493).

15. ASF, *Strozz.*, 4th ser., 76, fol. 150 (23 February 1515). See also in the trousseau of Gostanza Benci in 1518 "una fighura di rilievo rapresentativa di Cristo in pueritia bello, coperto di taffettà rosso et verghato" (a fine figure representing Christ in beautiful infancy, dressed in striped red taffeta) (L. Pagliai, "Una scritta nuziale del secolo XVI," *Nozze Schiaparelli-Vitelli* (Florence, 1904). My thanks to Diane Cole Ahl for this citation.

16. Biblioteca Laurenziana, *Acquisti e Doni*, 229, 2, fol. 2v (23 June 1493).

17. ASF, *Strozz.*, 2d ser., 23, fol. 131 (7 August 1499). See above, n. 14.

[and] a garland with a wide red fringe; it is accompanied by a tabernacle of painted wood, with a small altar and altar ornements, cloths, and other small objects for this altar."[18] All this pious apparatus, therefore, surrounded a *bambino* which, like others more expressly designated, very probably represented a "Messire Lord God" as an infant. One last text explicitly attests to the purpose of one of these holy dolls. In 1459, in his wife's trousseau, Bernardo di Stoldo Rinieri found "a large pine box containing one of those *bambini* that are set up on altars." It was perhaps this same doll that followed one of his daughters, Antonia, when she went to her husband in 1486—a doll characterized, as we have seen, as made "in the image of Our Lord."[19]

To tell the truth, the existence of these effigies of the Infant Jesus is less surprising than their presence in women's trousseaux in the fifteenth century. Historians of art or religion have in fact found many examples in the plastic arts of devotion to the divine child before the seventeenth century, and at that time the cult spread with the popularity of the multi-person crèche, or *presepio*, presenting the baby Jesus naked, swaddled, and lying in a crib.[20] Unlike the Germanic countries and northern Europe, Italy gives few examples of the full manger scene before the seventeenth century, and anything more than Jesus in the cradle is rare.[21] Prominent in Tuscan art of the fifteenth century was an image of the Christ child standing in triumph—an image that was placed on the altar during the important feast days, particularly at Christmas, or integrated into the new tabernacles of the Holy Sacrament. Otto Kurz has studied the variants of this baby Jesus, the glorious bearer of the symbols of the Passion, emerging from a chalice; and he has described them in terms of the technical and

18. ASF, *Strozz.*, 2d ser., 16 bis, fol. 16v (June 1452). See also the mention in 1417, in a Medici inventory (ASF, Mediceo avanti il Principato, henceforth abbreviated MAP, 129, fol. 59), of "uno tabernacolo di legno, entrovi uno bambino Nostro Signore con dalmatica in dosso di velluto azzuro e camisce e altro habito da diacono" (a wooden tabernacle, in which an infant Our Lord wearing a blue velvet cassock and robe and other deacon's vestments) found in the bedchamber of Cosimo (I owe this notation to the kindness of K. Lydecker). And the mention of "uno bambino, venne da Madonna Nibia (?), fornito di perle con una crocetta di perle, valeva fior. 10 e piu i' una zana" (a child doll, which came from Madonna Nibia, complete with pearls with a little pearl cross, worth over 10 *fiorini*, in a basket) (Innocenti, *Estranei* 633, Ricordi di ser Andrea di Cristofano Nacchianti, fol. 94v). These objects followed a young nun to the convent.

19. ASF, *Conventi soppressi* 95, 212, fol. 154 (31 January 1459) and fol. 169v (1 February 1486).

20. On the cult of the *presepio* and its antecedents in the thirteenth to the sixteenth centuries, see van Hulst, "La storia della divozione," 38–44; Berliner, *Die Weihnachtskrippe*, 14–18.

21. See also the examples of cribs cited in ibid, 156, nn. 24 and 25, and by van Hulst, "La storia della divozione," 42–44. A misinterpretation of a letter of Saint Catherine of Siena makes her the founder of the *bambini* industry in Lucca (see below, note 50) that was to develop and spread widely during the second half of the sixteenth century and to flourish in the seventeenth century. See the recumbent *bambino* from the Museo Bardini, Florence, reproduced as plate 14.4.

iconographic problems that the liturgy of the Eucharist posed to artists in the fifteenth century.[22] Artists of the time were invited to conceive receptacles worthy of the host and to integrate them into the high altar. Their efforts led, after 1450, to two solutions devised by Desiderio da Settignano: the wall tabernacle and the freestanding *tempietto*, prototypes for a great number of works up to the sixteenth century. Indeed, Desiderio's sculpted wall tabernacle in the church of San Lorenzo in Florence repeats and enhances the very ancient motif—more literary than iconographical—of the infant Jesus arising from a chalice, a miraculous and symbolic prefiguration of the Passion. This infant was to have an enormous vogue at the end of the fifteenth century.

Vasari reports that during his day this handsome infant had been removed from its place on the tabernacle "and is now wont to be set upon the altar on the feast of the Nativity, as an extraordinary thing; and in its stead another was made by Baccio da Montelupo, also in marble, which stands constantly on the tabernacle of the Sacrament"[23] (see plate 14.1). Baccio was known as a Savonarolan,[24] and it is probable that Savonarola and his followers were primarily responsible for the substitution. Pseudo-Burlamacchi reports that in the great procession of February 1497, the Dominican's "boys" carried all through Florence, hoisted "on a portable altar borne by four very beautiful angels . . . a most holy *bambino*, full of splendor, standing, on a gilded base, [and] giving a blessing with his right hand and with his left displaying the crown of thorns, the nails, and the cross: a work of remarkable beauty which was from the hand of the most excellent sculptor Donatello."[25] The infant sculpted by Desiderio corresponds to this description in almost all particulars, whereas no analogous work of Donatello's is known.

The immediate success of Desiderio's *bambino* (the book of *ricordanze* of the painter Neri di Bicci mentions the tinting of three *bambini di rilievo*

22. Otto Kurz, "A Group of Florentine Drawings for an Altar," *Journal of the Warburg and Courtauld Institutes* 18 (1955): 35–53. D. Lamberini has brought to my attention (too late for inclusion in the present study) Giovanni Previtali, "Il Bambin Gesù come immagine devozionale nella scultura italiana del Trecento," *Paragone* 21 no. 249 (1970): 31–40 and illus. 21–29. During the fourteenth century, Tuscan and Umbrian statues of the *bambino Gesù* gradually shifted from the standing, "triumphal" position to the lying position more frequent in the fifteenth century.

23. G. Vasari, *Vite de' più eccellenti pittori, scultori, e architettori*, ed. G. Milanesi (Florence, 1878–85), 3:108 (*Lives of Seventy of the Most Eminent Painters, Sculptors, and Architects*, ed. E. H. and E. W. Blashfield, A. A. Hopkins [London, 1897], 2:127–28). The substitution took place in any event before 1510.) (Kurz, "A Group of Florentine Drawings," 49, n. 3.) See G. Richa, *Notizie istoriche delle chiese fiorentine divise ne' suoi quartieri* (Florence, 1754–62), 5:1:28, on the later destiny of the *bambino*. Berliner, in *Die Weihnachtskrippe*, 18 and 160, nn. 51–53, cites inventories of the sacristy of San Lorenzo dating from 1453 and 1677 in which there figures a *bambino* richly dressed destined to the altars at Christmas time before and after the period in which the Jesus of Desiderio was used for this purpose.

24. According to Pseudo-Burlamacchi, *Vita del beato Jeronimo Savonarola*, edition attributed to P. Ginori Conti (Florence, 1937), 201–2.

25. Ibid., 131. See Kurz, "A Group of Drawings," 49.

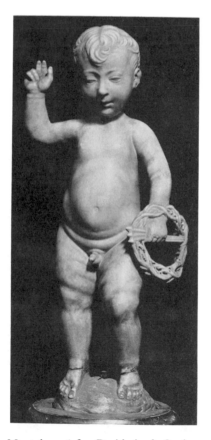

Plate 14.1 Baccio da Montelupo (after Desiderio da Settignano), *Christ Child.*
Museo dell' Opera del Duomo, Prato. (Photo Alinari 10041)

ordered for two nuns and one monk)[26] is attested by the many copies of
it that can be found in museums in Florence, in other Italian cities, and
in foreign countries and, more generally, of this sort of devotional statuette.
The custom of setting up an infant Jesus on the altar at Christmas seems
to have spread at the end of the fifteenth century. And, since Florentines
did not possess relics as precious as the *Santo Bambino* of Ara Coeli,

26. A sampling made by D. Lamberini and A. Lillie in the analytical files of the Kun-
sthistorisches Institut of Florence brought out no fewer than eleven of these variants of the
*bambino* of Desiderio (Florence: Acton collection, Museo Bardini, and Palazzo Davanzati:
see plates 14.1–14.3; Naples, Milan, New York, Detroit, Paris, Berlin, and Cambridge have
other examples). Kurz, "A Group of Drawings," 49, notes other copies in Fiesole and
Amsterdam. Comparable statuettes attributed to Benedetto da Maiano and to Francesco di
Simone are conserved, respectively, in Arezzo and Monteluce. Neri di Bicci, *Ricordanze*, ed.
B. Santi (Pisa, 1976), 170–71 (9 June and 28 September 1461), 192 (19 January 1463).

Plate 14.2 Attributed to Benedetto da Maiano, *Christ Child*. Museo Bardini, Florence. (Photo Amanda Lillie)

miraculously transported across the sea in 1591 and "shown to the people on the day of Christmas,"[27] the kidnaping of Desiderio's precious marble child and its innumerable copies in stucco, wood, and *carta pesta* obviously responded to the expectations of the followers of the divine infant. A passage from a book of *ricordanze* cited earlier refers to "one of those *bambini* that are set up on altars" (see plate 14.2).

The *bambini* included in Florentine trousseaux are important because they widen the area of this form of devotion to include the private houses of middle-class families. They also show that the cult of the infant Jesus may have spread earlier than had been thought on the basis of the few instances documented by historians of art. But what can we surmise of

27. Van Hulst, "Storia della divozione," 42–43.

the use those young wives and those nuns behind their convent walls made of their holy dolls? Were the dolls exposed temporarily on certain important holy days, for moments of contemplation and worship that were widely separated in time and of brief duration? Did laywomen and nuns make use of them in the same ways? By what learning processes were their emotions and their ritual behaviors shaped and turned toward devotion of the divine child? And what do the dolls teach us about this devotion?

According to our texts, these "dolls" were intended for and, it seems, owned by women: the statuettes went from one woman—lay or religious— to another. The mother transmited her *bambino* to her daughter, whether the daughter entered a monastery (as with the Guidetti doll, between 1482 and 1505) or moved under the authority of a husband (as with the Rinieri doll, between 1459 and 1486). The dolls were notable items in a girl's trousseau, often listed among the things appraised by a professional.[28] The *bambini* were always associated with women; it is always women who appear as owners or potential users of these divine or saintly figures. They were not given to little girls but to young women, and at the moment at which their matrimonial destiny was decided, either as terrestrial spouses or *spousae Christi* (see plate 14.3). Thus their wedding, of the flesh or mystical, had to have been celebrated before they could receive their wood and brocade "child." The holy dolls were the "toys" of adult women delivered up to a spouse.

In 1881 Giuseppe Marcotti advanced a hypothesis, which we should examine, to explain the *bambino Gesù* discovered in the trousseau of a Medici daughter. "The custom of giving wives a beautiful wax, sugar, or plaster doll," he says, "can also be explained by something other than devotional purposes: that is, by the belief that the woman would engender a child analogous to the image that she keeps before her eyes during her pregnancy."[29] The magical function assigned to the nuptial doll, according to this theory, was aimed at transferring the virtues of the object contemplated during the delicate period of gestation to the person looking at it or to the child she was carrying. The future mother, in other words, would be impregnated, by visual contemplation, with the power and the qualities of the magical object. To this day the custom of placing a richly dressed doll on the conjugal bed is probably meant to insure the fertility of the couple and the material success of the children. These practices would

28. In two out of eleven cases, these dolls count among the *donora* expressly called *non stimate*, and, in a third case, the family journal does not specify whether the doll was appraised with the rest of the trousseau. The reason for this difference in treatment for the moment escapes me.

29. Marcotti, *Un mercante*, 121, n. 43. The author cites A. de Gubernatis, *Storia comparata degli usi natalizì in Italia e presso gli altri popoli indo-europei* (Milan, 1869), and D. G. Bernoni, *Credenze popolari veneziane* (Venice, 1874). Aby Warburg, "Bildniskunst," in *Gesammelte Schriften*, 1:342, refers in turn to the other work of A. de Gubernatis, *Storia . . . degli usi nuziali* (Milan, 1878), 175, on magic for alliance and fertility.

Plate 14.3 Bernardino di Antonio Detti, called del Signoraccio, detail from *Madonna del Pergola*. Museo Civico, Pistoia. (Photo Caroline Elam.)

include the infant Jesus, the Saint Margaret (according to van Gennep, the major patron saint of childless women), and, more oddly still, the Mary Magdalen of our Florentine trousseaux among the magical agents of the fertility rites associated with the celebration of weddings.[30] The

30. A. van Gennep, *Manuel de folklore français contemporain* (Paris, 1972), 1:1:116, nn. 6 and 7; bibliography, ibid., 3:488–89. According to the Golden Legend, Mary Magdalen

hypothesis is not implausible. Van Gennep cites many examples of French country marriages at which, during the wedding banquet or that night, at the bedding of the newlyweds, a doll was presented to the couple, to be swaddled and embraced by the woman, and sometimes even fictively baptized.[31] These propitiatory anticipations of a more recent folklore seem to find an echo in the appearance of a child in Florentine nuptial ritual of the fourteenth century. The Florentine practice is well documented: sumptuary statutes in 1388 regulating wedding procedures prohibited the servant who brought the coffer containing the husband's presents to his wife from being accompanied by or carrying "a small child, boy or girl, of any age whatsoever," or the family would incur a fine of ten *fiorini*.[32]

Might the real child of flesh and bones—promise of fertility and forbidden by the authorities—have been replaced by a wooden, stucco, or wax doll that played the same role? There are two objections to this hypothesis. First, the *bambino* did not appear among the husband's gifts but was included in the trousseau sent by the bride's parents. A shift of this sort should make us hesitate at the idea of a simple substitution of a simulacrum for a child playing a ritual role.[33] Furthermore, even if the dolls did not have a religious identity, could it have been normal that they were included, as a fertility object, in the equipment of a young nun? Thus it seems to me implausible that the dolls were a simple substitute for a magical practice carried on during the wedding period. I would retain one part of Marcotti's hypothesis, however: the idea of a magical transfer of virtues and forces from the effigy to its user. An effigy is never innocent when the person looking at it knows how to put the right questions to it.

---

aided a sterile couple to conceive a child, watched over the child's survival, and resuscitated the mother, who had died in childbirth. She is associated with the Enfant Jésus as a sort of older sister in several regions of France.

31. Van Gennep, *Manuel*, 1:2:516–17 and 581. See H. Bächtold-Stäubli, *Handwörterbuch des deutschen Aberglaubens* (Berlin and Leipzig, 1927), s. v. 'Bild, Bildzauber,' 1, col. 1282–1306. Yvonne Verdier, in *Façons de dire, façons de faire* (Paris, 1979), 278 and 289, mentions these farcical rites in Burgundy today.

32. The *ordinamenta* of July 1388 were published by D. Salvi in appendix to G. Dominici, *Regola del governo di cura familiare* (Florence, 1860), 221–37; the passage cited can be found on p. 233. The custom is, in fact, corroborated by the *ricordanze*; see ASF, *Strozz.*, 2d ser., 4, Ricordi di Paolo di Alessandro Sassetti, fol. 70 (1384): "per dare al fanciullo posto in collo"(to give to the little boy he gave her to kiss). Ser Lapo Mazzei, *Lettere d'un notaio a un mercante del sec. XIV*, ed. C. Guasti (Florence, 1880), 2:247, notes the same custom in November 1407 (one *fiorino* "per dare a uno fanciullo che si pone in collo alla donna novella" [to give to a little boy who is put in the arms of the new wife] ).

33. On the exchange and circulation of gifts on the occasion of marriages in Tuscany see chap. 10 above, "The Griselda Complex." When Tommasa Delli marries Giovanni Niccolini 1 June 1353, her trousseau is brought by a servant "with a little boy" to whom Giovanni gives one *fiorino* (G. Niccolini da Camugliano, *The Chronicles of a Florentine Family, 1200–1400* [London, 1933], 64, 66). Here the child went — as did the dolls — from the house of the bride's father to the house of her husband. The substitution thus seems more plausible.

How did our Florentine women—whether they took the veil or remained in the world—play with their wedding dolls? What attitudes had been inculcated in them? How had they been taught since childhood to regard sacred images?

"Set up on altars," the *bambini* went to embellish a family oratory, like the *Nostra Donnas* or *Domeniddios* so often listed as part of the furnishings of the master bedroom, described in the inventories of Florentine dwellings.[34] This was where the devotions of all who lived in the house were concentrated: this was where the devotional image allowed exchanges with the realm of the sacred. Such exchanges were based on a virtue that the Church traditionally granted to the image: "to excite the sentiments of the soul to devotion where words do not suffice."[35] One work written in 1454 taught young girls the paths to devout emotion. While they contemplated the scenes and the actors in the image, they were to try to give an affective "charge" to the picture by imagining familiar landscapes, situations, and figures. Then, concentrating their thoughts on the mental images that moved them most strongly, they could hope to enjoy those states of *dolcecia e divotione* (enchanting sweetness and devotion) to which the sacred image was supposed to lead.[36] Devotional painting, then, which underwent such extensive development in Tuscany in the fourteenth century,[37] was not directed at adults alone. The apprehension of the sacred through images was taught children from their earliest years by the example of their elders' spontaneous attitudes, but also by adults' conscious efforts. The advice of the conservative Dominican pedagogue, Giovanni Dominici, to one mother of upper-class Florentine society at the beginning of the fifteenth century is well known, but the text deserves to be cited once again. According to Dominici, the mother should place representations of child saints before her babies, "pictures . . . in which your child . . . may take delight . . . Jesus nursing, sleeping in His Mother's lap or standing courteously before Her, drawing while His Mother embroiders according to His drawing. So *let the child see himself mirrored* [emphasis added] in the Holy Baptist clothed in camel's skin," etc. This pictorial program was addressed particularly to boys, but it was completed by an iconography reserved for girls.[38]

34. The *ricordanze* of the Florentine, Tribaldo dei Rossi, give one example in 1481 of a painting of *Nostra Donna* ordered immediately after marriage to decorate the conjugal chamber (Biblioteca Nazionale Centrale, Florence, henceforth abbreviated BNF, 2, 2, 357, fols. 4, 5. On family prayers, see Trexler, *Public Life*, 160, 353.

35. M. Baxandall, *Pittura ed esperienze sociali nell'Italia del Quattrocento* (Italian translation, Milan, 1978), 52–53.

36. Ibid., 57. He is speaking of the *Zardino di Oration*, written in 1454.

37. On these tendencies in Italian painting see F. Antal, *La pittura fiorentina e il suo ambiente sociale nel Trecento e nel primo Quattrocento* (Italian translation, Milan, 1960) , esp. pp. 200ff.; M. Meiss, *Painting in Florence and Siena after the Black Death* (Princeton, 1951; Harper Torchbooks, 1964), 125–26).

38. See full quotation in chapter 5 above, "Childhood in Tuscany"; Dominici, *Regola*, 131–32 (quoted from Arthur Basil Coté, trans., *On the Education of Children* [Washington,

By means of such representations—some of which, like the slaughter of the Innocents, were frankly negative—even babies in their cradles were to be led to identify with the figures in the icon. Is it fair to accuse our Dominican of unrealistic attitudes and pious deams? When he aroused the child's imagination in this manner, he was playing on the same reactions that inspired devotion in the adult, simply chosing images that corresponded to the child's sensitivities. Dominici proves more innovative in this than many humanist thinkers and accords greater respect to the unique characteristics of childhood. Certain texts reveal in unexpected ways that his recommendations rested on fairly consistent practice, and that pious images may have been present in private houses to satisfy the needs of children. Such texts do in fact illustrate a kind of devotional pedagogy. In 1482, for example, Niccolò Strozzi lent one *fiorino* to his servant woman, who wanted to acquire a "Virgin Mary." Two years later (although she still owed him the *fiorino*) the good woman left him the image, which, as he says, "she left in my house, thinking to give pleasure to the children."[39] Thus the sacred image was to satisfy the needs of less cultivated spirits in the household, from the servant woman to the young; it was to "instruct the ignorant," as the Church would say, and to become a prop for a female or childish devotion that the father judged, apparently, with some condescension.

This passive, visual impregnation of the child or the woman was completed by more active educational behaviors. Sometimes, in fact, private altars were used for a real apprenticeship in devotion through play. Here again, Dominici's pedagogical advice, which might seem theoretical or somewhat stuffy, finds an echo in real practices that can be confirmed, here and there, by other texts. Giovanni Dominici wanted the mother to incline her son toward religion by keeping him occupied around a domestic altar, which he should decorate, illuminate, and serve like a real accolyte.[40] The child should even learn to mimic the priest in front of the altar—after observing him in church—by ringing a bell, singing, saying mass, and preaching. The priest's "good example" justified the make-believe suggested by our Dominican, who saw no irreverence in it. He also had suggestions for decorating the altar at which the child was to officiate. "Sometimes they may be occupied in making garlands of flowers and greens with which to *crown Jesus* [emphasis added] or to decorate the picture of the Blessed Virgin, they may light and extinguish little candles, etc." Here is a familial Jesus, then, and we can imagine him in this context

---

D.C., 1927], 34). See J. B. Ross, "The Middle-Class Child in Urban Italy, Fourteenth to early Sixteenth Century," in Lloyd de Mause, ed., *The History of Childhood* (Harper Torchbooks, 1975), 204–11.

39. ASF, *Strozz.*, 4th ser., 71, fols. 78v and 79 (1 June 1484): "per una Vergine . . . la quale lasciò in casa, ritenneva per contento di fanciugli."

40. Dominici, *Regola*, 146 (Coté, trans., *Education*, 42).

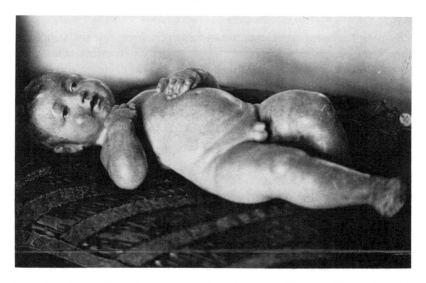

Plate 14.4 *Christ Child*. Anonymous, fifteenth century, Tuscany. Museo Bardini, Florence. (Photo A. Lillie)

of women's and children's devotions depicted as a young child, like the *bambini* that belonged to the mothers of these apprentice Christians (see plate 14.4). A few decades later, Savonarola, when he was still a little boy—*fanciulletto*—"amused himself enormously all by himself, busying himself setting up little altars and [engaging in] other devotions of the same sort."[41] The fully equipped altar that accompanied the *bambino* sent in 1452 to Francesco Giovanni's daughter seems at first sight to fit in with this type of religious education through play and imitation.

Identification and participation thus underlay the devotional practices proposed to Florentines from early infancy. When the emotions of the worshiper reach a certain intensity, the force of the image—the Infant Jesus, "Our Lady," or the crucifix—becomes effective and transfers some of its power to the worshiper.[42] A Florentine recluse of the beginning of the thirteenth century, the blessed Umiliana dei Cerchi, was in the habit of losing herself in prayer before an image of the Virgin, and it was the pressure exerted on the image that induced the miracle when the spent flame revived in the lamp burning before the icon.[43] The same pious effusion can be seen in confraternities at the end of the fifteenth century that joined together "around the little Jesus before whom [their members]

41. G. F. Pico della Mirandola, *Vita R. P. Hieronimi Savonarolae* (Paris, 1674), 6; Ps. Burlamacchi, *Vita*, 6.

42. Trexler, "The Sacred Image," 16ff. See also his analysis of the spiritual exercises of Giovanni Morelli (whose motto was *fammi partecipe*—Let me share) in *Public Life*, 174–85.

43. "De vita beatae Aemilianae seu Humilianae viduae," *Acta sanctorum*, Maii IV, 395–418.

offered their prayers, not without shedding many tears."[44] In offering sacred images of young saints to the offspring of the Florentine bourgeoisie and in appealing to their imaginations, Dominici was acting exactly like the spiritual leaders of the lay and religious communities who, from the thirteenth century on, had invited Christians to participate in Biblical dramas by acting with, or taking the place of, their sacred participants.[45] The Franciscan author of the *Meditations on the Life of Christ*[46] and his fourteenth-century imitators[47] opened up to pious souls and to artists a huge repertory of attitudes and emotions that made the image into the Christian's immediate partner. The author of the *Meditations*, directing the devotions of a Poor Clare, tells her: "You also, kneel and adore your lord God, then his mother, and salute the holy and venerable Joseph respectfully. Then kiss the feet of the infant Jesus who is laid in his bed, and ask Our Lady to give him to you and allow you to pick him up. Receive him and hold him in your arms. Look at his face with attention and kiss it with respect, take joy in this with confidence. . . . Then give him back to his mother and look well how she suckles him, cares for him, and serves him in all things with solicitude and wisdom. Thus, you also, keep yourself ready to help her if you can . . . serve Our Lady and the child Jesus as much as you can."[48] The mental image ends here in a fantasized manipulation of the sacred figure. Some surprising applications of these devotions can be found in the ritual life and the fantasy life of the faithful.

There is evidence that these spiritual behaviors were quite often dramatized and simulated in the fifteenth century by pious confraternities and religious communities. The most common ritual practice was the exposition of the infant Jesus, not only on the altar, standing in triumph, but lying in a cradle or a crib at Christmas time. The faithful came to adore him and to kiss his feet.[49] There is one of these figures of Jesus of the fifteenth century in the Museo Bardini in Florence, a chubby baby whose right foot has been worn away by the kisses of the devout (see plate 14.2). This custom was sometimes enlarged into a real theatrical production that

44. Ps. Burlamacchi, *Vita*, 95.

45. On the influence of the Dominicans and the Franciscans on Italian art see Antal, *La pittura fiorentina*, esp. p. 203; Meiss, *Painting*, 125–31.

46. Long attributed to Saint Bonaventura, then to Giovanni da Calvoli. I quote from the anonymous edition of Saint Bonaventura, *Meditationes vitae domini nostri Jesu Christi* (Arras, 1884).

47. Particularly Ludolphus the Carthusian, a Saxon prior at Strasbourg, who wrote during the first third of the fourteenth century a *Vita Jesu Christi*, edited by L. M. Rigollot (Paris and Brussels, 1878), that often follows the text of the *Meditations* word for word. There are many versions of the latter in the vernacular, in rhymed verse, etc., on which see Meiss, *Painting* 125–26.

48. *Meditationes*, 60; Ludolphus, *Vita*, 1:77–78.

49. Berliner, *Die Weihnaschtskrippe*, 160, n. 53. Previtali, "Il Bambin Gesù," 37, emphasizes the "double use of the statuette (standing, in a tabernacle, and lying in a manger of the *presepio*) planned from the start."

permitted the entire congregation to relive evangelical scenes. In this way the reformed Dominican monasteries of San Marco in Florence, Fiesole, and Prato, under the guidance of Savonarola, played the Journey of the Magi and the Adoration of the infant Christ during Epiphany in 1498. The procession ended in a direct contact between each one of the monks and the effigy of the divine child, which was lifted out of the manger and placed on a portable altar inside the church, kissed by all, one after the other, on its feet, its hands, and its mouth.[50] But these infant Jesus figures used at Christmas, which recall the *repos de Jésus* of northern Europe, inspired other rites of mothering that were much more elaborate and increasingly widespread in the convents of Europe of the time.[51] The worshipers were not satisfied with cradling their Jesus: occasionally they bathed him, dressed him, and made him new clothes, thus taking literally the spiritual recommendations that encouraged the Christian to prepare his or her soul for these humble services. Nuns all over Europe, identifying with the mother of God, gently tended an effigy of Jesus at liturgical feasts. One confraternity was even created in seventeenth-century Italy to care for, wash, swaddle, and cradle the newborn Christ.[52] Here the effigy was not only interpreted and adored, but handled, coddled, and taken for walks through the convent, purifying the entire community by its gaze and its presence. The image truly came to life and became an actor in a drama played by all, bringing tears to the participants' eyes. The objects that served as a property for these rituals, the *bambini*, were made in the convents of Lucca, and after 1600 they were exported to the four corners of the world, accompanied by the maternal rites so characteristic of this new form of devotion. But the commerce in holy dolls did no more than diffuse practices and a cult that were already thriving at the end of the fifteenth century, when Savonarola denounced nuns' adulation of their *bambini* as smacking of idolatry.[53]

Rite and sacred imagery were not the only ways the child Jesus crossed the barriers of art to enable the faithful to see, or rather to feel and to relive, his childhood and his vulnerability. The exhortations of their confessors so imbued female mystics with the sort of images we have been discussing that these nuns elaborated on them and lent them reality in

50. Ps. Burlamacchi, *Vita,* 117ff. See Trexler, *Public Life,* chap. 6, particularly 189–90.
51. Berliner, *Die Weihnachtskrippe,* 15–18.
52. Ibid., 160, n. 48. An English clergyman also noted this in 1674.
53. Van Hulst, "Storia della divozione," 43–48. When a "bambino di legno bellissimo" (most beautiful wooden infant) was discovered in the Philippines at the end of the sixteenth century, some thought it the one that Pigafetta had offered to the queen of Cebu on the occasion of her conversion in 1521 by Magellan (see A. Pigafetta, *Primo viaggio intorno al globo,* ed. C. Amoretti [Milan, 1800], 88–89). On the figures of Jesus of the seventeenth century see van Hulst, "Storia della divozione," 48–53. Savonarola's criticisms of nuns can be found in his *Prediche sopra Amos e Zaccaria,* ed. R. Ridolfi (Florence, 1955), 1:373: "Lasciate, monache li vostri bambini, che sono gl'idoli vostri, venite e cercate me" (Nuns, leave off your infant [dolls], which are your idols, and come to find me).

their visions. Many a saintly nun, after long orisons before the holy image, merged with the mother of Christ and changed places with her for the duration of her ecstasy. Umiliana dei Cerchi so ardently desired to see Jesus at the age of three or four years old "with her corporeal eyes" (like Saint Francis[54]) that one day a *bambino* of that age visited her in her cell, and began to play. Like the Wise Man of later paintings, the saint dared to kiss his foot.[55] According to her biographer, this apparition was exceptional even among miracles since (in this first half of the thirteenth century) it was usually angels that God sent to saints rather than his only son. Later, with the diffusion of devotional practices analogous to those recommended in the *Meditations* or by Ludolphus, Franciscan and Dominican convents in Italy were to see more frequent apparitions of the holy child. Around 1310, Saint Sibylline, a Dominican nun from Pavia and blind from the age of twelve, is visited by the infant Jesus. In her vision she attempts to seize him and embrace him, but he always escapes her, and from that very frustration an immense joy is born in her that even the memory of her vision is enough to revive for the rest of her life.[56] At about the same time Saint Agnes of Montepulciano ardently desires to see Jesus "face to face" and to "find joy in his embraces." Mary appears to her at last, and she gives Agnes the child, but an hour later Agnes refuses to give him back "in spite of the flatteries and the threats" of the Virgin. The true mother and the temporary mother, transformed into tigresses, quarrel fiercely over the baby, pulling him back and forth until Agnes is bested. All that she manages to keep from this adventure is a small cross, a precious relic that the child wore around his neck.[57]

Narrations of these ecstatic visions, from which the visionary often awakened with appalling violence,[58] follow the details of texts like the *Meditations*, reinforced at each stage by devotional paintings. The endearments, the kisses, the fondling, and the loving attention that the mystics pour out toward the divine child echo the hypermaternal attitudes

54. According to the "Vita prima" of Saint Francis written by Thomas of Celano, the saint introduced an ox, a donkey, and a manger into the church of Greccio in 1223, but without placing the child in the manger, and it was only some of his followers who had the vision of a *bambino* lying there. See also the "Vita altera s. Francisci" of Saint Bonaventura, *Acta sanctorum*, Oct. II, 706–7, 770.

55. "Vita," *Acta sanctorum*, Maii IV, 397. See D. Herlihy and C. Klapisch-Zuber, *Les Toscans et leurs familles* (Paris, 1978), 568. Satan also understands her "desire" to see the Virgin and child and one day makes them appear diabolically before the saint ("Vita," 390).

56. "De sancta Sibyllina de Papia," by Thomas of Bozolesto, *Acta sanctorum*, Martii III, 69. For a recent and Lacanian presentation of desire among Christian mystics and ecstatics, see J. N. Vuarnet, *Extases féminines* (Paris, 1980) and its bibliography.

57. "De s. Agnete virgine ord. sancti Dominici Montepolitiani," *Acta sanctorum*, Aprilis II, 797.

58. When she awoke, Saint Agnes of Montepulciano "post magnos et horrendos clamores in terram ejulando decidit semimortua" (after great and horrendous shouting, wailing on the floor, fell half-dead) (ibid., 797). The same was true of Angela di Foligno (see Vuarnet, *Extases*, 80).

that the devotional texts attribute to the Virgin herself. Spiritual service
of the infant Jesus, the quintessential *bambino*, takes on forms that seem
just as down to earth as the rituals of mothering. At Christmas 1540,
when the Virgin appears to Saint Caterina de' Ricci, a Florentine nun in
Prato, and lends her the infant Jesus, the saint is astonished to find him
dressed: from the time of Saint Francis, the poverty, nudity, and humility
of our Lord at his birth had been celebrated in the adoration of the
newborn Christ. In her vision, Caterina hears the Virgin answer that "it
is indeed the swaddling cloths, the bands, and the cloak that she [Caterina]
made for him by her Advent prayers" that have clothed him.[59] One year
later the Virgin returns: this time the child is nude. The saint plays with
him in her bed, then returns him to his mother, who pulls some cloths
from a basket and diapers him, "saying that these were the swaddling
cloths and the diapers that the nuns of the convent had prepared by their
prayers during Advent."[60]

Nuns or laywomen, these women required contact—visual or physical—
with sacred images in order to have immediate access to the child
Jesus. Whether they were actresses or visionaries, their doll play had
an evident cathartic role. Some used the ritualized manipulation of a wooden,
papier-maché, or plaster simulcrum; others, the exaltation of ecstatic de-
lirium. These play activities permitted young women, shut up from childhood on in a convent[61] or subjected to a distant husband[62] and separated
from their own newborn children at birth,[63] to identify with the mother
of Christ and transmute their frustrations and tensions. The language of
these mystics when they speak of their visions also shows that the husband
so desperately absent was hidden in the baby of their dreams. Later the
child dolls brought by nuns in Germanic countries to their convents were
to be called *sponserl*, "little husbands."[64] In dreaming of themselves as the
servants and nurses of the Christ child, these "brides of Christ" attempted

59. Serafino Razzi, *La vita della ven. Madre suor Caterina de' Ricci*, ed. G. M. Di Agresti
(Florence, 1965), 108–9.

60. Ibid., 119–20. Should we see in the offerings that the faithful even today leave by
the *bambino* displayed at Christmas time a symbolic offering toward his spiritual clothing,
as D. Lamberini has suggested to me?

61. According to a small sampling of nuns known through the *ricordanze*, Florentine
women took the veil between 8 and 12 years of age (average of 24 cases: 10 years, 6 months)
and pronounced final vows between 14 and 18 years of age (average of 9 cases: 16 years,
1 month). This last figure is close to the one (16 years 11 months) obtained by J. Kirshner
and A. Molho, "The Dowry Fund and the Marriage Market in early Quattrocento Florence,"
*Journal of Modern History* 50 (1978): 422, table 5, for fifteen girls who became nuns after
1430.

62. See Herlihy, and Klapisch-Zuber, *Les Toscans*, 395–400, 594–95, 603–5.

63. See chapter 7 above, "Blood Parents and Milk Parents." Nearly half of the children
that Florentine parents put out to nurse outside of Florence went to their *balia* before they
were six days old.

64. Van Hulst, "Storia della divozione," 52. Childless couples gave dolls called *Sponsele*
(little brides) to religious communities, with a dowry and a trousseau (see one example from
the seventeenth century in the Musée Alsacien of Strasbourg).

to see and to feel their spiritual husband physically, to bear him in themselves and to suckle him (like the Ebner sisters), to touch him and to
"embrace" him, to "find joy in his embraces." This language reaches toward
the spiritual, but at the same time it translates the total overwhelming of
all the senses. Saint Agnes of Montepulciano levitates up to the crucifix
placed on the altar and remains there, hanging on it, "kissing and hugging
it, seemingly clinging to her beloved, so that all can see in manifest fashion
the spiritual union of her internal unity with Christ through her embrace
with a material image, and so that all can understand the elevation of her
spirit as they consider the miraculous suspension of her body."[65] Many a
nun, in fact, entered into a mystical alliance, under the auspices of the
Virgin—a great matchmaker for souls—with these infant Jesuses of their
visions and returned from the experience with a finger encircled by a ring
invisible to others.[66] The mystical union, the "embrace" and the ineffable
"joy" that made saintly women who experienced it fall panting or writhing
in pain when it ended—these overwhelming experiences were certainly
attenuated, but not eliminated, when their love for an adult "husband"
was shifted to the child Jesus. In fact, the infant Jesus allowed the recluse
her primary social function—the maternal function—and put her desire
and frustrations within limits that her male confessors recognized and
could accept. The child-husband allowed these women an experience that
their secluded life condemned them never to know.

It is not my intention to limit the cult of divine infancy to the maternal
and sexual frustrations of more or less secluded women and young girls,
however. This devotional practice also awoke profound resonances in a
male public, religious and lay. In the processions and the dramatizations
that he put on for the monks and the young novices of San Marco,
Savonarola used similar emotional means, and when the monks called the
Virgin "their mother," they were doing no more than repeating and inverting the relations between mother and son that the nuns cultivated in
their attitude toward their *bambino*.[67] After all, in the biographies of male
saints one finds ecstatic effusions of a holy man with a baby: the "Legend
of the Miracles" of Saint Anthony of Padua established a prototype for

---

65. *Acta sanctorum,* Aprilis II, 794.

66. They evidently were following the example of Saint Catherine of Alexandria, whose
mystical marriage with the infant Jesus was a theme widely developed around the first third
of the fourteenth century; see Meiss, *Painting,* 108–11. Catherine of Siena had the same
experience, according to the "Miracoli della beata Caterina," ed. R. Fawtier, *Sainte Catherine
de Sienne: Essai de critique des sources,* vol. 1: *Sources hagiographiques* (Paris, 1921), 219. Her
later and more official biographer, Raimondo of Capua, substitutes a more probable adult
Jesus for the infant Jesus (*Acta sanctorum,* Aprilis III, 881–82). Caterina de' Ricci also entered
into a mystical marriage with the *bambino Gesù* (S. Razzi, *Vita,* ed. Di Agresti, 129–30).
On the body of saints, see the recent A. Vauchez, *La sainteté en Occident aux derniers siècles
du Moyen-Age* (Rome, 1981). On forms of female religiosity, see the many studies of A.
Benvenuti-Papi.

67. Ps. Burlamacchi, *Vita,* 46. See Trexler, *Public Life,* 88–89, n. 8.

male baby coddling long before Saint Joseph, guardian of the holy infancy, was to be presented as a rival model.[68] Is it possible that the common denominator of the exploitation of the emotions on which these images, visions, and new rites were based might be a new open-mindedness, a loss of blindness concerning childhood, reflected in the chubby forms of our *bambini*?[69] Noting the presence of one of these dolls among the belongings of a nun, Richard Goldthwaite attributes the unusual intrusion of a doll in a convent to "a new sense of domesticity and fascination with children,"[70] and he interprets this as a sign of a profound mutation that affected familial structures and ways of thinking. Might not the *bambino* bring into the cloister an echo of new feelings that had matured within the bourgeois—and "conjugal"—family of the end of the Middle Ages? I wonder, in fact, whether the inverse is not true. At the root of this appetite for childhood, which the taste for *putti* engendered by the Renaissance was to leave unsatisfied, is it not the idea of the humility, nudity, and frailty of the newborn child lying in a crib that we find, rather than an exaltation of the bourgeois baby, which was sent off to a nurse immediately after birth and which, if it died in her care, would never even have been known to its parents? And when painters removed the Virgin of humility from her throne and placed her on a cushion on the ground,[71] did they not do more to rehabilitate maternity and its humble nursing tasks[72] than all the rehashed preachings of doctors and moralists who from antiquity had lauded the benefits of maternal nursing, or the reflections of a few humanists writing on conjugal relations and the role of the woman in marriage? Perhaps we should invert the accustomed reading of the relations between the reality of childhood and its representation in images. Florentines may have begun to take a better look at their own flesh-and-blood babies because their practice in the sphere of the sacred had led them to cuddle plaster and papier-mâché figures of Jesus. Paradoxally, it would then be among cloistered women and in the ritualization of their desire for a child that we would have to seek the origin, not only of a pedagogy

---

68. "Liber miraculorum b. Antonii," *Acta sanctorum*, Junii II, 729. The Provençal saint Elzéar de Sabran and his wife Delphine were reported to have worshiped a *Jésus-enfant* in the cathedral of Apt during the fourteenth century. Later legends turned this wooden effigy into the guardian of the chastity of this holy couple, who were said to have placed it between them in their bed (*Acta sanctorum*, Sept. VII, 572, 582).

69. See P. Ariès, *L'enfant et la vie familiale sous l'Ancien Régime* (new edition, Paris, 1973), chap. 2, "La découverte de l'enfance"; Herlihy and Klapisch-Zuber, *Les Toscans*, 568–70.

70. Goldthwaite, "The Florentine Palace," 1010.

71. On the Virgin of humility, see Meiss, *Painting*, 132–56.

72. What better indication of this motivating role of sacred images than the wonder expressed in the *Meditationes* (p. 81) before the Virgin tenderly suckling Jesus: "O quam libenter eum lactabat! Vix fieri potuit, quin magnam etiam, aliis foeminis inexpertam dulcedinem in talis filii lactatione sentiret" (see chap. 7 above, "Blood Parents and Milk Parents," epigraph).

of pious practices, but of an apprenticeship in what we call maternal attitudes.

To specialists in the history of dolls, our Florentine *bambini* may not seem to be very representative of the species. This is because they stand at the confluence of many needs; they spin threads, less tenuous and less futile than may at first appear, which bridge the gap between behavior patterns not usually assigned to the level of mere play. In the hands of a young Christian or of a nun, mimicking gestures foreign to them, under the eyes of a simple worshiper or an actor in a sacred representation, the *bambini* broke down the transparent wall that separates reality from its figuration—just as the doll of childhood does. When we play, there is always an image involved, and if the game is played to the limit, it is the image that ends up manipulating us.

# Index